THE

Saturday Review

GALLERY

IN WHICH SOME OF THE OUTSTANDING WRITERS
OF RECENT YEARS PRESENT REMINISCENCES
AND BIOGRAPHICAL PORTRAITS
OF IMPORTANT AND STRIKING FIGURES WHO HAVE
APPEARED ON OR NEAR THE LITERARY SCENE
OVER THE PAST CENTURY.
SELECTED FROM THE COMPLETE FILES BY
JEROME BEATTY, JR.,
AND THE EDITORS
OF THE SATURDAY REVIEW.
INTRODUCTION BY JOHN T. WINTERICH.

SIMON AND SCHUSTER NEW YORK 1959

PUBLISHED BY SIMON AND SCHUSTER, INC.

ROCKEFELLER CENTER, 630 FIFTH AVENUE, NEW YORK 20, N. Y.

FIRST PRINTING

LIBRARY OF CONGRESS CATALOG CARD NUMBER: 59-11202

MANUFACTURED IN THE UNITED STATES OF AMERICA

ACKNOWLEDGMENTS

"A Briton on a Rampage," from *Domestic Manners of the Americans* by Frances Trollope. By permission of Dodd, Mead and Co.

"Last of the Great Fairy-Talers," by permission of the author.

"St. Elmo, or, Named for a Best Seller," by permission of the author.

"The Eddie Guest of the Seventies," by permission of the author.

"The Incredible Dr. Bell," from *The Fabulous Originals* (retitled *The Real Sherlock Holmes*), copyright © 1955 by Irving Wallace. By permission of Alfred A. Knopf, Inc.

"Watson Was A Woman," copyright © 1941 by Rex Stout.

"Hardy at Max Gate," by permission of the Society of Authors.

"Some Literary Celebrities I Have Known," from *Autobiography* by G. K. Chesterton, copyright © 1936. By permission of Miss D. E. Collins and Sheed and Ward, Inc., New York.

"D. H. Lawrence: Ten Years After," by permission of the author.

"Memories of Yeats," from *Life and the Dream*, copyright © 1939 by Mary Colum. By permission of Doubleday & Co., Inc.

"Harlem Literati of the Twenties," from *The Big Sea* by Langston Hughes, copyright © 1940 by Alfred A. Knopf, Inc. All rights reserved by Langston Hughes. From *The Langston Hughes Reader*, copyright © 1958 by Langston Hughes. All rights reserved by the author.

"Frank Crowninshield," by permission of the author.

"The Joyce I Knew" and "They Think They Know Joyce," all rights reserved to Oliver D. Gogarty.

"Des Imagistes," by permission of the author.

"The Idler and His Works." From *The Idler and His Works* and other essays, copyright © 1957, by Daniel Cory. By permission of George Braziller, Inc., New York.

"Willa Cather, The Sunlit Peak," from *Books and People* by Marion King. By permission of The Macmillan Company.

"Maugham At Eighty," all rights reserved to the author.

"America's Philosopher." Max Eastman's tribute to John Dewey appears in an expanded version in his new book *Great Companions*, published by Farrar, Straus and Cudahy, copyright © 1959 by Max Eastman.

"All About Geoffrey T. Hellman," by permission of the author.

"Ross Lockridge, Jr.—Escape from Main Street," by permission of the author.

"The Literary Life at Seventy-five," all rights reserved to the author.

"My Father." Translated for Miss Mann from the German by Fred F. A. Jacobson.

"Walter de la Mare," all rights reserved to the author.

"The Odyssey of Nikos Kazantzakis," all rights reserved to the author.

"Hero of the Great Know-How," from *Turn East, Turn West,* copyright © 1951, Riverside Press, Cambridge, Massachusetts. By permission of Houghton Mifflin Co.

For

HENRY SEIDEL CANBY

without whom

there would have been

no *Saturday Review*

CONTENTS

vii

INTRODUCTION

Fifty-one days after James Boswell had been introduced to Samuel Johnson in Thomas Davies' bookshop in Russell Street, Covent Garden, Boswell was host at a small dinner which was to have been given at his lodgings in Downing Street, Westminster. But on Tuesday, July 5, 1763, Boswell had a row with his landlord, who "behaved very rudely to me and some company who were with me," and the tenant thereupon "resolved not to remain another night in his house." Since the dinner was planned for July 6, the contretemps called for an abrupt change of base. Boswell selected the Mitre Tavern and informed his guests: Johnson, Goldsmith, Davies, Mr. Eccles (an Irish friend of Davies), and the Reverend John Ogilvie, a Scot.

All went well, except that "Goldsmith, as usual, endeavored, with too much eagerness, to shine, and disputed very warmly with Johnson against the well-known maxim of the British constitution, 'that the King can do no wrong.' " Later in the evening, in no specified context, Johnson made one of his memorable observations: "Bayle's Dictionary is a very useful work for those to consult who love the biographical part of literature, which is what I love most." This is Johnson's only mention of Bayle in the whole of the Life.

Pierre Bayle's Dictionnaire Historique et Critique, *first published in 1697, is as inclusive a biographical compendium as one might well require. It embraces all times and all places, characters out of ancient mythologies along with notables of Bayle's own time. The arrangement of the* Dictionary *is alphabetical. It opens with "Aaron, high priest of the Jews, and brother of Moses," and it ends with "Zuylichem, Constantin Huygens, Seigneur de, secretary and adviser to the Princes of Orange (1596–1687)." Achilles, we learn, "was one of the great heroes of ancient Greece," and he may or may not have been reared on lion's marrow—Bayle is noncommittal on this point. Not far beyond Achilles we find Adam. This "father and founder of the whole human race was produced forthwith by God on the sixth day of the creation." The story of Eve, the apple and the expulsion is summarized, and then: "He became the father of Cain and Abel, and later of Seth, and of many other sons and daughters of whose names we are ignorant, and he died at the age of nine-hundred and thirty years. This is all we know for certain about him."*

The Saturday Review Gallery *would, I am sure, have delighted Dr. Johnson, even though he would not find it as comprehensive as Bayle's* Dictionary, *and I am equally sure that those of our time who "love the biographical part of literature most," or even a little, will be equally delighted.* The Saturday Review Gallery *is a group of nearly sixty portraits of men and women of varying degrees of importance in the field of letters—most of them near contemporaries, some of them actual contemporaries—and the portraits have been sketched, in all but a few instances, by men and women who were acquainted with the subjects, or even related to them, and in three instances by the subjects themselves. Associates, collaborators, classmates, a widow, a daughter, a brother, a secretary, a translator, a librarian—and by secretary I mean a secretary to the subject; by translator, a translator of the subject; by librarian, a librarian who scouted books for the subject—these are some of the portraitists. They saw Shelley plain—most of them more than once.*

How reliable are they as primary sources? Since the majority of them are themselves professional writers (in other words, reporters of one sort or another), I think we can rate their credibility pretty

*high. I will trust even the relatives. The official biographer, par-
ticularly the in-the-family biographer, may require checking against
the objective biographer, but the non-objective biographer has his
value and often writes a good book. In 1898 Hallam Tennyson
published a life of his father:* Alfred, Lord Tennyson: A Memoir.
*(A declared memoir is likely to be a shade less objective than a
declared biography.) It was a good book. In 1949 Sir Charles Tennyson published his* Alfred Tennyson. *It was a better book. The passage of half a century, and the intrusion of a new generation, lent
objectivity to a narrative which was still basically a family chronicle; moreover, the grandson could smile, and even laugh, at times,
whereas the son was apt to be, on occasion, a bit stuffy. But no
Tennyson student can ignore either book.*

A few of the papers in The Saturday Review Gallery *are not by
friends, relatives or associates of the subjects, or even by contemporaries. Frances Trollope died in 1863, thirty-one years after the first
appearance of her* Domestic Manners of the Americans. *Michael
Sadleir was not born until 1888, but as the first Trollopean of his
day he was the authority best qualified to write about her. Three
or four other reports are also by non-contemporaries whose qualifi-
cations far outbalance the mere adventitiousness of the calendar.*

*One of the charms of these portraits is that not all of them depict
great subjects. How many of our bright pupils, for instance, can
identify Augusta Jane Evans? In 1867 she published a novel called
St. Elmo. It was gooey with sentiment and righteousness; the public
wanted just that, and the book sold prodigiously (it is still in print).
"The name 'St. Elmo,'" reports James D. Hart in* The Popular
Book: A History of America's Literary Taste, *"was bestowed upon
subjects as various as girls' schools, a cigar, a blend of punch, hotels,
steamboats, and thirteen towns from New York to California. Even
little boys, poor fellows, were christened in honor of Edna's re-
formed lover" (whose last name was a rather prosaic Murray). One
of the "poor fellows" was Earnest Elmo Calkins, born in 1868 when*

the St. Elmo *furor was at its height. He tells about the novel, the novelist, and what it feels like to be named after a book. Julian Street introduces Oliver Herford to a group who may never have heard of him:*

> *My sense of sight is very keen,*
> *My sense of hearing weak.*
> *One time I saw a mountain pass*
> *But could not hear its peak.*

Frederick Lewis Allen outlines the un-Algerish career of Horatio Alger, Jr. "Minor author," applied to Alger fifty years ago, would have been a fighting word to any boy of Frederick Lewis Allen's generation.

In reading The Saturday Review Gallery *you will find yourself exploring your own recollectest thoughts in search of incidents to which you were witness or auditor. A familiar and treasured moment may owe its immortality to its inclusion in some unlikely repository of print. The universally known anecdote that describes how thirty-two-year-old General James Wolfe, seated in a rowboat in the St. Lawrence River in the twilight of September 12, 1759, "repeated nearly the whole of Gray's 'Elegy' . . . adding, as he concluded, that 'he would prefer being the author of that poem to the glory of beating the French tomorrow,' " was first set down in a paper on John Robison which appeared in the 1815 volume of* Transactions of the Royal Society of Edinburgh. *Robison, a midshipman of twenty, later professor of natural philosophy at the University of Edinburgh, was in Wolfe's boat in line of duty.*

I do not submit the following as an "anecdote"—let us settle for gloss, second-grade. Some two years or more ago I came up in the elevator in the building where The Saturday Review *has its offices. There was one other passenger—a tall, bespectacled, elderly man with a large envelope in his hand. I assumed him to be a member of that rather pathetic company of deliverers of whom anyone who frequents publishing offices sees so many. The errand boy has given way to the errand gaffer; every printer and photographer, everyone in America who supplies goods or services to issuers of books or magazines, seems to employ couriers who must be at least sixty-five in order to qualify for their peripatetic profession. I have often wondered why someone hasn't built a novel around one of them, just as Arnold Bennett, watching an equally pathetic elderly woman fussing with her packages in a third-rate Paris restaurant, produced, from that unlikely seedling,* The Old Wives' Tale.

The elderly man with the envelope got off the elevator at The Saturday Review's *floor. I was behind him as he walked to the receptionist's desk and extended the envelope, and called "McFee!" in a quarterdeck voice. The name is not, of course, unique (though there is only one example in the current Manhattan telephone book, along with a MacFee, a Macfie, a Mcphee, and seven McPhees), but I strongly suspected that this was William of that persuasion. This suspicion was confirmed a few weeks later with the appearance in* SR *of "The Literary Life at Seventy-five," which is included in the present collection. This may well be the only contribution to the book which was delivered to the publisher by the author's own hand.*

Merely recalling this trifling trifle brings to mind a McFee memento of slightly sturdier validity. Twenty-five years ago or more I was one of a group that visited Captain David W. Bone (later Commodore, and after 1946, Sir David) in his cabin on the old Anchor Line steamship Tuscania. *Captain Bone wrote half a dozen sound sea books, beginning with* The Brassbounder, *and in 1955 he published an autobiography,* Landfall at Sunset. *The cabin had extensive shelfage, and the shelfage was filled with books—inscribed Conrads, that sort of thing. I pulled out a McFee title (*Pilgrims of Adversity, *I think) and read the inscription (which I quote from memory, with all the dangers likely to be attendant thereunto): "To Captain David W. Bone from Engineer William McFee, who wishes he were a captain and had nothing to do but write."*

This sort of thing, you see, is catching. Read the units that compose this fine and vivid gallery and you will want to get in on the act. All right—let's.

During the late 1920s I had some correspondence with Richard Henry Dana III, son of the author of Two Years before the Mast. *He invited me to visit him at his home in Cambridge, Massachusetts, any time I was in the neighborhood. The opportunity came in the fall of 1930, when business took me to Boston.*

I did not know Cambridge well—in fact, I did not know Cambridge at all beyond such slight acquaintance as one might gain from attendance at an occasional football game in Harvard Stadium, where events had usually gone counter to my hopes. The address 105 Brattle Street, therefore, to which I had been directed, meant nothing to me beyond the probability that 105 would be opposite a hypothetical 104. Picture, then, my astonishment and delight at discovering that 105 Brattle Street was one of the most familiar edifices in America—a dwelling as immediately identifiable as the White House or Mount Vernon. This was Craigie House, where Henry Wadsworth Longfellow had lived for forty-five years. I walked up the long path to the front door, alongside which was posted a notice announcing that the study and grounds were open to visitors at stated hours. This notice did not, of course, apply to me, who had come not as a raw tourist but as one having affairs to discuss with the present occupant.

The door was opened by a gentleman who introduced himself as Henry Wadsworth Longfellow Dana, one of the two sons of the proprietor of 105 Brattle Street (the other being, inevitably, Richard Henry Dana IV). For the moment the fact that Richard Henry Dana III had married Edith Longfellow had escaped me. H. W. L. Dana received me cordially and informed me that his father was in Europe. I deserved this, of course, for not making an appointment. But Mr. Dana invited me inside, and we sat down in the study. He started to explore a closet under the stairway which held some of

Longfellow's books—one, I recall, was his copy of the first issue of
Leaves of Grass, *with the owner's card pasted inside the front cover
(these books are now in the Houghton Library at Harvard). We
chatted pleasantly, more about the Danas than about the Longfel-
lows, for after all the Danas were the object of my visit.*

*A door opened and closed at the back of the house, and a woman's
voice spoke lively greeting, presumably to the cook, who answered
in kind.*

*"That's Aunt Anne—Mrs. Thorp," explained Mr. Dana. "She
lives nearby. Would you like to meet her?"*

*Just who Aunt Anne might be was a mystery to me. Mr. Dana
caught a suggestion of my bewilderment and came to the rescue.*

"She was christened Anne Allegra, but she's Aunt Anne to us."

*Anne Allegra! I was about to meet laughing Allegra, sister of
grave Alice and of Edith with golden hair. She came into the study
—a smiling, gray-haired lady of medium height and seventy years,
with a striking facial resemblance to Mrs. Franklin D. Roosevelt
and with a comparable charm of expression. Introductions were
made, and the purpose of my visit was explained. When meeting the
son or daughter of a famous man or woman, I have made it a rule
not to bring the parent's name into the conversation, on the theory
that the topic may grow a little tiresome with the years, regardless
of how decent a sort mama or papa may have been. It was Mrs.
Thorp who brought in Longfellow—I have forgotten just how—and
she was soon telling me that neither the poet nor his family had
ever reached a definite decision on the pronunciation of Hiawatha.
Some favored* hee, *others* high, *and the question had often produced
amicable debate at the dinner table.*

*I asked Mrs. Thorp if visitors were much of a nuisance. (Coming
on Dana business, I considered myself several cuts above the run-
of-the-mill sightseer, and well out of the nuisance class.) Yes, she
intimated rather than said, sometimes they were. From the street
they could not read the notice beside the door, which was no bigger*

than a good-sized nameplate. I suppose it was not placed at the gate for the reason that the house was, after all, a private dwelling. By the time casual pilgrims reached the door, however, they probably felt they were entitled to some reward for their pains. I could not see Aunt Anne putting her foot down and refusing to let anyone in.

"One time I did decide to be firm," she said. "It was not a visitors' day. The bell rang and I answered it, and there stood a woman who asked if she might come in. I pointed out the notice. 'Oh, that's too bad,' she said, 'after I've come such a long, long way.'"

That melted all of Aunt Anne's resistance, of course. The visitor was escorted through Craigie House by Longfellow's only surviving daughter—a circumstance that cannot befall again. "All the time," Aunt Anne went on, "I was curious about what that long, long way might be. Somehow my mind fixed on Oklahoma. When we were back at the front door I asked, 'You said you had come a long way. Do you mind telling me where your home is?' 'Not at all,' she answered. 'I live in Fall River.'"

For the benefit of those who may be unfamiliar with the compact geography of southeastern New England, let it be explained that Cambridge and Fall River are some forty-five miles apart.

The reader, having progressed to this point, has already rung the door bell and been admitted to the interior of The Saturday Review Gallery—*an interior which he will, we think, find attractive and hospitable. The house is peopled with men and women whose names are familiar but whom you may have met only in their writings (which is a perfectly sound way in which to meet people). Make yourself at home, and prepare to be introduced to these men and women by other men and women most of whose names will also be familiar to you. You will enjoy your visit.*

—JOHN T. WINTERICH

THE

Saturday Review

GALLERY

A BRITON ON A RAMPAGE

by Michael Sadleir

Today, what Mrs. Frances Trollope said about the behavior of Americans would probably seem harmless and amusing. But in 1832, when she published Domestic Manners of the Americans, *her opinions set the two nations at each other's throats and brought down on the author the wrath of her own people as well as that of the sensitive inhabitants of the New World. Bewildered, she knew only that she wrote books to provide food, clothing, and medical care for her fatherless children (one of whom, Anthony, was to be the famous novelist). Here is the strange story of how an English gentlewoman caused what might almost be considered an international incident.*

AUGUST 20, 1927

THE TALE OF FRANCES TROLLOPE and the curious circumstances which led to the writing and notoriety of *Domestic Manners of the Americans* have precisely those qualities of piquancy and paradox most agreeable to the malice of posterity.

On November 4, 1827, an English lady in early middle age, charged with the fantastic duty of preparing for the establishment of a department store in Cincinnati, was dispatched by her eccentric husband from Harrow Weald to the Middle West of America. She took with her three small children and a certain amount of ready money. After three years the money was spent; the store, before even its building was complete, had come to bankruptcy; and one of the children had fallen so ill that he had perforce to be sent home to England. The distracted mother and her remaining offspring were left stranded in America, to live in abject poverty and to become ever more unfavorably impressed with their surroundings.

At this crisis of her fortunes, and with a faint hope of earning a few pounds on her ultimate return to England, the forlorn and harassed lady began to jot down her impressions of the United States, to tell the tale of her adventures. It was a desperate experiment in bookmaking, and should, by all the canons of literary suit-

3

ability, have failed rather than triumphed. But Frances Trollope's luck had changed at last. By the middle of 1832 her jottings had been published under the title *Domestic Manners of the Americans;* and she herself—having turned author from compulsion and not at all from inclination or from belief in her own talents—had become the scandal or the heroine of two hemispheres.

In the queer hazard that led to her choice of theme lies at once the cause and the irony of Mrs. Trollope's leap to world-wide reputation. No one could have been more innocent of deliberate sensationalism. She wrote about America, because America was the only subject she was capable of treating; she wrote with bitterness, because her own experiences had been bitter. And yet, because at the moment of her writing the United States and their republican experiment were among the most topical and provocative questions of the day, her book and its virulence set two nationalisms at loggerheads and almost caused an Anglo-American "incident." And the second stage of this involuntary imbroglio was, so far as it concerned Mrs. Trollope, no less strange and contradictory. She had no sooner grown accustomed to the indignation of America over her book than she encountered an equally bitter hostility among her own compatriots. This hostility grew into a vendetta. Of the English enemies of Frances Trollope the nucleus was composed of serious persons of radical tendency, holding America for sacrosanct and her loud democratic vauntings for the battle cry of liberty, and the later recruits indignant representatives of the vested interests, roused by her propaganda novels against child labor in factories and other cruelties. All turned fiercely on the bustling, ordinary little woman who had dared to trespass on their idealism and their profits. From the moment of her first book's publication to the end of her prolific writing life this motley company pursued her with calumny and declared her a monster of dishonest prejudice and coarse ill-breeding. So it came to pass that Frances Trollope, whose chief accusation against the Americans had been that they lacked the refinement and elegance of Londoners, came herself to be vilified for an indelicacy most unfeminine, most unladylike, and most un-English.

Modern opinion will find little cause for fury in the pages of *Domestic Manners of the Americans.* Not only have many of Mrs. Trollope's criticisms the staleness to which only out-of-date caricature can achieve, but her very enthusiasms tend to prejudice the self-conscious twentieth-century mind against those qualities of

American enterprise and landscape that she was most concerned to praise. When, however, into the strained atmosphere of the early thirties these two volumes of tart fault-finding and rather superior approval blundered noisily, there was immediate explosion. At home the pro-American Radicals cried out against the hide-bound prejudice of snobbery, while Jingo-Conservatives cheered Mrs. Trollope to the echo, feted and flattered her, made of her Yankee slang a nine days' chic. In America, every journalist and politician howled execration at the latest and most unashamed example of the patronizing Briton on the oversea rampage. It cannot be denied that much of Mrs. Trollope's offense lay in her truthfulness. The Middle West in those early days was (and one must needs judge it on all available evidence from *Martin Chuzzlewit* downward) of a crudity, a tedium, and a boastful squalor inevitable to a certain stage of national development. As certain strata of society in England seemed to the cultivated French during the last half of the eighteenth century, so did the scenes witnessed by Mrs. Trollope during the first part of her sojourn in America appear to one brought up in the London of the eighteen-twenties. She has been blamed for generalizing on the basis of a very limited experience; but careful reading of her book will exonerate her from this charge. She is careful to disclaim any knowledge beyond the radius of her actual journeyings, and her record contains passages of generous compliment once she reaches Baltimore and New York. But to the contemporary American reader the whole body of her praise was as nothing beside her criticism of manners, her exposure of male selfishness and greed, her taunt at American provincialism and false prudery, and her vivid descriptions of crude religious mania and revivalist hysteria.

The anger of the United States gave such pleasure to those English folk who were of anti-American temper that a pamphlet was printed of extracts from American reviews of "Domestic Manners." But these extracts—selected deliberately to gratify a quarrelsome English nationalism—are less interesting than a more spontaneous and more amusing comment affixed by a so-called "American editor" to a pirated edition of the book, which, of course, was immediately issued in New York. This editorial comment is the more pointed (although unconsciously so) because of the great services which were actually rendered to Mrs. Trollope in her inexperienced dealings with publishers and public by Captain Basil Hall, a naval officer who had already given deep offense to Americans by a book about their country.* Here are some characteristic paragraphs from the American preface:

> I have satisfied myself [writes the American Editor] of the impossibility of this book being the production of an English lady. I think it quite impossible that an English lady should condescend to become a spy into the domestic habits and economy of the females of any country, with the views to expressing them to the world. . . . An English lady would scarcely descend to that singular minutiæ of painting in which our author so frequently indulges herself. I allude to the stories of the "bugs"; the curious description and innuendoes of the camp-meeting scene; the episode of the amorous parson; the dialogue between Miss Clarissa and Mr. Smith, illustrated so happily by the accompanying plate, and above all the representation of the scene at the theater and the young lady half dressed at her toilet. . . .
>
> No lady, I will venture to say, of any nation would stand godmother to a book embellished with such illustrations as accompany *Domestic Manners of the Americans.* . . .
>
> To complete the proofs which this work everywhere exhibits of the utter impossibility of its being written by an English lady, I shall merely advert generally to the entire absence of all the characteristics of female writing which it exhibits. There is a total want of delicacy in style and sentiment; a coarse disregard of all those nice decorums which are sacred in the eyes of a well-bred lady; a flippant ignorance of genteel life; and above all a daring, reckless meddling with scenes and topics, which we hope for the honor of old England, precludes the possibility of any English lady having the least agency in its production. . . .
>
> I set industriously about ascertaining the real author. In this pursuit I have been eminently successful. I have ascertained beyond all reasonable doubt that the real author is no less a person than Captain Basil Hall, or 'All, as he is called in the literary circles of London, where he moves with such distinction. . . .
>
> If there really are two such distinct individuals as Captain 'All and Mrs. Trollope, I congratulate the English nation on possessing another pair of Siamese twins.
>
> Some persons, of no contemptible sagacity, have hinted to me the possibility of Captain 'All being Mrs. Trollope, instead of Mrs. Trollope being Captain 'All. The idea is

---

* *Travels in North America,* by Basil Hall. London.

feasible, and deserves a passing examination, although the result is of little or no consequence to us; for whether the captain is Mrs. Trollope, or Mrs. Trollope the captain, concerns only the English ladies, who will doubtless be grateful to me for attempting this vindication of their manners and character. That they are one and the same is certain, but I confess there is some difficulty in ascertaining the sex of these twin gossips. When I listen to the garrulous foppery of the captain, I feel irresistibly inclined to pronounce him to be Mrs. Trollope, or some such ugly old woman in the disguise of a man; but when I ponder over the coarse delineations, the indelicate allusions, and bug and spitting stories of Mrs. Trollope, I am as irresistibly drawn in the conviction that it is some conceited ignorant Jack Tar, breaking his forecastle jests, with a quid of tobacco in his mouth, and his canvas hat knowingly adjusted on one side of his head. Thus am I again brought back to the region of doubt, and thus am I obliged to leave the subject to the industry of some future inquirer. Enough I trust, however, hath been said to prove, to the satisfaction of every impartial reader, either Captain Basil 'All is Mrs. Trollope in breeches, or that Mrs. Trollope is Captain Basil 'All in petticoats.

Domestic Manners earned for its author some six hundred pounds and a notoriety of a very piebald kind. She was herself more interested in the money than in the reputation. The family finances were in chaos, and although her first lucky venture relieved the immediate pressure, there was much more of earning to be done before she could have leisure even to think herself a literary lion. And when the leisure came, it brought no thought of vanity. By the time that money had been won, she was too old, too weary, and too indifferent to anything but peace to care whether her name in the annals of contemporary letters was bright or mud-bespattered. But to posterity—to such part of it, at least, as plays the amateur of irony and savors the quaint fevers of the past—the perpetual quality of irritation that her book possessed (how faded are now the great majority! what slapstick geniality seems even her most enduring satire!) provides an intriguing problem in changing standards of literary taste. Mrs. Trollope's long list of novels includes some twenty tales of fashionable life, rich in sensibility, painfully genteel, occasionally amusing, always rapidly observed; four stories of America—among them the moving anti-slave-trade novel *Jonathan Jeffer-*

son Whitlaw (1836) and the still excellent fooling of *The Barnabys in America* (1843); a savage satire on evangelical Christianity—*The Vicar of Wrexhill* (1837); an exposure of Jesuit intrigues in England—*Father Eustace* (1847); and two books as frankly propagandist as ever Dickens himself wrote—*Michael Armstrong* (1840), a fierce attack on child slavery in north-country mills, and *Jessie Phillips* (1843), an appeal for public protest against the administration of the New Poor Law. Thus summarized, the bulk of her fiction sounds commendable and praiseworthy enough; to read, the books are pleasant where they are not dull. And yet in the opinion of her contemporaries Frances Trollope was so violent, so unscrupulous, above all so vulgar, that even to read her was more daring than genteel.

How might this be? The explanation is little creditable to the England of the thirties and forties. Those persons who were angered by her anti-Americanism or by her assaults on their freedom to wring wealth from helplessness chose, as means of revenge, an intense though indirect campaign against her breeding and her sense of decency. That their disingenuous intrigue should so thoroughly have succeeded can only be attributed to the snobbery of their compatriots and to a prevalent desire to shirk unpleasant facts. For indeed, save by the prejudice of snobbery and by false refinement, the widespread shudder at the gross nature of her books cannot be interpreted. Her non-British acquaintances did not find her vulgar. She was one of the privileged few invited to hear Chateaubriand read his memoirs aloud at Madame Récamier's; while in Vienna she became an intimate friend of Mme. Metternich. But in her own country the respectable drew in their skirts. Thus, for example, a contributor to R. H. Horne's critical symposium, *A New Spirit of the Age,* who is at once sensitive to outrages against elegance and highly conscious of the fact that Mrs. Gore was of the *beau monde* but Mrs. Trollope of the middle class:

> If we want a complete contrast to Mrs. Gore, we have it at hand in Mrs. Trollope. The class to which she belongs is, fortunately, very small; but it will always be recruited from the ranks of the unscrupulous so long as a corrupt taste is likely to yield a trifling profit. She owes everything to that audacious contempt of public opinion, which is the distinguishing mark of persons who are said to stick at nothing. Her constitutional coarseness is the natural element of a low popularity, and is sure to pass for cleverness, shrewdness, and

strength, where cultivated judgment and chaste inspiration would be thrown away. She takes a strange delight in the hideous and revolting, and dwells with gusto upon the sins of vulgarity. Nothing can exceed the vulgarity of Mrs. Trollope's mob of characters, except the vulgarity of her select aristocracy.

The suggestion that this vulgarity was as much profit-seeking as self-expression was first made by Fenimore Cooper in his book on England. But he had, at least, the provocation of *Domestic Manners,* which Horne's contributor had not; nor Mary Mitford either, who, for all her long-standing intimacy with the Trollopes and her many protestations of friendship, could yet allow herself this little genteel sneer:

> I really cannot read the present race of novel writers, although my old friend Mrs. Trollope, in spite of her terrible coarseness, has done two or three marvelously clever things. She was brought up within three miles of this house and is, in spite of her works, a most elegant and agreeable woman.

So the tale went, from mouth to cultivated mouth, parroted from one decade to another; thus the irony that attended the reception of *Domestic Manners* persisted throughout Mrs. Trollope's life and even after it. She wrote her books from bleak necessity; she ground out library fiction to buy her children food, to pay her doctor's bills. As theme for bread-and-butter novel writing, any experience, absurdity, or abuse was welcome. Americans, evangelicals, mill-owners, old maids, parvenu vulgarians—all of these were to her hurried, anxious mind subjects as good as each or any other. Nothing she said of them was bitterly or even very deeply meant; but much of it was taken with a tragic indignation.

Her first encounters with such unlooked-for hostility left her bewildered and a little breathless. But time and her temperament accustomed her to the experience. A cheerful, unreflective creature, she was one to whom livelihood was more precious than vain speculation, and pretty clothes more lovely than idealism. Wherefore she rattled through her strenuous life, only concerned to keep her family in food and shelter, at once incurious and uncomprehending when the world cried out against her methods of breadwinning.

One may indeed liken her to a flustered and perhaps incautious starling who, home-seeking, builds a nest in a mansion chimney. The nest and chimney take fire; the mansion is burned and with it an important will; there follow family and legal complications of an alarming kind. But, were the starling to be charged with the responsibility for all these dreadful things, she would not understand her sin nor let it worry her. "I had to build a nest," she would protest. "That chimney seemed as good a place as any other."

LAST OF THE GREAT FAIRY-TALERS

by Rumer Godden

The stories which are read and enjoyed by a child are self-per-
petuating; they persist in his thoughts and speech through his adult
years, too. Not only Mother Goose and Santa Claus but the char-
acters found in profounder works accessible to children—men of
the Gospels, beasts of Grimm's tales, or the carefully contrived
figures of Perrault, La Fontaine, Lewis Carroll, and Hans Christian
Andersen—all these are as immortal as any literary creations can
be. Rumer Godden, novelist and playwright, writes about the last
of the great storytellers, Andersen of Denmark.

DECEMBER 25, 1954

ON HANS ANDERSEN'S STATUE in the King's Garden of Copenhagen
are the words "H. C. Andersen. Digter," meaning poet, or writer;
that word often comes as a surprise; we are all so accustomed to
think of him as a storyteller for the nursery that we forget that the
Tales were conceived, worked over, polished by a hard-working
writer. They seem so natural and easy that few of us realize that
Andersen, by scholars and thinking people, is ranked among the
great writers of the world.

Does that reputation rest only on the Tales? Yes, only on the
Tales. Andersen wrote many other things, among them a novel that
was immensely popular in its own day, *The Improvvisatore;* there are
three other novels, as well as travel books, plays—some of them produced at the Theater Royal in Copenhagen—and books of poems
but, except for a few of the poems, none of these is read now by
anyone but students of Andersen; it is for the Tales that he has his
place. On the surface it seems unlikely that such world fame should
come from fairy tales, little stories for children, but if we go deeper
it is easy to see how and why it came.

The word *fairy* has become associated in our minds so much with children that we have forgotten its real meaning; it is from the old French word *faerie* that meant "enchantment," which, in its turn, came from the Latin *fata* or *fate*, something inexorable and strong.

Andersen himself once explained what a fairy tale could mean. "In the whole realm of poetry no domain is so boundless as that of the fairy tale," he said. "It reaches from the blood-drenched graves of antiquity to the pious legends of a child's picture book; it takes in the poetry of the people and the poetry of the artist. To me it represents all poetry, and he who masters it must be able to put into it tragedy, comedy, naïve simplicity, irony, and humor"—all qualities of Andersen. "At his service are the lyrical note, the childlike narrative, and the language of nature description." Andersen used them all. He also said, "In a small country a poet must of necessity be poor so that he must try and catch the golden bird of honor." He added, half disbelieving it, "It remains to be seen if I can catch it by telling fairy tales."

In the 120 years since the first of Hans Andersen's Tales were published they have sold, taking the length of time into consideration, more copies than any other book in the world except the Bible, Shakespeare, and *Pilgrim's Progress*—there have been over 2,000 editions—and this is not only as an author for children; grown-up people from artisans to kings read him and keep his books on their shelves; scholars have given their lives to study him—one Japanese professor was so dissatisfied with the translations that he learned Danish only to read Andersen in the original; his Tales are in Japanese, Chinese, Hindustani, Arabic, Swahili, Hebrew, Yiddish, Russian, as well as all the European languages and Esperanto; they have been made into ballets, plays, films. He kept an album as a record of his friendships and the names in it read like an inventory of the most brilliant and famous people of the Europe of his time. Thorvaldsen the sculptor, Frederika Bremer the Swedish novelist, Grieg, Bøgh, Schiller, Heine, Chamisso, Tieck, Schumann, Mendelssohn, Weber, Cherubini, Victor Hugo, Dumas the Elder, Lamartine, De Vigny, George Sand, Rachel, Brandes, Liszt, Lord Palmerston, Dickens, Wilkie Collins, Lady Blessington, Jenny Lind, the Grand Duke of Saxe Weimar, the King of Prussia, the kings and queens of his own Denmark, were his personal friends.

Hans Andersen wrote in his autobiography, "Life itself is the most wonderful fairy tale." For him it certainly was. He started with every possible disadvantage: his father and mother were very humble and poor, a cobbler and a washerwoman. He came to

Copenhagen from the country when he was only fourteen years old, and wandered a destitute waif about the city; he had no real schooling until he was seventeen, when the directors of the Royal Theater, attracted by his strangeness and his queer persistence in attaching himself to the theater and writing extraordinary and unactable plays, applied for a state grant to educate him. Added to all this he was so tall and thin and ugly that he might almost have been a freak, and so thin-skinned and nervous that he wept at criticism, burst out into violent rages, and was a torment to his friends, while his naïveté would have been laughable if it had not been disarming. Yet he ended as a quiet, dignified, learned, and gentle man, his ugliness mellowed into a nobility that struck everyone who saw him; he was given the title of State Counsellor, with a state pension; he had orders and decorations. He became an accomplished courtier; it is told that once, at table, King Frederik VII raised his glass to Andersen; the drinking of healths in Denmark is a serious business and Andersen had only water in his glass; he thought the green color of the goblet would hide this and raised it in return but the King said, "When you drink to your King you drink wine."

"When I drink to my King water is made wine," said Andersen.

He was equally honored abroad; when he visited Portugal the ships in Lisbon harbor ran up their flags for him, and while he was in Scotland he lost his walking stick and it traveled safely back to him all over the Highlands, labeled simply "Hans Andersen, the Danish poet."

What was there in these fairy tales to merit all this? Was it simply popularity? No, because it has lasted; Hans Andersen is as much read now as when he was alive, or even more. Kings and queens, artists and statesmen still read him as children do. But why? What is it that makes him so different from Perrault, for instance, or from Grimm?

Andersen's countryman Kai Munk, the poet and playwright, has remarked that there are two kinds of writing: writing of entertainment, which is ephemeral, and writing of existence, which can be very entertaining as well. It would seem that a fairy tale must of necessity belong to the first group, but the tales of Hans Andersen are writing of existence—they have their roots in eternal truths.

In the Bible we are told that God formed Man out of the dust of earth and breathed into his nostrils . . . and Man became a living soul. Without irreverence it might be said that Hans Andersen did something like that, too; he formed his stories of the dust of earth: a daisy, an old street lamp, a darning needle, a beetle, and made them live. His breath was unique; it was an alchemy of wisdom, poetry, humor, and innocence.

He was adult, a philosopher, and a lovable man; his stories are parables and have meanings that sound on and on—sometimes over our heads—after their last word is read. He was a poet and knew the whole gamut of feeling from ecstasy to black melancholy and horror. People call him sentimental; in a way he was, but in the first meaning of the word, which is not "excess of feeling" but an "abounding in feeling and reflection." He was a child; children have this godlike power of giving personality to things that have none, not only toys, but sticks and stones, bannister knobs and footstools, cabbages; it dies in them as they grow up, but Andersen never lost this power. "It often seems to me," he wrote, "as if every fence, every little flower is saying to me, 'Look at me, just for a moment, and then my story will go right into you.'" "Right into you," that is the clue. The daisy, the street lamp, the beetle—they are suddenly breathing and alive.

> Once upon a time there was a bundle of matches; they were tremendously proud of their high birth. Their family tree—that's to say, the tall fir tree that each little match stick came from—had been a huge old tree in the wood. And now the matches lay on the shelf between a tinderbox and an old iron cookpot, and they told the other two about the time they were young. "Ah, yes," they said, "in those days, with the velvet moss at our feet, we really were on velvet. Every morning and evening we had diamond tea; that was the dew. And all day we had sunshine. . . . But then the woodcutters arrived; that was the great upheaval, and our family was all split up. Our founder and head was given a place as mainmast on board a splendid ship that could sail round the world if she liked; the other branches went to other places and, as for us, we've got the task of lighting up for the common herd; that's how we gentlefolk come to be in the kitchen."
>
> "Well, things have gone differently with me," said the cookpot which stood alongside the matches. "Right from the time I first came into the world, I've been scrubbed and boiled again and again. I've got an eye for the practical and, strictly speaking, I'm Number One in this house. My great delight, at a time like after dinner, is to sit clean and tidy on the shelf and have a nice little chat with my friends. But except for the waterbucket, who now and then goes down into the yard, we

spend all our time indoors. Our one news-bringer is the market basket, but that goes in for a lot of wild talk about the Government and the people. Why, the other day there was an elderly jug so flabbergasted by what the basket said that it fell down and broke in pieces. It's a red Radical, that basket, mark my words!"

"How you do chatter!" said the tinderbox; and the steel let fly at the flint, so that it gave out sparks. "Come on, let's have a cheerful evening!"

"Yes, let's discuss who belongs to the best family," said the matches.

"No, I don't like talking about myself," said the earthenware jug. "Let's have a social evening. I'll begin. . . . On the shores of the Baltic, where the Danish beech trees . . ."

"It does sound interesting the way you tell it," said the broom. "One can hear at once that it's a lady telling running through it all."

"That's just how I feel," said the basket, and it gave a little hop of sheer delight, and that meant "splash!" on the floor. Then the cookpot went on with its story, and the end was every bit as good as the beginning.

The plates all rattled with joy, and the broom took some green parsley out of the bin and crowned the cookpot with it, knowing this would annoy the others and "if I crown her today," she thought, "then she'll crown me tomorrow."

"Now I'm going to dance," said the tongs, and dance she did—my word, what a high kick! The old chintz on the chair in the corner fairly split himself looking at it. "Now may I be crowned?" asked the tongs, and crowned she was.

"After all, they're the merest riffraff," thought the matches.

That is a whole live kitchen world. After reading it a kitchen never seems the same place again; one is almost afraid to take a shopping basket out for fear of what it might think; it is almost as if the dustpan might speak; and notice in how few words it is told.

All the stories have this economy, this startlingly quick effect. Andersen is verbose and boring in his novels and autobiography, but the Tales are his poems. Each story has the essence of a poem and a poem is not prose broken into short lines, but a distilling of thought and meaning into a distinct form, so disciplined and finely made, so knit in rhythm, that one word out of place, one word too much, jars the whole. With Andersen we are never jarred and it is this close knitting and shaping that give the Tales their extraordinary swiftness—too often lost in translation—so that they are over almost before we have had time to take them in and we have had the magical feeling of flying. The children, he remarked, always had their mouths a little open when he had finished; that is the feeling we have too.

But they were not written swiftly, were not the happy accidents that some people think them; anyone who has studied one of the original manuscripts from the first short draft of a story, through all its stages, the crossings out, rewritings, and alterations in Andersen's small spiky handwriting, the cuttings and pastings together, until it was ready for the printer, can see how each word was weighed and what careful pruning was done, what discipline was there. Even the discipline was skillful; Andersen never let it kill the life in his style.

That life is his hallmark. A sentence from one of Hans Andersen's Tales is utterly different from a sentence by anyone else. "The children got into the coach and drove off," Perrault or Grimm would have written but Hans Andersen wrote: "Up they got on the coach. Goodbye, Mum. Goodbye, Dad. Crack went the whip, whick, whack, and away they dashed. Gee up! Gee up!"

"It's not writing, it's talking," the irritated critics had said but, one after another, serious writers have found in it a source of inspiration: "From that moment," said Jacobsen, "a new prose was born in Danish literature; the language acquired grace and color, the freshness of simplicity."

It is this freshness and simplicity that are lost in most English translations, but the newest, by R. P. Keigwin, Danish scholars say, catch the essence of Hans Andersen as never before; American and English people brought up on the sentimental verbose Andersens we have all known may find these a surprise. "But he makes the kitchenmaid in 'The Nightingale' say 'Gosh!'" said one American critic. Precisely, because *Gosh* or *Lawks* is nearest to the Danish of what she did say. "Where's your spunk?" the witch asks the Little Mermaid. That critic would no doubt have preferred "Where is your courage?" but *spunk,* its one syllable snapped out so quickly, is nearer to Andersen. The difference in translations can be shown by studying the story of "The Tin Soldier." He has been called "The Dauntless Tin Soldier," "The Constant," "The Steadfast"; Mr. Keigwin uses "The Staunch." That small taut firm word *staunch* is exactly right for a little tin soldier and it has the quickness and economy of the Danish; and with all their slang the stories keep their beauty; Andersen is one of the few writers who uses slang beautifully.

He always had a turn for phrases. "She is like a little black coffee pot boiling over," he once said of a plump, small, dark and talkative woman.

Not everyone liked the Tales. There were some bad reviews: "Although the reviewer has nothing against good fairy tales for the grownups," said one, "he can only find this form of literature entirely unsuitable for children. . . . Ought their reading, even out of school, to be merely for amusement? . . . Far from improving their minds," he said severely, "Andersen's Tales might be positively harmful. Would anyone claim that a child's sense of what is proper would be improved when it reads about a sleeping princess riding on the back of a horse to a soldier who kisses her? . . . or that its sense of modesty be improved by reading about a woman who dined alone with a sexton in her husband's absence? Or its sense of value of human life after reading 'Little and Big Claus'? As for 'The Princess and the Pea,' it is not only indelicate but indefensible as the child might get the false idea that great ladies must be terribly thin-skinned. . . ." The critic ended by saying, " 'Little Ida's Flowers' is innocent but it has no moral either."

We smile at such criticism, but there are others that threaten Andersen just as seriously; for instance, there is an idea now that children should be given books without shadows, books of brightness and lightness, and laughter, nothing else; perhaps the reason why such books are so lifeless is that living things have shadows.

This has led to what can only be called a desecration of Andersen's work; judicious editors have cut it, changed the endings, in some cases simply taken the plot away from the story and told it again, until, as Professor Elias Bredsdorff says, what we have is Andersen murdered.

No one can deny that Andersen has his dark side; he could hardly escape it; he was writing in the first half of the nineteenth century and had been brought up among crude and ignorant people. As a child he was told macabre stories and superstitions; he had been terrified of his grandfather, who was mad, and, when he went to the asylum with his grandmother, he had seen dangerous lunatics kept in cells. In his day Denmark had capital punishment and as a boy he was taken to see an execution, supposed then to be an edifying sight for children; in Copenhagen, in his early days, he lived among the dregs of the city; besides all this, as a true poet, once he began to write a Tale he became possessed by it.

Stories as vividly horrid as "The Girl Who Trod on a Loaf," as sad as "The Shadow," should perhaps be kept away from children altogether but to expunge parts of them, to tell them in another way, is to destroy them, not too strong a word; and almost always it is safe to trust the children to Andersen. "The Little Mermaid," for instance, has terrible parts, but the ultimate feeling is of joy and tenderness, the story is one of the saddest on earth but it is also one of the very best loved.

In pictures and statues of Andersen tiny children are shown listening to the stories; this is sentimentally false. The stories were not meant for them. In the 1840s, 1850s, and 1860s very little children were kept in the nursery when visitors came to the house; it was not until they were seven or eight years old that they were allowed to go down to the drawing room or in to dessert to meet Mr. Hans Andersen and perhaps hear his Tales. Even then they did not understand the whole; they were not meant to; all Andersen wanted was that they should love them.

In "The Apple Bough" the apple branch realizes the difference in people. "Some are for ornament, some for nourishment, and some we could do very well without," it thinks. A poet, if he is a good poet, is for both ornament and nourishment and the world would be a poor place without him.

Andersen charms and pleases us and he feeds our hearts and minds and souls; he has few conventional happy endings. Terrible things happen, but no matter what happens the ultimate pattern comes clear and a wholeness is reached that is better than happiness because it satisfies.

When Denmark was at war with Prussia, a friend wrote to Andersen and told him how in a house that had been ruined with cannon and grapeshot a storks' nest on the broken roof held a new stork family. It seemed to Andersen a symbol of the great pattern in which he believed. He had glimpsed it before. When King Christian VIII had died and all Denmark mourned, a swan had flown against the spire of Roskilde Cathedral, where all the kings and queens have their sarcophagi; it brushed its breast and fell but soon it was able to fly again. When Oehlenschlager the poet died a songbird built its nest in one of the wreaths, and once Andersen, in a black mood, wrote with his cane in the snow, "Snow is like immortality. In a little while there is no trace." He went away, there was a thaw, and when he came to the place again he found all the snow had melted, except for one spot, where remained the word *Immortality*.

It was Spinoza who said, "The more we understand individual things, the more we understand God." For Hans Andersen every fence, every small flower, seemed to say, "Look at me and my story will go right into you"; a thistle, a tin soldier, a snail, opens a breadth of vision and understanding; he knew that the little is part of the big and it is this sense of largeness, of infinity, that comes to us; the stories do not need a moral for they are each a parable.

ST. ELMO, OR, NAMED
FOR A BEST SELLER

by Earnest Elmo Calkins

*Right after the Civil War along came a book that swept the nation:
St. Elmo, a Novel, by Augusta Jane Evans. The brief description
of the plot given here makes one wonder why. In any case, here
are the odd circumstances of the writing of this novel, of its publication, and an explanation by Mr. Calkins of his middle name.*

DECEMBER 16, 1939

IN 1867 and for some years thereafter ministers of the gospel charged
with the duty of affixing given names to the newborn progeny of
their parishes were astonished at the number of male infants presented at the baptismal font to be christened with the novel and
romantic name of St. Elmo. And not only children. Such was the
amazing vogue of that exotic appellation that plantations in the
deep South, steamboats around the bends of great rivers, girls'
schools, hotels, various articles of merchandise, and thirteen American towns were likewise designated by that latest fad in nomenclature. Everything was St. Elmo.

The cause of the outbreak was *St. Elmo, a Novel,* as it was
demurely styled on the title page, by Augusta Jane Evans, patrician,
pedantic, and prudish daughter of the South, that became a best
seller in the years following the Civil War. It was translated into
most of the literate languages of the globe, and its success is comparable with *Gone with the Wind,* due allowance being made for
increase of population and better distribution of books. It lay on the
marble-topped center tables in all cultured homes; only *Uncle
Tom's Cabin* topped it in sales; its author was hailed as the American Brontë, and it was seriously suggested that she be called Beulah
Evans—after the heroine of one of her previous books—to distinguish her from that less famous Marion Evans of England, better
known as George Eliot.

Men forsook lives of sin and wrote the proud author they had been "saved" and "converted" by its chaste and pious pages, and a far-traveled observer recorded that he had discovered a Parsee boy reading it in the shadow of Taj Mahal, a striking coincidence, for a scale model of that famous tomb figures in one of the crises of the book. It attained the eminence of burlesque, and *St. Twel'mo*, by Charles Henry Webb, had a mild success of its own. And it may still be discovered, in the form of a melodrama, in the repertoire of jitney theatrical stock companies.

St. Elmo is the story of St. Elmo Murray and Edna Earl. Edna was the daughter of the village blacksmith of Chattanooga, whose

> flexible lips curved in lines of orthodox Greek perfection . . . while the broad, full, polished forehead with its prominent swelling brows could not fail to recall . . . the calm, powerful face of Lorenzo di Medici.

Orphaned and left alone in the world by the death of her grandfather, she is rescued from a train wreck at Columbus, Georgia, by Mrs. Murray, proud, ambitious, snobbish widow of a wealthy planter. Mrs. Murray takes Edna into her home, brings her up, and educates her. Allan Hammond, pastor of Mrs. Murray's church— no denomination given, but the parsonage beside the cathedral-like sanctuary suggests Episcopalian rather than the Methodist Church South—was placed in charge of Edna's education.

St. Elmo, Mrs. Murray's son, arrogant, wicked, was

> prematurely old . . . the fair chiseled lineaments were blotted with dissipation, and blackened and distorted by the baleful fires of a fierce, passionate nature and a restless, powerful, and unhallowed intellect . . . [until] . . . sin had reduced him to a melancholy mass of ashy arches and blackened columns.

St. Elmo gives one look at what mother brought home and flees to Edfu, to be gone four years. By the time he returns Edna has been brought to such an intellectual pitch by the learned minister that she is familiar with Sanskrit, Hebrew, Chaldee, Arabic, and Cufic, not to speak of Greek and Latin. Her learning is a match for the unhallowed intellect. St. Elmo falls in love with Edna. Her pure faith penetrates the ashy arches. But she rejects him with scorn.

> "I would sooner feel the coil of a serpent around my waist than your arms."

The duel is on. St. Elmo is able to quote appositely from the most
obscure sources, indulge in the most cryptic and recondite allusions,
and does so on every possible occasion. They converse in a language
coruscating with brilliance, studded with quotations; and their
lightest remarks would furnish posers for Mr. Fadiman's group of
pundits. As follows:

> "I have faced alike the bourrans of the steppes and the Sam-
> jeli of Shamo, and the result of my vandal life is best epit-
> omized in those grand but grim words of Bossuet: *'On trouve
> au fond de tout le vide et le néant.'* Nineteen years ago, to
> satisfy my hunger, I set out to hunt the daintiest food this
> world could furnish and, like other fools, have learned finally
> that life is but a huge mellow gilden Osher that mockingly
> sifts its bitter dust upon our eager lips. Ah! truly, *'on trouve
> au fond de tout le vide et le néant.'* "
> "Mr. Murray, if you insist on your bitter Osher simile, why
> shut your eyes to the palpable analogy suggested? Naturalists
> assert that the Solanum, or apple of Sodom, contains in its
> normal state neither dust nor ashes; unless it is punctured by
> an insect (the Tenthredo), which converts the whole inside
> into dust, leaving nothing but the rind entire, without any
> loss of color. Human life is as fair and tempting as the fruit of
> 'Ain Jidy' till stung and poisoned by the Tenthredo of sin."

Touché! She had him there. Thus throughout the book. No
matter how striking the figure or obscure the allusion that St. Elmo
dug out from the depths of his appalling education, Edna came
back with one more recondite, more abstruse. Not many of the
thousands thrilled by this book could offhand define such words as
epoptae, thanatoid, chrysolegent, androsphynx, lotophagi, lachry-
matoria, bath-kol, Zaarach, diamastigosis; or identify Alfrasiab,
Eponina, Ezzolino, Cyranides, Megilloth, Aurungzebe, Aphœa, Mt.
Byelucha, Demophoön; or get the full significance of such allusions
as "Peruvian Quieppo," "Neshki lore," "Bechuana of the desert,"
"Moleschott's dictum," "vineyards of Axarquia," "Basilidian
tenets," "skeleton of Atures," "caves of Atarpue," "cool cloisters of
Coutloumoussi," "reviewing the Bhuda-Gagna," "refugee Yerzidees,"
"incipient Isotta Nogarole." But with such and many more the
conversation of the two principal characters is loaded, not introduced with pomp and circumstance, but casually, as a matter of
course. The book is a gold mine for compilers of crossword puzzles.
Edna writes erudite novels (in the same vein as Augusta Jane's

own *St. Elmo*) that create a stir and bring her fame and money. Augusta Jane's faith in this scrapbook method is reflected in the advice the learned pastor gives his precocious pupil:

> He encouraged her to seek illustrations from every department of letters . . . assuring her that what is often denominated "far-fetchedness," in metaphors, furnished not only evidence of the laborious industry of the writer, but is an implied compliment to the cultured taste . . . when properly understood.

There must be a catch in those last three words.

St. Elmo presses his suit; Edna rejects him from her lofty stance as a perfect Christian, and after each session they must perforce have sought their dictionaries, thesauri, anthologies, and gazetteers to prepare for the next onslaught. Edna's hand is sought by other suitors from both sides of the Atlantic, who, while not in St. Elmo's class in that "information please" style of conversation, have a line sufficiently encyclopedic to keep Edna on her toes. One earnest young man insists on reading with Edna a Talmudic Targum in hopes of softening her heart, but to no avail.

Meanwhile, St. Elmo, failing to overwhelm her with his odd bits of esoteric learning, tries telling her the melancholy story of his life, how he became a "mass of ashy arches," or as he aptly put it, "roll away the stone from the charnel house of the past and call forth the Lazarus of [his] buried youth." Finally he plays the trump card, the only way to break through Edna's fierce religious intolerance, renounces his wayward, cynical, atheistic life, becomes a Christian, and immediately, without the tiresome necessity of a course in theology, the minister of the Gothic pile he himself had built before his fall from grace.

> "God has pardoned all my sins," he cries triumphantly, "and accepts me as a laborer worthy to enter his vineyard. Is Edna Earl more righteous than the Lord she worships?"
>
> "Oh, sir, do not think about it. . . . Never was more implicit faith, more devoted affection, given any human being than I now give you, Mr. Murray; you are my first and my last and my only love."
>
> He drew her closer to his bosom, and laid his dark cheek on hers, saying fondly and proudly:
>
> "My wife, my life. Oh! we will walk this world,
> Yoked in all exercise of noble end,

And so through those dark gates across the wild
That no man knows. My hopes and thine are one.
Accomplish thou my manhood, and thyself,
Lay thy sweet hands in mine and trust to me."

Such, briefly, is the plot of *St. Elmo*. The author of this remarkable
effusion, Augusta Jane Evans, was born in 1835 at Columbus,
Georgia, not far from Warm Springs. The old mansion house that
still stands has been built up into something of a local shrine,
though most of the stories told about it are legends. It is often
pointed out as Augusta Jane's birthplace, but actually it was the
home of her aunt, Mrs. Seaborn Jones; and the Evanses, poor
relations, occupied a cottage on the estate.

Nor could it have been, as is hopefully maintained, the original
of "Le Bocage," the home of the Murrays in the novel, for no such
mansion as Augusta Jane describes existed in the South, or anywhere
in the United States. It was like something from the Arabian Nights
with its domes, arched ceilings, vaulted corridors and arcades, its
doorways guarded by Bacchus and Bacchante, by Boeotian monsters
and Trimurti, adorned with an architrave from the Cave Temple
of Elephanta, a marble miniature of the Taj Mahal at Agra, two
black rhyta from Chiusi and a cylix from Vulci, bijouterie and
objets d'art scattered everywhere to fill a dozen pages, and a
menagerie consisting of deer, reindeer, llamas, Cashmere goats, and
a large white cow from Ava.

For the claim that some parts, at least, of Augusta Jane's *magnum
opus*—pardon me, great work; this book does corrupt one's style—
were written in this house, there is some ground. The Evanses were
living in Mobile when it was being written, but Augusta often
visited her aunt and may have worked on it there. In Mobile only
one of her three homes is still in existence. It has a tablet, and is a
shrine for the few surviving knights of St. Elmo to visit, but there
is glory to spare for the Georgia house.

Augusta Jane's father was Matt Evans, her mother was a
"Howard," if you know what that means, and Augusta was the eldest
of eight children. Things did not go well with Matt—they seldom
did—and he moved as much of his family as existed in 1845 to San
Antonio. The tragic history of the Alamo, fresh in the minds of the
citizens, deeply impressed the young girl. She had had no formal
education other than her mother's teaching, but fired by desire to
surprise her father, and inspired by a miscellaneous but carefully

expurgated reading, she wrote at fifteen her first book, *Inez, a Tale of the Alamo.*

She worked in her own room late at night when she should have been in bed. The old mammy, rising at dawn to bake the hot bread without which no Southern breakfast is complete, saw her light still burning, and reported it to Mrs. Evans. Her mother kept the secret, and her father was greatly surprised, and so proud and pleased he later persuaded Harper's to publish it, in 1855, when Augusta was twenty. As might be expected, it brought the young author neither fame nor money.

Matt Evans found Texas no better for his purposes than Georgia, though what his lines of endeavor were the record does not state. He moved to Mobile, where, nothing daunted by the failure of *Inez* and actuated by zeal to help her father in his financial difficulties, Augusta Jane wrote another book, *Beulah,* on the religious problems of the day. She herself took the manuscript to New York to find a publisher, but did not go alone, of course. That was unthinkable for a Southern young lady. She was chaperoned by her cousin, young, stalwart, and chivalrous (he was a Howard, too), who during the entire interview with J. C. Derby kept his hand on a large book, determined to hurl it at the publisher's head if he had the temerity to refuse Cousin Augusta's work.

His championship was unnecessary. Derby was charmed by Augusta Jane's frankness in confessing the ill success of her first book— though how he, a publisher, could be ignorant of that is strange —and also the further admission that the present work had already been refused by Appleton's. Derby's wife and daughter read it; its religious fervor impressed them favorably, and it was published by Derby & Jackson in 1859. Its success was immediate. Appleton's, who were booksellers as well as publishers, placed an initial order of a thousand copies. During the struggle that Southerners insist on calling "the war between the States," a Confederate camp near Mobile was christened "Camp Beulah," and in the adjoining hospital Augusta Jane nursed wounded soldiers, and sang to them.

While the war continued to rage, she wrote her third book, *Macaria, or, Altars of Sacrifice;* its history is picturesque. Though written in wartime, it is not a war book; the Civil War comes in incidentally—Augusta Jane was curiously aloof from contemporary life —but its dedication to the soldiers of the Confederacy was so fierce and fervid it was required reading throughout the Confederate army. Nor did the characteristic legend fail of the soldier whose life was saved when the book in his breast pocket stopped a Yankee bullet. He must have had a large pocket, but at least the book was tough enough to stop any missile, for it was printed on wall paper instead of the conventional book stock.

It was published by West & Johnson, a firm of booksellers in Richmond. It was printed at Columbus, Georgia, in the shop of Walker, Evans & Cogswell—the name suggests a possible connection with Augusta's family. Because of the blockade, no print paper was obtainable, and, as said, wallpaper stock was used, as yet unadorned, of course, with the floral patterns that were its original destiny. This curious item of Americana is now very scarce, but at least two copies still exist: one belonging to the family now occupying one of Augusta Jane's former homes in Mobile; the other, appropriately, in the Howard Memorial Library at New Orleans.

If *Macaria* was used to pep up the Confederate soldiers, it had just the opposite effect on the other side. General George Henry Thomas, commanding the Army of the Tennessee, declared it contraband, forbade his men to read it, and confiscated all copies found, lest it destroy what we have since learned to term their morale. A copy was smuggled through the lines, however, and coming to the hands of one Michael Doolady in New York, he promptly got out a pirated edition, copyright by the Confederate States of America having no validity.

Meanwhile, the author had sent a copy to her publishers by way of Cuba to avoid the blockade. Derby, his firm having gone out of business, was making arrangements with Joshua B. Lippincott to publish it, when they learned of Doolady's venture. Derby asked Doolady what royalty he intended to pay the author.

"None," said Doolady, "so arch a rebel is entitled to no royalty and will get none."

Lippincott was called in and proposed withdrawing his edition if Doolady would pay the regular royalty to Derby in trust for Augusta Jane, and Doolady agreed.

In the summer of 1865 Derby was sitting in his office in Spruce Street, New York, when a heavily veiled woman was ushered in. It was Augusta Jane. Her brother had been wounded in the war, her father ruined, and when Derby, noting her seedy appearance, suggested some new clothes, she replied that, alas, she had no money.

"But you have," cried Derby, and she was told of the large sum earned by *Macaria,* a pot of rainbow gold, she called it. She had brought with her the manuscript of another book, which was to become her best-known work, bring her the greatest financial return, and influence nomenclature in this country for a decade. That book was *St. Elmo.*

It was brought out by G. W. Carleton (whose imprint and cipher monogram on the title pages of popular novels were to become well known in the seventies), copyrighted 1866 but not published until 1867 "affectionately dedicated to J. C. Derby." Its green cloth cover, with the gold shield lettered *St. Elmo,* was a familiar sight in homes all over the country. Its success was immediate. My parents in a small Illinois town had a copy before 1868, and that was rapid distribution in those days.

It is difficult now to understand the vogue of that strange book, with its *Jane Eyre* plot, its stilted mannerisms, its pages peppered with words and allusions not one in a thousand readers could comprehend. It lacked the lure of realistic descriptions of St. Elmo's wickedness, for the author had neither the experience nor the imagination, nor would there have been a publisher or a public, for such characterization. St. Elmo was a profane, blasphemous man, but his strongest expletive was apparently "What the d—l," always discreetly fig-leaved with a 3-em dash. His sins, as he confessed them to Edna in the great scene, were that he had shot in a duel his best friend for luring his sweetheart away, and thereafter revenged himself on womankind by making love to them and jilting them, sometimes at the church door. But aside from faithlessness, there was nothing to show that his relations with women were other than circumspect. To the author of *St. Elmo,* and to most of her readers, his dominant sin was skepticism of the Christian religion. In this respect *St. Elmo* was in the spirit of a contemporary series of preposterous juveniles found in all Sunday-school libraries, in which the little girl heroine, Elsie Dinsmore, equally priggish and self-righteous, stood off her father and everyone else according to the dictates of an exacting conscience. *St. Elmo* was an Elsie book for adults.

A new vocable was thus given wide currency, and was seized upon as a name for every entity from boys to villages. Towns in Alabama, Tennessee, Georgia, California, Colorado, Illinois, Kentucky, Louisiana, Mississippi, Missouri, New York, Texas, and Virginia were named St. Elmo in memory of a now forgotten best seller. Alabama, Tennessee, and Georgia were obvious, being localities associated with the book or its author. The others are merely examples of the impact of an odd name on everybody's mind. None of the towns became large, and two of them have been absorbed by the nearest large cities, Chattanooga and Mobile. The boys so named grew up; most of them are dead now. I once attended an advertising meeting at which four of the members were named Elmo or St. Elmo. In some cases the name survives into the second generation.

She lived until 1908, dying the day after her seventy-fourth birthday. She wrote five more books, *Vashti, Infelice, At the Mercy of Tiberius* (a detective story), *A Speckled Bird,* and *Devota,* but none made much of a splash. She was for her day an advanced woman—Southern ladies did not write books—but she was bitterly opposed to "woman's rights." In *St. Elmo* occurs this stinging paragraph:

> At least, sir, our statesmen are not yet attacked by this most loathsome of political leprosies. . . . I think, sir, that the noble and true women of this continent earnestly believe that the day which invests them with the electoral franchise would be the blackest in the annals of humanity, would ring the death knell of modern civilization, national prosperity, social morality and domestic happiness, and would consign the race to a night of degradation and horror infinitely more appalling than a return to primitive barbarism.

In 1868 Augusta Jane married Colonel Lorenzo M. Wilson, a wealthy man, president of the Mobile & Montgomery Railroad, one year her father's senior. For that reason Matt Evans had opposed the match, and it was not until after his death that Augusta married. At Ashland, a palatial southern galleried mansion on Spring Hill Avenue, Mobile, then a suburb, now a residential development in that city, she lived with her husband until his death; devout, systematic, following a set daily routine, active in the Methodist church and its choir. On his death in 1891 she moved to the house that is now the sole landmark of St. Elmo in Mobile.

St. Elmo may still be seen at times as a melodrama in the repertoires of ten-twenty-thirty-cent stock companies, along with *East Lynne* and *The Lady of Lyons*, playing small towns and show boats. The author was reluctant to permit it to be dramatized, and vetoed vigorously a proposal to introduce Negroes, pickaninnies, a colored quartet, to lighten the gloom of the story. In her books she had side-stepped slavery as resolutely as if it had not existed all around her, as she ignored the Civil War, and no slaves appear as characters in her books. A dramatization was finally approved, having its première at Cleveland with E. D. Stair in the title role, to be given later at Mobile, but Augusta died without seeing it.

Where did she get the name? Who was St. Elmo? Apparently there never was such a saint, though the name has existed in folklore for some three hundred years. Popularly, St. Elmo is the patron saint of sailors, particularly in the Mediterranean. The strange blue lights that appear on rigging and yardarms during electrical storms have been known for ages as St. Elmo's fires. In Naples there is a Castel Sant' Elmo.

There were at least three originals. First, St. Erasmus, affectionately shortened to Ermo, and corrupted to Elmo by the Italian tongue. Then, St. Anselm of Lucca—Anselm, Anselmo, Elmo. The connection with Peter Gonzales is more remote, and his history more exciting. He was the holy man who preached against the licentiousness at the court of Ferdinand III of Spain with such vigor that the young nobles decided to stop his tongue by hiring a courtesan to seduce him. Peter proved himself a second St. Anthony, resisted her wiles, and in his agony threw himself into the fire. The now contrite nobles rescued him, repented their sins, of course, and Peter devoted his life to preaching to sailors in Italian seaports. He became Elmo something like this. Spanish and French sailors call the blue lights St. Telme's or St. Helme's fires. Spoken rapidly it becomes St. Elme, then St. Elmo, and this new appellation was in turn applied to Peter. All of which means that the origin is lost in the mists of ecclesiastical history. To thousands in the seventies it was simply the name of a novel about a wicked scoffer at religion, saved by his love for a pious woman.

"WHEN IN DOUBT, FIGHT!"

by Earl Schenck Miers

Ulysses S. Grant, who raced death to finish his Memoirs and save his family from poverty, was an enigmatic, unsuccessful President but a great general. Though he never rivals Lincoln's splendor, his personality has its own bite, and those who know him say he has never been given his due. None loves him more than historian Earl Schenck Miers, who here speculates about Grant and Lee, and concludes that the silent, noble Northerner was a wonderful figure in our history.

JULY 9, 1955

ON THE DAY Ulysses S. Grant died thunder shook the hills around his summer home at Mount McGregor, New York, and lightning knocked down eight people at the railroad station. In ancient Greece a poet would have created an epic around this celestial disturbance as the old general walked across the dark valley with hand outstretched in greeting to former comrades-in-arms. But Grant already had written his own legend, in deed and in prose, and in both instances had achieved a magnificent, virile simplicity.

Rediscovering that legend today, one wonders if it may not be the equal of any legend America has produced.

In the South Lee always has stood alone as the untarnished hero of the Lost Cause, whereas Lincoln and Grant have shared a common role in saving the Union and demonstrating to the world that a constitutional republic could endure against foreign and domestic foes. Lee's place in the sun was never seriously contested by Jefferson Davis, who, to his last breath, remained the same severe, cantankerous, argumentative face on a Confederate postage stamp. His quarrel ten years after the war—when the testy Sherman's *Memoirs* suggested that Joseph E. Johnston may have been a capable general—revealed Davis hopelessly as unobjective as ever. There he sat at the bitter end, bickering to the point of weary cussedness, an exiled Achilles sulking over a breezeway in Biloxi.

Today, where no one thinks of Lee and Davis as being of equal stature in life or history, Lincoln and Grant emerge as powerful co-leaders in the ageless struggle for the rights of man. Both understood thoroughly that the essential issue which produced the American Civil War was, in Lincoln's phrase, whether one man should live by the sweat of another man's brow. Slavery, in its ugliest terms, amounted to this perversion of basic Christian concept; and Lincoln and Grant, typical citizens of the high-spirited, individualistic Midwest, looked upon human bondage in any form as repugnant. Yet neither would have disturbed the "institution" as long as it remained in the states where it had existed at the time the Constitution was adopted, for under these circumstances, as Lincoln contended the founding fathers had intended, slavery faced ultimate extinction. Southern insistence on extending slavery deeper into the territories ended this hope and drove Lincoln, in full conscience that the struggle was whether wrong should triumph over right, to take the stump against Douglas.

The Southern argument was that it fought for "states' rights"—specifically, in the Northern estimate, for states' rights that protected the "institution" for all time and against all moral, political, and judicial persuasion. Just how the secessionists intended to convince the objective student of the Constitution that it could claim a right of rebellion under a document that never once mentioned sovereignty as a characteristic of any state was a problem that baffled Lincoln. Whence came this independence to undo with bullets what had been determined by ballots? Whence did this power derive among states who, in the Declaration of Independence, had been "United Colonies" declaring that they were "Free and Independent States" pledged to the common cause of throwing off a tyranny, and who, under the Articles of Confederation, had plighted their faith in a Union that should be perpetual? Lincoln called the Southern contention what he believed history must judge it to be, a sophism. A state that could, under claim to a *local* right, defeat the *general* will of the nation destroyed the nation. And Lincoln asked:

> . . . Our adversaries have adopted some Declarations of Independence; in which, unlike the good old one, penned by Jefferson, they omit the words "all men are created equal." Why? They have adopted a temporary national constitution, in the preamble of which, unlike our good old one, signed by Washington, they omit "We, the people" and substitute "We, the deputies of the sovereign and independent states."

Why? Why this deliberate pressing out of view of the rights of man and the authority of the people?

If these seem like old issues and old emotions, the author is not asking the reader to find modern parallels between the Southern nullifiers and the more recent Dixiecrats; or between the secessionists and the Southern governor who, in effect, recently told a television audience that, the Supreme Court be damned, he hoped his state could maintain segregated schools for at least the next thousand years.

In 1860-1861 these were valid issues and valid emotions, resulting in the bloodiest civil war the world ever has witnessed and creating the point at which the United States of America began to rebuild the constitutional republic we have inherited. These were the issues and the emotions that divided Grant and Lee and brought them as antagonists into the decisive duel to decide our national destiny, whether (as Lincoln believed) Grant fought Lee in what was "essentially a people's war" or Lee fought Grant in the War for Southern Independence.

When the decision had to be faced, between the strong national government represented by the Union or government by disintegration which was the end where secession seemed to lead, Grant possessed the advantage of being an ancestor whereas Lee bore the burden of being a descendant. One followed the irresistible logic of intellect, the other yielded his mind to his heart. Douglas Southall Freeman, tracing Lee's distinguished Virginia background, speaks of the decision Lee was born to make. Even this predestination, however, was not without its price. Through those spring months, as war approached, Lee writhed in mental torment. He saw secession as revolution, as virtual insult to the memory of Washington, and as a refusal to read the Constitution correctly; he despised the very thought of disunion. He employed no pretty words on slavery, labeling it a social and moral evil and declaring that if he owned 4,000,000 slaves he would gladly free them all to end the quarrel between North and South.

Most of all, Lee had no wish to renounce his love for the United States Army, which he had served for more than thirty years. In the month before Sumter he refused a brigadier-generalship in the Confederate army, and did not even answer the letter that proffered him this position, a significant act for any correspondent as conscientious as he. Instead, in a commission signed by Lincoln, he accepted the lesser rank of colonel in the U. S. cavalry. As long as Virginia did not secede Lee faced no compromise between mind and heart; and as a man who had practiced piety through a lifetime, he was not ashamed to pray that his mother state would keep her head in the crisis.

Actually during this period no one symbolized more dramatically than Lee the dread that must have been gnawing at the heart of Jefferson Davis. The Confederacy was still only a provisional government, suspended upon the very thin thread of its own insensibility to fear. With reflection, with time, the danger existed that the influence of men like Lee, who obviously doubted the Cause, could lead many to drift back into the Union. If tempers ever subsided, if powerful Virginia (which in convention on April 4, 1861, voted two to one against secession) continued to hedge, the Confederacy became even less significant in world affairs than one of the more remote Swiss cantons.

So the shooting war started. All over the South church bells rang; people ran through the streets, shouting the news. With gay hearts Southerners rushed to self-destruction, never once truly analyzing the possibility that they might be waging war not only against the North but also against the most desperate aspirations of humanity. For always the enslaved Negro stood before the world: the captive sold into bondage for profit, his human quality destroyed for profit, his existence of soul denied for profit. Southern diplomats, cooling their heels in foreign courts and finding with each passing year that their feet grew colder, must have glimpsed the ugly possibility: had the South lost step with the civilized world?

Soon after Sumter, Virginia seceded. Robert E. Lee was in Alexandria, paying a bill in John Mosby's drugstore, when he read the news. "I am one of those dull creatures that cannot see the good of secession," he said, and Mosby wrote the remark in his ledger beside the amount Lee had paid him. At home in Arlington Heights, Lee paced yard and bedroom, and toward midnight his wife heard him kneeling in prayer. He knew what, as a Virginian and the son of a Revolutionary War hero, he must do. Sumter and the triumph of the secessionists in the Virginia Convention began the tears of blood that Lee must weep until the end came at Appomattox four years later. Forced to the choice, he never again tried to analyze, he never again doubted. This magnificent self-possession of the man not even a Lost Cause could destroy. No passion for self-gain or for self-justification motivated him. He fought for a love.

Edmund Ruffin, who pulled the lanyard to fire the first shot of the war at Sumter, took his own life after the surrender at Appomattox, and between this swinging of the Confederate pendulum from excitement and joy to bewilderment and humiliation four factors shaped the decision.

Lincoln always had been a shrewd politician, a talent that he first manifested during those callow years in New Salem; in the White House he emerged as a supreme statesman, endowed with a sense of history unsurpassed by any President in our national life.

But the Union survived also through Lincoln's superb intelligence; he learned quickly and thoroughly, and from a rank amateur he became a master of war, whose advice in letters to his generals offered a deeper knowledge of the craft of Mars than, apparently, most of them had learned from their classes at West Point, their stints in Mexico, or their tiffs in the territories with the Indians.

Combining these qualities of insight as statesman and commander-in-chief, Lincoln made of the Emancipation Proclamation a triumph of psychological warfare: its impact was upon mankind, reducing the Confederacy to a pitiful little stockade, virtually alone and friendless in its struggle. From the English workingmen in Manchester, hard hit by the shutting off of Southern cotton, came stanch approval of this act that repudiated "the ascendancy of politicians who not merely maintained Negro slavery, but desired to extend and root it more deeply." The workingmen of Manchester were willing to pull in their belts and stand by Lincoln for this purpose —"an instance of sublime Christian heroism," wrote Lincoln in warmhearted reply.

The fourth and final factor insuring the doom of the Confederacy was the emergence of Grant, the quiet, thoughtful, undramatic little general who reduced war to four words: "When in doubt, fight." In life, as in history, Grant simply kept coming on, confounding his critics and his enemies, always better than they suspected (and most always a lot soberer). On occasion he could drink like an Irishman in a Frank O'Connor story—he could *really* drink; and history isn't too much concerned over whether it was luck or prudence that he always managed to have a clear head when he needed one.

Stuck during the early months of the war in the mudhole of Cairo, Illinois, Grant, who had loved horses all his life, dreamed of how fine it would be to command a brigade in the cavalry of the

Army of the Potomac. For a time no one appeared willing to let Grant fight, so he began to force his own opportunities at Belmont and Paducah, and then at Henry and Donelson; he was a nation's hero long before his commanders sensed how good he was. His ascending star dipped sharply at Shiloh, where he was caught flat-footed and badly pasted; but the Vicksburg campaign followed, and suddenly he stood apart, a general who made up rules of war to fit the exigencies. He was bold, original, and smart, a man of success—and precisely what Lincoln most needed.

Grant's powers of concentration were enormous. Details of running his army he left to the members of the staff; his forte was chewing on half a cigar, tipped back on a camp stool, thinking—thinking. Invariably his field orders had to be read only once, they were so clear, so concise, so well thought through. He could move troops to the critical point in a battle with unequaled speed—"feeding a fight," he called it. The pertinacity of the man was in the message he sent after Spottsylvania: "I shall take no backward steps." Soldiers said of him: "Ulysses don't scare worth a damn."

Grant was innately modest, and success never turned his head. Arriving in Washington, to receive the rank of lieutenant-general and command over armies numbering more than a half million men, he simply wrote in the register at Willard's Hotel: "U. S. Grant and son, Galena, Ill." Then he called during a reception at the White House, quite unprepared to find official Washington so eager to see him that his mere presence nearly turned the occasion into a shambles. Asked later to dinner by the President the general declined politely but firmly: "I have become very tired of this show business."

But Lincoln understood—in fact, looking down from the advantage of an extra eight inches in height the President recognized in the unaffected Grant that he beheld, as Horace Porter said, someone who "had sprung from the common people to become one of the most uncommon of men." When Grant insisted on bringing Sheridan east to command his cavalry Lincoln commented that he was "rather a little fellow." Grant said quietly: "You will find him big enough for the purpose"—and Lincoln did. So Lincoln and Grant struck it off from the start, both good-humored and gentle men; and even Stanton failed to fluster Grant, no mean achievement considering that there were many Union generals who for years after the war shuddered every time they beheld Stanton's grim visage on a one-dollar treasury note.

To speculate whether Lee or Grant was the better general is sheer nonsense; both were fine generals, and since Lee was forced more than Grant to demonstrate his leadership both offensively and defensively it may be said unequivocally that he rose to both necessities with brilliance. Those who would detract from Grant's ultimate victory by saying that he fought with superior numbers and equipment must ignore Lee's advantage of thorough familiarity with every foot of the ground over which he fought, the ease with which he could guard supply lines in a friendly country, the prestige and morale of a fighting force that never had been defeated on Virginia soil, the rapidity with which the Confederates could move on interior lines, and the skill with which—at this point in the war— armies had learned to dig intrenchments overnight.

Again, such speculations are nonsense: it was always fated, in this contest of 9,000,000 people against 23,000,000, that time would give the North the military machine to overwhelm and to crush the South. Again, patience—that the moral and legal cause justified the sacrifice on the part of the North, that eventually the general would emerge who could use the spectacular fighting force Lincoln had created in the Army of the Potomac—was the crux of the war.

Many politicians were against Lincoln, but never the hard core of his people; he won the time, the patience for Grant to consummate the inevitable victory. Lincoln knew that the end came too slowly —and knew why when one of his messages would snap at McClellan: "Will you pardon me for asking what the horses of your army have done since the Battle of Antietam that fatigues anything?"; when one of his messages prodded Hooker: "I would not take any risk of being entangled upon the river, like an ox jumped half over a fence, and liable to be torn by dogs, front and rear, without a fair chance to gore one way or kick the other."

Year after year Lincoln pleaded with his generals to understand what they had in the Army of the Potomac, an organization of such strength that whenever it moved it was as though a city like Albany or Columbus or Indianapolis arose one morning and walked away with all its clothing, food, horses, wagons, medicine, ammunition, people. On its own soil, most of all, that army should be able to end the conflict, but twice Lee crossed the line of the Potomac—into Maryland at Antietam and into Pennsylvania at Gettysburg—and despite reverses succeeded in escaping to Virginia. If these were circumstances to drive a President to distraction, so they did with Lincoln.

And then came Grant . . . that slouchy little man with the wart on his cheek and the squint in his eye. There Grant was all at once . . . pitching along with his odd, unmilitary gait, smooching with his wife in full view of staff officers, and batting the hell out of everybody in a new kind of war that saw his armies imitating the old man's restlessness, his need to keep moving, to keep fighting, to risk anything rather than be forced on the defensive.

Was he, as many charged, needlessly a butcher because he was always "hammering" his opponent? "Who's shedding this blood, anyhow?" soldiers said, reading the papers in the trenches. "They better wait till we fellows down at the front hollo, 'Enough!' " With a shrewd understanding of Grant, Longstreet told Lee: "We must make up our minds to get into line of battle and stay there; for that man will fight us every day and every hour till the end of the war." This quality in Grant was also in Lincoln; after Sumter the President never stopped trying to win. Like Grant, he saw in the Confederacy a military despotism that could be defeated only by destroying its resources for waging war. Day and night Lincoln devoted himself to this purpose, and when in Grant he found a general ruled by the same passionate dedication he gave him his blessing and a free rein.

Lincoln's affection for Grant was shared by veterans of the GAR and the majority of the American people. Few men in their lifetime ever have known more demonstrative love and respect. Abroad wherever Grant traveled after the war he was hailed as a hero without perhaps understanding why, but the survival of the American constitutional republic shook the solid resistance to liberal reforms that long had dominated the monarchies of Europe. The American democracy, standing the bloody test of civil war, vitalized everywhere the aspiration for government of the people, and by the people, and for the people.

At home, too, the appeal of Grant was irresistible, for all the cold critics of his two terms as President were able to say, then and since. When the third-term prejudice finally swung the nomination to Garfield it was obvious early in the campaign that this lackluster Republican candidate was in trouble. So Grant came out of quasi-retirement to take the stump. With characteristic directness he usually had completed what he had to say in five or six minutes; really wound up he might last for ten. Wavering Ohio and Indiana swung back into the GOP column. In New York, the real battleground of the campaign, Grant spent the last ten days thumping for

Garfield, but more often talking about "the nation" than his candidate. When every citizen could vote, he said, and political parties didn't line up on a sectional basis, it wouldn't make much difference to him whether the Republicans won. He swept the North with him in politics just as he had in battle. Old veterans cheered and hooted and sang "John Brown's Body." The people preferred Grant but elected Garfield to please the uncommon common man.

Lee, whom the South found to be noble in war, the North judged to be noble in peace. He accepted the verdict of war with the same wholeness of character that led him to the necessity of war in devotion to Virginia. There was not in Lee any of the post-bellum posturing of those who wanted to carry on the resistance by guerrilla tactics, none of the blustering threat of emigrating to foreign lands, none of the festering bitterness of a Davis brooding in Biloxi. He tried in his own quiet, manly way to lift from the South the iron curtain which for a generation had warped its judgment and obscured its vision. Often this was the loneliest battle he ever fought; truly, at times, he floundered in a wilderness more forbidding in its deep shadow than the one through which he had fought Grant on the road to Appomattox.

Grant, sitting in his stocking cap and muffler on the porch at Mount McGregor, fighting the cancer that sapped his vitality for enough time to finish his *Memoirs* and save his family from the privations of poverty, summed up the difference between his army and Lee's: "The Army of Northern Virginia became despondent and saw the end. It did not please them. The National army saw the same thing, and were encouraged by it." This judgment was a fufillment of a prediction. Lincoln had always believed that secession must dissolve rather than sustain its supporters. Eventually it must break under its own weight, returning to the ashes of disintegration whence it sprang. The rebellion against the United States, said Grant, concluding his memoirs, "will have to be attributed to slavery." IIc had not seen this fact as early as Lincoln, and confessed it; but when there was nothing left but death he reduced life to the simple truths he wanted to maintain in this world where man proposes and God disposes. Unless the South could control the general government slavery was doomed. So the war that no sane man ever had wanted to fight was fought—by none more grudgingly, more unremittingly than Grant. Now, in the dwindling hours, he thought: "The war has made us a nation of great power and intelligence. We have but little to do to preserve peace, happiness, and prosperity at home, and the respect of other nations. Our experience ought to teach us the necessity of the first; our power secures the latter."

With these words the old general was about ready to close the pages of his life. Soon the thunder would rumble, the lightning flash.

THE LOST YEARS OF
W. H. HUDSON

by Edwin Way Teale and
R. Gordon Wasson

The whereabouts and activities of W. H. Hudson, during one twenty-year period of his life, are mostly unknown to us. Naturalist-author Teale and banker-author Wasson have done some detective work which provides clues enough to solve at least a part of the mystery.

APRIL 12, 1947

THROUGHOUT THE WORKS of W. H. Hudson there runs a singular paradox. His pages reveal at the same time so much and so little of his life. Virtually every book he wrote contains paragraphs of autobiography, nostalgic recollections of bird choruses of long ago, or great thistle years on the pampa. Yet these memories are timeless; they are linked to no calendar; they might have occurred on any one of a long succession of dawns or summer seasons. Hudson is at once bountiful and niggardly—lavish in memories that are vivid and charming, grudging in the precise placing of events.

Hudson rarely dated his letters. He misled friends as to the year of his birth. He seemed striving all through his later years to forget or ignore the passing of time and the fact that the beauty of the earth which he loved so passionately was slipping from his grasp. To the end, Hudson remained secretive about many events in his past. His friend and biographer, Morley Roberts, could only guess at the year in which he left the land of his birth for England, and he guessed wrong by four years. There are blank spaces, lost years, in the chronology of W. H. Hudson's life.

When the reader lays down *Far Away and Long Ago,* he parts company with young Hudson as the boy is attaining manhood. The time is 1860 or thereabouts and the place Argentina. In sources hitherto available we scarcely pick up contact with him again until about 1880, years after he had arrived in England. Sometime during the intervening period he journeyed to Patagonia. In the main, however, the years are veiled. Faced with this absence of information, inventive admirers of Hudson have suggested all sorts of wanderings and adventures and romances.

Anyone who will take the trouble to seek out the annual report of the Board of Regents of the Smithsonian Institution for the year 1866 will find a clew as to what W. H. Hudson was really doing during at least a portion of this period. On page 27 he will discover what is probably the earliest reference to Hudson in print. The item could hardly be more brief: "In South America, explorations have been made and collections transmitted by Mr. W. H. Hudson, in Buenos Aires. . . ." That dusty tome offers us nothing more, but in the reports for the three years immediately following, there are fuller acknowledgments of accessions of bird skins sent in by Hudson. Then, beginning with the 1870 volume, his name appears no more.

During the second World War, we inquired of Dr. Alexander Wetmore, now Secretary of the Smithsonian Institution in Washington, D. C., whether the archives there might still hold correspondence with W. H. Hudson concerning those bird-collecting activities of long ago. In the card catalogue Dr. Wetmore discovered a number of entries indicating the existence of such letters. But for the duration of the war the archives of the institution were stowed away in an inaccessible place. Now, with the war over, and thanks to Dr. Wetmore's courtesy and the hospitality of the Smithsonian Institution, we have examined a sequence of eight letters, six in Hudson's hand, that have been lying buried for some eighty years in the files in Washington. These letters are the earliest writings from Hudson's hand known to survive.

Two days after Christmas, in the year 1865, in Buenos Aires, Hinton Rowan Helper, the United States Consul, addressed a letter to Dr. Spencer Fullerton Baird, then assistant secretary of the Smithsonian Institution, commending to his attention a young man named William H. Hudson, who was then twenty-five years old. The American official who wrote that short and simple letter of presentation, introducing Hudson to a larger world, was himself a famous person at the time. He was the author of *The Impending Crisis,* a widely circulated attack on slavery, published in 1857. It contributed notably to the emotional ferment leading to the Civil

War. Describing, as Mr. Helper's letter does, a man now famous who was then unknown, it is pleasing to observe that the terms of the letter reflect credit on all concerned, and across the span of the intervening years the words of the American Consul will leave no Hudson admirer unmoved:

United States Consulate,
Buenos Aires, Dec. 27, 1865

MY DEAR SIR:
Professor Burmeister has sent me a Mr. Wm. H. Hudson, of Conchitas, Partido de Quilmes, in this Republic—a sort of amateur ornithologist, who would like to be employed in collecting birds, either for the Smithsonian Institution or for any museum, in the United States or elsewhere. Mr. Hudson has been recommended to me as quite capable in what he professes; and it is believed that he would give satisfaction to anyone who would employ him. I have asked him for his terms, but he says he has never made any collections except as a matter of mere interest to himself; and does not, therefore, know how to charge for his services. Should you feel disposed to employ him, paying him so much for such and such birds, or otherwise, I shall be happy to be, if possible, the medium of any understanding or arrangement that would meet the wishes of both you and himself.

Yours very truly,
H. R. HELPER

Spencer F. Baird, Esq.
Smithsonian Institution,
Washington, D. C.

"The maps I have do not show where Conchitas is," wrote Dr. Baird in his reply to Mr. Helper, "but very little is known of the birds of any portion of the Republic. . . . It will give me much pleasure to see Mr. Hudson's collections and aid him in disposing of them." He pointed out that small, inconspicuous birds were of the greatest scientific interest and discussed possible prices. His letter was dated February 20, 1866.

More than a year went by before a letter from W. H. Hudson was delivered to Dr. Baird. It bears the Smithsonian stamp of February 12, 1867. It was written on September 5 of the previous year in Conchitas. This small community, lying a dozen miles from Buenos Aires, was in the township of Quilmes, where, in 1841, Hudson had been born on the immortal *estancia* of the Twenty-Five

Ombu Trees and whither his family and he returned to live when he was sixteen years old. From the newly discovered letters we now learn that Hudson was still living there when he was in his middle twenties.

In contrast to the difficult scrawl of later years, the penmanship of this initial letter was executed with copybook care. The paper, lavender-tinted, appears to have been cut from a notebook about seven by nine inches in size. A number of the letters show evidences of originating in notebooks; in some instances the holes left by the binding threads are apparent. Of the six letters from Hudson, this first one is the longest and perhaps the most interesting. But all of them convey a vivid impression of the eagerness with which he sought a place for himself as a field worker in the natural sciences. In this letter we have the earliest writing from W. H. Hudson's pen now known to survive.

Conchitas; Sep. 5, 1866

DEAR SIR,

Mr. Helper kindly favored me with a copy of your letter to him, in reference to my collecting birds. I hoped then, to have had, before September, two or three hundred specimans, but I have been disappointed: winter birds, which I tried to collect, were so very scarce this season, that several times I have ridden leagues without being able to obtain, or even see, a single speciman. Most of the birds I now send are of those that remain with us all the year, and are probably well known to naturalists: it is too early yet for summer birds, and as I will not collect any more for two or three weeks I think it best to send the few I have got.

I am not confident that they will reach you in a good state of preservation, as I have no experience in this kind of work; however, they are not many to lose, if they should be lost, and by the time your answer reaches me, I hope to have many more ready to send. I will also try to obtain some ostrich eggs, and a box of snail shells, of which I believe there are only four species in this country.

As you have not required the names of the birds, I have only thought it nessisary to mark the sex of each one, on the margin of the paper in which it is wraped; but if you desire it, in future, I can give with each species, a concise account of its habits. As to the locality in which they were killed, I shot them all within eight leagues of Buenos Ayres city.

You remark that the birds best to get are the small inconspicuous ones, as they are better for scientific purposes. By diligently searching through the swampy forrests along the river, I can obtain many birds of this description. There are here many species of the certhia, an extensive genus of small and homely birds. And it is reasonable to expect, that in a country so little explored by naturalists as this, many species may be found unknown to science.

You must know from the physical conditions of this country—the Province of Buenos Ayres—that it posesses a very scanty Fauna. Wide as is its extent, it is but one vast, level and almost treeless plain, affording no shelter to bird or beast from the cold South winds of winter or the scorching North winds that blow incessantly in summer: while the yearly droughts banish all the aquatic birds to great distances. But it is not only that there are few species that makes the work of a mere taxadermist unprofitable but these are often so widly seperated that vast tracts must be traversed to obtain them all. Though I am not a person of means, it is not from want of other employment I desire to collect, but purly from a love of nature. It would, however, be eisier for me to devote all my time to these pursuits, if I was required to collect other natural objects besides birds, as fossils, insects, grasses &c. and this would enable me to make thorough collections of all the birds. I am, Sir,

respectfully yours
WILLIAM H. HUDSON

Prof. Spencer Baird

We have retained in this letter the mistakes in spelling that Hudson made: wraped, forrest, taxadermist, widly, purly, eisier, nessisary, seperated. The observant reader will notice that at one point, where Hudson describes the pampa near his home, his style begins to take literary wings, but the fledgling in letters quickly drops back to earth again. It may be noted that instead of there being only four species of snails in Argentina, as Hudson imagined, there are nearer 400.

In this first letter Hudson refers to the *Certhia*. Small and inconspicuous, birds of the *Certhiidae* group are related to the North American brown creepers. The young collector does not hide his hope of finding among them, or among the other birds he shipped north, "many species . . . unknown to science." In a second letter, written from Conchitas in June 1867, Hudson notes that some "blackbirds" in a pasteboard box are being included with another batch of bird skins. He wishes Dr. Baird to examine them with special care; he is sure they represent a new species. Nine months pass. Then, in his fourth letter—also from Conchitas and dated March 15, 1868—we hear Hudson's cry of disappointment. No word has come from Dr. Baird about his "blackbirds." He reports that Dr. Burmeister, the head of the natural history museum in Buenos Aires and the man who introduced him to Mr. Helper, "desires much to know what name you will give the species." We may permit ourselves to believe that it was Hudson, more than Dr. Burmeister, who was anxious about the name and that he hoped it would be derived from his own.

Twenty-five years later, as Hudson began to write his *Idle Days in Patagonia,* he recalled these dreams of his bird-watching years on the pampa.

> It was [he records] my hope to find some new species, some bird as beautiful, let us say, as the wryneck or wheatear, and as old on the earth, but which had never been named and never even seen by any appreciative human eye. I do not know how it is with other ornithologists at the time when their enthusiasm is greatest; of myself I can say that my dreams by night were often of some new bird, vividly seen; and such dreams were always beautiful to me, and a grief to wake from; yet the dream-bird often as not appeared in a modest grey coloring, or plain brown, or some other sober tint.

In those lines we listen to a poet recalling emotions of long ago. It is seldom given to us, in such circumstances, to make the clock of the years run backward until we are in the very presence of those emotions themselves. But this is precisely what the perceptive reader will discover behind the veil of these early letters of Hudson's that we now publish. The "blackbird" was a bird of his dreams. The bitter disappointment that lay behind those simple words to Dr. Baird is easy to understand. Although there is no further mention of the "blackbird" in the Smithsonian letters, the story does not end there. We now know the bird was one of the Argentine cowbirds, *Molothrus rufoaxillaris.* It had received that name when it was added to the lists of ornithology by an American scientist only a few months before Hudson wrote his letter. By this small margin he missed the realization of his early dreams. It is pleasing to note that only a few years later, during his Patagonian days, he collected a species of tyrant bird unknown to science. It was named in his honor *Cnipolegus hudsoni*.

At the Smithsonian Institution, in Washington, among the birds ranged in rows in metal drawers, there are still a number of specimens sent in by W. H. Hudson in the eighteen-sixties. Even an uninitiated observer can quickly pick out the bird skins he prepared. Unfamiliar with the practices of conventional taxidermy, he folded the legs so they project forward instead of to the rear. Among these skins there are several specimens of the Argentine "blackbirds," the winged creatures that eighty years ago filled the head of the youthful collector with dreams of scientific achievement.

Another souvenir of those early days, linking us with Hudson, rests in the archives of the Smithsonian. The fourth letter to Dr. Baird contains this arresting sentence: "I enclose a card photograph of myself as desired. . . ." Those words led us to a search in the photographic files of the Institution, and resulted in the discovery of an unpublished photograph, the earliest known likeness of William Henry Hudson. This picture, taken at the studio of "Meeks y Kelsey, fotógrafos, 74 Belgrano, Buenos Aires," shows the young naturalist as he appeared, replete with full beard, in his mid-twenties.

There are frequent references in the later letters to troubles, political and domestic. In 1868, Argentina was at war with the formidable tyrant Lopez of Paraguay. Hudson suggests Dr. Baird address his letters to Buenos Aires rather than to Conchitas as " . . . postal regulations with us, like everything else, are out of joint." In February 1868, he reports: "For several months I have not collected any birds at all, as I have had other occupations at home, besides we have not been exempt from the afflictions that have come on almost every household in this country. . . ." If Morley Roberts is correct, it was in 1868 that Hudson's father died. That event, leading to the break-up of the family and eventually to W. H. Hudson's departure from Argentina, must explain his veiled allusion.

Leaving Conchitas was a thought that was uppermost in Hudson's mind during the period covered by the Smithsonian letters. As early as June 1867, he was writing: "It is impossible for me to make complete collections while I remain at home." The following March he reported: "I shall perhaps leave the Conchitas. . . ." By June 3, 1868, his mind was made up. "At present," he concludes his final letter, "I am so occupied with other matters that I do not collect, but still cherish the hope that I will soon be able to give my whole time to a pursuit that affords me so much pleasure: I will, of course, leave the Conchitas, as I think you will not require more duplicates of the species to be obtained here."

What travels followed, except for the Patagonian adventure, we do not know. The curtain drops once more after 1868. But for a brief span—the years between December 1865 and June 1868—that curtain has been lifted by the letters in the Smithsonian file. They reveal the hopes, plans, uncertainties of some of Hudson's lost years, of a period when as a scientific field-worker he was adding birds from the pampa to the collections of the Washington museum.

THE EDDIE GUEST OF
THE SEVENTIES

by Earnest Elmo Calkins

Will Carleton could really pound them out. His homespun ballads,
teary or humorous, as the case may be, were eaten up by the public.
"Over the hill to the poorhouse—my child'rn dear, good-by!"

JULY 24, 1943

ONE AFTERNOON IN 1871 a young newspaperman sat in a courthouse in western Michigan reporting a small-town divorce case for the Detroit *Tribune*. Something pitiful in the story being thus judicially unfolded so moved him that almost without premeditation he began to put his feeling into verse:

> *Draw up the papers, lawyer, and make 'em good and stout;*
> *For things at home are crossways, and Betsey and I are out.*
> *We who have worked together so long as man and wife*
> *Must pull in single harness for the rest of our natural life.*

The poem, for such it must be called, however pedestrian, ran to some twenty-one verses. In it the old farmer tells of the quarrel that opened a breach between him and his wife, but soon memories overcome him; he recites Betsey's good qualities, instructs the lawyer to make generous provision for her, and winds up—

> *And when she dies I wish she would be laid by me,*
> *And lyin' together in silence, perhaps we will agree;*
> *And, if ever we meet in heaven, I wouldn't think it queer*
> *If we loved each other the better because we quarreled here.*

This tender effusion was printed in the Toledo *Blade* with the title "Betsey and I Are Out," and was soon reprinted in countless newspapers. There were no syndicates in those days to make circulation easy and profitable to rhymsters who touched the popular heart, but it is safe to say that these lines eventually became familiar to every literate inhabitant of the country. The softhearted American public reacted to them as it always does to a sentimental appeal. Indeed, its feelings were so lacerated by this pathetic ditty that the author was moved to soften the blow. It will be recalled that Dickens was deluged with letters begging him not to kill Little Nell; that Thackeray was subjected to the same pressure over the death of Colonel Newcome. This author was more amenable, for he wrote a sequel, "How Betsey and I Made Up," supplying the happy ending so tearfully demanded, and the divorce proceedings were metrically quashed.

The author of "Betsey and I Are Out" was William McKendree Carleton, a name he cannily shortened to Will Carleton as soon as growing fame required a more easily-spoken monicker. He was born on a farm in western Michigan October 21, 1845. His father, John Hancock Carleton, was a Yankee pioneer with several New England generations behind him who had built with his own hands the log cabin in which his son was born.

His mother, Celestia Smith, used to sing old English ballads as she rocked him to sleep, and that early influence may have given direction to his subsequent career. A dreamy lad, he showed little aptitude for farming, but spouted declamations to the patient and respectful cows as he milked them, absorbed what education he could from the country school, and entered Hillsdale College not far from his birthplace. There he devoted some of his spare time to metrical composition, and was elected class poet at his graduation in 1869.

He found immediate employment on *The Standard,* the local Hillsdale sheet, transferred the following year to the Detroit *Weekly Tribune,* and thus we find him in the courthouse composing the piece that was to start him on his typically American career and bring him widespread if not lasting fame.

In 1871 *Harper's Weekly* was the leading American publication. Its crusading cartoonist was Thomas Nast, inventor of the tiger, elephant, and donkey as symbols of political parties, whose bitter and stinging lampoons were smashing the Tweed ring and helping to send its corrupt boss to jail. Its editor was S. S. Conant, over whose head hangs an unsolved mystery. It took a bit of research to learn that his initials stood for Samuel Stillman, for he always appeared in print, even in J. Henry Harper's copious history of the House of Harper, as "S. S." But that is not the mystery. Conant was the shrewd and successful editor of the *Weekly* from 1869 until 1885. And then one Saturday morning he left his home in good spirits ostensibly for his office and was never seen or heard of again. To this day no one knows what became of him.

No sooner had a copy of the Toledo *Blade* reached New York than Conant spotted the "Betsey" ballad, recognizing its human interest value whatever its literary qualities. He not only printed it in the *Weekly*, he wrote Carleton for more—and got them. The first to arrive was a poem written out of the emotion Will had felt when the old log cabin his father had built and in which he himself had been born was sold, preparatory to a move into a more stately mansion. He dwelt on the familiar scenes its walls had witnessed:

> *Out of the old house, Nancy—moved up into the new;*
> *All the hurry and worry is just as good as through.*
> *Only a bounden duty remains for you and I—*
> *And that's to stand on the doorstep, here, and bid the old house good-bye.*

Then came the most successful tear-starter of the entire series, "Over the Hill to the Poor-house," the soliloquy of a poor old unwanted mother, as she tramps her weary way to the pauper's final home. Eight children she has, most of them successful, one well-to-do, but none want her. She has been shoved around from one to another until there is no place to go but—

> *Over the hill to the poor-house—my childr'n dear, good-by!*
> *Many a night I've watched you when only God was nigh;*
> *And God'll judge between us; but I will al'ays pray*
> *That you shall never suffer the half I do today.*

This poem proved to be effective propaganda. The population of the almshouses of the country shrank noticeably after its publication, as conscience-stricken children rushed to take parents from the poorhouse and give them homes. And again Will Carleton bowed to a public that cannot take its tragedy undiluted, for he wrote a companion piece in which the black sheep of the family, the ne'er-do-well son, who has made a strike in the West, rescues his mother and gives her a good home. "Over the Hill from the Poor-house" dried many weeping eyes.

There is an O. Henry touch to "Gone with a Handsomer Man," for in it the faithful John comes home to find the house empty, his somewhat skittish wife gone, the conventional note propped up on the kitchen table, its message the title of the poem. Poor John has a tantrum, throws things around, and apostrophizes the empty walls:

> *A han'somer man than me! Why, that ain't much to say;*
> *There's han'somer men than me go past here every day.*
> *There's han'somer men than me—I ain't of the han'somer kind;*
> *But a lovin'er man than I was I guess she'll never find.*

In the midst of his wailings in walks the smiling wife on the arm of her good-looking old father (though the artist fails to give him much of an edge on John at that) who is of course the "handsomer man," and the phrase "gone with a handsomer man" is added to our popular sayings.

The mild humor of the lighter of these bucolic ballads reached the farcical in such skits as "The Three Lovers" or "The Schoolmaster's Guests." In one Bessie the coquette tried to keep three beaux on the string. The hired man is favored by the old folks, but the neighboring farm lad and the village lawyer are forbidden the house. Bessie hides the small one in the churn, the tall one in the attic, and the dénouement is lively unadulterated slapstick:

> *And there let us leave them, 'mid outcry and clatter,*
> *To come to their wits, and then settle the matter;*
> *And take for the moral this inference fair:*
> *If you're courting a girl, court her honest and square.*

In the other piece, the selectmen call in a body on the schoolmaster and tell him what's what, while the giggling pupils look on. The head selectman "stomps" so hard to emphasize his points that the stovepipe, cunningly adjusted by "Jim, the heaven-born mechanic," falls on their heads and covers them with soot.

> *And the squire, as he stalked to the doorway, swore oaths of a*
> *   violet hue;*
> *And the four district fathers, who followed, seemed to say,*
> *   "Them's my sentiments tew."*

These extracts will give an idea of the content as well as the style of the poems. *Harper's Weekly* published them as fast as they were written, the press clipped and reprinted them, and the people ate them up. They were carried around in wallets. They became platform favorites at Friday-afternoon speakings in the schools, and were added to the programs of those popular entertainers, the itinerant elocutionists.

Harper's wisely decided that such popularity called for a book, and in 1873 the first batch of poems was published, handsomely gotten up for those times—*Farm Ballads by Will Carleton,* the title no doubt in memory of the old English songs his mother used to sing, for the book is dedicated to her. At a time when $1.25 was the standard price for a novel, 40,000 copies of *Farm Ballads* were sold at $2 a volume, or, with gilt edges, $2.50.

In 1875 *Harper's* published *Farm Legends,* similar in format and price to the first book, dedicated to his father, and in 1881 *Farm Festivals,* dedicated to his one brother and his sisters. In 1878 Carleton moved to Boston and attempted to do for the town what he had done for the country with *City Ballads,* 1885, *City Legends,* 1889, and *City Festivals,* 1892. The first book in the City series is dedicated to the author's wife, who was Adora Goodell. The trilogy never attained the popularity of the farm ditties. The pieces are less spontaneous, more mannered, and an attempt was made to tie them together into one narrative by various literary devices, but no one quoted or spouted them, and they gave no sayings to current speech. Will Carleton's heart was in the rural western country where he was born and bred, but nevertheless the total sales of all his books reached 500,000 copies.

While the poems were appearing in the *Weekly, Harper's* called in their best artists to illustrate them, and later the same blocks were used in the books. Artists received scant credit from publishers in those days, and some of the earlier illustrators are anonymous, but names, or at least initials, can be deciphered on many of the cuts (which are of course wood blocks), though the engraver usually managed to make his own name more prominent or more legible than the cipher of the artist. However, it is evident that the books of the series exhibit early work of such distinguished men as Edwin A. Abbey, C. S. Reinhart, A. B. Frost, Th. Nast, W. A. Rogers, W. T. Smedley, and Frederick S. Church. To those of us who conned these poems as they appeared, learned them by heart, and spoke them at rhetoricals, the conceptions of the artists were as veritable portraits of Will Carleton's character as Sir John Tenniel's pictures are of Alice and her strange friends.

In the spring of 1873 when "Betsey and I Are Out" was at the high tide of its popularity, Will Carleton was made the object of a fantastic attack. Its authorship was claimed by a Mrs. (or Miss) K. E. Emerson (she also went by the name of French). Her publishers, G. W. Carleton & Co. (no relation to Will) backed her

claim and published in *The New York Times* a defamatory advertisement charging Carleton with "literary piracy." The story of the
Emerson woman was that she was a "medium," that she had composed the poem in a state of trance under the influence of George
D. Prentice (deceased), that she sold the poem to Carleton for two
dollars, and that he had published it in the Toledo *Blade* as his
own, and was about to include it in his forthcoming book, *Farm
Ballads*.

When confronted by the fact that Will Carleton had never been
in New York she changed her story, and asserted that she wrote
poems merely for amusement and allowed her friends to make
manuscript copies of them; that "Betsey" had thus circulated
around the country and fallen into Carleton's hands, and he had
appropriated it. *Harper's* stood firmly behind their poet and urged
him to bring suit against Mrs. Emerson-French and her publishers
for criminal libel, there being no ground for action for infringe-
ment as "Betsey" in the *Blade* had not been copyrighted. But Will
gave no attention to the matter. The Emerson book was published
with the title *A Thanksgiving Story*, with "Betsey" among its contents, slightly altered textually from the original. This book was
sufficient evidence the Emerson woman could not have written the
disputed poem, for the other pieces in her book were drivel or
doggerel, without the slightest resemblance in style or matter to
Carleton's work. It had no effect on *Farm Ballads,* which appeared
shortly afterward and was, as has been stated, a tremendous success.

Will Carleton was living in Brooklyn, and editing a publication
called *Every Where* that he had founded in 1904, when he died of
bronchial pneumonia December 18, 1912, at the age of sixty-seven.
He lies in Greenwood Cemetery beside his wife. The gold-stamped
gilt-edged quartos once seen lying on the marble-topped center
tables in nearly every parlor turn up occasionally in the second-
hand bookstores. A set of first editions brings about thirty dollars.

MATTHEW ARNOLD

by C. E. Montague

"A tall, oldish man with the shapeliest features, the stoop of a scholarly Jove, and an air of the most distinguished melancholy"
—Matthew Arnold as remembered by a novelist and dramatic critic who, as a youth, saw him walking the streets of Oxford.

MAY 12, 1928

WALKING WITH AN ELDER BROTHER in the streets of Oxford in my youth, I was struck by the looks of a tall, oldish man with the shapeliest features, the stoop of a scholarly Jove, and an air of the most distinguished melancholy. "That's Matthew Arnold," my brother said when we had passed him. My heart had already told me that it was someone illustrious.

It was wet at the time: I could not kneel down on the Merton Street cobbles. Still, I turned round at the name and adored the Olympian back with all my eyes till it vanished round the corner of Oriel. For no italics, no capitals, not all the massed resources of typographical emphasis could tell you the fervor with which we swore by Arnold in those remote eighties, unless we were such as swore by the rival and comparatively sulphurous godhead of Swinburne. Was it not Arnold who in one famous and beautiful sentence of prose had doubled, to our sense, the beauty of our own Oxford, "whispering from her towers the last enchantments of the Middle Ages"? And was it not he who had taught us the delicate fascination of doubt, and the tremors, the thrills, the delicious venturings and flutterings of spirtual trouble?

Remember, Arnold flourished at a time when people of education had pretty well lived down the original shock and distress that were caused by the first serious work of scholars on the Bible. The process, as someone had called it, of robbing millions of pious souls of their hope of eternal damnation had already entered on its second stage. It had almost ceased to be seismic or cyclonic. It was becoming more tranquilly detergent, erosive or decompository. And now, as promoted by Arnold, it had a sensuous beauty that charmed the young mind. Lit with the softened light of an imagination more tender and brooding than fiery, lustrous with the burnished older scholarship, twinkling with quiet ironies that seemed to take you ever so flatteringly into the confidence of a spirit august beyond words, the skepticism of Arnold had beautiful manners and entrancing tones. We are told that Ophelia could turn "Hell itself" to "favor and to prettiness." Arnold went one better and extracted those delights from the tragic decline of that institution.

The late George Russell, the last of great Whig wits, and himself a devoted High Churchman, told a friend that "Arnold's wish to believe, coupled with his inability to do so, was one of the most pathetic things I have ever known." The good Russell need not have grieved. Many men and women derive enjoyment from ill health; but to the proper temperament a congenial complaint in the body is, as a source of agreeable emotions, nothing to a gentle malady of the soul. "Let us sit upon the ground," says the most human Richard the Second of Shakespeare, "and tell sad stories of the death of kings." Let us sit, says Matthew Arnold to himself, upon the window seat of our hotel at Dover and tell sad stories of the death of faith. And so he does, and writes the lovely lines of "Dover Beach."

> *Listen! you hear the grating roar*
> *Of pebbles which the waves draw back, and fling,*
> *At their return, up the high strand,*
> *Begin, and cease, and then begin again,*
> *With tremulous cadence slow, and bring*
> *The eternal note of sadness in.*
>
> *The Sea of Faith,*
> *Was once, too, at the full, and round earth's shore*
> *Lay like the folds of a bright girdle furl'd.*
> *But now I only hear*
> *Its melancholy, long, withdrawing roar.*

And he enjoys himself immensely, as anybody would who was writing such good lines. And if anything had interrupted him while doing it, even the first trump of a new and completely reassuring revelation, he would have murmured, like Richard, "Beshrew thee, that dost lead me forth From that sweet way I was in to despair." For no one is unhappy in the act of writing delightful things. Nature makes no mistake about that. She wants to have everything good and takes care that man, at any rate, shall have more pleasure than pain in carrying out this admirable purpose.

A writer will often tell you that this or that meritorious production of his has been written in agony. A classical case is Tennyson saying in "In Memoriam" that the composing of it was a mere

> *mechanic exercise,*
> *Like dull narcotics, numbing pain.*

Don't believe him. Nothing so good as the good parts of "In Memoriam" was ever done like that. To say that it was is like Boswell's saying that he would suffer vexation if he were in Parliament and saw things going wrong, "That's cant, sir," said Johnson.

> Clear your *mind* of cant. You may *talk* as other people do: you may say to a man, "Sir, I am your most humble servant." You are *not* his most humble servant. You may say, "These are bad times; it is a melancholy thing to be reserved to such times." You don't mind the times. You tell a man, "I am sorry you had such bad weather the last day of your journey, and were so much wet." You don't care sixpence whether he is wet or dry. You may *talk* in this manner; it is a mode of talking in Society: but don't *think* foolishly.

In Tennyson's and Arnold's age, and in the company they kept, there was a mode of talking as if artists of every sort ought to go about studded with visible and audible tokens that their heart was in their work and that every emotion to which they offered an expression was genuinely gnawing at their souls. In this way poor Irving, the great tragic actor, had to go about, all his life, with a manner and look that almost amounted to a suit of sables; Tennyson had to be always the mourner for Hallam, Browning the optimist, virilist sage, and Arnold the heartbroken outcast from the snug household of faith, wearying in spiritual wastes of sand and thorns. They all kept it up very well, and none better than Arnold. But it must have been, at bottom, just what Johnson called a mode of talking. When any one of them was working at his craft, at the top of his form, he must have been in ecstasy, as every other artist is, as Fra Angelico was when he painted a picture of Heaven, and as Orcagna was when he painted a picture of Hell.

It was this ecstasy, too, and not merely certain charges of new theological explosives, made in Germany, that Arnold, in prose and in verse, could communicate to our minds. That was how he gave us medicines, as Falstaff says, to make us love him. Under his winning conductorship there was intellectual luxury to be got out of tottering creeds and melting rigidities. Walter Pater, though his mind was traveling at the time in the direction opposite to Arnold's, had lately ventured to diagnose an exquisite fascination in states of decay—a faint and fine aroma as of immemorial oak paneling and fading tapestries. Arnold taught our adolescent sense to snuff up some such delectable fragrance among the fragments of the orthodoxy which he shattered for us with a grace and courtesy so remarkable. It is important, says Bacon, to have in your garden some plants of the sort that smell sweetest when trodden upon; Arnold filled our gardens with a scent of nice crushed Fundamentalism in an age when that redoubtable word was yet unborn.

There was another suave chain that bound us to Arnold. I mention it with some diffidence in a much-altered world. We were notably serious, and Arnold's seriousness kept us in countenance. You may say there are always some serious young men. Yes, there are, even now. Some men are born to be serious, others achieve it, and others have it thrust upon them by economic and other forces. But seriousness was "the done thing" at the English universities in the eighties. It was the mode of the day. Carlyle had sown the seed; Browning had watered it; Ruskin had helped to give it increase. T. H. Green was dominating Oxford with a philosophy that escorted you straight to the life of good works and honest endeavor. Arnold Toynbee was founding a whole school of new social service. Rossetti, Watts, Burne-Jones, diverse in other ways, seemed to be wholly at one on the point that the cult of beauty was a most serious, if not an anxious and mournful, affair. So seriousness became the only wear. If you were of the kind that conforms, you soon decided that life was real, life was earnest; you took horse to hunt the Beautiful and Good with your young friends—just as persons of similar temperament are deciding today, like the Jolly Beggars of Burns, that "life is all a variorum: little reck we how it goes." Even the reprobated disciples of Swinburne practiced their loyal little dissipations with some gravity. So Arnold was the very man for us— Arnold with his "stream of tendency making for righteousness"; Arnold who called all the world's poets up to be judged by their measure of "excellent seriousness" and ordered off the muse of Burns himself to the house of correction because of her shortage of this solid quality.

I never saw Arnold again. He died a year or two after. And presently I had to turn to and work—a novel experience—and found that work was a heavenly game and that everything was remarkably well with the world, so far as it dealt with me, though some of its other arrangements seemed to admit of improvement. In this Elysian condition I somehow lost the habit of reading my Arnold and gazing with a luscious melancholy at

> *this strange disease of modern life,*
> *With its sick hurry, its divided aims,*
> *Its heads o'ertaxed, its palsied hearts.*

I could not tell why. I could only suppose that, as Benedick said of his failure of relish for bachelorhood, a man loves the meat in his youth that he cannot endure in his age. But after a time I knew better, or thought so. For something was said which, as soon as I read it, I felt to be just the truth that I had been missing.

It was said by William Watson, the poet. Arnold had been buried close to the Thames, and Watson was praising the choice of that bland and composed countryside for the site of the grave in preference to the stern Cumberland hills, which the dead had loved too,

> *'Tis fittest thus! for though with skill*
> *He sang of beck and tarn and ghyll,*
> *The deep, authentic mountain-thrill*
> *Ne'er shook his page.*
> *Somewhat of worldling mingled still*
> *With bard and sage.*

Yes, I said to myself; that was it. And perhaps it was just what had most charmed one's uncritical youth. For youth itself is apt to be worldly, unsure of its own presentableness, timid lest it be out of the swim and remote from the center, wherever the center may be. And Arnold had never failed, in one's youth, to give one that peace which the world *can* give—the restful sense of snuggling up close to a center, of being taken right into a perfectly irreproachable "set." Oh! of course a most unmaterialist set; a set cultured up to the nines; a set as grandly free from mere gross common snobbishness as it had been from the raucous uncouthness of any poor "Philistines"—"outside our happy ground." But always a true set, elatingly exclusive, heartwarmingly superior. You felt, while you read, as if the right people had taken you up. In your glee at his majestic chaffing of spiritual boors and intellectual guys, of the young lions of popular journalism and the grim ways of Black

Countries and of crude reformers, you melted agreeably into a set which you felt to be supremely eligible. Of course you were no common intellectual climber, but still you had sensations distinctly allied to those of Thackeray and his Arthur Pendennis on coming to town and finding themselves securely elected to Brooks or to the Megatherium Club. You too were enormously "in it."

"Why not?" you may very well ask. "Has not the art of every considerable writer a core to be reached? And must not the joint quest of this heart of the rose become a conscious fellowship of souls in some sense or other elect? And what else is a set?"

And yet there is something more in it. I fancy it arises from a certain special tinting of Arnold's own consciousness while he wrote —a delicate suffusion of his genius with charity toward what is dominant in the polite lettered caste, the caste which has mastered the secret of making the things of the mind—a favorite phrase of its own—live at peace with what Burke calls the pomps and plausibilities of this world.

"But," you may object again, "was not Arnold the tireless critic of his country and his age, the lifelong arraigner of British limitedness and complacency, the crier of woe upon the darling mental vices of the principalities and powers of his world?"

Yes, he was a quite sincere and quite good-sized Isaiah. And yet he wore the prophet's robe with a difference. He never let it look outlandish, as so many prophets have done, in the extravagance of their absorption in the primary business of saving mankind. Arnold's camel's-hair raiment was always extremely well cut and he ate his locusts and wild honey with conspicuous refinement. It seems to have been necessary that Moses should kill an Egyptian before he could lead Israel out of Egypt with adequate authority. But Arnold would never have killed an Egyptian—nor even a Philistine. He would have dined out with all the best people in Egypt or Philistia, appraised their fleshpots with intelligence, and delighted them with his vivacious conversation. As the adroit William Penn described—and possibly invented—by Macaulay found means to stand well at the court of the persecuting James the Second, so did Arnold keep in with the world that he chid. It liked entertaining him and he must have given, in these polite exchanges, as good as he got, for he could be charming.

Long after I had first read that revelatory stanza of Sir William Watson's, Arnold's letters were published. And they, too, threw a

light. For I found an unexpected resemblance between their effect
on my mind and the effect of the extremely different letters of Dickens. You may remember the all but religious ecstasy that fired the
pen of Dickens whenever he touched upon the remarkable satisfac-
toriness of the box-office receipts at his lectures. We all like money,
unless we are fools, but greater love hath no man for money than
glowed in those artless cries of the great heart of Dickens. In some
of these letters of Arnold's I seemed to feel glowing—not indeed
that ingenuous gusto of Dickens, but something distantly akin to
it—a pure white gemlike flame of delight in knowing all that was
nicest in the great world of his days. No arrant tuft-hunting, of
course; no downright stalking of lions, as lions; only something re-
motely related thereto, as the practice of Shakespeare's Old Gobbo
was to actual rapine—"indeed, my father did something smack,
something grow to, he had a kind of taste." Arnold was always a
rather poor man, as things went at that time in England, though
among French civil servants and poets he would have counted as
rich. And "depend upon it, my boy," as Major Pendennis said to
his nephew, "for a poor man there is nothing like having good
acquaintances." Like many other men of high intellectual gifts,
Arnold was ballasted with a just proportion of Major Pendennis'
practical wisdom.

No shame to him, either. At any rate, he that has in him no grain
of the staple alloys of this world, let him throw the first stone, for
I am not throwing. I touch on the matter only by way of exploring
the origin of a just perceptible flatness afflicting at times the fine
bell-like voice which was engaged in crying "Woe!" here and
"Woe!" there so engagingly and so often. People, especially very
young ones, warn us today to keep out of the error of thinking that
a man's life and his art have much to do with each other. And yet—
so obstinate is nature, so careless of current critical fashions—there
does somehow creep into R. L. Stevenson's elegant family prayers
and handsome harangues on practice and on morals a very slight
queerness of *timbre*. It may not amount to a positive crack in the
soul-animating trumpet. It only goes far enough to commute the
last thrill, the supreme dose of awe in our minds, for a sup of
savorsome amusement as we think what manner of man this
moralist was in his life—how equally prone with us all to walk in
the ways of his heart and in the sight of his eyes. Those who knew
Thackeray in the flesh had consumed with the same piquant sauce
the full meals of domestic virtue served up in his novels. And even

those who had not known him, but still were sensitive readers, had been either tickled or put off, according to their several natures, by a certain still, small falsity of intonation that infests his celebrated commination services against the pomps and vanities of the great world. For the waters of moral elevation refuse, as flatly as do other waters, to rise higher than their source. No Stevenson can, by any elocutionary skill whatever, produce the authentic thunders of a Knox. And Arnold, too, had his appointed or acquired limits. He could never be tremendous. If he tried, you felt something was wrong, though you might not be able to say what it was till you read, long afterwards, one of his letters and thought to yourself that his were not the social valuations of the major prophets.

Within these limits, set, perhaps, by a natural vein of timidity and by the best English upper-class education, what power he had! What beauty he commanded! And, in the main, how thoroughly he was on the right side. It is easy work to poke fun at his habit of crying up "sweetness and light"; but, after all, is there much to be said, on Europe's postwar experience, for the alternative cult of sourness and gloom? And if Arnold were not a distinguished Victorian, but a young author just rising above the horizon, what a refreshing spice of originality we should find in his frank preoccupation with matters of conduct and in his unconventional preference for conduct that is reputable.

Our literary criticism now is passing through a lively little epidemic of inverted priggishness. In fiction the rather lecherous hero, the gallant young fellow who forges a check, the charming woman with several young children who commits adultery for some tenuous reason, are very much in the mode. And the critic who wants to be in mode lays it down that on no excuse is an imaginative author to betray a warmer liking for straight livers than for scrubs or polecats. Now, "this sort of thing," as the attitudinizing critic and poet says in the comic opera, "takes a deal of training." It is like pirouetting on tiptoe. It is not natural to man. The natural man quite simply and frankly prefers those bus conductors who do not steal people's change to those who do. He has an unreasoned general liking for monogamic women and for the man who can keep a hold on himself. Scold him as you may, he feels an unaffectedly greater enjoyment in the company of people whom nobody would want to blackball at a club. He finds such company more interesting. When he tries to acquiesce in the fashionable theory that the words "good" and "bad" in the moral sense are obsolete solecisms, he feels as if he were trying on an extremely tight boot. What a thrill he would get from any unconventional pioneer who let fashion go hang and said that conduct was three-fourths of life, that most of us spend the greater part of our time in thinking out what we ought to do in this or that case, and that literature is only losing the way and going off to dawdle in blind alleys when it ceases to take count of the fact! Let him come to Arnold with a fresh mind, and that thrill will be his.

His, too, will be a liberal measure of poetry's most characteristic delight. What the greater genius of Scott did for the Lowlands of his country, and that of Hardy for Wessex, that Arnold did, as De Wint did it in paint, for the southern English landscape of meadow, river, down and beach, with its contained and friendly amenity and the mild melancholy that becomes an heirloom of a countryside long settled and intensely humanized. His poems not only give this landscape reality; they give it a share of the trans-figured, enchanted reality attained by the river gardens of Bagdad when a boy first sees them in the *Arabian Nights*. We are all heirs to the loveliness of the visible world; but only by process of art can we be inducted into possession of this large estate. Some authentic poet or artist has to intervene and give the property its rights and empower it to attain perfection in our sight. Whatever his limita-tions, Arnold was poet enough to do that to the country he knew. From the Cotswolds to Dover, England shines with an increase of beauty that is of his giving.

ED HOWE VERSUS TIME

by Wilbur L. Schramm

In the books and magazines of 1883 life was romantic, quaint, and sweet. The Story of a Country Town *broke into this delusion like "an elephant in a china shop." Ed Howe, the Middle Western small-town newspaper editor, dared say that life was a lot different from the way other novels were painting it. He stripped the hides off the small town and its inhabitants thirty years before* Main Street *came along with a similar message. Wilbur L. Schramm delves into the theories between Howe and Lewis, and how each of them saw the ills of the country town in quite a different light.*

FEBRUARY 5, 1938

LET THIS AT LEAST be said as obituary for Ed Howe: that he had a legitimate quarrel with time and uttered never a word of complaint during eighty-four years.

He built a career which, a century before and under the right conditions, might have made him known as another Benjamin Franklin, but which in his own day made him merely a five-cent Carnegie. He was ensaged, as the Sage of Potato Hill, only at a time when bankers and politicians had become far more important to American life than wise men. He wrote one of the significant books of a literary movement thirty years before the movement started; by the time it had caught up with his book, his philosophy was no longer in sympathy with the movement; and now, in the winter of his death, there are unmistakable signs that the country is coming around once more to his way of thinking.

Of these three anachronisms the last is the most serious, for it becomes more and more clearly apparent that Ed Howe will be remembered not as a sage, nor a self-made man, nor an editor, but as an interpreter of the village and author of *The Story of a Country Town.*

Set his topsy-turvy history, for a minute, beside the career of that other interpreter of the small town, Mr. Sinclair Lewis. Mr. Lewis published *Main Street,* in 1920, when Spoon River and Winesburg

63

were already places well known and when the country was in full
tide of what Mr. Carl Van Doren called "The Revolt from the Village." He published *Babbitt* two years later, at a time when the problems of business and advertising were central in his readers' thinking. *Arrowsmith* came when biological research had already been
dramatized for the layman, when phages and serums had entered the
headlines. *Elmer Gantry* appeared at the height of the sacrilegious
twenties. And so on throughout the list, to *It Can't Happen Here*,
which rode the wave of fascist-phobia. Somehow, Mr. Lewis has
managed to march with his times.

But consider *The Story of a Country Town* against the backdrop
of its times. Ed Howe wrote that book when he was not quite thirty,
when his days were filled from dawn to dusk with newspaper work
and he was forced to struggle by lamplight, at home in the late evenings, with the unfamiliar problems of fiction. As he wrote he remembered the romantic village idyl that filled the pages of contemporary literature with wistaria and honeysuckle, and he remembered,
too, the dismal pioneer village in which he had spent his own youth.
He wanted to tell the truth about this kind of village.

He told it in a bitter, powerful book which was so true that no
publisher would take it. When Howe finally rolled the book off his
own newspaper press, in 1883, readers found a hissable villain, a
beautiful girl, a heart-rending separation, and a melodramatic ride
through storm and night, with bells tolling and wind shrieking. But
all these ancient melodramatic devices were overshadowed by an unforgettable portrait of the great actor in the book, the village. Covered wagons no longer carried romance to this village. The hope,
trust, brotherly love, optimism, beneficent nature had fallen out of
the frontier eulogy. The people were tired and discontented, the
men sullen and rough, the women pale and fretful. Defeatism was
in the air. "I don't want to be like the people here," one character
said, "for none of them are contented. . . . I cannot believe but
there is a better way to live than that accepted at Fairview, and that
somewhere . . . happy homes may be found, and contented people." Another declared:

> I never formed a good opinion of a man there that I was
> not finally told something to his discredit by another citizen,
> and if I said a good word for any of them, it was proved be-
> yond question immediately that he was a very weak, a very
> worthless man. There were no friendships among them, and

they all hated each other in secret, there being much satisfaction when one of them failed. . . . The only real ability
any of them ever displayed was in looking up the previous
history of each other, which they carried on with great vigor,
and frequently with alarming results.

This has a familiar sound to us who have read Lewis and Masters,
but it was not familiar in 1883. It was a bull in a china shop. It was
an elephant in a china shop. In 1883 the local colorists were flood-
ing the magazines with dialect, quaintness, romantic settings, Kentucky colonels, and Tennessee ha'nts. The New England renaissance
had grown mellow and harmless. The favorite novels of the day were
usually bound in white leather, emblazoned with gold or lavender
titles. The fictional West was a land where Indians existed merely to
bite the dust, where white folks lived in joyous simplicity close to
nature, either in charming communities or in picturesque isolation
on prairies overhung by snowy mountains. And in the midst of all
this sweetness, a Middle Western small-town newspaper editor
dared to say in a harsh awful voice that life isn't the way books
paint it.

The novel was mostly negative. But about the time when Masters,
Anderson, and Lewis were discovering the Country Town, Ed Howe
felt called upon to advance a positive program to improve village
and small-town life, and he broadcast the program by means of
aphorisms which were syndicated from Potato Hill to newspapers
throughout the country. The wisdom from Potato Hill is exceedingly interesting.

"In thousands of years," saith the sage, "there has been no advance in public morals, in philosophy, religion or politics, but the
advance in business has been the greatest miracle the world has ever
known." Man cannot serve God and Mammon? Stuff and nonsense!
Man *must* serve Mammon; dollar-chasing isn't a crime but a virtue.
Poverty is a social crime; the rich are the best citizens. "Every great
improvement in the world's history is due, directly or indirectly, to
the munificence of some man successful in the world's affairs."

For complex interpretations of life, for metaphysics and abstruse
reasoning, he had little sympathy. "I do not care what Plato who
lived a long time ago says. But what Joe Smith says, if he lives today, and is fairly intelligent, may be important: at least it is up
to date, like a real-estate abstract you can depend upon. . . . Select
the wisest and best man in your community, and he knows more

than Adam Smith. . . . Did Shakespeare, or Goethe, or Whitman, or Buddha, or Tolstoy, or Confucius, or Rousseau ever teach you as important lessons as you learned from your parents, from your worthy and intelligent neighbors, from the leading men of practical affairs in your own country and age?" Thoreau, Alcott, and Emerson were "Consecrated Cranks." Of Fruitlands: "Think of four robust loafers taking a music lesson the first thing in the morning, and the next enjoying a long and dreary conversation about Friendship, instead of going to work." "What we need is not shorter hours but longer hours." "Any law enjoining me to love my enemy is too much duty. . . . A better doctrine is: 'An eye for an eye, a tooth for a tooth'; except it isn't strong enough. To accord with civilized life, it should read '*Two* eyes for an eye; *two* teeth for a tooth.' " Religion, he believed, generally tends to the public good, but the time will come when "the world's religion will consist of five words: Fairness, temperance, thrift, industry, politeness."

So spoke the sage of Potato Hill, proud of his materialism. "What is wrong with materialism?" he demanded. "Nothing under God's high heaven, except that it is true."

In many ways it is an admirable doctrine that comes from Potato Hill, admirable for its sanity, common sense, practicality, simplicity. Of course, it is neither new nor unique. The same things were said by the businessman Franklin. The same things were said by the Gilded Age: keep your feet on the ground, your hand on your purse, your eye on a bargain. The same things have become familiar to us more recently through the satire of Sinclair Lewis. It is the "Pep, Punch, Go, Vigor, Enterprise" of Honest Jim Baussler in *Main Street*. It is the people of Gopher Prairie speaking: "There would be no more trouble or discontent in the world if everybody worked as hard as Pa did when he cleared our first farm." It is George F. Babbitt defining the Ideal Citizen for the Zenith Real Estate Board in terms of zip and Regular Guys and four to ten thousand a year and adding machines and bathtubs and automobiles per hundred people and distrust of professors and "intelligentsia."

What a strange commentary on the progress of human events it is that the prescription which Dr. Howe wrote out for the Country Town should be the very poison which Dr. Lewis found in Gopher Prairie and Zenith! Howe would save America by converting it to the glorious gospel of American Business; Lewis would save it by rescuing it from the standardized religion of business. Howe recommends that America be peopled with Babbitts; Lewis, that America be saved from Babbitts. Most of the aphorisms which Howe collected into a book in 1919 might have been sprinkled into Babbitt's famous speech, in 1922, without any disturbance other than a stylistic one. Agreeing on the symptoms, the two physicians still chose antithetical remedies.

So Howe was caught off base again. But he might have smiled his ironical smile this winter if he could have heard Henry Wallace making love to the small businessman, if he could have heard the regionalists preaching individual initiative as opposed to mass action and urban collectivism, if he could have heard Sinclair Lewis advising the Middle West, from a Cedar Rapids lecture platform, to hold on to its Babbitts. For the chief spokesman of the revolt against Chambers of Commerce and chain-store thinking and synthetic zip no longer waves his fiery pen over the small town. The hero of *It Can't Happen Here*, Doremus Jessup, is more like Babbitt than perhaps even Mr. Lewis recognizes, and in *The Prodigal Parents*, the identification is complete and deliberate.

Thus the final anachronism of Howe's career is that he was taken away at the moment when it seemed that he might after all not be anachronistic.

MEMORIES OF
OSCAR WILDE

by Ford Madox Ford

One year he was a popular idol, the next he was being tried and sent to jail on criminal charges that stunned the world he lived in. Such was the career of Oscar Wilde, poet, wit, dramatist, and celebrity on both sides of the Atlantic. Wilde visited the Ford household when he was at the height of his fame. Ford ran across him later in Paris when he was a wreck of a man. Here is an intimate glimpse of the tragedy that was Wilde, with a theory as to how he misjudged his public as well as himself.

MAY 27, 1939

In December of the year before the trial of Oscar Wilde the writer's uncle called the male children of his family together and solemnly informed them that if any older man made to us "proposals or advances of a certain nature," we were morally and legally at liberty to kill him "with any weapon that offered itself." The person speaking thus was not merely the brother of Dante Gabriel Rossetti, the pre-Raphaelite poet, but also her Majesty's Secretary of the Inland Revenue; one of the most weighty and responsible of Great Britain's permanent officials, and the most reasonable human being ever sent on this earth.

From that you may understand that London parents of adolescent male children of the end of '94 saw "perverters" lurking in all the shadows; and Wilde and Oscarisms, in their several kinds, were the preoccupation of that metropolis almost to the exclusion of all other intellectual pabula. And, beneath the comfortable strata of Society, growled the immense, frightening quicksand of the Lower Classes and the underworld, with ears all pricked up to hear details of the encounters of their own Fighting Marquis, a toff called Wilde, and the riffraff of the Mews. Every two or three days, inspired by the generous port of his lunch, the Home Secretary issued a warrant against Mr. Wilde; but in the mists of before-dinner indigestion ordered it withdrawn. The Queen and Mr. Gladstone, then retired, were mercifully shielded from these whisperings—or Heaven knows what they would not have done!

The writer, however, was conscious of none of these things . . . until the first night of *The Importance of Being Earnest*. Instances—or indeed knowledge—of what was called "perversion" had never come his way; even Mr. Rossetti's exhortation had seemed nearly unmeaning. And that any blame could attach to Mr. Wilde would have seemed fantastic. Mr. Wilde was a quiet individual who came every Saturday, for years, to tea with the writer's grandfather—Ford Madox Brown. Wilde would sit in a high-backed armchair, stretching out one hand a little toward the blaze of the wood fire on the hearth and talking of the dullest possible things to Ford Madox Brown, who, with his healthy colored cheeks and white hair cut like the King of Hearts, sat on the other side of the fire in another high-backed chair and, stretching out toward the flames his other hand, disagreed usually with Mr. Wilde on subjects like that of the Home Rule for Ireland Bill or the Conversion of the Consolidated Debt.

Mr. Wilde was, in fact, for the writer and, as far as he knows, for his cousins, the younger Rossettis, what we should have called one of the common objects of the countryside. Like Ford Madox Brown's other old friends or protégés and poor relations he had his weekly day on which to pay his respects to the Father of the pre-Raphaelites. He had begun the practice during a long period of very serious illness on the part of the older man and he continued it, as he said later, out of liking for the only house in London where he did not have to stand on his head.

Certainly, there, he could be as quiet as he liked, for, as often as not, he and Madox Brown would sit silent for minutes on end in the twilight. So that the painter was accustomed to deny that the young poet who sat at his feet possessed any wit at all and, since Madox Brown died the year before the Wilde-Queensberry trial, he went to his death without any knowledge at all of the singular nature of the bird of paradise who had nestled on Saturday afternoons in the high-backed *bergère* beside the fire. Thus the only utterance of that date that comes back to the writer as at all weighty on the part of Mr. Wilde, the private gentleman, was an admission that he had been mistaken in a political prophecy. The Tory Government of that day had decided to reduce the rate of interest on Consols. Mr. Wilde had prophesied that that "conversion" would be disastrous to the finances of the country. The rate was, however, reduced from 3 to 2¾ per cent without any panic on the Stock Exchange. The Government had triumphed, and the writer still remembers very vividly the by then extremely bulky figure of Wilde as he entered the studio in a Saturday dusk, came to a standstill, loosened his great overcoat, removed his gloves and in the fashion of the day, smacked them against his left-hand palm, and exclaimed in a voice of unusual sonority: "I see I was wrong, Brown, about Consols!"

And the writer might add that the last poem of Christina Rossetti—the manuscript of which he happens to possess—is written on the back of a used envelope on the front of which the poetess had made a number of jottings—as to fluctuations in the price of Consols. So much did that day resemble our own!

Thus, the first intimation of what, whether it were irresponsible or sinister, Wilde meant to London and later to the world came with Lord Queensberry's presentation of his bouquet to Wilde on the first night of *The Importance of Being Earnest*. That was an occasion! The writer may have been obtuse or may have been merely inexperienced. But it was impossible during the performance of the play not to feel that both the audience and the quality of that audience's emotions were something different from those of any other first night he had attended. That audience was almost infinitely "smart." It consisted, presumably, one half of "decadents" more or less reckless and irresponsible, and of rich, more or less cultured and titled people who were, at least, in the know and presumably did not disapprove of what Wilde represented. What exactly Wilde represented at that moment it would be too complicated here to analyze.

On the fall of the curtain, Wilde appeared, rather pallid, blinking against the glare of the footlights and singularly prophetic of what Mr. Morley looked like in *Oscar Wilde* at the Fulton Theater the other day. He said some words, in the voice of Mr. Morley, that singular mixture of Balliol and brogue. Then unrest in the audience made him hesitate. His eyes, always uneasy, roved more uneasily than usual over the whole audience from gallery to pit. An immense pink and white bouquet was being carried down the gangway between the stalls.

That alone was sufficient to cause tittering emotion—because bouquets were only handed to women. But when the bouquet reached that solitary black figure with the pallid face and the audience could realize of what it consisted, then an extraordinarily black undertone of panic surged right through that semi-oval bowl. You saw men starting to their feet and women pulling their ermine cloaks hastily up over their shoulders—as if they felt they must incontinently flee from a scene on which violence was about to burst out.

For that bouquet consisted, plain to the view, of carrots and turnips framed in a foam of coarse lace paper. The panic in the face of Wilde exceeded the final panic that came over him under the cross-examination of Sir Edward Carson in *Wilde vs. Queensberry*. He shook and his lips bubbled. During the trial his breakdown was very gradual; there behind the footlights he was struck by a thunderbolt. For he and all the hundreds in the theater had realized within a second that this was Queensberry's final insult to the author of that play. The whole matter *could* no longer keep under ground. And the hurried exit of all that audience from the theater was like a public desertion of that unfortunate idol of the unthinking. You saw people running to get out and the cries of encouragement of the few decadents who had the courage to take it were completely drowned in the voices of those departing who were explaining to each other what it all meant. And next day all whispering London heard that the Marquis had left in the hall of Wilde's club a card of his own bearing an unmistakable insult.

Thus, the libel action of Wilde against the Marquis was a really horrible occasion. It was not so much Wilde as the spirit of irresponsibility that was on trial and so many of us all—all London that in the remotest degree counted—had been guilty of sympathizing with the spirit of irresponsibility.

And there was another feature. It should be remembered that for the first and last time in the whole history of London the Arts, at least of painting and poetry, had really for a year or so counted as one of the important attributes of the metropolis. We, the poets and painters of London, had for the first time in the history of the world, become front-page news. Our hearths, our bookshelves, our favorite dogs, our back yards, were photographed for publication with all the honors of flashlights. Yes, the very pen of this writer here writing was reproduced in the shiny papers of the capital's weeklies and his inkpot, too.

This accounted for the hesitation of the Home Secretary in issuing and withdrawing his warrant. People who then used the pen in London were a clan with whom one must very seriously take account. And the same fact accounted for the final downfall of Wilde. He could not believe that the Victorian state would dare to measure itself against the chief pre-Raphaelite poet and the foremost playwright of the day.

His breakdown at the Queensberry trial came very slowly and was, therefore, the more agonizing. The cross-examination at the hands of Carson lasted at least as long as the whole play of *Oscar Wilde* at the Fulton. And it was obviously impossible that our sympathies should not go out to that doomed rat in that rat pit without issue. Every time that he got back on Carson—as when he said: "No, it is not poetry when you read it"—one breathed with relief as if a sorry hero had achieved the impossible. For in the arid panoply of English law procedure the dice are so weighted in favor of the cross-examiner that one would doubt if the archangel Michael or in the alternative Machiavelli could ever finally get back on learned counsel. Wilde, however, came very near it once or twice.

No, your sympathies were bound to be with Wilde in that place and on that occasion. It is a detail that is by no means a criticism of the art displayed on the Fulton stage that the cross-examination there shown in no way duplicated the process of the London law courts. There was none of the shouting and parading about the court by counsel that the Fulton stage showed. Sir Edward Carson spoke from a sort of a box, at some distance from the plaintiff and in a quite low if very clear voice. It made it the more horrible when suddenly you saw that pallid man's left hand begin to quiver along the lower edge of his waistcoat. And then a long time afterward his right hand, holding his gloves, quivering on the lapel of his coat. You just waited and waited for the next sign of discomfiture until finally it came with his throwing his gloves hysterically into the well of the court, his lips bubbling with undistinguishable words until they ended in silence. The whole three stages of breakdown took perhaps an hour and a half to accomplish.

Yes, Wilde overestimated the position in the Victorian hierarchy of a poet-playwright who was the cynosure of two continents. He felt behind him all the reckless and unthinking of London, Paris, New York, and why not the boundless prairies of the Middle West? Chicago had given him a king's reception.

Thus, immediately after the end of the Queensberry trial, the Home Secretary let it be signified to Robert Humphreys, who was Wilde's lawyer—and happened also to be the writer's—that a warrant would be issued for the arrest of Wilde at 6:51 that evening.

That was a word to the wise, its significance being that the boat train for Paris left Victoria station at 6:50. There was a sufficient crowd of the smart that left by that train but Wilde unfortunately was not one of them. He came into Humphreys' office about two o'clock that afternoon and before Humphreys could get words spoken, he had sunk into a chair, covered his face with his hands, and sobbingly deplored the excesses of his youth, his wasted talent, and his abhorred manhood. He spread himself in Biblical lamentation. But when Humphreys, coming round his table, was intent on patting him on the shoulder and telling him to cheer up and be a man and cut his stick for Paris, Wilde suddenly took his hands down from his face, winked jovially at Bob, and exclaimed: "Got you there, old fellow."

And no persuasions of Humphreys could make him leave for Paris. No. He drew himself up, assumed his air of an autocrat and exclaimed: "Do you think they dare touch me! The author of *Lady Windermere's Fan!* I tell you the Government must fall if they did it. Why, the French would declare war. Even America!" He really believed it.

He was, by the bye, much more erect in figure than Mr. Morley made him. The writer remembers seeing him in the sunlight at the Bishop of London's garden party at Fulham in a white top hat and a gray frock coat with black buttons and braiding, much too tight across him. And he seemed, as we have said, very erect, a rather virile figure, if much too stout. The writer has very strongly the vision of Mr. Wilde, who was a common object of the countryside, who sat in a high-backed chair, consuming tea and muffins with the luxury of a great Persian cat coiled up before the fire. And wasn't that in all probability the real Wilde? The man who sighed with relief to find himself in the one house in London where he did not have to stand on his head?

Even today, the writer or painter who is to secure even the modicum of thin oatmeal that will keep the skin over his bones has to perform a sufficiency of antics in the securing of publicity for himself. But in Victorian days those antics must be still more fantastic because press agents did not yet exist and the public was even more indifferent to the Arts. Almost no Victorian great poet or painter did not owe at least half of the impress that he made on the public to one singularity or another of costume or one or another eccentricity of behavior in public. The process was called alternately *épater les bourgeois,* or "touching the philistine on the raw." And since Wilde was determined and was successful in keeping himself monstrously in the center of the picture, it would seem to have been inevitable that he should have landed where he did whether on account of his personal taste or the remorseless logic of publicity.

The writer is hardened in his half conviction that Wilde *pêchait par snobisme* by the nature of his few contacts with Wilde in Paris during the latter days. Certainly Wilde, weeping and slobbering and surrounded by teasing students, was a sufficiently lamentable spectacle of indigence, solitude, and alcoholism. The students carried on with him an almost nightly comedy. Those were the days of the great Apache scares. Wilde possessed only one thing of value and that he treasured excessively. It was a heavy black ebony cane with a crook for a handle, inlaid with numerous little pinpoints of ivory. The students would come up to his table and would say, "You see Bibi la Touche, the King of the Apaches, there? He has taken a fancy to your fine stick. You must give it to him or your life will not be worth a moment's purchase."

And after they had kept this up for a long time, Wilde, weeping still more copiously, would surrender his stick. The students would take the trouble to take it home to his hotel in the Rue Jacob and next morning, Wilde, who was presumed to have forgotten the overnight incident, would find his stick, sally forth to Montmartre, and the whole thing would begin all over again.

And one may be quite uncertain as to whether the whole thing was not one last, or nearly last attempt to *épater les bourgeois*. Wilde was so obviously—so almost melodramatically—degenerated, deserted, and soaked in alcohol that one was apt to suspect that that lamentable *mise en scène* was put up for the benefit of the bystander. The writer's contacts with him at that date limited themselves solely to buying him rather rare drinks, or, if the hour were very late and Wilde quite alone, to taking him to the Rue Jacob in a *fiacre*.

One doesn't, of course, know to what extent Wilde was really deserted by his friends. He did, perhaps, tire out the patience of people. But it pleases the writer to consider that, perhaps, Wilde, in all this, was really scoring a world at which he had consistently mocked.

At any rate, one night very late, the writer found Wilde, hopelessly drunk, sprawled over a table outside of one Montmartre bistro or another. The writer was in the embarrassing position of having at the moment only exactly two francs. Wilde might be presumed to be completely penniless. It was, therefore, necessary to walk him quite a long way before arriving at a place that would be a reasonable two-franc cab fare from his hotel. It was at first very difficult to rouse the poet; but when he realized who was talking to him he came to himself rather suddenly, exclaiming, "Hey, oh yes, I'll come without resistance." He staggered for some yards, true to character, and then threw back his shoulders and we walked quite a distance side by side down the dark Rue Pigalle, he talking with quite sensible regret of the writer's grandfather and the great old house in Fitzroy Square. He seemed to retain even then quite an affection for the memory of Madox Brown, who was by that time dead. The walk comes back to this writer as having been excruciatingly painful. He was very young at the time, and that the quiet gentleman of Madox Brown's Saturdays should have fallen so low seemed to him terribly a part of the tears of things. Suddenly Wilde exclaimed, "Hello, what is all this? Why are we walking? Man was not made to walk when there are wheels on the streets."

I said, "I'm very sorry, Mr. Wilde; I haven't got the money to pay for a cab."

He said, "Oh, is that all?" And thrusting his right hand deep into his trouser pocket produced quite a respectable roll of small notes. He waved to a cab, got into it and drove off, like any other English gentleman, leaving the writer planted there on the curb.

So one may take it as one likes. And as far as this writer is concerned he likes to take it that Wilde did in the end get a little of his own back—out of this writer and all us other imbeciles—and that he died as he lived, not beyond his means, but keeping, as the phrase is, his eyes quite consummately in his own boat. It is at least pleasant to think of him winking at St. Peter as before he winked at Bob Humphreys and exclaiming, "Had you there, old fellow."

POETESS OF PASSION

by Jenny Ballou

*For many years Ella Wheeler Wilcox's poetry inspired, advised
and sometimes shocked her admirers and followers, many of whom
believed the sun rose and set with their "Queen." In this piece
Jenny Ballou describes the triumphant behavior of the author of
Poems of Passion.*

JANUARY 20, 1940

FROM THE CRESCENT BEACH a wayfarer may have stopped on that
hot summer night, dazed, to see the naphtha launch transformed
into a legendary barge. There, under the dangling lanterns, stood
the Junoesque Julie Opp Faversham, Goddess of Liberty. Thirteen
girls in Grecian draperies formed a patriotic tableau of the original
states of the Union. And, as the cool salt waves of the Sound carried
the fleet to shore on the strains of "Columbia, the Gem of the
Ocean," Ella Wheeler Wilcox, American poetess of passion,
alighted, followed by her costumed attendants, the good neighbors
of Short-Beach-on-the-Sound.

As undisputed queen of her court, she had chosen Julie for
Goddess of Liberty; but Ella herself was all the goddesses she had
ever heard of, as she was all the heroines she wrote about. In her
fluttering chiffons she must have seemed to herself the first incarnation of Cleopatra. This was not Long Island Sound on a
Fourth of July at the close of the nineteenth century, A.D. It was
the ancient Nile; and there on the sands, her lover awaited her.
What if her Antony was seen by the world in the guise of a silver
merchant, tipping the scales not far from two hundred pounds?

To her eyes, to which the russet rocks off the Sound were pink,
to her vision, before which all history and all personal experience
were finally to be seen through yellow journalistic glasses, Robert
was all the ancient heroes rolled into one. Among his contemporaries—for though he did not, like his wife, write for publication, he
was a contemporary—whose lanuginous tufts made Rip Van
Winkle seem by comparison simply unshaven, his face, with the

76

sole ornament of twirled mustachios, must have appeared de-
nuded, almost defenseless. And to modern eyes, unschooled in the
tonsorial experiments of that period before Freud, when the saying
went that to be kissed by a man without a mustache was like eating
an egg without salt, Robert, from his photographs, gives the impression of a documentary desperado, corrected by the benign expression of his glance. But there he was, with his fine voice, and
direct eyes, always solid behind Ella—more than her Antony.

Their child lived only a few hours; but did not the Sunday
supplement beauty, Maurine, whose mother had read Ella Wheeler's "Maurine," come and smile to her, and was this not a child of
their own, then, smiling? All the girls in the Maurine Club in Chicago were her children; and the thousands upon thousands who
read in her poems, syndicated by Hearst, that "Love Rules Triumphant" and "Life Is Eternal." And those too, whom she took to
that warm, heaving bosom, so graphically described in her *Poems
of Passion* and comforted for the loss of their loved ones, for their
gray hairs, for being out of a job, they too were her children. And
the bereaved mothers she consoled during the First World War,
they were her children too, those for whom she wrote in her New
York *Journal* column that Death was the most loyal, the last, the
best lover of all, the never-failing friend. Later, when she went to
the Front herself, to France, obeying an astral message from Robert,
who had "passed on to a larger and more wonderful plane"—were
not the boys to whom she ministered and read her oft-quoted
poems, her sons? Might not any one of them be her own son who
had not lived to die for democracy?

Her own parents had been her children, when she took on, with
the burden of her success, that of being a daughter twice over.
From the beginning she had helped the family on that bleak
Wisconsin farm, with the verse that flowed so easily, far too easily,
from her exalted temperament. For Ella Wheeler Wilcox belonged
to that buoyant race to whom Mark Twain would have reared
his heathen statue to Energy; though she ended by saying that all
the optimistic props she had given others failed her. But while the
show lasted, she awakened each morning reborn.

No matter what happened the day before, there was always with
the dawn—for she was a morning person—the renewed "undertone
of rapture," there was always "the balm." Each summer she wrote
her friends that this was the best summer of all. Like Mark Twain,
and like Jack London, she lived in the moment, safely close to the

surface. Her adolescent dreams, excepting for one thing—she was possessed of the same passion for fame and adulation that consumed Marie Bashkirtseff—her longings were entirely those of the average American girl; lovely dresses, travel, feminine accomplishments, summers by the sea, the compelling lover. And she wanted everybody else to have everything and to be happy and beautiful. In "Being Alive" she expostulated, with more truth than prose, that "in every thousand people who are living on this earth, not more than one is alive."

She herself was avid for life. Would she ever make up for those lonely nights on the farm, when she pinned her curtains against the moon's rays, crying: "Another beautiful night of youth wasted and lost"? She was not content with what Robert Frost and the Greeks call samples of life; she wanted big slices of it—with the loud pedal on. She wanted, like Hemingway's bullfighter hero, to live "all the way up." And she balked at the woman's role of waiting with clasped fingers for life to come; she ran eagerly toward it, as far as a woman can.

Hankering, like London, for "life" above art, she confused both mortally by separating them—as though the one did not flower from the other. She could easily have said with Jack London that "I have always stood for the exalting of the life that is in me over art, or any other extraneous thing." For with her, too, art was the extraneous thing. In her lonely childhood she had presentiments that "hosts of rare souls were approaching" and that "splendid banquets were in preparation for me." But when the routine of being successful palled, when she was no longer hungry at the banquets, and the time arrived to come to terms with herself, without excuses, the whole bric-a-brac would tumble. Both art and life would fail her. But until that day, when all her values went shipwreck, she always had her defenses ready.

But while an interloper on the literary front, her letters and public apologics arc a definite contribution to the literature of self-defense. American letters might be silent about her; American inarticulated life was full of her. Standing for something beneath and beyond the intellectual life of the country, a pure phenomenon of democracy, she considered herself, and was considered, a star in that sky where the barefoot girl makes good. And she took the role of Ella Wheeler Wilcox so seriously that she considered it a patriotic duty to appear always triumphant and joyous. In her autobiography she puts the joyousness on thick; but her pride in her humble origins, in which she always gloried, contributed to the effect of an imposing dignity. She never tried to hide her wide, soft plebeian feet from the aristocratic New England worshipers of success who surrounded her in Connecticut. For she knew she belonged to the rising aristocracy; and she was queen.

James Whitcomb Riley, with whom she had a correspondence, and a few meetings that ended disastrously, criticized her for her "frivolous appearance" and asked her how she thought "that god-woman Mrs. Browning would have looked in a fashionable gown and a bang." After which, having replied "that I thought she would have looked very much better than she did with the cork-screw curls prominent in the pictures," she stuck to her guns, and continued through the years to adorn herself in costumes of new color schemes each spring, as carefully planned with her dressmaker as a military campaign.

She might rival all; she would emulate none. And she fought like a tigress against the advice of any kind, whether it came from Riley or Lucy Larcom, the gentle authoress of "Idyl of Work"; or from the woman who had warned her that *Poems of Passion* were "calculated to spoil all chance of a desirable marriage," and whom Ella, with uncharacteristic spite, called Madame de Staël of Milwaukee.

No, nobody could make a Mrs. Browning of her. She wanted, only, and above all, to be that god-woman Ella Wheeler Wilcox. And later, when she became noted, or, as a well-meaning but somewhat unlettered neighbor in Short Beach put it, notorious, she was herself an announcement of Ella Wheeler Wilcox wherever she went, a magnetic annotation of her photographs and illustrated verses in the New York *Journal*.

Henry James may have found our continent "unentertaining." For Ella Wheeler Wilcox it was a continual pageant, to be celebrated with all the fireworks. She did not have to wait until Illumination Night in Short Beach to celebrate love, life, and democracy. There was something of the Fourth-of-July spirit even in her "Sonnets of Abelard and Heloise"; and when, in France, she made the pilgrimage to Argenteuil (that "battlefield of love"), to worship at the shrine of those poets of passion of the twelfth century, it was with a reverence with which she would have gone to Bunker Hill or Gettysburg.

She had a genius for worship; love was her specialty; heart came before art. But she only gave evidence against herself when she confronted her critics with those "sonnets" (which, she wrote a critic, who had been particularly cruel, "are regarded my most ambitious work in a literary way"). As to her prose description of Abelard and Heloise, in which she proves "how much greater is a lover than a philosopher," it is a masterpiece of its kind. The classic characters to whom she alludes with great abandon have a misplaced air; just as her more extended studies in spiritualist phenomena somehow lack substantiality. (She translated a part of Leon Denis' "The Problem of Life and Destiny," encouraged by an astral message from Robert during the World War.) But just as her worst novels were her best, so was she at her most inimitable when she was most maudlin.

In a language easily accessible to the weary and semi-literate, she told her readers, hungry for easily swallowed half-truths, that it was unhappiness, and not happiness, that was the exception. She warned them, knowing too well their anonymous hopelessness, that the suicide was "a spiritual pauper." She goaded them to the Broader Life, in huge capitals: "We must climb, stumble, fall and try again and again." They were all as she had once been, and any of them might become as she was, an Ella Wheeler Wilcox. "No force of circumstances can keep you down if you are strong enough to rise up."

The subway-riders might not, after a grinding day of work, be strong enough to rise up. But what if the work was enervating, distasteful? Keep at it: "until you feel yourself bettered and strengthened by it . . . Unless you are learning self-control and patience and cheerfulness you have not become large enough for a larger occupation." No less than Emerson, she was telling them to hitch their wagons to a star.

And it was not enough that she encouraged these thousand invisible ones. In her own life, though there might be a few who left her with a vague feeling of insult upon being hailed too enthusiastically as genius, there were many who carried away an energizing ray that did not leave them all their lives. They had seen a masterpiece of heart. For with her heart was art. If a neighbor apologized for interrupting her in her work, she would not listen, crying that what, after all, is there in the world, more important than people?

And this was too true. There was nothing more important than people for her. She won the wide world over; and in Short Beach it was said that the sun rose and set with Ella Wheeler. Here she walked in and out of neighbors' houses without knocking, looking for her Angora cats (she had preferred cats to dolls when she was little, and feeling she had been a cat in some other incarnation, said she would not even care to go to heaven if there were no cats there). She gave the young girls books on the Facts of Life, and the little boys dishes of ice cream they remembered with the greatest tenderness when they grew up. On the trolley to New Haven she would dash up to a startled and embarrassed young mother and read phrenologically her baby's future, to the entertainment of the passengers who knew by the action, though they might not yet have seen her, that this was certainly Ella Wheeler Wilcox.

She was able to practice, sure of an appreciative community, her Little Efforts at Brotherhood; and to give full sway to civic raptures by organizing the Short Beach White Wings, although this was speedily abandoned when it appeared to have a feminist tinge. For Ella Wheeler was not among those women who winged their way, flat-heeled, into a man's world. She wore very high heels; and though temperamentally so different from Lucy Larcom, her idea was not essentially unlike the New Englander's who "always regarded it as a better ambition to be a true woman than to become a successful writer." In fact, Ella's attitude on the burning woman question of the day was quite on a par with her Sunday-school solution of economic problems by being kind to beggars and peddlers, and training her servants never to turn them away, until the trolley built from New Haven made this continual reminder of life on the other side of the tracks not so easy to handle, after Ella's kindness was broadcast.

The famous author, philosopher, and gentlewoman, as Ella Wheeler Wilcox was called, gave costume balls and Sunday-afternoon musicales and pageants that turned into regional festivities. Eva Gautier sang her Javanese songs for Ella's guests; Ruth St. Denis (whom Ella considered "lovelier and greater in character even than as an artist") danced for them. Ella, reclining on her Oriental couch —a hang-over from the wistful Omar Khayyám craze—surrounded by trophies from the long travels she and Robert took during the winters, would remember the carved papercutter he had given her in Wisconsin, and that had roused half-visions of these high moments, which now shaped themselves before her very eyes.

She won the wide world over, and lost, so to speak, her own soul. The world had been too much with her; the impulse had been lost in the speech that went with the saying; feeling had too often drowned the phrase. For much as she would have liked to believe that heart came before art, she learned too well, when the summing-up came, that heart had been an excuse for her art.

Yet even at her most blatant, it can be said for her that she ended by fooling herself almost as much as she helped fool the public. Scarcely possessing Brisbane's quotation-book knowledge, she did not write down; and in place of his high counterfeit thinking, we have, in her, the direct expression, however crude, of a genuine democratic experience in which thousands basked. Close to her readers, she knew—she had lived—their lives. There was not a mood that passed over the country which she did not reach, reflect, and express. One of our first syndicated advisers, she wrote on love, morals, labor, and manners.

She warned girls not to telephone their lovers; she reproved the elderly for sighing for bygone days, advising them to "Keep Love and Sympathy and Faith alone in your Soul and you can Defeat Time." She preached that "morals is something quite apart from chastity" and she gave the Victorian ladies, who complained about the Oneida Community in Short Beach, a pleasant shudder, by declaring in "The Creed" that

> *Whoever was begotten of pure love*
> *And came desired and welcome into*
> *life,*
> *Is of immaculate conception.*

Always generous, she consoled the ungraceful that Beauty was not All; she told the poor that money carried its own poison; and she warned the sanctimonious that

> *Sometimes it takes the acid of a sin*
> *To cleanse the clouded windows of*
> *our souls.*

Intensely religious by temperament, she subscribed to no fixed religion. (She wrote her brother Marcus: "In my tour of the world I went into every temple of the different countries and worshiped according to their methods. In that way I get all the vibrations of faith and reverence to add to my own.")

Her own mentality curiously characteristic of her day, it was as though her own life had been the autobiography of America. And when Robert died, she was no more reluctant to share her astral experiences with those who were also suffering during the World War from the same loss than she had been to share her earthly ones. And she spoke to her followers of her spiritualistic excursions, as she had of everything else she had ever lived.

She believed herself divinely inspired; and she could have said with Emerson: "I am surrounded by messengers of God who send me credentials day by day," fully as well as she could have claimed kinship legitimately with "that Somebody" who helped John Philip Sousa compose his patriotic marches. And anonymous America listened, through her, to its own experiences; and heard in her, its own voice.

HORATIO ALGER, JR.

by Frederick Lewis Allen

He wrote well over a hundred books that sold some 25,000,000 copies. In all of them poor boys overcame tremendous odds and rose to positions of wealth and power through clean living and remarkable good luck. For half a century these moralistic and monotonous stories influenced the thoughts and actions of millions of young boys, probably for the better. But the life of the author, Horatio Alger, Jr., left much to be desired when weighed against the success and apparent happiness of his fictional heroes. Historian Frederick Lewis Allen pointed out in this article the sad aspects of Alger's existence and questioned the validity of the advice to be inferred from what the man wrote.

SEPTEMBER 17, 1938

IF YOU RELISH paradoxes, consider the career of Horatio Alger, Jr. He made his fame writing books in which boys rose "from rags to riches"—yet he himself did not begin life in rags and did not die rich. The boys in his books got ahead by outwitting thieves and sharpers—yet he himself, a mild and generous little man who gave freely of his earnings to newsboys and bootblacks on the New York streets (the sort of boys who were his favorite heroes), was an easy mark for impostors. His books were, and are, generally regarded by the critical as trash—yet their sales mounted into the millions, he was one of the most popular of all American authors, if not of all authors of all time; and there can be little doubt that he had a far-reaching influence upon the economic and social thought of America—an influence all the greater, perhaps, because it was innocently and naïvely and undogmatically exerted.

Alger wrote always about boys who were on their own, making their way for themselves, usually in the big city. His own boyhood was quite different. It was highly protected and regimented. He was born in 1834 in Revere, Massachusetts, a town which has become one of the northern suburbs of Boston; Horatio Alger, senior, his father, a Unitarian minister, was a bleak, God-fearing man who fought the

84

sins of the flesh and wanted to rear up young Horatio to join him in the spiritual leadership of America. Young Horatio was kept away from all playmates who might prove naughty influences; was put through such a strict course of study that by the time he was eight years old he could explain the Revolutionary War, add fractions in his head, and write the synopsis of a sermon; and became such a little prig that the neighbors' children called him Holy Horatio. When he was fourteen he was sent away to school and learned for the first time the joys of natural play and of mischief; but even after he reached Harvard his primness remained. He fell in love with Patience Stires of Cambridge when he was nineteen, and wanted to marry her, but gave her up—to his lasting regret— when his father told him that marriage would prevent him from continuing his preparation for the church. And later he left a boarding house at college because, seeing his landlady scantily dressed in the doorway of her room, he resolved to "move to where there is greater respect for decency." Yet, earnest puritan though young Alger was, he did not want to follow his father into the ministry. He wanted to write.

After he left Harvard college he went through a long period of false starts and indecision and frustration. He tried to write but failed miserably. He completed a long theological course but hated it. He went to Paris, tasted the Bohemian life, tasted briefly also the delights of the flesh (because, as he wrote in his diary, genius had prerogatives and he would have prerogatives too), but went through agonies of shame over his affair with Elise Monselet—and produced in Paris nothing of any literary moment. He returned to America and became a minister at Brewster, Massachusetts. But still he was so obsessed by his literary ambition that he would sketch out plots on the margins of his sermons; and in 1866—when the Civil War had ended and he was thirty-four years old—he gave up the church once and for all and went to New York to write boys' books.

There he remained most of the rest of his life. He never married; there was a period when he was pathetically in love with a married woman, but even then he did not apparently hope to win her from her husband, though he so adored her that when she tired of him he went into a mental breakdown. One of his closest attachments was to a Chinese boy whom he befriended and fathered for three years, until the boy was tragically killed in a street accident. Another close attachment was to Charles O'Connor, who ran the Newsboys' Lodging House in New York. It was at this lodging house that he spent most of his time, for he was devoted to the ragged boys who frequented it, and found in them a constant gold mine of the sort of literary material that he could use. And year by year he turned out Horatio Alger books in profusion— always wanting to write important books for adults, always dreaming of the novel (to be called *Tomorrow*) that he would someday produce, but always unable to make a go of anything but the boys' stories which flowed from his pen in a torrent.

The truth seems to be that Horatio Alger never fully grew up to adult life, that he shunned its passions and battles and hard realities. Always, deep down in his heart, he wanted a boy's life—not a boy dominated by a stern father and dressed up in neat and proper clothes, but rather a boy free from parental supervision, free to soil and rumple his clothes, free to make a living for himself and test his budding self-reliance. Alger wanted also to be a man of letters, but could not achieve this ambition because his mind, while clear and logical, was childishly naïve, unimaginative, and bewildered by the complexities of mature life. After his books had become widely known, and people began to turn to him as an authority on slum conditions in New York, he was asked to serve on charitable and civic committees, but though he was happy to be treated as a person of importance he usually sat silent at board meetings; either he was too self-distrustful to speak or the problems discussed there took him beyond his depth.

Once, to be sure, he briefly plunged into city affairs with ardor and courage. Having learned how the Italian *padrones* in New York kept little Italian immigrant boys in virtual slavery, lived on their earnings, and thrashed them cruelly, Alger not only wrote a book exposing the *padrone* system (*Phil the Fiddler*), but conducted a campaign of public protest, made speech after speech, and was instrumental in ending the abuse, though more than once be was beaten up by irate *padrones* or their hired thugs. But most of the time, what Alger most enjoyed was to shun adult society and play with the lodging-house boys: to go dashing off with them to fires, to beat the drum in their children's band, to ride on the open horse cars, to go to Barnum's Museum, to work at organizing a children's theater. One excited entry in his diary, about an especially splendid fire, ended with the triumphant words, "Rode back on engine." As he made money with his books he would spend it on the boys—giving them presents, setting up a bootblack in business, helping a newsboy's mother with the rent payments. He died in 1899, at the age of sixty-five—still a nice boy, hard-working, generous, friendly, innocent of heart.

It was this perpetual youth's singular fortune to have just that simplicity, that elementary directness of approach to fiction writing, which would make his books a joy to immature minds. From the moment when William T. Adams, the author of the "Oliver Optic" books, encouraged him, in 1865, to write *Ragged Dick*, the way was clear for him. *Ragged Dick* was followed by over a hundred other volumes—exactly how many, it would take an indefatigable bibliographer to discover. (Herbert R. Mayes, writing Alger's biography, ran the total up to 119, and later found that he had left out several.) Some of the titles, such as *Bound to Rise, Luck and Pluck, Sink or Swim, Do and Dare, Strive and Succeed,* will evoke nostalgic memories in many an older reader today. And almost all of the books were essentially the same—variations upon an invariable theme.

The standard Horatio Alger hero was a fatherless boy of fifteen or thereabouts who had to earn his way, usually in New York City. Sometimes he had to help support a widowed mother with his bootblacking or peddling; sometimes his parentage was unknown and he lived with an aged and eccentric miser, or with a strange hermit who claimed to be his uncle. It might even be that his father was living, but was having trouble with the mortgage on the old farm. Always, however, the boy had to stand on his own feet and face the practical problem of getting on.

This problem was set before the reader in exact financial detail. On the very first page of *Do and Dare,* for example, it was disclosed that the young hero's mother, as postmistress at Wayneboro, had made during the preceding year just $398.50. Whenever "our hero" had to deal with a mortgage, the reader was told the precise amount, the rate of interest, and all other details. When our hero took a job, the reader could figure for himself exactly how much progress he was making by getting $5 a week in wages at the jewelry store and another $5 a week tutoring Mrs. Mason's son in Latin. Our hero was always a good boy, honest, abstemious (in fact, sometimes unduly disposed to preach to drinkers and smokers), prudent, well-mannered (except perhaps for the preaching), and frugal. The excitement of each book lay in his progress toward wealth.

Always there were villains who stood in his way—crooks who would rob him of his earnings, sharpers who would prey upon his supposed innocence. His battles with these villains furnished plenty of melodrama. They tried to sell him worthless gold watches on rail-

road trains, held him up as he was buggy-driving home with his
employer's funds, kidnaped him and held him prisoner in a New
York hide-out, chloroformed him in a Philadelphia hotel room,
slugged him in a Chicago alley-tenement. But always he overcame
them—with the aid of their invariable cowardice. (There must be
many men now living who remember the shock of outraged surprise
with which they discovered that the village bully did not, as in the
Alger books, invariably run whimpering away at the first show of
manly opposition, but sometimes packed a nasty right.) The end of
the book—or series of books, for often several volumes were devoted
to the varied adventures of a single boy—found our hero well on his
way toward wealth: a fortune which might reach to more than a
hundred thousand dollars, which, to the average boy reader of the
seventies and eighties, was an astronomical sum.

The Alger style was incredibly simple, matter-of-fact, and un-
original. Whenever Alger turned aside from plain literal fact for a
bit of analysis or description, he became a fountainhead of eighth-
grade clichés. Nothing whatever was left to the reader's imagination.
The dialogue, though it had little relation to the confusing way in
which people speak in real life, had at least the merit of trans-
parency. When young Rufus wanted to take Miss Manning and his
little sister Rosie out for an evening's diversion, for instance, there
would be no beating about the bush:

"Miss Manning," he said, "have you any engagement this
evening?"

"It is hardly necessary to ask, Rufus," she replied; "my company is not in very great demand."

"You have heard of the Japanese jugglers at the Academy
of Music?"

"Yes; Mrs. Florence was speaking of them this morning.
She and her husband went last evening."

"And we are going this evening. Wouldn't you like to go,
Rosie?"

"Ever so much, Rufie. Will you take me?"

"Yes, I have got tickets; see here"; and Rufus drew out the
three tickets which he had purchased in the morning.

"Thank you, Rufus," said Miss Manning. "I shall like very
much to go. It is long since I went to any place of amusement.
How much did the tickets cost?"

"A dollar and a half apiece."

"Isn't that rather extravagant?"

"It would be if we went every week; but now and then we can afford it."

The reader, you will see, always knew just where he was. No frills, no literary antics; always the story moved with elementary clarity.

Nor did any subtleties of character-drawing prevent one from determining immediately who were the good characters and who were the bad ones. They were labeled plainly. When Andy Grant, the poor farmer's son, met Conrad Carter, the rich squire's son, and said to him, "That's a new bicycle, isn't it?" Conrad replied,

"Yes; I got tired of the old one. This is a very expensive one. Wouldn't you like to own a bicycle?"

"Yes."

"Of course, you never will."

From that moment on, the reader could feel sure that Conrad would never say a decent word or do a decent thing; that Andy would outdistance Conrad in the boat race and Conrad would whine excuses for his defeat; that Conrad would try to burn up Andy's boat and burn his own by mistake; and that when Andy's hard work in New York at last enabled him to pay off Squire Carter's mortgage on the Grant farm, Conrad would go into a dreadful rage, as all thwarted villains do. Similarly, the good characters were always definitely noble and uttered splendid sentiments. And always virtue triumphed. Thus the reading of an Alger story was like watching a football game in which you knew the names and numbers of all the players, and the home team made all the touchdowns.

Any writer who in thirty-three years turned out well over a hundred such books and whose memory (especially as he got on in life) was often faulty must have been expected to make mistakes. Alger made them. Frequently he got his characters mixed, to the dismay of his publishers, who had to rearrange the names. But he had a talent for improvisation. When his hero was to be taken out for a ride on the savage horse Bucephalus—which the villain hoped would run away and kill him—it would suddenly be divulged that the boy had been taking riding lessons the preceding year and had won a reputation as a rider of surpassing skill. Nothing had been said in preceding pages about this course of instruction, but Alger didn't bother to go back and insert a reference on page 45; the accomplishment was sprung upon the delighted reader, Bucephalus was mastered, and the story roared right ahead, to the triumph of the young Jehu and the downfall of the villain.

When one considers that the period in which these books were the delight of millions of American boys was that very period when the economic expansion of the United States was going on full tilt, to the accompaniment of every sort of financial knavery and speculative excess; and when one realizes that to most of these millions of young readers the Alger books provided their first intelligible picture of economic life and the making of an individual fortune, one looks again, with an analytical eye, to see how the Alger hero's fortune was achieved. And one notes, not without amusement, that the boy never got rich from the direct fruits of his industrious labor. How could he, starting in at $5 a week, even with rapid increases in pay? No; he got his hands on capital.

Sometimes this capital was inherited: the supposed orphan, ragged though he was, proved to be the son of a man whose supposedly worthless mining stock was good for $100,000. Sometimes the capital was a gift: rich Mr. Vanderpool was so impressed with the boy's pluck that he made over to him the $50,000 that the boy had helped him to save from the robbers. Or the boy was out in Tacoma, buying lots as a real-estate agent (on his boss's inside information that the Northern Pacific was to be extended to the Coast), and in a Tacoma hotel he befriended an invalid gentleman, who out of gratitude gave him a part interest in some lots that promptly soared in value and put him on Easy Street. The method varied; but when the time came for our hero to get into the money, it was a transaction in capital which won the day for him.

Yet always he was so good, and husbanded so prudently the $175 in his savings account (though he was generous, too, to the poor washerwoman and to the other bootblacks), that to the casual reader the lesson of these stories was not that hard work brings in but a pittance, or that the way to succeed is to stand in with the men who have the capital, but something quite different. The lesson was that capital comes as a reward from heaven to him who labors mightily and uses his head all the time. Work, save, be a good boy, shun the fleshpots, and presently the mining stock will fall into your lap and all will be well.

Possibly this explains something about the Gilded Age—when Americans worked furiously, and opened up the West, and accomplished wonders in invention and manufacturing; when the average American of moderate means was hardheaded, diligent, and on the whole fairly scrupulous; but when the ethical level of the big operations in capital was often well-nigh barbaric. Once capital began to fall into a man's lap, he did not inquire unduly whence it came. He had labored meritoriously; merit was always rewarded— was it not?—and now his reward was at hand; obviously it must come from heaven. One remembers Rockefeller saying, "God gave me my money," and one knows that other men of millions felt as he did. Who knows but that to some of them—and to some of their successors in more recent times—this conviction grew, in part at least, out of early lessons in economics from *Andy Grant's Pluck* or *Tom the Bootblack*—lessons learned when the man of millions had been a farm boy reading in the shade of the barn, or a grocer's clerk hiding under the counter the latest enthralling volume in the "Brave and Bold" series?

The total sale of the Alger books will probably never be known, for he had numerous publishers, many of the publishing firms were short-lived, and the books went through many editions—in cloth at $1 or $1.25, in paper at 40 or 25 or 10 cents. But one can get at least a clue from the fact that M. A. Donahue Company of Chicago, who did not begin publishing them till after Alger's death, estimate their own total, very roughly, at close to ten million copies; and that Street & Smith's estimated total, likewise very roughly computed, would be above two million. The John C. Winston Co. estimate their total sales at five million. Probably it is safe to guess that the grand total must have been well beyond twenty million copies, and may have been far greater. One seldom sees an Alger book nowadays; when the Children's Aid Society questioned seven thousand boys in 1932 (on the hundredth anniversary of Alger's birth), it found that less than twenty per cent of them had ever heard of Alger, only fourteen per cent of them had ever read an Alger book, and not a single boy owned one. But during the Alger heyday, from about 1870 to about the time of the first World War, the results of any such inquiry would have been far different. Parents who were people of cultivation generally frowned on the books as rubbish of a low intellectual order; some parents frowned on them as likely to tempt boys to run away from home (a charge that so distressed Alger that he inserted in many of his later volumes an explicit warning that boys in happy homes had better stay there); but other parents welcomed them as valuable incentives to thrift and ambition. And boys of all ages and condition ate them up.

As they read, they must have dreamed of success—which included wealth, of course, and power, and the thrill of being on the way up, of being prominent, being envied—and also, presumably, a chance to marry happily, and live in a fine house, and enjoy the good things of this earth. What would they have thought, one wonders, had they been able to see, through those dreams of theirs, the man Alger himself—scribbling away in his room in the bare, dour-looking building of the Newsboys' Home in a dingy part of downtown New York; leaving his labors to play with the little newsboys and bootblacks, and perhaps to take a group of them to the circus; a man disappointed in the defeat of his real literary ambitions, disappointed in love, awkward in the society of mature men and women, and apparently almost unaware, as he went innocently and obscurely about the city, that his influence was reaching into millions of families and helping to determine the trend and tradition of American business life?

HERO OF THE GREAT KNOW-HOW

by Henry Seidel Canby

Dr. Canby, founder of The Saturday Review, *considers Mark Twain and his machine-age Boss, the hero of* A Connecticut Yankee in King Arthur's Court.

OCTOBER 20, 1951

NEXT TO *Tom Sawyer*, Mark Twain's *A Connecticut Yankee in King Arthur's Court* was for a while (and in the time of my youth) one of a half-dozen most famous books in the English-speaking world. Published in 1889, it has gone down in critical estimation as fast as *The Adventures of Huckleberry Finn* has come up. Bernard De Voto, in his recent volume in The Viking Portable Library Series, abbreviates it heavily, although in his preface he says that it contains some of the best as well as some of the worst in Mark Twain, and elsewhere describes it as the last of Mark's books of the first rank. Its taste, indeed, is often worse than a barker's in a circus side show. What lover of Twain has not tried to forget those shameful knights, cursed of chivalry, who ride about the kingdom like Fuller Brush men advertising tooth paste? It is a parody of Malory's *Morte d'Arthur*, which was one of Twain's favorite books. It is not a satire based on Tennyson's too noble Arthur. It is a burlesque which dirties the idea of chivalry.

Twain attacked the processes of representative government in *The Gilded Age* with a fierce humor, fierce because in Congress he could see how men of sawdust and solder could make a democratic-republican government a corruption and an absurdity. Yet, like Whitman, he never lost faith in the ideas and the ideals of democracy. Chivalry and feudalism he never understood as necessities for their time—which is strange since he grew up within touching distance of their last stand in the English-speaking world, the old South. Colonel Grangerford, that champion of feudist honor, he could admire, yet only because his absurdity as a sentimental fire-eater made him too pathetic to be dangerous. Yet King Arthur, I should say (Mark says he has seen him on the Mississippi), is studied from a *good* slaveholder. Arthur is lovable and truly noble on his own plane, but roaring in astonishment when his privileges are denied. Then he becomes a kind of stupid dinosaur heedlessly trampling common men into the mud. And in Mark's book the Knights of the Round Table and the dirty, superstitious monks become offensive obstacles to progress. No wonder his British readers were shocked and wished that he had not written the book.

Mark had no idea whatsoever of the inner ideals or the outer responsibilities of feudalism, as, for example, his fellow American Henry Adams was to describe them twenty years later in *Mont St. Michel and Chartres*. His contrast is between a purely literary and romantic version of certain ideas and actions described in the *Morte d'Arthur* and what he himself decided, and not always wrongly, the resulting medieval society must have been like.

In this society (say of the twelfth to thirteenth century—not, of course, Arthur's sub-Roman sixth century) only two elements are reasonably accurate: the state of the peasant (the French, however, rather than the English, peasant) and the predatory greed and blood of the knights. The Church is false, except in its baser aspects. The simple-hearted rulers, such as Arthur, are, historically, nonsense. The contrast, therefore, is between a burlesque of feudal institutions and democratic republicanism as one found it in Connecticut. The book belongs with *Gulliver's Travels* and Butler's *Erewhon* and should so be read. Nevertheless, its philosophy is at least 50 per cent right—and 100 per cent in its emphasis upon the importance of soap and the absurdity of fighting except as a sport.

And yet my generation of young Americans read the *Yankee* with passionate delight. And not merely because we thought some of the episodes the funniest ever written. Perhaps they were, and we have just got a little too sophisticated for the horseplay of a fireworks show pretending to be a miracle. It is Huck's subtler unconscious humor that goes so much deeper that still makes us laugh. And yet, even though lassoing a panoplied knight made even us squirm a little, there was something in the story that warmed our hearts and flattered us to the depths of our being. That is what I wish to try to explain.

Mark did not intend to write this kind of book. He planned merely to illustrate his own ideas of progress, with no sneering, no absurd burlesque of great figures of the imagination. Here is what he said while the book was just begun to "Mother Fairbanks," his friend of *The Quaker City*, a journalist like himself. Dixon Wecter published his letters to her in 1949.

HARTFORD, Nov. 16, 1886.

The story isn't a satire peculiarly, it is more especially a *contrast*. It merely exhibits under high lights, the daily life of the time & that of today; & ncessarily the bringing them into this immediate juxtaposition emphasizes the salients of both. . . . Of course in my story I shall leave unsmirched and unbelittled the great & beautiful *characters* drawn by the master hand of old Malory (if he drew them—at any rate he gave them to *us*)—I am only after the *life* of that day, that is all, to picture it; to try to get into it; to see how it feels and seems. I shall hope that under my hand Sir Galahad will still remain the divinest specter that one glimpses among the mists & twilights of Dreamland across the wastes of the centuries; & Arthur keep his sweetness & his purity, and Launcelot abide and continue "the kindest man that ever strake the sword, yet the sternest knight to his mortal foe that ever put spear in rest"; & I shall grieve indeed if the final disruption of the Round Table & the extinction of its old tender & gracious friendships, & that last battle—the Battle of the Broken Hearts, it might be called—should lose their pathos & their tears through my handling.

Well, he could not write it that way, and if he had been Henry James he would have known it. In *The Prince and the Pauper*, which was a preliminary workout for the archaisms of the *Yankee*, and so kept sweet and calm for Olivia and the children for whom he wrote it, the shrewd Howells detected a "bottom of fury." After the first few chapters of which he wrote Mrs. Fairbanks, the fury began to break the crust of humorous contrast in the *Yankee*. Arthur stays at least noble, Launcelot devoted and courageous, the humor of modern man in case armor, and science vs. magic, remain. But the opportunity to see the "damned human race" in one of its noblest fancies, slaughtering, exploiting, in the name of courtesy and for the benefit of a stupid elite, is too tempting. He strikes at the present by destroying as far as he can the illusions of the past. Does it by a furious humor rather than by a furious satire. For he wanted to be read.

If this were all, there would be little more to say of this once so famous story except in praise and criticism of this outburst of economic humanitarianism. On the contrary, there is another and entirely unexpected element in this story, new for Mark, new in literature, prophetic in history, ominous in its philosophy. And it is this which far transcends in interest a mere contrast of new and old. A new man appears in the *Yankee,* called by everyone the Boss, for it was as a boss that he worked in an arms factory in Hartford until in a fight one of his workmen banged his head in—and he woke up in the Middle Ages. The Boss as a workman had learned to make anything a body wanted, and if there wasn't any quick, new-fangled way to make a thing, he could invent one, and do it as easy as rolling off a log. His father was a blacksmith, his uncle was a horse doctor, and he was a mixture of both. The Boss is, of course, Tom Sawyer grown up part way and thoroughly satisfying his desire to show off. Note the kingdom he proposed to make when he got round to it, precisely in the Tom Sawyer manner. He is Huck in his ingenuity only, with the technique of a machinist substituted for the skills of the river. It is the Yankee himself that explained much of our passionate interest in the book.

He had fallen through the Time Machine by a device common to many writers of fantasy into a world familiar to him only by legendary literature. There he was at first regarded only as another product of some wizard's enchantment. Actually, however, this skilled mechanic from a mechanized world and a materialistic society of infinite tool-making skill is a far stranger creature in these Middle Ages than would be a devil or angel, and more powerful. Soon they are calling him the Boss, and rightly. For every problem, every danger, in this naïve age of Europe, except morals, he had one only, but sufficient answer: applied science. To the simplicities of the Age of Faith he offered his rather naïve, but powerful simplicity. Give the poor peasants, exploited like cattle, the tools they need. Give them self-respect and the idea of equality. Do it by a decent currency and machines to increase production, by laws to secure their gains, by weapons to defend themselves against tyrants, by knowledge of science to defeat superstition. Give them everything that the American workman had in Connecticut and presto! dark ages become light. Destroy the prestige of the clergy by a few scientific miracles, break up the charges of those human tanks, the knights, by precision gunfire and a defense by electricity, train peasants technologically until they can make anything for anyone, meet any emergency, whether a broken bridge, an unpenetrable jungle, or a pestilence, by a know-how that only they possess—and the world is made safe for democracy, Europe reorganized, and all by a few workers and executives out of Hartford. Afterward—well, that was not Mark's business.

The Boss's great plan was wrecked by a moral breakdown at home. He did not know what to do about Launcelot and Guinevere. Morals and morale, which are at least as important as know-how, he had neglected in his idea of progress, with other things quite as important. It was typical of the Tom Sawyer in Mark. And Mark himself was really a humanitarian, not a reformer, and most of all a novelist. His job was to create what Walt Whitman called an eidolon, an imaginative type which men could imitate, and make it true and prophetic. He had created in the Boss an eidolon a half century before this machine-age man became triumphant in history in two great wars. Once a slave, the common man is armed with the terrible by-products of science. He is irresistible—yet still the common man!

I have kept in mind in this description the phraseology of the correspondents of the last war as they wrote of the extraordinary ingenuity, the know-how of the American GI, wondered at throughout all the armies—and have not forgotten the failures of the same type of mind in handling the greater complications of peace. I have no intention, however, of pushing the analogy too far. It is enough to say that Mark, who was neither a sociologist nor a philosopher, was writing prophetically, nevertheless, of obvious aspects of what proved to be the near future, and particularly of Americans. This is why we youngsters brought up in the American tradition of success read the *Yankee* like a dime novel of whites and Indians when the kind of fellow we saw every day became the Boss by using just the kind of science we were being taught at school; organized an underground; and proceeded to enforce civilization. It was as powerful a medicine as Dickens' warm hearts, and much more timely. For Mark, without knowing it, had found a hero (the Great Know-How) for the Industrial Revolution. And the Boss's imitators are enlisting in millions in high schools and colleges today—to the alarm of humanists, philosophers, and historians.

A Connecticut Yankee in King Arthur's Court is in some ways the most American of Mark Twain's books. Yet it makes a cartoon of both Jeffersonian democracy and the Age of Chivalry, a cartoon with the deadly truth of a comic strip. The Yankee of the Industrial Revolution has somehow lost his sense of the dignity of man on the way up through the great New World experiment. He has kept pity and courage and a passion for human rights. But his formula for making a perfect democracy has shifted to the centers of the brain which control only the hands and the eyes. He proposes to make democracy safe by gadgets. As a result he is brash, if not quite so brash now as in Mark's Wild West; and he has brought with him the manifestations of history, a sense of superiority, which is curious because it is neither arrogant, nor predatory, but sprung from his technical efficiency, and based on extreme self-confidence, and not much self-knowledge. The reader feels sympathy with Henry James and his passion for the "refinement" of culture (and religion) when Mark hangs signboards of consumers' goods on the towers of Camelot and the spires of the cathedrals.

This is no fantasy. The Soviet dictatorship, with far greater political and scientific efficiency than the Boss possessed, is quite as brash, and in a much more dangerous fashion. It is providing the common man not only with the tools and a political idea, but with their own brand of pseudo-religion and their carefully controlled culture. The police state is a gadget state also, and in its mechanical ideology is closer to the Industrial Revolution than is old-fashioned agrarian democracy.

But if the Boss was politically naïve, so, on a long term and in all probability, is the Politburo, which expects to build a thousand years on a harsh dogmatism. The Boss is far more human than the present leaders of the Russians, in the sense that our ancestors of the West have given the word for so many centuries—more humorous, more humanitarian, more conscious of the rights and needs of the individual. It is encouraging to know that for many decades *Huckleberry Finn* has been a widely read book, if not by Stalin, by the masses in Russia. And certainly the Boss is a far more engaging figure than any that Russian literature has produced since the overthrow of Russian feudalism. He is the prototype of the skilled laborer with brains as hands, the applier of science who has made his country for the time being the most powerful in the world, although not necessarily, or probably, the wisest.

I will go to any length to set up Mark Twain as that rare phenomenon—an unquestionable genius, as lovable as he was neurotic, as powerful in imagination as he was uncontrolled in art. I do not for an instant propose him in this article as another Jefferson or

Marx. But he could make a man (not a woman) into which Shakespeare called an epitome, and make him a living document that both proves and in a real sense shapes history. I shall be accused by some of taking the humor out of a humorist. Well, Mark himself often wished in later years that he was not so irresistibly funny. He wanted to be regarded as a serious person, which at bottom he certainly was, and forgot that humor is one of the best ways of describing a society without analyzing the life out of it. We young readers had the damosel Sandy to amuse us—Sandy who was so bemused by what she had been told was true that she could see an enchanted princess in what the Boss knew was a pig, who once she began a story could not be stopped except when she had to slosh out her knight errant's helmet with cool spring water to keep his brains from frying. But we did not miss the triumphant Yankee with a gadget in his hand (and a bulldozer in his mind) that warmed us to a country so inventive, so successful as ours, and so easily understood by a boy.

COLONEL WOOD: GRAND OLD REBEL

by Sara Bard Field

Soldier, lawyer, explorer, poet—that was Charles Erskine Scott Wood. His writings weren't published until he was in his sixties. His satirical Heavenly Discourse is still in print. His prolific output, published under a variety of pseudonyms, almost alone saved The Pacific Monthly from failure in the early days of this century. This story was written by his wife, herself a distinguished poet, once prominent in the woman suffrage movement and champion of liberal causes.

MARCH 24, 1935

WHEN THE POPULAR BOOK, *Life Begins at Forty,* appeared, Charles Erskine Scott Wood remarked, "Why forty? Mine began at sixty."

He was nearing sixty when circumstances permitted him to give all, rather than fractions of himself and his time, to writing. His remark placed his own discriminating emphasis on the occupation which, after brilliant careers in the military and legal professions, he knew to be his true, hence his most satisfying, self-expression.

It was, however, no leap into the unknown he made when he turned from writing his last legal brief to the completion of *The Poet in the Desert,* and of *Heavenly Discourse* (satires which last year, seventeen years after publication, went into their twenty-fifth printing). Whether he was exploring Alaska, engaging in Indian campaigns, carrying important secret documents from General O. O. Howard to President Hayes, or, later, engaged in brilliant legal battles which gave him place with the foremost Admiralty lawyers on the Pacific Coast, he was always writing something. There is a file of early, racy ballads about the Indian wars, some of which he composed on horseback when a young lieutenant in the field. There were, later, vigorous verses sent to *The Public,* a forthright liberal magazine published in Chicago by Louis Post, verses which elicited hearty commendation from Mark Twain, with whom he had a robust friendship. His *Indian Tales,* later published by the Vanguard Press, were early collected into a charming volume printed by his young son and a friend on their "attic press." This and a three-year-later private printing of his *Masque of Love* are now collector's items.

Indeed, as one surveys the life of this poet and many-sided prose writer one sees that writing was a necessity to him. His other professions gave him a living. Writing gave him life. This *aqua vitae* bubbled up between any and every conceivable crack in his other imperative preoccupations. There is no more convincing evidence of the truth that one finds time for the fundamentally necessary work in spite of all obstacles than the record of Colonel Wood's writing during years of his greatest activity in legal and social fields. With the support of a large family, a crowded daily docket, exhausting hours in court where he argued his case "with leonine passion if a principle was involved," with a participating interest in all liberal movements and legislation, he also found time for his many unique contributions to *The Pacific Monthly.*

The Pacific Monthly was launched in Portland, Oregon, in 1899 with the hope it might become to the Pacific Coast what *The Atlantic Monthly* was to the Eastern shore. Between the date of its first issue and 1903 Colonel Wood contributed many articles covering a wide range of subjects. Because of the hungry reception given these educative articles, he was urged to undertake a monthly contribution of comment on current events. Always eager to spread his cultural and liberal ideas, he agreed to do this. From 1904 till the suspension of the magazine at the close of 1911, with but few breaks, his columns appeared. They were called *Impressions, A Department of Individual Opinion,* a necessary qualification for a struggling magazine to make when turning loose on a highly conservative public so fearlessly unorthodox a pen. In the eight years he conducted this department he covered over two hundred subjects, not by mere brief comment but by longer or shorter essays.

At the close of 1907, *The Pacific Monthly* faced disaster. Its good angel, Mr. Charles Ladd, had put $300,000 into the magazine and stood to lose it. He refused longer to meet its deficits. Mr. Lute Pease, now cartoonist of the Newark *Evening News,* who had become editor at this inauspicious time, talked the situation over with Colonel Wood. He pointed out that the small financial margin on which the magazine must now be published would not enable him to offer attractive pay for top writers' work. Colonel Wood did not want his close friend, Mr. Ladd, to lose all the money he had contributed to the magazine. He did not want the magazine to fail. Good contributions it must have, especially good fiction. Just what happened is best told in the words of a letter from Mr. Pease:

> One day a little gnome of a man called at my office in response to a request from me to an unknown person named Felix Benguiat. I had received from a writer signing that name a manuscript of such superlative quality, an Oriental tale, richly imaginative, masterly and brilliant with poetry, that I was certain none but a famous writer could have been the author, though I had never heard of Felix Benguiat. I was convinced that somebody was fooling me. The little gnome of a man who appeared said his real name was Rosenthal and attempted to prove to me that he could have written the story; showed me a book by him which only proved beyond a doubt that he never could have been the author of the story. I went after him so savagely that he finally explained Colonel Wood had persuaded him to pose as the author. In short, Colonel Wood, with characteristic delicacy, had tried to avoid subjecting my editorial decision to any influence of friendship or of anything other than consideration of the availability of his story.

After the success of this story Mr. Pease tells me he went to Colonel Wood's office and said:

> Colonel, I feel sure you must have a whole trunkful of unpublished manuscripts. No writer can turn out a thing like this without having back of him a lot of good work. Finally the Colonel agreed to furnish as many stories, poems, etc., as I cared to use, stipulating only that he should sign various names when more than one of his things was printed in the same number. Further, he would take no pay. Was ever an editor in such luck?

The field of fiction was not new to Colonel Wood when he promised this largesse to *The Pacific Monthly,* a largesse he was to supply not from "a whole trunkful of unpublished manuscripts," in spite of his immense activities elsewhere, but from a hitherto untapped reservoir. Under the pseudonyms of Felix Benguiat and Francis du Bosque he had been contributing stories to Benjamin R. Tucker's famous magazine, *Liberty,* published in New York City. Mr. Tucker was then, I believe, the leading exponent of philosophical anarchism in America, a man of much learning. His magazine is full of both meat and ambrosia. The late Mr. Brownell of Scribner's told me he thought the stories Colonel Wood contributed to *Liberty* "unique in flavor, revealing an original style and a delightful personality" and in some instances faithfully preserving the atmosphere of New York's Washington Square in the eighties and nineties, a section of the city in which Colonel Wood lived while studying law at Columbia University.

With this experience in fiction writing behind him and still sheltered under the name of Felix Benguiat, he began feeding the magazine nourishing tales. They were curiously enough of completely opposite types: fairy tales with a Persian flavor, the so-called "escape literature," or stories of grim reality wherein the hero or heroine was victimized by an evil social and industrial system. Sometimes a tale would not sit appropriately under the Felix Benguiat disguise. It then appeared under Orrin Seaman. Felix Benguiat, privileged by pseudonymity of foreign flavor, also conveniently reviewed books particularly controversial or provocative. New verse writers for the magazine appeared: Jared Mallet, William Maxwell, Gustave Korter—"*e pluribus unum.*" At particularly gaunt times in the magazine's life a single number might contain a story, a book review, both by Felix Benguiat, verse by William Maxwell or Jared Mallet or Gustave Korter and Impressions by Charles Erskine Scott Wood without the uninitiated public's suspecting the one hand in the multiple contribution. Sometimes a poem appeared under his own name. His contributions and the able editorship of Mr. Pease increased the magazine's circulation from 60,000 to 100,000.

Early in 1915, aroused by Anthony Comstock's efforts to suppress Margaret Sanger's birth-control movement, Colonel Wood sent a satirical discourse on this subject to *The Masses*. The editors liked it and wanted more. They wanted more even when one particularly provocative discourse took the magazine off the newsstands. The Government suspended publication of *The Masses* because of the magazine's open hostility to World War I, but the Vanguard Press printed a small, cheap edition of the collected dialogues, with a few additions, under the title *Heavenly Discourse*. In printing after printing, this small book, later brought out in a larger, more expensive edition, has encircled the English-speaking world. It spread like small grass fires through college campuses. Nor have campus paths and restaurants been the book's only experience with higher education. *Heavenly Discourse* is on college library shelves and in some colleges is taught in courses covering English satire.

Early in my acquaintance with Colonel Wood, he asked me to examine the contents of a large chest of manuscripts to see if I could find anything of special worth. The chest's contents, much prose and more verse, were the accumulation of many years. I turned the manuscripts over with increasing disappointment—too many trifles, too much *vers de société*, too many lines of occasion, too much imitative style. Then I came to a yellow-sheeted, paper-covered notebook containing free verse sketches of the desert, written long before the school of free verse had become articulate. To the broad bosom of the desert Colonel Wood had returned again and again for summer camping since the days when, a young army officer fresh from the East, he, with his company, had crossed there. In the notebook, the desert was painted with words that in later careful revision were to be printed in many anthologies and school readers. Here, too, were the matured thoughts, born long ago under the stars when he first felt the desert's compelling power—thoughts about Nature's ways contrasted to man's, about war and peace, poverty and plenty, bondage and freedom—thoughts that, from youth to old age, stung him creatively wide awake whenever his head rested on that sage-pungent earth. At that time no one had celebrated either in poetry or painting (he later brought Childe Hassam out to paint it) the American desert, nor had any certain aspect of Nature stirred a poet to make, in this particular manner, the probing, insistent, inventoried comparison between Nature in her largesse, freedom and beauty, and man in his poverty, enslavement, and ugliness.

I leave critical judgment of this poem, which has aroused so much praise and censure, to qualified pens, and turn to the history of *The Poet in the Desert,* more colorful than that of most books of poetry. Colonel Wood first printed the poem at his own expense in 1914 under the dreary title, *Civilization.* A year later it appeared under its present title. In 1918 a new, much-revised edition was printed. It has delighted me to call this edition "the Prince and the Pauper" for, while a portion of the edition was printed on fine, handmade linen paper in the best black ink and bound in substantial boards, the other, far larger portion, at Emma Goldman's request, was printed on cheap paper with indifferent ink and paper-bound. Emma Goldman was lecturing to large, mostly proletarian, audiences all over America. She wanted a cheap edition of *The Poet in the Desert* to be sold, with other literature, at her lectures. I have not the exact figures but I know that in this way several thousand were sold. It is my belief no poem, with the possible exception of Markham's "Man with the Hoe," has been so widely read and loved by the working class of this country as *The Poet in the Desert*. It went into the trenches of World War I. It has circulated in lumber camps and hobo "jungles." Our library contains one of the paper-bound copies rebound in oilcloth to protect it from weather, for it was carried like a lamb in the bosom of an itinerant tinker who traveled up and down the Oregon and Washington Coast repairing small machines. It had been carefully indexed. There were many marginal notes and much text underlining. The tinker, whose name was Frasier, referred to it always as "the good book." He told us of once riding a boxcar with men automatically made hoboes by the depression. Being hungry, they had all decided to leave the train at Sacramento in search of food. Meanwhile, Frasier told us, to distract them from their hunger, he began to read from his worn copy of *The Poet in the Desert*. Whenever he paused the men would yell, "Go on!" He was in the middle of one of the longer sections when the train reached Sacramento. "Hell, let's go on to San Francisco and finish this," one of the men said. They all agreed and so went on to the big city while Frasier read to the end. "As soon as those men got a job," Frasier said, his face glowing, "each one bought a copy of the good book." Colonel Wood offered to exchange this worn copy for one of the better-made books but Frasier refused, saying his copy was part of him. Yet one day, years after we had first seen it, he climbed our hill and laid the little book in Colonel Wood's hands, saying he would now like to leave it with him as he had premonitions of death due to a recent illness. I think Colonel Wood prized it more than his Shakespeare Folio.

Such stories could be multiplied. We have in our files many touching letters from men and women in the labor ranks who felt the beauty of the poem because of its social challenge and the social challenge because of its beauty.

In 1929 The Lantern Press published *Poems from the Ranges,* containing, with other purely Western verse, the famous "First Snow" which was originally published in the immediate ancestor of *The Saturday Review, The New York Evening Post Literary Review.* Except for two other privately printed books, *Selected Poems* (with Sara Bard Field) and *Sonnets to Sappho,* Colonel Wood made no effort to publish more of his poetic work. Indeed he made no effort to publish anything. If publication came in the natural flow of events, well and good. If not, equally was it well and good. "Uncaring praise or blame," he once truly wrote of himself. Poetry, if worthy, would take care of itself. Meanwhile there were immediate social issues of grave importance about which he was aflame. So he constantly interrupted his poetic writing to protest passionately against growing interference in personal liberty in *Too Much Government* and against other social sins in *Earthly Discourse*. He was eighty-four when he wrote the latter. When one considers the powerful irony in *Satan and the Publisher*, the identification of himself with tender romance in *King Cophetua and the Beggar Maid*, the vigorous review of *The Supreme Court* which elicited praiseful letters from many able jurists, one is amazed to realize what high emotional and intellectual flames burned under the snow. I am glad that a renewed demand for *Earthly Discourse* is causing its republication even though new plates have had to be made.

Colonel Wood has left many unpublished manuscripts, among them several dramas. Of these the most important is *Circe*, which Maurice Browne has called "one of the seven noblest plays of our time." For all his writings, published and unpublished, completed or uncompleted, his notebooks, journals, diaries, etc., the Huntington Memorial Library is offering a safe home where they will be accessible to the future historian of the social and cultural aspects of this coast. Only after a lapse of time can the stature of "that grand old rebel," as the late Senator Phelan always called him, be properly measured and his far-reaching contribution to thought and culture be adequately understood.

THE INCREDIBLE
DR. BELL

by Irving Wallace

*When Conan Doyle invented a new kind of fictional detective, he
had in mind his old medical instructor in Edinburgh, Dr. Joseph
Bell, who had an odd knack for spotting details about people he
met. Irving Wallace tells how the eminent surgeon was a real-life
inspiration for Sherlock Holmes, the great detective.*

MAY 1, 1948

ONE EVENING, about the turn of the century, after a week-end shoot
in Scotland, a dozen guests sat around a dinner table discussing
human monsters, famous murders, and unsolved crimes. One of the
guests, Dr. Joseph Bell, the eminent Edinburgh surgeon and medical instructor, had the others wide-eyed with his deductive acro-
batics.

"The trouble with most people," he said, "is that they see, but
do not observe. Any really good detective ought to be able to tell,
before a stranger has fairly sat down, his occupation, habits, and
past history through rapid observation and deduction. Glance at a
man and you find his nationality written on his face, his means of
livelihood on his hands, and the rest of his story in his gait, mannerisms, tattoo marks, watch chain ornaments, shoe laces, and in
the lint adhering to his clothes."

The guests were skeptical. One challenged Dr. Bell to give an
example of applied observation. Happily, Dr. Bell obliged.

"A patient walked into the room where I was instructing the
students, and his case seemed to be a very simple one. I was talking
about what was wrong with him. 'Of course, gentlemen,' I happened to say, 'he has been a soldier in a Highland regiment, probably a bandsman.' I pointed out the swagger in his walk, suggestive
of the Highland piper; while his shortness told me that if he had
been a soldier, it was probably as a bandsman. But the man insisted
he was nothing but a shoemaker and had never been in the army

in his life. This was rather a floorer, but being absolutely certain, I told two of the strongest clerks to remove the man to a side room and strip him.

"Under his left breast I instantly detected a little blue D branded on his skin. He was an army deserter. That was how they used to mark them in the Crimean days. You can understand his evasion. However, this proved my first observation correct. He confessed having played in the band of a Highland regiment in the war against the Russians. It was really elementary, gentlemen."

Most of the guests were impressed. But one listener chidingly remarked, "Why, Dr. Bell might almost be Sherlock Holmes."

To which Dr. Bell snapped, "My dear sir, I *am* Sherlock Holmes."

Dr. Bell was not jesting. He was, indeed, the original Sherlock Holmes, the real-life inspiration for the immortal detective of fiction. "It is most certainly to you that I owe Sherlock Holmes," A. Conan Doyle wrote to Dr. Bell in May 1892. Thirty-two years later, still grateful to Dr. Bell, Doyle publicly admitted, "I used and amplified his methods when I tried to build up a scientific detective who solved cases on his own merits."

Unlike the detective, Dr. Bell wore neither deerstalker cap nor ankle-length cape coat and used neither magnifying glass nor cocaine. Where Sherlock Holmes was the eccentric bachelor in his cramped room at 221-B Baker Street, Dr. Bell was entirely the family man with a son, two daughters, and two sprawling gabled homes of his own. Where Sherlock Holmes dwelled in a shadow world bound by Moriarty and Watson, Dr. Bell was a surgeon whose courage won compliments from Queen Victoria, whose crusades for nurses earned the friendship of Florence Nightingale, whose classroom wizardry influenced five decades of Edinburgh University undergraduates including not only Doyle but Robert Louis Stevenson and James M. Barrie.

The rules of Sherlock Holmes merely echoed the real-life gospel of Dr. Joseph Bell. "I always impressed over and over again upon all my scholars the vast importance of little distinctions, the endless significance of the trifles," Dr. Bell once told a reporter.

"The great majority of people, of incidents, and of cases resemble each other in the main and larger features. For instance, most men have apiece a head, two arms, a nose, a mouth, and a certain number of teeth. It is the little differences, in themselves trifles, such as the droop of the eyelid or what not, which differentiate men."

What were some of these "infinitely little" factors Dr. Bell regarded as important in observation? "Nearly every handicraft writes its sign-manual on the hands," contended Dr. Bell. "The scars of the miner differ from those of the quarryman. The carpenter's callosities are not those of the mason. . . . The soldier and sailor differ in gait. Accent helps you to district and, to an educated ear, almost to county. . . . With a woman, especially, the observant doctor can often tell what part of her body she is going to talk about."

While Dr. Bell felt the development of observation was a necessity to doctors and detectives, he felt as strongly that it was a thrilling sport for laymen. Every man, argued Dr. Bell, can transform his world from one of monotony and drabness into one of excitement and adventure by developing his faculty of observation.

Throughout his life, he continued to amaze his circle with the observation game. "When the family traveled in a train," his surviving sister, Mrs. Cecil Stisted, recalls, "he would tell us where all the other passengers in the carriage were from, where they were going to, and something of their occupations and their habits. All this without having spoken to them. When he verified his observations, we thought him a magician."

One afternoon he was at his desk, in the Royal Infirmary, working. Someone knocked at his study door.

"Come in," he called. The man entered. Dr. Bell stared at him. "Why are you worried?"

"How do you know I am worried?"

"The four knocks. Unworried people content themselves with two, or at the most three."

Dr. Bell had hit the nail on the head. The man *was* worried.

Years after Dr. Bell's death, Conan Doyle told an interviewer, "Dr. Bell would sit in his receiving room, with a face like a red Indian, and diagnose people as they came in, before they even opened their mouths. He would tell them their symptoms, and even give them details of their past life, and hardly ever would he make a mistake."

Inside the spired Royal Infirmary of Edinburgh, in the packed lecture amphitheater beneath the flickering gas lights, Dr. Bell daily tried to prove to his pupils that observation was not a magic but a science.

In the Royal Infirmary wards, in the dispensaries, especially in the out-patient department where ailing citizens were brought forward by student-clerks, Dr. Bell practiced what he preached. Glancing at a newcomer, Dr. Bell remarked, "A cobbler, I see." He explained to his students "that the inside of the knee of the man's trousers was worn; that was where the man had rested the lapstone, a peculiarity found only in cobblers."

Students would remember, for years after, some of the master's deductive feats. One former student, Dr. Harold E. Jones, recalled that Dr. Bell would summon his charges up front to try their own hand at observing. "What is the matter with this man, sir?" Dr. Bell once asked of a quaking student. "No, you mustn't touch him. Use your eyes, sir, use your ears, use your brain, your bump of perception, and use your powers of deduction."

At sea, the confused student blurted, "Hip-joint disease, sir."

Dr. Bell scowled, shook his head. "Hip-nothing! The man's limp is not from his hip, but from his foot. Were you to observe closely, you would see that there are slits, cut by a knife, in those parts of the shoes where the pressure of the shoe is greatest against the foot. The man is a sufferer from corns, gentlemen, and has no hip trouble at all. But he has not come here to be treated for corns. His trouble is of a much more serious nature. This is a case of chronic alcoholism. The rubicund nose, the puffed, bloated face, the blood-shot eyes, the tremulous hands and twitching face muscles, with the quick, pulsating temporal arteries, all show this. These deductions, gentlemen, must however be confirmed by absolute and concrete evidence. In this instance my diagnosis is confirmed by the fact of my seeing the neck of a whisky bottle protruding from the patient's right-hand coat pocket. . . . Never neglect to ratify your deductions."

At one time, when the young Conan Doyle was Dr. Bell's student assistant, a patient entered. "Did you like your walk over the golf links today, as you came in from the south side of town?" inquired Dr. Bell. The patient replied, "Why yes, did your honor see me?" Dr. Bell had not seen him. "Conan Doyle could not understand how I knew," Dr. Bell related later, "but on a showery day such as that had been, the reddish clay at bare parts of the golf links adheres to the boot, and a tiny part is bound to remain. There is no such clay anywhere else. . . ."

But the most famous example of Dr. Bell's skill was the one Conan Doyle retold in his autobiography. A civilian out-patient, a total stranger to Dr. Bell, came into his ward. In silence, Dr. Bell studied the visitor, then spoke.

"Well, my man, you've served in the army."

"Aye, sir."

"Not long discharged?"

"No, sir."

"A Highland regiment?"

"Aye, sir."

"A non-com officer?"

"Aye, sir."

"Stationed at Barbados?"

"Aye, sir."

Dr. Bell turned to his students. "You see, gentlemen, the man was a respectful man, but he did not remove his hat. They do not in the army, but he would have learned civilian ways had he been long discharged. He has an air of authority and he is obviously Scottish. As to Barbados, his complaint is elephantiasis, which is West Indian and not British." Years later Conan Doyle was still sufficiently impressed by this incident to reproduce it in his Sherlock Holmes story "The Greek Interpreter."

Conan Doyle, after five years as a struggling medical student, graduated from Edinburgh University in 1881. He nailed up his oculist shingle and waited for patients. Six years later he was still waiting. Lacking a practice, desperate for any kind of income, Doyle turned to writing. After one false start, and under the influence of Gaboriau and Poe, he decided to try a detective story. And for it he wanted a new kind of detective.

"I thought of my old teacher Joe Bell, of his eagle face, of his curious ways, of his eerie trick of spotting details," Doyle recollected in his autobiography. "If he were a detective, he would surely reduce this fascinating but unorganized business to something nearer to an exact science. . . . It was surely possible in real life, so why should I not make it plausible in fiction? It is all very well to say that a man is clever, but the reader wants to see example of it— such examples as Bell gave us every day in the wards. The idea amused me. What should I call the fellow?"

He called him Sherlock Holmes after an English cricketer and Oliver Wendell Holmes.

With Bell as his model, Sherlock Holmes became the familiar tall, stooped, hawk-faced, intense, and inscrutable human bloodhound. His first appearance, in *Beeton's Christmas Annual* in 1887, was inauspicious. But as a result, an American editor, two years later, ordered more Sherlock Holmes stories, and the detective was on his way to literary immortality.

Sherlock Holmes's deductive tricks thrilled readers on both sides

of the Atlantic. Each Holmes stunt was discussed and repeated by
fans everywhere. In "The Adventure of the Norwood Builder," when
a frantic young man burst into the room on Baker Street and announced himself as John McFarlane, Sherlock Holmes lazily replied, "You mention your name as if I should recognize it, but I
assure you that, beyond the obvious facts that you are a bachelor, a
solicitor, a Freemason, and an asthmatic, I know nothing whatever
about you."

Joseph Bell, product of five generations of surgeons, was the eldest son of a devout and renowned physician. At the age of twenty-
two he took his medical degree at Edinburgh University, and two
years later became house surgeon in the Royal Infirmary. His courage was amazing. On one occasion, at a time when diphtheria was a
little-known disease, an ailing child suffering diphtheria was oper-
ated upon. After the operation, poison accumulated, and, since
there were no instruments for suction, the child was given little
chance to live. Without a moment's hesitation Dr. Bell put his lips
to the child's, sucked the poison from its throat, and saved its life.

As a result, Dr. Bell himself caught diphtheria and impaired his
voice for life. When elderly Queen Victoria, visiting Edinburgh,
heard the story, she personally congratulated Dr. Bell. "The dear
old lady was so friendly," he reported afterward, "and I was not one
bit flustered."

Dr. Bell devoted much of his medical career crusading for nurses,
and through this crusade he won Florence Nightingale as one of his
closest friends. At a time when nurses were little better than street
women, with no interest whatsoever in their patients, Dr. Bell
fought to dignify the profession. Later, when nursing became fashionable, Dr. Bell fought equally hard to keep out pretty girls who
were only interested in wearing uniforms.

In company he had very definite opinions on all matters. "Hysterical people are generally liars," he would say. Or, "I have no
patience with bigots. There is always some hypocrisy in conjunction with bigotry." Or, after visiting the remains of Wellington and
Nelson, "I should not have liked to know them. One should not
see a hero too near." He was Empire-minded, defending the Boer
War to a friend, "You surely don't want us to be kicked out of
South Africa. Once a nation begins to give in, it is a dying nation,
and soon will be a dead one."

Yet Dr. Bell was not infallible. Moreover, he had a sense of
humor. When visitors begged him to recount tales of his deductive

prowess, he liked to relate the story of his visit to a bed-ridden patient. "Aren't you a bandsman?" Dr. Bell asked, standing over the patient. "Aye," admitted the sick man. Dr. Bell turned cockily to his students. "You see, gentlemen, I am right. It is quite simple. This man had a paralysis of the cheek muscles, the result of too much blowing at wind instruments. We need only inquire to confirm. What instrument do you play, my man?"

The man got up on his elbows. "The big drum, doctor!"

WATSON WAS A WOMAN

by Rex Stout

Most Sherlock Holmes fans consider the great detective and his companion, Dr. Watson, as real as life. This is reason enough to include in this collection a controversial portrait of the doctor.

MARCH 1, 1941

GASOGENE: TANTALUS: Buttons: Irregulars:

You will forgive me for refusing to join your commemorative toast, "The Second Mrs. Watson," when you learn it was a matter of conscience. I could not bring myself to connive at the perpetuation of a hoax. Not only was there never a second Mrs. Watson; there was not even a first Mrs. Watson. Furthermore, there was no Doctor Watson.

Please keep your chairs.

Like all true disciples, I have always recurrently dipped into the Sacred Writings (called by the vulgar the Sherlock Holmes stories) for refreshment; but not long ago I reread them from beginning to end, and I was struck by a singular fact that reminded me of the dog in the night. The singular fact about the dog in the night, as we all know, was that it didn't bark; and the singular fact about Holmes in the night is that he is never seen going to bed. The writer of the tales, the Watson person, describes over and over again, in detail, all the other minutiae of that famous household—suppers, breakfasts, arrangement of furniture, rainy evenings at home—but not once are we shown either Holmes or Watson going to bed. I wondered, why not? Why such unnatural and obdurate restraint, nay, concealment, regarding one of the pleasantest episodes of the daily routine?

I got suspicious.

The uglier possibilities that occurred to me, as that Holmes had false teeth or that Watson wore a toupee, I rejected as preposterous. They were much too obvious, and shall I say unsinister. But the game was afoot, and I sought the trail, in the only field available to me, the Sacred Writings themselves. And right at the very start, on page 9 of "A Study in Scarlet," I found this:

. . . It was rare for him to be up after ten at night, and he had invariably breakfasted and gone out before I rose in the morning.

I was indescribably shocked. How had so patent a clue escaped so many millions of readers through the years? That was, that only could be, a woman speaking of a man. Read it over. The true authentic speech of a wife telling of her husband's—but wait. I was not indulging in idle speculation, but seeking evidence to establish a fact. It was unquestionably a woman speaking of a man, yes, but whether a wife of a husband, or a mistress of a lover . . . I admit I blushed. I blushed for Sherlock Holmes, and I closed the book. But the fire of curiosity was raging in me, and soon I opened again to the same page, and there in the second paragraph I saw:

> The reader may set me down as a hopeless busybody, when I confess how much this man stimulated my curiosity, and how often I endeavored to break through the reticence which he showed on all that concerned himself.

You bet she did. She would. Poor Holmes! She doesn't even bother to employ one of the stock euphemisms, such as, "I wanted to understand him better," or, "I wanted to share things with him." She proclaims it with brutal directness, "I endeavored to break through the reticence." I shuddered, and for the first time in my life felt that Sherlock Holmes was not a god, but human—human by his suffering. Also, from that one page I regarded the question of the Watson person's sex as settled for good. Indubitably she was a female, but wife or mistress? I went on. Two pages later I found:

> . . . his powers upon the violin . . . at my request he has played me some of Mendelssohn's *Lieder* . . ."

Imagine a man asking another man to play him some of Mendelssohn's *Lieder* on a violin!
And on the next page:

> . . . I rose somewhat earlier than usual, and found that Sherlock Holmes had not yet finished his breakfast . . . my place had not been laid nor my coffee prepared. With . . . petulance . . . I rang the bell and gave a curt intimation that I was ready. Then I picked up a magazine from the table and attempted to while away the time with it, while my companion munched silently at his toast.

That is a terrible picture, and you know and I know how bitterly realistic it is. Change the diction, and it is practically a love story by Ring Lardner. That Sherlock Holmes, like other men, had breakfasts like that is a hard pill for a true disciple to swallow, but we must face the facts. The chief thing to note of this excerpt is that it not only reinforces the conviction that Watson was a lady—that is to say, a woman—but also it bolsters our hope that Holmes did not through all those years live in sin. A man does not munch silently at his toast when breakfasting with his mistress; or, if he does, it won't be long until he gets a new one. But Holmes stuck to her—or she to him—for over a quarter of a century. Here are a few quotations from the later years:

> . . . Sherlock Holmes was standing smiling at me. . . . I rose to my feet, stared at him for some seconds in utter amazement, and then it appears that I must have fainted. . . ."
> —*The Adventure of the Empty House,* page 4.
> I believe that I am one of the most long-suffering of mortals.
> —*The Tragedy of Birlstone,* page 1.
> The relations between us in those latter days were peculiar. He was a man of habits, narrow and concentrated habits, and I had become one of them. As an institution I was like the violin, the shag tobacco, the old black pipe, the index books, and others perhaps less excusable.
> —*The Adventure of the Creeping Man,* page 1.

And we have been expected to believe that a man wrote those things! The frank and unconcerned admission that she fainted at sight of Holmes after an absence! "I am one of the most long-suffering of mortals"—the oldest uxorial cliché in the world; Aeschylus used it; no doubt cavemen gnashed their teeth at it! And the familiar pathetic plaint, "As an institution I was like the old black pipe!"

Yes, uxorial, for surely she was wife. And the old black pipe itself provides us with a clincher on that point. This comes from page 16 of "The Hound of the Baskervilles":

> . . . did not return to Baker Street until evening. It was nearly nine o'clock when I found myself in the sitting room once more.
> My first impression as I opened the door was that a fire had broken out, for the room was so filled with smoke that the light of the lamp upon the table was blurred by it. As I entered, however, my fears were set at rest, for it was the acrid

fumes of strong coarse tobacco which took me by the throat and set me coughing. Through the haze I had a vague vision of Holmes in his dressing gown coiled up in an armchair with his black clay pipe between his lips. Several rolls of paper lay around him.

"Caught cold, Watson?" said he.

"No, it's this poisonous atmosphere."

"I suppose it *is* pretty thick, now that you mention it."

"Thick! It is intolerable!"

"Open the window, then!"

I say husband and wife. Could anyone alive doubt it after reading that painful banal scene? Is there any need to pile on the evidence?

For the last-ditch skeptic there is more evidence, much more. The efforts to break Holmes of the cocaine habit, mentioned in various places in the Sacred Writings, display a typical reformist wife in action, especially the final gloating over her success. A more complicated, but no less conclusive, piece of evidence is the strange, the astounding recital of Holmes's famous disappearance, in "The Final Problem," and the reasons given therefor in a later tale, "The Adventure of the Empty House." It is incredible that this monstrous deception was not long ago exposed.

Holmes and Watson had together wandered up the valley of the Rhone, branched off at Leuk, made their way over the Gemmi Pass, and gone on, by way of Interlaken, to Meiringen. Near that village, as they were walking along a narrow trail high above a tremendous abyss, Watson was maneuvered back to the hotel by a fake message. Learning that the message was a fake, she (he) flew back to their trail, and found that Holmes was gone. No Holmes. All that was left of him was a polite and regretful note of farewell, there on a rock with his cigarette case for a paperweight, saying that Professor Moriarty had arrived and was about to push him into the abyss.

That in itself was rather corny. But go on to "The Adventure of the Empty House." Three years have passed. Sherlock Holmes has suddenly and unexpectedly reappeared in London, causing the Watson person to collapse in a faint. His explanation of his long absence is fantastic. He says that he had grappled with Professor Moriarty on the narrow trail and tossed him into the chasm; that, in order to deal at better advantage with the dangerous Sebastian Moran, he had decided to make it appear that he too had toppled over the cliff; that, so as to leave no returning footprints on the narrow trail, he had attempted to scale the upper cliff, and, while he was doing so, Sebastian Moran himself had appeared up above and thrown rocks at him; that by herculean efforts he had eluded Moran and escaped over the mountains; that for three years he had wandered around Persia and Tibet and France, communicating with no one but his brother Mycroft, so that Sebastian Moran would think he was dead. *Though by his own account Moran knew, must have known, that he had got away!*

That is what Watson says that Holmes told her (him). It is simply gibberish, below the level even of a village half-wit. It is impossible to suppose that Sherlock Holmes ever dreamed of imposing on any sane person with an explanation like that; it is impossible to believe that he would insult his own intelligence by offering such an explanation even to an idiot. I deny that he ever did. I believe that all he said, after Watson recovered from the faint, was this: "My dear, I am willing to try it again," for he was a courteous man. And it was Watson who, attempting to cook up an explanation, made such a terrible hash of it.

Then who was this person whose nom de plume was "Doctor Watson"? Where did she come from? What was she like? What was her name before she snared Holmes?

Let us see what we can do about the name, by methods that Holmes himself might have used. It was Watson who wrote the immortal tales, therefore if she left a record of her name anywhere it must have been in the tales themselves. But what we are looking for is not her characteristics or the facts of her life, but her *name,* that is to say, her *title;* so obviously the place to look is in the *titles* of the tales.

There are sixty of the tales all told. The first step is to set them down in chronological order, and number them from 1 to 60. Now, which shall we take first? Evidently the reason why Watson was at such pains to conceal her name in this clutter of titles was to *mystify* us, so the number to start with should be the most *mystical* number, namely seven. And to make it doubly sure, we shall make it seven times seven, which is 49. Very well. The 49th tale is "The Adventure of the Illustrious Client." We of course discard the first four words, "The Adventure of the," which are repeated in most of the titles. Result: "ILLUSTRIOUS CLIENT."

The next most significant thing about Watson is her (his) constant effort to convince that those things happen exactly as she (he) tells them; that they are on the *square.* Good. The first square of an integer is the integer 4. We take the title of the 4th tale and get "RED-HEADED LEAGUE."

We proceed to elimination. Of all the factors that contribute to an ordinary man's success, which one did Holmes invariably exclude, or eliminate? Luck. In crap-shooting, what are the lucky numbers? Seven and eleven. But we have already used 7, which eliminates it, so there is nothing left but 11. The 11th tale is about the "ENGINEER'S THUMB."

Next, what was Holmes's age at the time he moved to Baker Street? Twenty-seven. The 27th tale is the adventure of the "NORWOOD BUILDER." And what was Watson's age? Twenty-six. The 26th tale is the adventure of the "EMPTY HOUSE." But there is no need to belabor the obvious. Just as it is a simple matter to decipher the code of the Dancing Men when Holmes has once put you on the right track, so can you, for yourself, make the additional required selections now that I have explained the method. And you will inevitably get what I got:

> *Illustrious Client*
> *Red-headed League*
> *Engineer's Thumb*
> *Norwood Builder*
> *Empty House*
>
> *Wisteria Lodge*
> *Abbey Grange*
> *Twisted Lip*
> *Study in Scarlet*
> *Orange Pips*
> *Noble Bachelor*

And, acrostically simple, the initial letters read down, the carefully hidden secret is ours. Her name was Irene Watson.

But not so fast. Is there any way of checking that? Of discovering her name by any other method, say *a priori?* We can try and see. A woman wrote the stories about Sherlock Holmes, that has been demonstrated; and that woman was his wife. Does there appear, anywhere in the stories, a woman whom Holmes fell for? Whom he really cottoned to? Indeed there does. "A Scandal in Bohemia" opens like this:

> To Sherlock Holmes she is always *the* woman. . . . In his eyes she eclipses and predominates the whole of her sex.

And what was the name of *the* woman? Irene!

But, you say, not Irene Watson, but Irene Adler. Certainly. Watson's whole purpose, from beginning to end, was to confuse and bewilder us regarding her identity. So note that name well. Adler. What is an adler, or, as it is commonly spelled, addler? An addler is one who, or that which, addles. Befuddles. Confuses. I admit I admire that stroke; it is worthy of Holmes himself. In the very act of deceiving and confusing us, she has the audacity to employ a name that brazenly announces her purpose!

An amusing corroborative detail about this Irene of "Scandal in Bohemia"—*the* woman to Holmes according to the narrator of the tales—is that Holmes was present at her wedding at the Church of St. Monica in the Edgeware Road. It is related that he was there as a witness, but that is pure poppycock. Holmes himself says, "I was half-dragged up to the altar, and before I knew where I was I found myself mumbling responses. . . ." Those are not the words of an indifferent witness, but of a reluctant, ensnared, bulldozed man—in short, a bridegroom. And in all the 1323 pages of the Sacred Writings, that is the only wedding we ever see—the only one, so far as we are told, that Holmes ever graced with his presence.

All this is very sketchy. I admit it. I am now collecting material for a fuller treatment of the subject, a complete demonstration of the evidence and the inevitable conclusion. It will fill two volumes, the second of which will consist of certain speculations regarding various concrete results of that long-continued and—I fear, alas—none-too-happy union. For instance, what of the parentage of Lord Peter Wimsey, who was born, I believe, around the turn of the century—about the time of the publication of "The Adventure of the Second Stain"? That will bear looking into.

MEMORIES OF
A. E. HOUSMAN

by Laurence Housman

The author of A Shropshire Lad *came from a large family where writing poems was as much a part of childhood as ordinary fun and games. Here Laurence Housman, who became an artist-author-poet in his own right, tells some revealing things about the early days of his eldest brother, Alfred.*

SEPTEMBER 19, 1936

OF THE EARLY YEARS of an eldest brother, six years my senior, I know little except on hearsay from himself and others. In a brief autobiographical note, which he supplied to a French translator of some of his poems, he gave the following account of himself:

> I was born in Worcestershire, not Shropshire, where I have never spent much time. My father and mother were respectively Lancashire and Cornish. I had a sentimental feeling for Shropshire because its hills were our western horizon. My topographical details—Hughley, Abdon-under-Clee, etc., are sometimes quite wrong: but I know Ludlow and Wenlock.
>
> I took an interest in astronomy almost as early as I can remember: the cause, I think, was a little book we had in the house.
>
> I was brought up in the Church of England and in the High Church party, which is much the best religion I have ever come across. But Lemprière's *Classical Dictionary,* read when I was eight, made me prefer paganism to Christianity; I abandoned Christianity at thirteen, and became an atheist at twenty-one.
>
> I never had any scientific education. I wrote verse at eight or earlier, but very little until I was thirty-five.

That last statement needs qualification. He had a great facility for verse-writing, and not only wrote poems of a serious character but was prolific in *vers d'occasion*. In early years his compositions so much exceeded his own use for them that he sometimes palmed them off on others, and my first sonnet, written when I was about six and before I knew what constituted a sonnet, was dragged out of me, or squeezed into me, by a process of hypnotic suggestion which left me entirely convinced at the time that the poem was mine, though I know better now.

Under his leadership, in a family of seven, we all wrote poems, even the unpoetic ones: lyrics, ballads, sonnets, narrative poems, nonsense-rhymes, and compositions to which each contributed a verse (not always in the same meter) occupied almost as much of our playtime as the more active games of childhood, in which also, as often as not, he led and we followed.

His early education was first under a governess, then at a small dame-school, where a slipper was the regular instrument used for corporal punishment; at the age of eleven he was elected to a Foundation Scholarship at Bromsgrove School, where he remained to the end of his schooldays.

Having gained an open scholarship at St. John's College, Oxford, in 1877, he went up in the autumn of that year. There was no particular reason, except the need for a good scholarship, why that college should have been chosen. Unfortunately there were parental reasons against two others which might have suited him better. His father would not allow him to try for a Balliol Scholarship from disapproval of the theological views of Dr. Jowett, the Master; Cambridge was ruled out unless he could obtain a scholarship at the college (St. John's) where uncles and grandparents had graduated, and where one had become Dean.

It is probable that Cambridge, with its Classical Tripos, would have opened for him a better course of study than Oxford, where after gaining a First in "Moderations" in 1879, he failed in "Greats" two years later—so bringing his university career to a catastrophic end, which, for the time at any rate, destroyed all chance of a scholastic appointment at Oxford or Cambridge, and compelled him to accept as an alternative the uncongenial work of a civil servant in H. M. Patent Office, where he remained for ten years.

An explanation of his failure in "Greats" has recently been given by one of his friends and contemporaries at Oxford. Finding himself unable to deal to his full, honest satisfaction with certain of the set papers, he gave no answers at all, thus, as he himself declared, leaving the examiners no alternative to the course they took. But to the best of my recollection, for home consumption (where the disappointment was naturally very great) he gave no explanation at all.

On leaving Oxford he remained a member of the university, and having in a subsequent year passed the necessary examination, took his B.A. and his M.A. together in 1892, when, on the strength of the reputation which he had built up for himself, by his classical contributions to the learned journals, he was appointed Professor of Latin at University College, London.

In the autobiographical note from which I have already quoted, "Oxford" wrote Alfred, "had not much effect upon me, except that I there met my greatest friend." A statement which can hardly be as true as he would have liked it to be; since this, at any rate, can be said for certain—he came back from Oxford a changed character. It was probably the blow of his failure which caused him from that time on to withdraw so completely into himself, and he became a silent and impenetrable recluse in the midst of his own family, during the year which elapsed before he left home to take up his Civil Service appointment in London. Up to the beginning of his university career he had been our social and intellectual leader, the inventor of our games, the composer and producer of our plays (impromptus devised only on the day of their performance), the editor and chief contributor to our *Family Magazine,* and the instigator of all our attempts in prose and poetry. When he came back, and for a good many years afterward, we ceased to know him—mainly, if not entirely, because he was determined not to be known. If sympathy was what he feared to receive on his return from Oxford, he took the best means to deprive himself of it; and only very occasionally at first, and then gradually as the years went on, did he allow a breaking-down of the barrier.

But in those first years while up at Oxford, his correspondence with members of the family was lively and amusing; and during vacation there was no diminution of his social affability. It must have been during those intervals of college life that he delighted us with some of his best pieces of nonsense-verse. Our evening diversions, almost as long as I can remember, had often been of a semiliterary character. One of these was the writing of short poems, containing a collection of nouns, each member of the company supplying one. Here is a sample of the sort of thing which Alfred was able to turn out in the course of fifteen or twenty minutes. The nouns were: hat, novel, banker, cucumber, yacht, and abridgment. Obviously the last was the crux; and this is how Alfred tackled it:

> *At the door of my own little hovel,*
> *Reading a novel I sat;*
> *And as I was reading the novel*
> *A gnat flew away with my hat.*
> *As fast as a fraudulent banker*
> *Away with my hat it fled,*
> *And calmly came to an anchor*
> *In the midst of the cucumber bed.*
>
> *I went and purchased a yacht,*
> *And traversed the garden tank,*
> *And I gave it that insect hot*
> *When I got to the other bank;*
> *Of its life I made an abridgment*
> *By squeezing it somewhat flat,*
> *And I cannot think what that midge meant*
> *By flying away with my hat.*

One Christmas (1879, I think), we attempted something more ambitious, which produced a memorable result. Each wrote a story, and on Christmas Eve, or thereabouts, the stories were read out to the assembled family. Alfred's contribution was a domestic sketch in verse and prose entitled "A Morning with the Royal Family," the opening sentence of which ran: " 'Pigs on the front lawn!' cried the King, 'Lend me a cannon, somebody!' Nobody lent him a cannon, so seizing a teaspoon from the breakfast table he rushed from the apartment." The whole story—the only complete work of fiction, I think, which he ever produced—was published a year or two later, without his permission, in the school magazine, of which at that time another brother was editor: and it has remained ever since a prized but rather private family possession, republication having been strictly forbidden by the author.

While at University College, Alfred contributed occasional nonsense-rhymes to the *College Magazine,* three of which (though not his best) he allowed to be privately reprinted in 1935. He also gave, about once a year, a written paper on one of the British poets, before the College Literary Society; his chosen poets were: Tennyson, Matthew Arnold, Burns, Campbell, Erasmus, Darwin, Swinburne, and "The Spasmodic School." He was only quite kind to two

of them—Matthew Arnold and Campbell; all the others were subjected to varying degrees of satirical criticism—so severe, in the
case of Burns, that a Scottish professor, rising in wrath, declared
he would never forgive the lecturer for what he had said of him.
It would be unkind on my part to excite the interest of my readers
any further in material which I am under orders to destroy. These
papers have to share the fate of a very much better one—the
Inaugural Lecture which my brother gave on his appointment, in
1911, to the Kennedy Professorship of Latin at Cambridge University, and which he would not allow to be published because of his
inability to retrace his authority for a statement which he had
made concerning a Shelley manuscript; as to which later investiga-
tion has gone rather against him.

In the autobiographical note from which I have already quoted,
Alfred writes of his years in London as follows:

> While I was at the Patent Office I read a great deal of
> Greek and Latin at the British Museum of an evening. While
> at University College, which is not residential, I lived alone
> in lodgings in the environs of London.
>
> *A Shropshire Lad* was written in Byron Cottage, 17 North
> Road, Highgate, where I lived from 1886 to 1905.
>
> *A Shropshire Lad* was offered to Macmillan, and declined
> by them on the advice, I have been told, of Mr. John Morley,
> who was their reader. Then a friend introduced me to Kegan
> Paul; but the book was published at my own expense.

It was to this friend (Alfred W. Pollard) that he owed a change
in the proposed title of the book, which must have had a considerable effect on its fortunes. He had intended to call it *Poems of
Terence Hearsay*. Pollard suggested *A Shropshire Lad* as better,
a piece of good advice which the author was luckily not above
taking.

> The *Shropshire Lad* [the note goes on to say] is an imagi-
> nary character, with something of my temper and view of
> life. Very little in the book is biographical.

As regards the influences affecting his poems, he added:

> "Reader of the Greek Anthology" is not a good name for
> me. Of course I have read it, or most of it, but with no
> special heed; and my favorite Greek poet is Aeschylus. No
> doubt I have unconsciously been influenced by the Greeks
> and Latins, but I was surprised when critics spoke of my

poetry as "classical." Its chief sources of which I am conscious are Shakespeare's songs, the Scottish Border Ballads, and Heine.

In answer to an inquiry whether *A Shropshire Lad* had been the product of "a crisis of pessimism" he replied that he had never had any such crisis.

In the first place I am not a pessimist but a pejorist (as George Eliot said she was not an optimist but a meliorist); and that philosophy is founded on my observation of the world, not on anything so trivial and irrelevant as personal history. Secondly, I did not begin to write poetry in earnest until the really emotional part of my life was over; and my poetry, so far as I could make out, sprang chiefly from physical causes, such as a relaxed sore throat during my most prolific period, the first five months of 1895.

Finally, to the same correspondent, he writes:

I respect the Epicureans more than the Stoics, but my man is Aristippus of Cyrene, who was not afraid of words. Of the writers you mention, the only two I have read and admired much are Pascal and Leopardi. For Hardy I had a great affection, and admiration for some of his novels and a little of his poetry.

As some of the questions which you ask in your flattering curiosity may possibly be asked by future generations, and as most of them can only be answered by me, I make this reply.

The one English novelist whom Alfred preferred to Hardy was Jane Austen. When he told Hardy so, Hardy replied, "Well, of course it's the greater thing." "What he meant by that," said Alfred, "I'm sure I don't know."

Another of his rather unexpected admirations was Christina Rossetti, of whom he said that posterity would probably place her above Swinburne. It was an admiration which we shared; twice I had the pleasure of introducing him to poems by her which he did not know; of one he asked me to send him a copy; of the other (a poem called "The River of Life") he said, "Yes, it's the sort of nonsense that is worth writing": a remark which somewhat consoled me for his having described certain devotional poems of my own as "nonsense-poems." Some years later he said he thought they were the "cleverest" I had ever written; from which I gathered that with him "nonsense" as applied to poetry was not a word of opprobrium.

During the years preceding his appointment at University College, London, Alfred remained for most of the members of his family a somewhat distant acquaintance, and neither from our occasional meetings, nor from our quite formal correspondence, have I anything to record that seems now worth telling. Indeed it was not until after *A Shropshire Lad* was published that our correspondence became fairly frequent, and that his letters began once more to be individual and amusing. The astonished exclamation of a member of the family, after reading the first six or seven of the *Shropshire Lad* poems, "Alfred has a heart!" is sufficient indication of the pains he had taken to conceal it during the years of his bitter disappointment over the finish of his university career. But even while he lived so far removed from the familiar association of early days, he still had his eye on us, as regards our literary activities, and when any of them pleased him, he let us know it. When his sister Clemence's story "The Were Wolf" appeared in the Christmas number of *Atalanta* in 1889 she got from him a letter of warm appreciation beginning "Capital, capital, capital!" And quite early, with my own stories, poems, and plays, I was conscious of more regard for what Alfred would think and say of them than for what any other critic or the general public might think or say.

It so happened that I sent him the manuscript of my first book of poems for criticism, at the very time when, without my knowing it, he was preparing his own for publication; and I got from him two long letters of detailed criticism—sometimes scathing in its terms, but also considerate and kind where it seemed to him that kindness was deserved. Shortly after our two books had been published, I received a letter from him, the terms of which will be better understood if I explain beforehand that I had designed for the cover of my own book *Green Arras* a very elaborate and as I thought beautiful cover of gold scrollwork. "The other day," wrote Alfred,

> I was sitting at dinner next to a man who thought to interest
> me by talking about *you* and *your* poems. He said he liked
> *Green Arras;* he added that *A Shropshire Lad* had a pretty
> cover. I am your affectionate brother, A.E.H. P.S. He did not
> say that *Green Arras* had a pretty cover; nor has it! P.P.S.
> I was just licking the envelope when the following enven·

omed remark occurred to me: I had far far rather have my poems mistaken as yours than your poems mistaken as mine.

This was the sort of thing which he enjoyed writing; and to me it was done less maliciously than to others, because he knew that I also enjoyed it, having reason to know that sometimes he said kinder things about me behind my back than he wrote to my face. But there can be no doubt that he did greatly enjoy writing and saying bitter and contemptuous things about people who seemed to him to deserve them; and he had in his notebook pages stocked with phrases which were apparently waiting a suitable victim to whom they might be applied. Many of these found a place in his critical writings—the introductions to his own editions of the classics and his reviews of books by other scholars whose claim to that term he would not admit; and one does not doubt that the more highly established their reputations, the more did he enjoy bringing them down into the dust.

Without naming names I give here just a few samples of the gentle ferocity with which he put into their places certain people of supposed importance in the scholastic world, in order that those who are not readers of the edited classics may here get an idea of that gift for invective which made him the most feared, and perhaps also the most hated, among the pedants (his own pet phrase) of his day.

> I can easily understand why Mr. —— should not tell the truth about other people. He fears reprisals: he apprehends that they may tell the truth about *him*.

> If Mr. —— were a postage stamp he would be a very good postage stamp; but adhesiveness is not the virtue of a critic. A critic is free and detached.

To put a finish to this pillorying of unnamed victims, here is one more pronouncement which would miss its point were its subject left nameless:

> Swinburne was as good a critic as a rhinoceros can possibly be—a much better critic than his fellow rhinoceros Macaulay. But to be a good critic you must be more sensitive to pain than either of these illustrious pachyderms. . . . Swinburne reading Shakespeare was like a bear rifling a bees' nest; he eats and enjoys the honey, and the bees cannot sting him through his hide.

What all this goes mainly to show is that while Alfred considered truth the first duty of a critic and a scholar, he enjoyed telling the truth provocatively. Illustrative of which (on a matter not of literature but of morals) was his remark that the rarest of sexual aberrations is chastity! It is quite true, but it could hardly be said in a more provocative way.

Alfred's minute insistence on accuracy is well exemplified in his reply to a friend who regretted that she had been unable to obtain a first edition of *Last Poems* and had been obliged to content herself with the second. "In that case," he wrote, "you have got the more valuable edition. In the first a comma is missing."

People seem to have got the impression that Alfred disliked being questioned about his poems. That was not my own experience; if the question had any interest in it he liked answering it. I asked him once whether as a rule, his so-happily-chosen adjectives had come to him spontaneously or after labor and with difficulty; and I gave as an instance "colored counties," a phrase which has become famous. "Now that you should have picked that out," he said, "is interesting. When I wrote the poem I put down a quite ordinary adjective, just to fill up for the time, which didn't satisfy me. Then with the poem in my head, I went to bed and dreamed, and in my dream I hit on the word 'painted'; when I woke up I saw that 'painted' wouldn't do, but it gave me 'colored' as the right word."

This is confirmed in the first draft of the poem, which I found in one of his notebooks where the alternatives run: sunny, pleasant, checkered, patterned; "painted" is left out; it was not necessary for that to be written down.

I have given, in the preceding pages, instances of Alfred's ruthless treatment of intellectual foolishness, more especially of foolishness which gave itself the airs of learning. In that direction he could be cruel with relish: but toward moral foolishness, especially toward the foolishness of troubled youth, his inclination was all the other way. Even deflections from rectitude which he would not have tolerated in himself caused no withdrawal of aid when once it had been proffered; and in a case known to me, conduct which he described as nefarious did not alter relations of real personal friendship between him and the offender, though the offense was to himself. Certain "laws of God and man," with their socially imposed sanctions, he disliked heartily, and with recognition of human nature's imperfect material, made a wide allowance for its failures. This is shown clearly in many of his published poems.

Two years ago, when we were taking a holiday together, I found Alfred more communicative than I had ever known him before. Of the poem called "New Year's Eve" which he published in a magazine while at Oxford, he wrote it, he said, in his twentieth year. "I was then a deist." "And now," I asked, "what do you call yourself—agnostic?" "No, I am an atheist," he said, decisively. He then went on to say that he thought the Church of England the best religion ever invented; it was less disturbing than other forms, and eliminated "so much Christian nonsense." Christianity, he added, was most harmful in its social application.

Belief in immortality was quite unnecessary, he said, for good morals. The Hebrews had a higher code of morals than the Egyptians, and did not allow themselves to be perverted from the non-belief in a future life by Egyptian superstition.

Of certain things published under a pseudonym during his undergraduate days he said he would be very much obliged to me if I would let them rest in oblivion; they were less good than his home-productions because they were written to order, not for pleasure.

Of the reputation which his poems won for him he wrote to an American correspondent: "Though it gives me no lively pleasure, it is something like a mattress interposed between me and the hard ground."

Those words were written when life was ceasing to have any comfort for him.

For several years he had persistently declined all the academic honors offered him by various universities, at home and abroad. The proposal from his own University of Oxford to confer on him the honorary degree of Doctor of Letters he had twice refused, in 1928 and 1934.

It was about five years ago that he admitted to me another refusal, which, till then, he had kept secret. I had for some time felt a brotherly concern that the one honor which I thought he would be willing to accept, the Order of Merit, had not been offered him. Since others were feeling as I did, I broached the question—would he accept it? He replied that he would not, and when, disappointed, I asked why, he said that, though he had always known that it would be offered him if he lived to the age of eighty, he had decided against accepting any honor, and against this particular one because it was not always given to the right persons. He had condoled, he said, with Robert Bridges for having had to receive the honor at the same time as John Galsworthy, whose writing they both disliked, and Bridges had admitted that the circumstance had not given him pleasure.

I suppose I pressed him further, for suddenly he blushed (an unexpected gift which he had retained from the days of his youth) and said:

> Well, as a matter of fact, Mr. Baldwin did write to me not long ago to say that the King was ready to offer it; and I believe it was offered at the same time to Bernard Shaw. But for the reason I have already stated, and because I could not have the trouble of going to be received by the King, I declined. But [he added] I don't want it to be known: it wouldn't be fair to the King.

Who first gave away the secret I do not know. It was only after my brother's death that I found that others knew of it, and that word of it had gone to the press.

Three years ago his health began rapidly to decline, and his walking powers, which all his life had given that quiet companionship of nature which suited him best, had considerably diminished.

Early in January 1936, his condition became so serious that he was not expected to live more than another week; but when term approached, he announced his intention of leaving the Nursing Home and returning to his rooms to give his lectures. His doctor told him that this was impossible. "It is my duty and my pleasure," he replied, "and I shall do it." At the end of term, writing to a member of the family, he said that he had never lectured better in his life. But the effort sent him back to the Nursing Home, from which he went, at the commencement of the Easter Term, and gave two lectures, sitting down. That was the end.

Over the grave, where his ashes have been laid under the north wall of the parish church at Ludlow, is a tablet bearing these words:

> In Memory of Alfred Edward Housman, M.A. Oxon. Kennedy Professor of Latin and Fellow of Trinity College in the University of Cambridge.
> Author of "A Shropshire Lad."
> Born 26 March 1859. Died 30 April 1936.
>
> Good night. Ensured release.
> Imperishable peace:
> Have these for yours.

THOMAS BEER

by Monty Woolley and
Cary Abbott

*Iowa-born Thomas Beer was the highly successful writer in the
1920s and 1930s who turned out innumerable popular pot-boilers
for the magazines—who can forget the Egg family?—so that he
might spend more time on the novels and studies which many of
his admirers declare will make his name immortal. His friends, on
the other hand, felt that his wealth simply allowed him more time
for talking. He was an incurable, lovable, prodigious talker. Two
friends who remember him warmly and well are the actor Edgar
Montillion Woolley and Cary Abbott, Beer's classmates at Yale,
1911.*

SEPTEMBER 13, 1941

THE APPEARANCE OF Thomas Beer's three studies on the men and
activities of the nineties and the early 1900s, *The Mauve Decade,
Stephen Crane,* and *Hanna,* in the recently published omnibus
volume, recalls to the minds of two of his oldest friends a number of
Tom's highly individual and curious traits and practices. In the
midst of composing a story for the *Saturday Evening Post,* or in the
throes of writing *Hanna,* he was a remote, morose, coffee-drinking,
sleepless figure, alternately pacing restlessly through the spacious
rooms of his house overlooking the Hudson at Yonkers, and throwing away an almost completely typed page—to be laboriously rewritten—because he had omitted a comma in a necessary place. It
was agony to watch him, so meticulous was he in all literary detail
of a manuscript.

However, when he had finished a *Post* story, for example, he
would gleefully fold it in an envelope, stamp it, and seal it by licking
the flap, put an encyclopedia on it, and tramp on that to make sure
the glue would stick. Then his chauffeur would have to take
it all the way to the main post office in New York—for no particular
reason—after which Tom would watch the mail like a hungry hawk

until he had the assurance that the manuscript had reached its destination.

The news of its acceptance often resulted in Tom's rushing from Yonkers into New York, and in Prohibition days, to such a place as the Meadowbrook Club, a spot where very good wine and delicious food were served in quiet surroundings. Whoever was lucky enough to be his guest then listened to a fascinating potpourri of gossip, history, travel, interspersed with anecdotes, with perhaps an informal lecture on Egyptian art or the husbands of Joanna of Naples. If he was at someone's house, he was apt to deliver a monologue on any subject from the genealogy of the Adams family to the effects of the Code Napoléon on American jurisprudence. His ironic humor, coupled with a truly formidable store of knowledge, made him a magnet to all whom he regarded as his friends.

Sometimes, when he was asked about some point or subject, he would have to cover his confusion by a good deal of stuttering and having to spin some exaggeration to divert his questioner. Many years ago, in college, he was asked in all innocence what was ambergris. His friends were hoping that he knew nothing about ambergris but would tell a tall tale to cover his ignorance. Tom, nothing daunted, went on about its somewhat nauseating origin and its uses. When he had finished, the entire crowd piled their watches, fraternity charms, cuff links, and money on the table to pay off the biggest tale since Baron Munchausen. Tom fled, but upon looking it up, his audience found to their great chagrin that he had actually furnished them with a true and detailed account of this product of the sea.

He loathed large gatherings of people, preferring to meet new acquaintances who were under the aegis of this or that familiar. Comparatively speaking, it was a small circle whom he cared for, but they were drawn from a highly variegated assemblage made up of literary and dramatic authors and critics, actors and actresses, politicians, "social registerites," men and women from widely separated sections of America, and a sprinkling of foreigners.

These friends were carefully selected for their backgrounds as well as for their personalities, as Tom was insatiably curious about obscure local idioms, customs, odd bits of history and lore, particularly pertaining to America; and the answer to a casual question by him often found its way into print some years later in one of his novels or biographies. A strange usage of English in western Pennsylvania or northern Mississippi, or the reason why Senator Blank's wife managed to "crash" the Cave-dweller set in Washington were grist for his mill. Many of his circle were famous and important persons; an equal number of them were not. Snobbery was a hateful thing to him, literary and social.

Possessed of a photographic memory, Tom's reading was swift. From long and probably secret practice he seemed to be able to extract and remember some important or well written passage from a book—a passage that no one would ever have been able to uncover without difficult research or a flair for the unusual. He was forever telling his friends to read some forgotten novel, or odd piece of history, or a neglected dissertation on art so that they should be properly posted. As an example, he once found an out-of-print memoir by an army officer's wife telling a thrilling story of her experiences at a now deserted fort on the lower Colorado River in the eighties, a unique work that deserves a better fate as a literary and historical "find."

Besides having a penetrating knowledge of history and literature, Tom was always absorbed in painting and sculpture. He had a passion for many of the moderns, and in his later years he hung a Thomas Benton over the mantelpiece facing the desk where he did his writing. His love for Egyptian art was almost an obsession, matched only by his interest in the "stately homes of England," and old American houses and objects. He had a large collection of pictorial volumes on the plastic arts which he used to mull over, generally by lying crosswise on his narrow bed, turning over the leaves of the book which reposed on the floor, and dropping cigarette ashes in or near a tall receiver nearby.

Tom's love for music was somewhat limited to the vocal, dramatic forms. He was very fond of opera, and equally fond of modern popular music. His wide knowledge of the theater seemed to be responsible for his liking such diverse works as *Die Walkuere* and *Show Boat,* and even such ribald ballads as "Frankie and Johnnie." He was not highly interested in the more abstract types of composition. But here again, as in his chosen profession of letters, he was always ahead of his contemporaries in discovering odd but pertinent facts. At home he was often heard humming an aria from such a forgotten opera as *Maritana,* or singing verses from hillbilly songs long before the latter found their way to their present vogue.

Tom had always hoped to put on paper the book on modern aesthetics which was to have been called *Form, Color, and Desire,* and for some years his publishers announced its forthcoming appearance;

but, alas! it apparently never reached a first draft. There were times when he wished that in the future he might have departed from writing novels and studies of American manners and men, in order to devote his talent and energy to other subjects that appealed to his imagination. One of these ideas was a work on the culture and civilization of Celtic Ireland. His library contained much material on the subject, most of it written years ago, and Tom felt that an up-to-date book on that Golden Age was needed. Another subject dear to his heart was Scottish political and social history during the seventeenth and eighteenth centuries. But his pet idea was a biography of the before-mentioned Joanna of Naples with her several husbands and her goings-on at the Papal Court at Avignon, because she and her contemporaries appealed both to his sense of humor and to his appreciation of the pageantry and corruption of the fourteenth century.

Tom was at his best as a host, when his shy public manner would thaw, and he was surrounded by his family and a small company of friends. At Christmas dinner, after he had distributed a gold piece to each guest—the gold pieces had been hanging from the traditional tree—he sat down to a table loaded with all the usual Yuletide bounty, fortified with magnificent wine, and garnished with such delectables as oyster sauce and pineapple ice with the turkey. And later in the day, after family and guests had dozed for a soporific two or three hours, and a cold supper of perhaps smoked Westphalian ham, foie gras, champagne, and brandied peaches was about to be served, Tom would avoid the conventional reading of Dickens' *Christmas Carol,* and instead turn to the Bible. It was not the story of Bethlehem he would read, but the tale from Ezekiel of those two jaunty harlots Ohalah and Ohalibah, sometimes following that up by the one about old King David and the beautiful Shulamite. Then off to New York the guests would go, full to the gorge with a feast for body and soul, and a memory of our host that never dims.

NOTES ON THE FAILURE
OF A MISSION

by Elmer Davis

H. G. Wells had a realistic—perhaps hopeful—view of the human race. He tried his best to make the human race understand what he had in mind for it. Elmer Davis examined the Wells prophecies and their applicability in this article.

AUGUST 31, 1946

I DID NOT KNOW Wells and do not know what he was thinking about toward the end of his life, but he might very reasonably have been thinking that nothing fails like success. He grew up in a great age, the nineties, which it was once fashionable to laugh at but which now begins to look like the Lost Paradise; when the flood tide of nineteenth-century progress and optimism was still running, and when science was beginning to open up such possibilities as men had never dreamed of before. True, the human race did not seem entirely prepared to take advantage of its new opportunities; but that was because it was walled in by outworn orthodoxies. Wells, a poor unknown young schoolteacher, set himself to blast away these barriers to progress, with such success that when he died half a century later, so orthodox an institution as *The New York Times* editorial page could call him the greatest public teacher in the world.

So he was, and look at the world. Even in his youth it had tensions that he understood; twice he predicted their resolution in a world war. Well, since he wrote we have twice gone to Armageddon; twice the cause of right has triumphed and the devil has been bound in the bottomless pit; but we rise victorious over old perils only to find new perils, even more ominous, looming over the next hill. Wells the Socialist, living under a regime he despised, died in an England at last gone Socialist—but not because Socialism was the best way to control and distribute an unprecedented prosperity; only because Socialism seemed the desperate last resort to avoid complete collapse. As for Wells the reformer of private manners and morals, most of his revolutionary heterodoxies have become the commonplaces of everybody's mental and emotional background; yet it may be doubted if the human race is notably happier today than it was in the age of Grover Cleveland and Lord Rosebery and Sherlock Holmes.

Were there Christian bishops in the latter half of the fourth century—midway between the jubilant anticipations of Lactantius and the painfully heroic reconstruction of Augustine—who uneasily contemplated just such a spectacle? Men who said to themselves, "Look, it has all come off; everything we hoped for has been realized; yet Apollyon still walks the earth"? I am not sufficiently read in the Church Fathers to know if anybody committed such thoughts to writing, but there must have been men who had them. It may be said that in those days the acceptance was official and superficial, that the essence of the new doctrines had not soaked into men's souls—and indeed has not even yet. Still, it could have been no more pleasant then than now to look at a world set free, and no better off. (On this point see Roark Bradford's *Kingdom Coming*—a book not of 1865 but of any age.)

What was the matter with this turn-of-the-century Reformation, whose prophets were Shaw and Wells, that it came to so sorry a conclusion? A dozen years ago, in these pages, I examined that problem from the standpoint of the generation which in all English-speaking countries was educated chiefly by Shaw and Wells—the generation which was to be the pioneers of a new heaven and a new earth; and could find no better excuse for our ineffectiveness than that perhaps there were not enough of us. I can find none better now. That generation, in England—I knew them well—was perhaps the finest lot of young people any nation has ever produced at one time (unless France in the early years of Louis XVI, when also there was a Reformation afoot); but most of them are buried at Passchendaele or on the Somme. As for other nations, in possibly greater need of education, the Germans used to read Shaw but got the wrong things out of him (except for Spengler, and the Germans got the wrong things out of him too); while those who now rule Russia seem to have done most of their reading in the gloomy labyrinths of Marxian theology. (For that matter, the Congress of the United States might legislate a little more intelligently if more than a few of its members had been permeated by the Wellsian and Shavian doctrines.)

There were not enough of us sons of the prophets; but our proph-

ets were pretty good, as prophets go. Both Shaw and Wells realized that the only obstacle to the realization of the Earthly Paradise
was human nature; and if they somewhat underestimated its cussedness, there was less evidence to go on in their youth than we have
now. "I who have preached and pamphleteered like any encyclo-
pedist have to confess that my methods are no use," wrote Shaw in
the Preface to *Major Barbara,* but that must have been a brief interlude of despondency; for he wrote that forty years ago and he has
been preaching and pamphleteering ever since. At any rate, as between the two, Wells was the more inclined to keep his feet on the
ground. Shaw thought that the best education was no education;
but Wells, who had taught school and known pupils, knew better.
(Much of *Joan and Peter* makes as much sense still as when it was
written, though it might be noted that both Joan and Peter had to
get their real education from experience.)

Wells had his visionary moments; in *The Shape of Things to
Come* he seemed to hope that war might finally be ended by a revolt
of aviators' consciences—something which has not yet happened, and
would have to happen simultaneously and equally in all nations if
it were not to leave us worse off than before; and in *The World Set
Free* he cut completely loose from all plausibility and hoped that we
might be saved by the sudden application of the collective intelligence of all humanity. (For commentary see the debates of the
United Nations Committee on Atomic Energy, *passim.*) But he never
indulged in any practical aspirations so fanciful as Shaw's dream of
a Catholic Church catholic enough to include Protestants—an idea
very attractive to everybody except genuine Catholics and genuine
Protestants; when Wells went off into fantasy he went all the way,
imagining the human race transfigured by the swish of a comet's
tail, loaded with a new gas conducive to brotherly love.

Another difference—Wells was, to use a bit of bureaucratic jargon,
much more of an operator than Shaw, at least in intellectual approach. Both men believed they were collectivists; but Shaw was
much more so than Wells, though even Shaw had little use for collectivism when it interfered with the conscience of such a sensitive
individual as Lavinia or Saint Joan. Wells's dominant desire always
seems to have been to find some way to make things work, even if
(sometimes it almost seemed preferably if) a strong individual had to
do it. The theme adumbrated in *The New Machiavelli* was pronounced, and amplified with variations, in *The Outline of History;*
history (or so it seems to memory—I have no books with me at the

moment) was a succession of strong men, each one of whom was about to remake the world when he was deflected by an amorous young woman. Shaw wrote about Caesar and Cleopatra too, but not like that. Yet it is notable that when an ostensible collectivism turned in practice into the rule of a strong individual, Wells was rather less sympathetic with it than was Shaw. But then Shaw still seems to believe in the perfectibility of human nature, however skeptical he may have become in its early practical realization; and as Crane Brinton has reminded us, Reigns of Terror are also Reigns of Virtue.

Wells was more dubious about perfectibility; he never played with it much outside of *The World Set Free* and *In the Days of the Comet,* and in the latter book he had to pass a miracle to make us perfect over night. Usually he was much more realistic; his very first book, *The Time Machine,* was a horrible warning of what might happen to us if we are not careful. *The War in the Air,* which must have been begun soon after Bleriot flew across the Channel and is the prototype of a hundred similar apocalypses, underestimated—as did its successors—the ability of the human race to take punishment, but not its persnicketiness; and imagined a war stubbornly fought out till every organized government in the world had been smashed as you can smash a saucer with a stick. And in *When the Sleeper Wakes*—one of his best pieces of writing, and sounder prophecy than some of its better-known successors—he saw mankind rebelling successfully against a tyrannous oligarchy, only to fall under the worse tyranny of the politician who had led the revolt. I do not imagine that book is read much in Russia.

Wells apparently never thought much of *When the Sleeper Wakes.* Years later he revised it, not entirely for the better, and among other things removed the hint of a happy ending which perhaps a young novelist had put in to help the sale. As he originally wrote it the People, thanks to the hero's sacrifice of his life, were about to beat the Boss; in the revision Wells said in substance (again I write from memory) that he ought to have realized that the struggle between the Boss and the People is unending. I wonder if he still thought that, at the last, if he saw that the dialectic which Hegel perceived as in a mirror enigmatically is valid in a sense; that no matter what positions are gained or lost in successive phases of the struggle, Arimanes and Oromasdes will be locked in perpetual conflict till the end, whatever the end may be. (Our grandfathers would never have dreamed that Arimanes might finally win, but we can-

not exclude that possibility.) How that prospect would seem to a
man who grew up in the Age of Hope I cannot conjecture; for our
more depressed generation, it is something to be able to feel that we
have a chance.

If we have a chance, we owe it to the fact that Arimanes and Oromasdes are inside us, not outside, and that (with all respect to the
Predestinarians) we may be able by intention to do something about
it; if the chance is thin, we owe it to the fact that (with all respect
to Socrates) virtue and knowledge are not necessarily the same thing.
Meliora dum video, proboque, deteriora sequor, said a man who had
undoubtedly studied Socrates and perceived that there was something Socrates had left out; and he has had plenty of successors. But
if the chance, though thin, is by no means hopeless, we owe some
gratitude to Shaw and Wells.

They cleared away a lot of cobwebs; if they replaced them, occasionally, by obfuscations of their own, the very training they had
given us helped us to see where they had gone off the track. If the
battles they won were episodes in an interminable campaign, they
at least enable us to fight on somewhat more favorable terrain hereafter. What they both gave us is the conviction that if the human
race is ever going to amount to anything, it has got to work out its
own salvation; that whether or not God helps those who help themselves, He certainly does not help those who don't; and that if Arimanes in his secular fight with Oromasdes should finally get the
upper hand, we shall have nobody but ourselves to blame for it. A
bleak prospect? Well, it is the prospect there is; whether we like it
or not, we had better learn to live with it.

HARDY AT MAX GATE

by H. M. Tomlinson

Not long after Thomas Hardy died in his eighty-eighth year the English journalist and author H. M. Tomlinson wrote this appraisal of him. It includes the story of Tomlinson's last visit to the Hardy home, Max Gate, and attempts to unravel some of the mystery about the character of the great poet and novelist who was so unlike the works he produced.

FEBRUARY 11, 1928

IT WAS JANUARY 12, 1928, and a winter sunrise that gave our empty suburban street an unrecognizable look of splendor. I think the chimneys of our houses were of gold, and the walls and roofs of jasper and amethyst, which is nothing like them. That glowing and unfamiliar vista was as if I had surprised a secret celebration of the earth and sky; we were not supposed to see it; it was to fade into our own place before we were about. As I looked out on my changed street I was repeating the haunting thought of the night: "Hardy is dead." But the knowledge that our own light had gone out accorded with the colors of that high dawn. Naturally we associate a thought of Hardy with the aspect of the earth and sky. The heavens and the earth were always the chief characters in the dramas of that poet; over mere mortals presided the eternal sky and the shadowy presence of the earth. So it seemed right for the street to be empty, and to be strange with a transfiguring glow. Hardy had gone.

Within an hour, as the sunrise foretold, came the wind and rain. Roofs and sky turned to lead. The spurts of rain thickened the glass of the windows. There was going to be plenty of time indoors to think about Hardy, yet to think to little purpose; not really to think, but to stare unseeing at the sullen clouds and the rain; for beyond them was a dream country more vivid and stable than the elements, a visionary land in which one had moved imaginatively in the reading of nearly forty years, and had watched there the tragic drama of men and women who were more significant than one's neighbors; and to remember the venerable little man, whose magic had conjured that sublimation of the real and changing world, as we saw him at Max Gate shortly before his fatal illness began, sitting with the flames of a log fire reflecting in his quick eyes while he talked blithely of poetry, speculated on the prehistoric earthworks to be seen from his house, and smiled at the gossip of the town.

But though there was all day to think about him there was no likelihood of making a contribution to wisdom, no chance of a critical adjustment which would help to place the poet's urn with precision. We cannot be dispassionate now. We cannot stand apart from our personal feelings, and so we cannot be critics; for in criticism, as we know, we ought to do what no one has ever done, and consider the work of a poet apart from mutable human opinions, and simply as an isolated and bereaved work of art. Luckily for Hardy's contemporaries they are not called upon to be critics who will be strictly just to him by all the fundamental laws of art which somehow include at our desire any curious deviation from precedent. It is not for us to attempt impartial justice, but only to exalt him, or otherwise—explain his sublimity, or his want of taste—as the moods take us, and this or that is consonant or not with the way we ourselves would have handled the matter; though certainly, as to one characteristic of the poet, most of us will agree. We cannot but mark, and with profound surprise, Hardy's pervasive sorrow. We have to question that perplexity. How could so great a mind, in the face of our beneficent progress, look sadly upon the happiness of our state? But it is not our business now to prove the poet's lifelong error by pointing to those late agreeable steps heavenward in the history of humanity which joyfully mock the pessimist.

Today we must have diverse views of Hardy, but it cannot be helped. Instinctively we shall attempt to separate—for we know what we want—the beauty of his work, which we desire, from the truth in it. Hardy cannot succeed where Jesus of Nazareth failed. That truth and beauty are mystically one need not concern those who prefer the simple method of separating what is comforting in a book from what is challenging and disturbing. We find it difficult to confess that a poet's thought may be beautiful in its contrast with the darkness of our perversity; for that would mean that beauty convicted us. It is not the province of poetry to do that. Poetry is an irrelevant solace at leisure, which is pleasant, as in wine, after the dustiness of a harsh and insistent world. Besides, its thoughts may be contrary to revealed religion, and a poet is not a prophet. We do not expect of him revelations. So it need not surprise us that one of our younger and brighter essayists—to whom good and evil are no longer difficulties, but are easily definable because his Church provides him with an infallible test—when his opinion was sought by a journalist on the news of the death of the poet, said of the author of *The Dynasts* that "he was a nice, courteous gentleman, rather simple-minded." Which is quite right, as far as it goes, and shows less religious intolerance than describing Hardy as "the village atheist mourning over the village idiot"; though the testimonial is applicable to so many men, fortunately, that it seems hardly worth the time of a journalist to record virtues so usual.

Then again, the London daily papers, by their various placards on the morning after Thomas Hardy's death, betrayed the fact that not every one of them was prepared on the instant to estimate the weight of the news. Some of them did not consider his passing to be more important than some other subjects of interest, subjects which I was compelled by surprise to note. One paper was anxious that we should "Read our new serial: 'Frail Wives.' " Another asked: "Who will give Jix £100,000?" The contents bill of another famous London daily paper bore simply the cryptic numerals "1857428"; though whether those figures referred to a successful feat of circulation, or were indeed a cabalistic advertisement of a fatal conjunction of numbers which made inevitable the passing of a great man, it was impossible for a nonreader to guess. Yet another of our daily papers placarded an outburst entitled: "Ambassadors' Cars." That may have been a special edition devoted to automobiles of luxury, but I cannot say, for I did not buy the paper. And later in the day one afternoon paper of the capital of the British Commonwealth, a paper once famous for its liberal outlook on the world, gave a bare half column to the news that the greatest figure in European literature, who happened also to be English, had gone, apparently because its editorial staff was too astonished by Mrs. Snyder's New Lease of Life. There were other periodicals, however, which did make the appropriate comment, and whose estimates of the significance of the principal news of the day were serious; yet these little aberrations show us that the stress of the exciting nature of the living day, its fears, dogfights, rumors, executions, crime, and market prices, tend to confuse our sense of the value of what is lovely and of good report. It is not easy to turn from the attraction of what takes our notice to the estimate of the worth of a creator of beauty. Beauty, if it be there, will last longer than the distractions about us, but that does not mean much to those who cannot see it. Said a London councillor once, in the peroration of his speech which demanded the destruction of London's finest bridge, "as for its beauty, I have never seen it." Yes, but he failed to see also that the very horses which plod over it daily are in the same cart with him.

Some of us are old enough to remember the violence of the attacks on Hardy and his morality when his last novels appeared. And besides immorality, he made plain his vulgarity; his taste was liable to deplorable lapses. But though that reception of his later novels decided him against writing any more prose for us, yet when I met him first, and this was referred to, he was reluctant to look back at it, but presently, finding that I could recall the controversies in some detail, he did begin to gossip of that phase of his past, but in so low and tolerant a tone that you might have thought he never had any feeling about it. Once I began to move uneasily at his recital of the course of one outrageous attack, but Hardy's face did not lose its good humor, nor his voice its gentleness. He was talking only of men in the abstract, and this was part of the evidence. I should doubt that Hardy was ever made angry, except by cruelty to the lowly and unimportant.

He was a great man, if a sign of that is simplicity and modesty so surprising that they might be innocence. It was a shock to talented visitors, to find, when they met him, that the man who wrote *The Woodlanders* and *The Return of the Native* seemed not so clever as they. A meeting with Hardy was comforting to self-esteem. He was venerable, he was indeed already a legend; his great epic which placed him next to Shakespeare was published over twenty years ago; yet it all seemed rather odd, for the little old man himself, as he entertained us, might have been the youngest and most innocent of us all. He appeared content to talk of the habits of owls, and of the signs of the weather, of local inns and crusted characters, and of hearing in Dorchester by wireless the dancers' feet when an orchestra was playing at a London festival. Trivial life interested him. Little things amused him. Little things, you could see, often had for him a significance which a clever listener failed to grasp. Hardy was a simple man. A meeting with Hardy made it possible to understand why those very clever men about Shakespeare left for us such scant testimony of the fellow who wrote *Macbeth*. The poet who wrote the sonnets was a smiling and good-natured man, we must suppose, who was so simple there was little to say about him. He never made epigrams, he never quarreled, and he never got excited, even when the Armada was scattered. Now and then perhaps, he would drop an odd remark which made a listener stare, and wonder what he meant. There seemed nothing but queerness in it, until later the phrase was remembered, because of an awkward coincidence in life, and then it became explicable, in a new light. Mere chance, that thought. It was the experience which brought the light. Shakespeare had spoken more wisely than he knew.

Hardy, too, had so innocent a divination into people and their motives that sometimes when talking to him you felt this child was as old as humanity and knew all about us, but that he did not attach importance to his knowledge because he did not know he had it. Just by chance, in the drift of the talk, there would be a word by Hardy, not only wide of the mark but apparently not directed to it. Nothing seemed to have suggested it. Why did he say it? Going home, or some weeks later, his comment would come back, with that revealing light on it.

Max Gate is a walled little island of trees on the road to Egdon Heath, just outside Dorchester. No house can be seen from the road. I fancy Hardy himself planted most of that screen of leaves. It suggests the hiding place of a recluse. There is an approach across the fields from the town, and in summer that was the way to go, with Came Hill lifting darkly beyond a sea of corn, and the isolated promontory sculptured by men long before the Romans landed, now called Maiden Castle, in the distance. The square tower of Dorchester Church and the chimneys of the town floated near on the tree tops of a hollow; you felt sure you would find Hardy in that country, even though the foot path was uncertain. But it was evening in sharp winter weather when we were there last. The house then was only a lantern in a dim porch. A spray of cotoneaster had left the mass of shadow to get into the light of the lantern; it was the only sign of a wall.

Mrs. Hardy always knew how to keep out intrusions such as easterly winds. Her house was as warm and comforting that evening as a quiet heart. The old man, brisk and youthful, showed us where we should sit to get the benefit of the fire. There was a lazy smoke-colored Persian cat—appropriately, Cobweb—who stretched and yawned, and was an assurance of the ease and rightness of the time and place. It was certainly the fireside to get to the heart of a matter, though leisurely. If our talk gave out, then in the interval the reflections of the lively fire played on the face of the old poet, who contemplated the bright logs, his eyebrows raised, his legs stretched out, his hands between his knees. That seamed face lost sight of the visitors for a while, and its nervous interest in the gossip changed to the compassionate look of a man who had brooded for long on the world but was not sure he had made out what it all meant, or could do it the good he desired for it.

It may be true that as a man thinks so is he, and that may be why Hardy's head was satisfying with expected beauty. Some who met him say that you would not have known Hardy for a poet. Perhaps that is because the younger poets frequent the town, and are so often seen and heard. We get to think that a poet should resemble the pattern of a poet. Hardy did not. He resembled in no particular any other poet you may have met. He might have been a retired solicitor of the country town, pursuing keenly in his leisure several hobbies, finding cheerful entertainment in the fact that his house was on the site of a patrician graveyard of the Romans, and that when gardening he sometimes turned up relics. He would describe the signs which hinted that men unknown had a grove to their god near his garden long before Caesar landed. He would startle you with the remark that Robert Louis Stevenson, when he saw him last, was sitting in your chair. He would admit, and it seemed strange for a man of his years, that he read poetry nowadays and very little prose, but that he enjoyed the styles of Sir Thomas Browne and Lamb, and preferred Sterne to Swift. It would not be odd, but quite in keeping, that a retired solicitor should have a shrewder knowledge of men and women than a fashionable novelist. His interests turned quickly with any change of the conversation. He would give you a rum story of a dog, and you had to admit it was stranger than your own anecdote; so very strange indeed that you fell silent, wondering what the clue to the mystery could be.

Yet when Hardy was in repose his face was that of a seer. There was no doubt then, no need to wonder what special privilege had admitted him to so intimate a knowledge of his fellows. That little man, with wisps of faded sandy hair on the back of the collar of his tweed jacket, blue-eyed, with a masterful nose that turned slightly from the straight, whose raised and questioning eyebrows pushed furrows up his forehead to his bald and globular cranium, had with his lifework taken the place in English literature next to Shakespeare; and it was always easy for me to feel that there was the very man. What those people were told who asked for signs and wonders we know. There the wonder was. There sat the author of *The Dynasts*. He looked like it. And here, while we are at Max Gate, is where we should acknowledge the debt we owe to Mrs.

Hardy, for she ordained that he should be with us longer than his frailty otherwise would have allowed.

While Hardy was with us he lent dignity to our day. His presence honored the temple of Athene. He was English; but because he was the embodiment of qualities which were essentially of the tradition, and because he belonged to the land as much as the heath and hawthorn of Egdon, and the dateless barrows on the hill tops about his home, and the stones of his village church, he represented us in a way that Parliament cannot, and so he belongs to those in every country who judge their neighbors by the best their neighbors have done. There is more of the salt of English life in the talk of the characters who move in Hardy's novels, and more of the English land in his scenes, than in all Hansard, and in all the controversies and guidebooks. If strangers wish to know us let them read Hardy; but then, they will see only themselves in his poems and stories. Hodge over his beer in a Dorset inn, even when his drink has been doctored by politicians and the press, sometimes drops a word which is more convincing than the upshot of a Parliamentary debate. It is not recorded, except in Hardy; and yet perhaps it may be the last word on the subject, though it may take a century for it to be repeated with sufficient emphasis. Such words are like the flints in the soil; they belong to it and are sure to show when the earth is moved.

Hardy himself never understood—or so it seemed to me, and in any case I suppose so simple a man would not find it easy to believe it—that the people of his tales and the scenes in which they move are part of the unconscious life of the present English world; that the light from the country of his dreams falls across reality and makes significant and so more easily endurable its garishness. We have forgotten Hardy as a great writer; he is already part of traditional landscape. We are to believe, on the best authority, that we betray our provincialism if, when speaking of novels and novelists, we permit the mention of the best of the English writers until after a long list of Russians have been named. There is, says the voice of authority, a virtue called characterization, and the Russian novels have it, but the English in but an inferior way. Very well. Yet suddenly we remember there is more characterization in the last popular novel by a candid young lady than in all Greek drama. Where are we now? There is more characterization in Proust than in all Shakespeare. So what of it? Modern novels are full of characterization, good and bad, but good and bad together they all soon die. There is a chance, as *Macbeth* still lives on, that we may be mistaken in supposing that characterization is as important as we have been told. We may as well be called provincial as anything else if we decline to displace the author of the Wessex tales. For it may still be true that the earth and the sky and the force we call life transcend in their mystery any character, however heroic or pitiable. The earth itself is the oldest of characters; it was here when the earliest of us arrived. What word was given to it?

We cannot learn that; but if you read again the first chapter of *The Return of the Native,* or watch at night with Gabriel Oak on the summit of Norcombe Hill, with its "ancient and decaying plantation of beeches," while he revives a newborn lamb by a fire in his hut and looks to the stars to see where the earth has got to in the heavens, then the shadow of Something which is greater than mortal life begins to fall upon your reading. There is an undertone to Hardy's great passages which is like the murmur of an unseen ocean. We have a conviction of continuity then, though the stars are passing Norcombe Hill, which is, perhaps, only an illusion. But we need not trouble to prove our conviction. A poet has evoked beauty, which cannot be proved. Yet it is there, even if it is undescribable. For a bare instant we feel the riddle can be solved. A light from nowhere transfigured, for a moment, our gray and accustomed levels, and though the light is withdrawn its revelation is remembered.

"YOU MUST DIG THE BAIT"

by John Masefield

In this short piece Great Britain's famous Poet Laureate reflects on the best advice he ever received.

MARCH 20, 1954

APPROPRIATELY for a poet, the best advice I ever had came to me in the form of a sententious little quatrain. It has been of inestimable value to me, and, so I have been told, to hundreds of others to whom I have passed it on.

I was only seventeen or eighteen. I had quit my life as a seaman and was working in a carpet factory in Yonkers, New York, while trying to learn to write. Having just read Keats and Shelley for the first time, I was on fire to be a poet, but, as everyone knows who has tried to compose a poem, the new task I had set myself was far more difficult than climbing masts or painting decks. I had almost despaired when I came upon this homespun sentiment:

> *Sitting still and wishing*
> *Makes no person great.*
> *The good Lord sends the fishing,*
> *But you must dig the bait.*

This easily remembered stanza somehow gave me the courage I needed to go on. I dug bait for months—and finally caught a publisher who accepted my first poem.

This counsel helped me every day and stood me in especially good stead on a particular occasion after I had returned to London. An admirer of the great Irish poet William Butler Yeats, I had written to him and he had replied with an invitation to one of his Monday evenings. The tall, stooped, cadaverous-looking Irishman with his pale hands and pince-nez seemed like a caricature of a poet. But his shortsighted eyes were full of fun; and witty, illuminating conversation cascaded from him like a cataract. Dozens of writers and artists crowded into his small quarters to sit at his feet and share his inspiration.

That night he urged us younger poets not to be content with writing fragments of verse but to attempt something long enough to have a beginning, middle, and end. Our minds must be stretched, he said, forced to produce an extended work. Then all our writing would come easier.

I went away intoxicated with ambition. Tomorrow I would begin to do great things. But the next night and many nights following found me still at my writing desk—without the anticipated masterpiece even started.

I grew terribly discouraged. I simply lacked the power, I told myself. I could not compose a large work requiring scope, imagination, and control.

But the prosaic quatrain kept singing in my brain. So, while continuing with poems and short stories, I turned to the vast sea for inspiration for a larger project. For background I read hundreds of accounts of voyages and tried to recall every character and conversation met with in my own years as a sailor. In picture galleries I studied innumerable seascapes to help me describe the ocean in its various moods. I walked up and down lonely streets until late at night, plotting my story.

Eventually, after some ten years of continual digging, I completed a novel which found favor with the critics and—more important to me—with Yeats himself.

It would have been very easy for me to sit and dream of being a writer, but I would never have been one without a constant goad. "You must dig the bait" gave it to me. To this day I do not know the name of the author of the simple lines. But I have been indebted to him many times for helping me see a job through.

H. L.: A WRITING MAN

by Booth Tarkington

"H. L." is Harry Leon Wilson, the author of, among other books,
Ruggles of Red Gap (1915). He had no illusions about himself or
his work. He could concentrate while Vesuvius was blowing off
within sight, or he could follow up a best seller with a dull novel
about a religious movement—because he wrote what he wanted,
when he wanted. Booth Tarkington, another writing man, worked
with him and admired him.

AUGUST 12, 1939

HARRY LEON WILSON was a writing man. He hated the phrase *English
prose* because he thought it pretentious; but English prose, made
American, was what he strove to produce. He was a craftsman, didn't
think or talk about the "art of writing," because he took his work too
seriously for that; and, because he was also really an artist, he'd have
borne severe torture rather than call himself one. His conviction was
that language is a means, not for self-expression but for communica-
tion; therefore he expressed himself with clarity. He never tried to
get either beauty or humor into his work; both will be found there
because they were in the temper and quality of the man himself.

Some of the kindly editorials written about him after his death
might have given him a momentary grimness, could he have read
them. He wouldn't have expected any editorials at all—he was a
vacuum about "publicity"—but if he could have imagined beforehand any obituarial comment he would have expected it to run
somewhat astray, and the moment's grimness just mentioned would
have been his substitute for a laugh and "I thought so!" He laughed
seldom, smiled rarely; his years of editing a professionally humorous
journal hadn't left him much capacity for the physical expression
of mirth—he'd investigated and corrected too many thousand jokes.
One of the editorials, though, would have drawn at a corner of his
mouth.

He'd have liked its friendliness, of course, because that quality was genuine. The editorial spoke of his singular genius in surprisingly introducing Lincoln's Gettysburg address into the filming of *Ruggles,* bringing that solemn note suddenly into the midst of jocose passages. The episode will be looked for in vain in Wilson's book, and its appearance in the film affected his stomach, because, as I've said, he was really an artist. A contract had left him powerless to suppress the director's inspiration. Wilson wrote to me that when the "picture people" told him of their great Lincolnian idea his impulse was to respond, "Why not use the Lord's Prayer, too?" He didn't say it, because he was afraid they'd do it.

Another of the admiring and genuinely friendly editorials said something that he'd have accepted unregretfully; it said rather wistfully that he'd never received special distinction or high honor "at the hands of the aristocrats of literature," possibly meaning that he'd never had a Pulitzer Prize or a great fuss made over him by metropolitan reviewers. Wilson would have agreed that the "aristocrats of literature" hadn't seen much in him; but he'd have done so because he'd forgotten. The National Institute of Arts and Letters, which, generally speaking, has contained the best names of American arts and letters since its foundation, elected him to membership about thirty years ago; but probably only a few times since then did Wilson remember that he was officially of that distinguished group.

Moreover, there was a literary aristocrat who in his lifetime represented royalty itself to the minds of almost every American writing man. He was William Dean Howells, the most authoritative and penetrating critic of writing our country has known, and a good word from him in his lofty literary department in *Harper's Monthly Magazine* was the accolade. He was late in "discovering" Wilson; but when he did find him, at last, raised him to the peerage. Howells' delight in *Bunker Bean* and in *Ruggles* was profound; in *Ma Pettengill* it was an ecstasy.

Wilson could write anywhere, even on Capri, where, in the autumn of 1905 and the winter and spring of 1906, he lived in the beautiful, unbelievable villa that Elihu Vedder had built there. Vesuvius was meditating an eruption, just across the bay, and the fireworks display from the mountain became more and more prodigious until the final great eruption of 1906. Wilson sat at a desk, unceasingly playing his own game of solitaire that he'd invented and at intervals setting down the cards to make a note for the novel that engaged him.

After the volcano had spent itself, he went to Paris, took rooms in the Boulevard Raspail, and wrote. He'd never seen Paris before and wouldn't look at it—he was writing. Every afternoon at four o'clock he walked a block or two to the Café du Dôme (not in those days a sight for tourists) and played cards during exactly two hours; then went home and wrote again. It took me about three months to convince him that he ought to spend a morning in the Louvre and at least half an hour in the Sainte Chapelle. He did, somewhat grudgingly, and immediately returned to his work in the Boulevard Raspail and his cards at the Dôme.

Then, being young and irresponsible, I lightheartedly coaxed him away from both, got him out to the country and a house over the Marne to write a play with me. One of the editorials I've mentioned spoke of this play, saying that it "glorified" a rustic American type, and this again would have brought Wilson a brief grimness, for it was a reminder of the unforeseen and rather absurd pure accident that made our first play written together outrageously "box office" and gave it a run of plethoric years.

A manager had asked for a play about Indiana to fit a "star" of his, and Wilson and I decided that an "Indiana type" would be theatrically effective if seen against an exotic background. Therefore we projected an untraveled young Kokomo lawyer of only local experience into Sorrento. Both Wilson and I had often delighted in the complaints and the innocent bragging of Americans who were abroad for the first time and looked upon the continent of Europe as uncomfortable and degenerate. We'd even collected expressions of strong feeling we'd heard uttered by some of these—bits of stalwart patriotism, which we put into the mouth of our Kokomo wanderer. Otherwise we made him as agreeable as we could and of course gave him a comedy-melodrama triumph in the end. Our feeling was that the audiences (if there came to be any) would laugh at him with us when he complained of Europe and bragged of America; but that they would indulgently forgive him his nonsense and like him in spite of it.

The American audiences, when the play was put before them, did nothing of the kind. When our young man announced from the stage that he wouldn't "trade our State Insane Asylum for the worst ruined ruin in Europe" they didn't laugh at him forgivingly, they applauded thunderously. In all such matters they felt as he did. Shocked play reviewers who had been abroad heard this applause and thought that Wilson and I had slyly planned to produce it; they announced that we had written "bunkum." Audiences promptly

increased in numbers and in noise; and the two astounded play-
wrights, as innocent of the critics' charge against them as they were
of inciting the audiences' 100 per cent enthusiasm, were besought to
write more plays.

We did—eight or nine, I think. Wilson, always workmanlike, took
up with me the task of filling orders. For several years we were
collaborating playwrights, and then, almost without forewarning, he
faded away. We'd written an honest little comedy that fell into the
hands of a much beloved actress who knew what the public wanted.
They wanted her, she said, just her, and what she did to our play—
to make it her—became with every rehearsal just that much more
upsetting. I think it was from Montreal, an evening or two before
the Poughkeepsie tryout, that I received a telegram from Wilson
mentioning that he was on his way to Banff. I didn't see him again
for nine years.

Then, after he'd written *Bunker Bean* and *Ruggles* and *Ma
Pettengill,* in California, he came to join me in Maine, to construct
some more plays. He waited to see a few rehearsals of the first ill-
fated little series we did then—and faded away again, this time
permanently from my sight. He went back to California to write
Merton of the Movies and to be vaguely astonished by its popular
success and by what was paid him for the subsequent serials that he
wrote. He gave most of it away.

In 1902 Wilson became a "best seller" with *The Spenders,* and, because he was really a writing man, he threw his best-sellerness away
the next year with that penetrating and somewhat somber historical
novel about the Mormons, *The Lions of the Lord.* Then he wrote
The Boss of Little Arcady, a novel obviously by a man charmingly
in love; and after that *Ewing's Lady.* These books are out of print,
of course, and may remain so. Probably they fall into the class of
forgotten novels, a matter understandable since such masterpieces
as *The Damnation of Theron Ware* and *The Grandissimes* are now
forgotten novels. *Ma Pettengill, Ruggles,* and *Bunker Bean* aren't
yet forgotten; it would be a pleasure to think that they won't be.
Such books are harder to write than are tragedies; they need a rarer
talent than do searchingly realistic explorations into toughness or
profoundly formless aphrodisiacs for the adolescent minds of the
physically adult. Wilson never dropped down into the easier kinds
of writing.

Once he stopped, did almost no work at all for more than a year;

and during that time I hadn't even a letter from him. Then he wrote me:

> I've been reading—reading some books I'd never read and rereading some I had. Hegel, Kant, Schopenhauer, Spinoza, Herbert Spencer, Tyndall, Huxley, Nietzsche; a dozen others. So now I know everything—the nature of matter, the law of life and the universe, all about what man is, whence he came, where he's to go, and why. It's a wonderful thing to know all this and to be sure that I'm now able to solve all questions.

He always ruggedly enjoyed his own discomfitures.

A few years ago his head was hurt in a motoring accident, and after that his memory began to fail him at times—times that were gradually more and more frequent. This was a calamity that he took in his own stride; no blow on the head or in the heart ever got a wince or a murmur out of him. He planned a novel—one that would say of this present world all that his life had given him to say of it —and, when he found the story to carry this burden, and made a synopsis, he sat down day after day to play solitaire and make his notes. At these he worked hard, pondering both deeply and eagerly, and some of them, now and then, he sent to me. I found them stirringly brilliant, noble in wisdom, and urged him to begin the manuscript. He couldn't, for now his memory grew so queer that he had to have somebody with him when he walked abroad, because by himself he couldn't find the way home. Still he worked, set down the cards as he dealt them, took notes and planned his book. He made notes, planned the book and worked upon his thought for it the day that he died. He was a writing man.

SOME LITERARY CELEBRITIES I HAVE KNOWN

by G. K. Chesterton

Shortly after his death Chesterton's reminiscences of Hardy, Mere-dith, Yeats, and others appeared in The Saturday Review. *They later became a part of his autobiography.*

SEPTEMBER 12, 1936

THE FIRST GREAT Victorian I ever met, I met very early, though only for a brief interview: Thomas Hardy. I was then a quite obscure and shabby young writer awaiting an interview with a publisher. And the really remarkable thing about Hardy was this: that he might have been himself an obscure and shabby young writer awaiting a publisher; even a new writer awaiting his first publisher. Yet he was already famous everywhere; he had written his first and finest novels culminating in *Tess;* he had expressed his queer personal pessimism in the famous passage about the President of the Immortals. He had already the wrinkle of worry on his elfish face that might have made a man look old; and yet, in some strange way, he seemed to me very young. If I say as young as I was, I mean as simply pragmatical and even priggish as I was. He did not even avoid the topic of his alleged pessimism; he defended it, but somehow with the innocence of a boys' debating club. In short, he was in a sort of gentle fuss about his pessimism, just as I was about my optimism.

He said something like: "I know people say I'm a pessimist; but I don't believe I am naturally; I like a lot of things so much; but I could never get over the idea that it would be better for us to be without both the pleasures and the pains; and that the best experience would be some sort of sleep."

I have always had a weakness for arguing with anybody; and this involved all that contemporary nihilism against which I was then

156

in revolt; and for about five minutes, in a publisher's office, I actually argued with Thomas Hardy. I argued that nonexistence is not an experience; and there can be no question of preferring it or being satisfied with it. Honestly, if I had been quite simply a crude young man, and nothing else, I should have thought his whole argument very superficial and even silly. But I did not think him either superficial or silly.

For this was the rather tremendous truth about Hardy: that he had humility. My friends who knew him better have confirmed my early impression. Jack Squire told me that Hardy in his last days of glory as a Grand Old Man would send poems to the *Mercury* and offer to alter or withdraw them if they were not suitable. He defied the gods and dared the lightning and all the rest of it; but the great Greeks would have seen that there was no thunderbolt for him, because he had no insolence. For what heaven hates is not impiety but the pride of impiety. The whole case for Hardy is that he had the sincerity and simplicity of the village atheist—that is, that he valued atheism as a truth and not a triumph. He was the victim of that decay of our agricultural culture, which gave men bad religion and no philosophy. But he was right in saying, as he said essentially to me all those years ago, that he could enjoy things, including better philosophy or religion. There come back to me four lines, written by an Irish lady in my own little paper:

> *Who can picture the scene at the starry portals,*
> *Truly, imagination fails,*
> *When the pitiless President of the Immortals*
> *Shows unto Thomas the print of the nails?*

I hope it is not profane to say that this hits the right nail on the head. In such a case, the second Thomas would do exactly what Prometheus and Satan never thought of doing: he would pity God.

I must leap a long stretch of years before I come to my meeting with the other great Victorian novelist so often bracketed with Hardy; for by that time I had made some sort of journalistic name, which was responsible for my wife and myself being invited to visit George Meredith. But even across the years, I felt the curious contrast. Hardy was a well, covered with the weeds of a stagnant period of skepticism, in my view; but with truth at the bottom of it; or anyhow with truthfulness at the bottom of it. But Meredith was a fountain. He had exactly the shock and shining radiation of a fountain in his own garden where he entertained us. He was already an old man, with the white pointed beard and the puff of white hair like thistledown; but that also seemed to radiate. He was deaf; but the reverse of dumb. He was not humble; but I should never call him proud. He still managed to be a third thing, which is almost as much the opposite of being proud; he was vain. He was a very old man; and he was still magnificently vain. He had all those indescribable touches of a quite youthful vanity; even, for instance, to the point of preferring to dazzle women rather than men; for he talked the whole time to my wife rather than to me. We did not talk to him very much, partly because he was deaf but much more because he was not dumb. On an honest review, I doubt whether we could either of us have got in a word or two edgeways. He talked and talked, and drank ginger beer, which he assured us with glorious gaiety he had learned to like quite as much as champagne.

Meredith was not only full of life, but he was full of lives. His vitality had that branching and begetting genius of the novelist, which is always inventing new stories about strange people. He was not like most old novelists; he was interested in what was novel. He did not live in the books he had written; he lived in the books he had not written. He described a number of novels that were really novel; especially one about the tragedy of Parnell. I do not think I agreed very much with his interpretation, for he held that Parnell might easily have recovered popularity, if he had been capable of wanting it; but that he was naturally secretive and solitary. But I doubt whether that Irish squire was really any more secretive than any number of speechless English squires, who were at the same moment conducting exactly the same sort of sex intrigue and would have been equally angry and equally inarticulate if they had been discovered. Only they never were discovered. For there was no hope that the discovery might delay the deliverance of a Christian nation. But that was the quality that struck me personally about Meredith. Ever on the jump, he could jump to conclusions; so great a man could never be called superficial; but in a sense, being so swift means being superficial.

The name of James Barrie dates also from my youth, though of course he was younger than Hardy; he has lived to be my very good friend; but he is of all friends the least egotistical; and I connect him largely with intensely interesting memories of these other men and their contemporaries. He remains especially as a witness to the greatness of Meredith, in a world which has rather strangely forgotten him; but he also told me many tales of the men I never met, such as Stevenson and Henley and Wilde. But there is one impression that has been left in my mind by such memories of such men; and that is the strangely fugitive character of the controversies even about the greatest literary men. Like anybody writing any memoirs, I find that my first difficulty is to convey how immensely important certain individuals appeared at certain epochs. For those men are no longer topics, even when they are still classics. I remember Barrie giving me a most amusing account of a violent scene of literary controversy, in which Henley hurled his crutch across the room and hit some other eminent literary critic in the stomach. That will illustrate a certain importance that seemed to attach to certain intellectual tastes and preferences. For this piece of creative critical self-expression was apparently provoked by the statement, during a discussion about Ibsen and Tolstoy, that one of these great men was great enough to hang the other on his watch chain. But what strikes me as the grand and grim joke of the whole business is that the narrator had apparently entirely forgotten whether Ibsen was to hang Tolstoy on his watch chain or Tolstoy to hang Ibsen on his watch chain. From which I venture to infer that neither of those giants now seems quite so gigantic to anybody as they then seemed to somebody.

Of course I have only noted here a name or two, because they are the most famous; I do not even say that they are the most worthy of fame. For instance, supposing that we each keep a private collection of our pet pessimists, I have always been more intellectually impressed by A. E. Housman than by Thomas Hardy. I do not mean that I have been impressed by anybody with the intellectual claims of pessimism, which I always thought was piffle as well as poison; but it seems to me that Housman had, more than Hardy, a certain authority of great English literature; which is all the more classic because its English is such very plain English. I could never quite digest Hardy as a poet, much as I admire him as a novelist; whereas Housman seems to me one of the one or two great classic poets of our time. I have had both friends and fellowship in discontent with the socialists; indeed, I was not discontented with them about conditions with which they were discontented; but rather about the prospects with which they were contented. And there was a sort of official optimism, when the collectivist ticket-collector of the Fabian tram called out, "Next stop, Utopia," at which something in me not merely heathen was always stirred to a sympathy with the words of that high heathen genius:

> *The troubles of our proud and angry dust*
> *Are from eternity and shall not fail.*

As everyone knows, the poet was also a professor, and one of the first authorities on the old pagan literature. I cherish a story about him which happens to concern this double character of the classical and the poetical. It may be a familiar story, it may be a false story. It describes the start of an after-dinner speech he made at Trinity, Cambridge; and whoever made it or invented it had a superb sense of style.

> This great College, of this ancient University, has seen some strange sights. It has seen Wordsworth drunk and Porson sober. And here am I, a better poet than Porson, and a better scholar than Wordsworth, betwixt and between.

I have known one or two isolated cases also of the mere man of imagination. It is always difficult to give even an outline of men of this kind; precisely because an outline is always the line at which a thing touches other things outside itself. I have already suggested very vaguely, for instance, something of the position of W. B. Yeats; but that is precisely because Yeats does touch some things outside his own thoughts; and suggests controversies about Theosophy or Mythology or Irish politics. But he who is simply the imaginative man can only be found in the images he makes and not in the portraits of him that other people make. Thus I could mention a number of detached and definite things about Mr. Walter de la Mare; only that they would not, strictly speaking, be about him. I could say that he has a dark Roman profile rather like a bronze eagle, or that he lives in Taplow not far from Taplow Court, where I have met him and many other figures in the landscape of this story. I could mention the fact that I once found a school, somewhere in the wilds of the Old Kent Road, if I remember right, where all the little girls preserved a sort of legend of Mr. de la Mare, as of a fairy uncle, because he had once lectured there ever so long ago. I've no idea what spells he may have worked on that remote occasion; but he had certainly, in the words of an elder English poet, knocked 'em in the Old Kent Road. But even a thing like this has not strictly speaking anything to do with the subject, the center and fullness of the subject. And I have never been able to say anything that is in that sense about the subject. The nearest I could ever come to judging imaginative work in that sense would be simply to say this: that if I were a child, and somebody said to me no more than the two words *Peacock Pie,* I should pass through a certain transforming experience. A sacramental instinct within me would give me the sense that there was somewhere and somehow a substance, gorgeously colored and good to eat. Which is indeed the case.

But among these literary figures, there was one figure whom I shall put last because I ought to put it first. It was the figure of a contemporary and companion of all that world of culture; a close friend of Meredith's; an artist admired as artistic by the aesthetes and even by the decadents. But Alice Meynell, though she preferred to be aesthetic rather than anesthetic, was no aesthete; and there was nothing about her that can decay. The thrust of life in her was like that of a slender tree with flowers and fruit for all seasons; and there was no drying up of the sap of her spirit, which was in ideas. She could always find things to think about; even on a sick bed in a darkened room, where the shadow of a bird on the blind was more than the bird itself, she said, because it was a message from the sun. Since she was so emphatically a craftsman, she was emphatically an artist and not an aesthete; but above all, she was like that famous artist who said that he always mixed his paints with brains. But there was something else about her which I did not understand at the time, which set her apart as something separate from the time. She was strong with deep roots where all the stoics were only stiff with despair; she was alive to an immortal beauty where all the Pagans could only mix beauty with mortality. And though she passed through my own life fitfully, and though her presence had indeed something of the ghostly gravity of a shadow and her passing something of the fugitive accident of a bird, I know now that she was not fugitive and she was not shadowy. She was a message from the Sun.

THE LEGEND OF
OLIVER HERFORD

by Julian Street

An unforgettable human being with a gift for delight and laughter, Oliver Herford possessed a wit that enlivened all who came in contact with him. His funny sayings and doings will be remembered for many a day, as will his whimsical writings, illustrated by his own drawings. In this tribute, Julian Street describes Herford humor.

JUNE 26, 1943

HE WAS FRAIL and gnomelike. His clothing hung from his shoulders with the empty look of clothing on a coat hanger, and by contrast with his meager body and spindling neck his head looked large. This disproportion gave him the appearance of a baby robin, and the suggestion was enhanced by the great, astonished eyes behind his glasses, and by the nimbus of fine, soft hair, like pinfeathers on a half-bald birdling.

Yet there was a certain style about him. His writings and drawings were full of style and he could wear an old gray homespun suit in a way that made it look newer and better than it was. Long ago, when I first knew him, fancy waistcoats were the fashion and I remember that his were of heavy woolen goods, for except in an overheated room he seemed always to be chilly.

He wore enormously tall, starched turnover collars of a style I remember from half a century ago, spats in cool weather, and a monocle which usually hung on a black ribbon against his vest. His voice was low, his diction distinct—as befitted the son of an English clergyman—and his smile slow and misty. He almost never laughed aloud; a smile was usually the best he gave; the rest of us, who listened to him, did the laughing.

Oliver Herford was rated the first wit of his time. Since his death in 1935 the legend of him has steadily expanded. His sketches and

162

water colors and the delightful little books he wrote and illustrated are collectors' items now; his verses are enshrined in the paper Westminster Abbeys of the anthologists; and Herfordisms such as "My wife has a whim of iron," "A woman's mind is cleaner than a man's—she changes it oftener," "They came to cough and remained to spray" (patients in a throat specialist's waiting room), "I don't know your face but your manner is familiar" (in rebuke to a back-slapper), and "I've always wanted to throw an egg into an electric fan" (his famous reply to a patronizing dowager who asked about his loftier ambitions) are classics of American quippery.

The coruscating side of him that caused him to be so widely quoted in the United States and England was far from being the whole show, and it is far from being the only reason why to me and many others who knew him Oliver Herford is the most unforgettable of men. His gift was the gift for creating delight and laughter. He never "built up" a story or had anything pat. He didn't *try* to amuse us.

It always seemed to me that the essential thing that made Oliver Herford completely an odd number was that he lived on two separate levels at the same time. Physically he trudged about this old boarding house of a world with the rest of us, but mentally he floated overhead.

This affair of dual levels, or of having been delivered to the wrong address by the celestial expressman, kept his friends enormously entertained and considerably concerned about him. But, though he seemed to the rest of us the most impractical of men, he thought himself as practical as Calvin Coolidge. It was others who were impractical: poor, plodding wretches who were so obsessed with notions about punctuality and the first of the month and checkbooks and columns of figures and rent bills and grocer's bills and light bills and telephone bills and other awful dullnesses that they never had time to think of worthwhile things such as the fairy patterns made by Jack Frost on winter windowpanes, and the fact that to an insect's eye the grasses were like the columns and arches in a Gothic cathedral, and that the right time to open Christmas cards was in July, when it was hot, and that the way to deal with unattractive-looking mail was to drop it unopened in the wastebasket.

One Sunday when he and his sister, Beatrice, were walking in the country in New England they came upon a little one-room schoolhouse in the woods. Thinking of the children who would trudge dismally to school next morning, Oliver managed to lift a window, climbed in, and, while Beatrice sat at a desk, spent a happy two hours drawing in chalk on the blackboard which ran round the room a droll mural decoration of wild animals. Later Beatrice chanced to hear of the delight of teacher and pupils when the drawings were discovered next day, and of the reluctance with which they were erased to make way for more practical and painful things, the so necessary things which in Oliver's special world weren't necessary at all.

And indeed one could sometimes see a sort of cockeyed practicality about Oliver's ideas. The earliest example I know of his special kind of practicality occurred when he was in his late teens. His father had brought his family here from England when Oliver and Beatrice— famous these fifty years for her humorous monologues, an entertainment form I believe she invented—were children, and Oliver went West and got himself a job on a Nevada cattle ranch, cooking for cowboys. He had to rise at 4:00 A.M., build the kitchen fire, and start breakfast, but his most difficult duty was to take the bunkhouse water barrel down to a spring, fill it, and get it up the hill again. Particularly on cold winter mornings he hated this task, and he formed the habit of filling the barrel the last thing at night to escape going out in the pitch-dark, freezing morning.

One morning when he started to get breakfast he discovered that a mouse had got into the water barrel and drowned.

"What did you do?" I asked when he told me of this episode.

"Well," returned Oliver the practical, "I didn't take coffee that morning."

As may be imagined, banks, public-service corporations, and other businesslike institutions presented something of a problem to Oliver, and he in turn presented something of a problem to them. When he received a letter from his bank saying, "Your account appears to be overdrawn," he answered, "Never trust appearances."

In the happy days of yore it was the beneficent practice of the Periodical Publishers Association to give an annual blowout of Arabian Nights proportions to some hundreds of writers and illustrators. The guests were wafted out of New York on a special train, put up for the night at a de luxe hotel, given a banquet at which leading figures of the period were speakers, and transported back to New York with their headaches next day.

Delighted with the sumptuous resort hotel at which one of these banquets took place, Oliver decided to remain there a few days after the mob went home. As he was about to leave he was shocked to learn from the clerk that he had been the guest of the publishers for one night only and was expected to pay the balance of the bill himself.

"I haven't that much money with me," he told the clerk.

"That's all right, Mr. Herford. Just give us a check."

"But I haven't any checks, either."

A blank check was supplied and Oliver filled it out.

"I'm sorry, Mr. Herford," said the clerk, passing the check back to him, "but you've neglected to fill in the name of the bank."

"Ah, yes," said Oliver. "Perhaps you can tell me the name of a good bank."

When his tailor once wrote him, expressing pained surprise that he had paid no attention to his bill, Oliver wrote back that far from paying no attention to the bill he had shown it every attention, taking it with him on a weekend visit to the Berkshires, to luncheon with a charming lady, and to a distinguished literary gathering. "I was about to take it to Newport for the yacht races," he wrote, "when your letter arrived."

As far as I know, Oliver had but one settled economic policy. Small checks for second serial rights and the like—"windfalls" he called them—he always gave to Peggy, his wife. Peggy was Irish, red-headed, peppery, and humorous. She had a beautiful appreciation of Oliver in all his phases, and she treasured every little note and verse he wrote her during their many years together.

I remember two items she showed me. One was a note he sent her with a little check: "Here is a little windfall, dear. Spend it wisely but not too often."

The other was a six-line verse. Oliver had found an eyelash on a piece of paper on which Peggy had been writing when called to the telephone. On her return to her desk she found the eyelash mounted on a card with these lines:

> *O many a lash have I*
> *Received from Peggy's eye*
> *And there are many more*
> *Mayhap for me in store;*
> *Pray God the others all*
> *As light as thou may fall.*

The dedication of his books were clever and sometimes tender, but at least one had a sting in its tail. When Woodrow Wilson was President he used to quote Oliver in his speeches. But Oliver did not admire his admirer, and when his book, *This Giddy Globe,* appeared it was dedicated

TO PRESIDENT WILSON

(With all his faults he quotes me still.)

Oliver's likes and dislikes were strong and he aired them freely. The story has often been told of the Farragut Club, and of how he would tell people he was proposing them for membership and later inform them that they had been blackballed. Ultimately it came to be known that Oliver held all the offices in the Farragut Club and was its sole member, and that the club's meeting place was the seat under the statue of Admiral Farragut in Madison Square. I once asked him what had put the idea of the Farragut Club into his head, and he replied that he had organized it for the sole purpose of blackballing Richard Harding Davis.

The late Childe Hassam, celebrated painter, detested careless superlatives. "Oliver," he once told me, "is one of the few men you can call a genius without making an ass of yourself"—and he quoted a definition of the term *genius* by Edward Simmons, the mural painter. "A genius," Simmons said, "is a man who can make you see stars in the daytime."

Oliver could do that. Usually the stars he made you see were pretty fireworks of the mind, but on provocation he could put more voltage into them and make them scorch.

He was fond of animals, particularly Persian cats, and loved to draw them, but Hassam wanted to interest him in bigger subjects. "Why do you all the time paint cats, Oliver?" he asked.

"Well, anyway," retorted Oliver crisply, "I don't paint cats and call them landscapes."

Simmons, who was also a member of The Players Club, said many clever things but he was such an incessant talker that he came to be regarded in some quarters as a bore; and several of the best-known Herford stories are of biting things Oliver said to Simmons in a well-meant effort to make him moderate his loquacity.

When Simmons wrote his autobiography he asked Oliver to write an introduction for the book. Oliver did so, but headed it "Interruption."

A member of The Players, fed up with Simmons' monologues, said to him, "I'll give you fifty dollars if you'll resign from this club."

"Don't take it," advised Oliver when Simmy told him of the insult. "You can get more."

His faculties for forgetting were incredible. He seemed to know nothing at all about things that had not interested him. I once asked him how old he was when he came to the United States and he told me he was about a year old. Since then I have learned that he was thirteen when he came. He had not enjoyed his schooldays in England and had, so to speak, shut the door on them. It was the same with Chicago, where he went to public school, and Boston, where he went to art school. He never liked his school anywhere and I never heard him mention Chicago or Boston except that he once remarked that when he went abroad he sailed from Boston because it was such a pleasant place to go away from.

Again I asked if he was a member of the National Institute of Arts and Letters. He said no. When I showed surprise he explained, "They say you have to be a citizen."

"My God, Oliver," I exclaimed, thinking of his interest in American politics, "aren't you a citizen?"

"I don't know," he replied with his dim look. "That's what they said."

Beatrice Herford tells me he was a citizen, and the yearbook of the National Institute of Arts and Letters tells me he was elected to that body in 1911—twenty years before I asked him about it.

Everyone wanted to know Oliver but Oliver didn't want to know everyone, and especially he didn't want to know people who would gush over him or use him as an exhibition piece.

Many years ago a society woman widely known as a collector of celebrities gave a large dinner party at which the guests of honor were Oliver Herford and a then-famous military man. Bulbous and beaming, the lady arose at the end of the meal and, without having warned Oliver, announced, "Mr. Oliver Herford will now improvise a poem in honor of the hostess."

Oliver, sunk down in his chair, seemed visibly to shrivel.

"Oh, no," he murmured. "Have the General fire a cannon."

With Gelett Burgess, Oliver once started a sophisticated little magazine called *L'Enfant Terrible* which Burgess tells me ran for one consecutive issue. Taking a copy of that issue, fresh from the press, Oliver called on the late William W. Ellsworth, president of the Century Company, and asked him to take advertising space in the new magazine.

Mr. Ellsworth declined, and Oliver demanded to know why.

"Because," said the prescient publisher, "your magazine will be ephemeral."

"Why should it be ephemeral?"

"You'll get sick of it and it will stop."

"Nonsense," said Oliver. "I got sick of *The Century* long ago and it hasn't stopped."

As Oliver aged he ate less and less, and his weight, little enough at best, dwindled until he became more than ever a mere "intelligence on legs." As his weight diminished colds and drafts disturbed him more, and the atmosphere of his apartment in the old "French Flats" in West Eighteenth Street was practically airless.

Into this situation came one winter Mr. E. J. Regan of London, Peggy's father, to pay the Herfords a visit. Mr. Regan brought with him a Briton's mania for fresh air. He went rushing about the apartment opening windows while Oliver rushed after him closing them.

Thoroughly irritated, the visitor went to the hall closet and ostentatiously put on his overcoat.

"Where are you going?" Oliver asked.

"Out to get some air," snapped the old gentleman.

"No use going out for it," said Oliver. "You've got it all in here now."

Oliver was not merely liked by his friends; he was treasured by them as a very special treasure. They loved to hold symposiums, to tell one another of things they had heard him say or seen him do, comparing notes, sorting the wheat from the chaff or, rather, sorting Oliver's chaff from other people's chaff—for his reputation was so great that the witty sayings of others were often attributed to him. This sorting process still goes on among the friends who have survived him, and the affectionate smiles that light their faces when his name is mentioned are at once their bequest from him and their memorial to him.

On a July day in 1935 Oliver, frailer than ever, walked slowly into The Players. A friend asked how he felt. "I know what's the matter with me," he replied. "I'm just fading out." And it was true. Less than a week later a black-bordered card posted on the bulletin board announced Oliver Herford's death. The card reminded many an old Player of what Oliver said when the name of George Barr McCutcheon was similarly posted.

"When I look out of my studio window," he said, "and see the club flag at half-mast, I hurry over and look at the bulletin board to see who it is; but it's always the wrong man." Oliver's own death notice had been on the bulletin board but a short time when someone who remembered pencilled on it: "Always the wrong man."

When I heard that Oliver was dead I could have wept, but when I read his obituary notices I laughed. No one could have helped laughing at such collections of Oliverish anecdotes.

After his funeral, which was at noon, there were things to be talked over, and a group of his pallbearers went to The Players for lunch. One story suggested another. Each man, it seemed, had some pet Oliver stories which were new to the rest of us, and the luncheon party quickly turned from an occasion of gloom into one of hilarity.

This expresses better than anything I am able to say the thing that makes Oliver so unforgettable. When those who loved him meet and mention him the inevitable result is gaiety.

ARNOLD BENNETT

by Francis Hackett

When Arnold Bennett died at the full height of his powers, Francis Hackett wrote this appraisal of the man and his works, with the provocative thesis that somewhere along the line Bennett had gone astray without fully realizing his own ability as a writer.

MAY 2, 1931

I THINK of Arnold Bennett as I last saw him, coming down the stairs of his own house. His morning's work was evidently done, his conscience clear, his manner leisurely and assured. He had that fresh English color and that sparkle of health which one hardly sees in a photograph. Though his hair was silvery it had a cocky curl in it, and the subtle shade of his blue suit enhanced the beauty of his eyes. He might have been a captain in the merchant marine coming off the bridge of his ship. He greeted his guests with a cordial yet pondering gaze; and then, very characteristic of something precise and critical in him, I remember how he adjusted the reversed collar of his friend Somerset Maugham's coat as we went in to lunch. "You are always so neat, Somerset," he murmured paternally.

Nature is sardonic. There was perhaps no literary career in England so robust and flourishing. This year Bennett was sixty-three-odd. He had produced a piquant film not so long before. He was writing weekly literary articles at half a crown a word that gave powerful impact to any book's success or failure. Every day an aspiring author sent his work to Bennett. "I receive two hundred books a year," he told me seven years ago. "I promise to read twenty. I read ten." But his criticisms and his general articles were mere hors d'oeuvres. He had just concluded an immense novel, *Imperial Palace,* which was lustrous with vitality. He was quoted. He was continually in view. He possessed the center of the stage in literary London. And suddenly this vigorous organism, of which he was so careful and so naturally proud, was attacked by the typhoid germ and the whole beautiful mechanism reduced to dust.

It is sad and shocking. It is sad to see a man die in full strength.

It is shocking to think that Arnold Bennett is no longer there. One counted on Bennett. The young men might disown him and Rebecca West might be amused by him as avuncular. But he was there. And now he is not there.

The suddenness of this catastrophe brings into relief the problem that Arnold Bennett had always deliberately presented to one's literary conscience—the problem of his expensive commercial success. Now that his work is over and the Rolls Royce empty, was it worth it? That is what any literary critic may ask.

I began puzzling about this problem in my own mind over twenty years ago. I always liked Arnold Bennett immensely. I liked him from the day I reviewed *The Old Wives' Tale* when I was a critic in Chicago in 1910, perhaps not the less because he wrote to me that mine was the review which had given him the most pleasure. I liked him when I came to meet him. He was too much of a literary magnate for me to become intimate, but there was something about him inherently rich, warm, genuine, and lovable. And yet I was always puzzled by his sense of values. . . . An extraordinary man.

Sometimes one opened a popular magazine to light on a short story by Bennett of simply atrocious quality—like bad chocolates in a beribboned box. Sometimes one read novels like *Accident* or *Strange Vanguard* that were hopelessly superficial. Sometimes he did things like *The Pretty Lady* that were spiritually obtuse. But just as one had "found him out" and ruled him out, he revealed the existence of an entirely different being—a rare, sensitive, generous, scrupulous, honest, and essentially incorruptible artist who didn't give a damn for the philistines.

In one mood, I think, Bennett hated and feared the aesthetic man. Himself from the clay of Staffordshire, he was of the uncouth Puritan English stock, set in prejudices like iron in cement, confined by the English caste system, detesting the self-betrayal of emotion, despising the least concession to the weakness of human nature, fortifying himself in truculent independence against his gaucherie; and trusting above everything to armor himself in cash. On this side of his character Bennett was tough will-to-power. He showed when he was a young man that he too could write for *The Yellow Book;* but he never submerged his will to inspiration. There was nothing of the "artistic temperament" about his conduct. He worked by the clock—an article in an hour. He told me proudly he had never been late with "copy" in his life. He could take regular

morning exercises, "jerks" as the English call them, or make regular
entries in his diary, no matter how vividly he was living. He was
methodic, positive, rational. He gloried in the solvency of his self-
control. He was an "executive," and he could avert a cocktail or a
liqueur with cool common sense. "Poison. How can you do it?"
This cool common sense ran through him as a commercial canal
might cut across a garden. He came of mercantile England and he
was basically utilitarian. Hence his utilization of his literary by-
products. He made trivial novels out of the exhaust of serious
novels. He produced stories with heroines in the latest frocks. He
wrote guides to literary taste, secrets of domestic happiness, how to
live on twenty-four hours a day, hints on efficiency—everything, in
fact, except politics and poetry. And he rejected poetry after an
experiment because, as he said, it cost too much effort and time.

   And yet this literary Benthamite, this man whose cool common
sense never completely forsook him, had the temerity, on occasion,
to love beauty and tell the truth. He was a professed Freethinker
in correct England, a declared Socialist before the war, an advocate
of birth control against cant and reticence, a friend to every kind
of new talent, an extraordinarily accessible man. It was his love of
beauty that, as a young man, sent him to France. He left the safety
of a London editorship (he, like Oscar Wilde, was once editor of a
ladies' journal) to create such a stupendous novel as *The Old Wives'
Tale* that could scarcely remunerate him—and to do this in the
exalted isolation of Fontainebleau. The mercantile prudence that
was in his bones could not stop him from it. The French helped him
to understand how deeply he had lived in the apparently trite and
squalid Five Towns, and he set himself with a kind of voluptuous
honesty to envelop his own unromantic experience. *The Old Wives'
Tale* is French in being completely emancipated from the moral
obsession that enslaved the English novel in Dickens, in George
Eliot, in Thackeray, in Meredith even—in everyone, one might say,
since Jane Austen. Bennett contemplated his unfashionable creatures with pure fidelity to their significance as against mere edifying
existence; and he did this on the grandest scale.

   The English did not see it. As English criticism twenty-five years
ago was still dominated by the mandarins, and as the lending libraries remained Victorian, *The Old Wives' Tale* fell comparatively
flat. It was not until America acclaimed it that it made its real
reputation in England.

   The man who had created *The Old Wives' Tale* was the man

who, in Bennett, always gave his disinterested heart to the best in literature. Little bohemian as he was, deeply as he mistrusted his impulses, he was always one of the first to see the real thing. When he wrote of books in those crisp letters to the "New Age," about 1910, names like Chekhov were introduced to hundreds of eager readers who could trust his generous discernment. The first day I met him, in 1920, the book that was open on his table was Proust. It was he who paid decisive tribute to the H. G. Wells of *Tono-Bungay*, to George Moore always, to the great Russian novels. Once he was at a lionizing reception to Joseph Conrad, whom he had never met. Bennett kept far away from the lion, but when Conrad was told who was there he broke through the circle. He rushed over and put both his hands on Bennett's shoulders, exclaiming, "Well, I've just heard you are Arnold Bennett. To think you've been my friend all these years, and I didn't know you." It was Bennett who said first of all, "D. H. Lawrence is a genius," which is true, just as it was he the other day who recalled the glorious mountain freshet of Robert Burns. Old or new, he saw authors for himself; he made his reservations about James Joyce. He saw sentimentality in Galsworthy twenty years ago. He insisted on the thinness of Henry James.

"After I read Chekhov," he said to my wife, "I put down my fountain pen and swear I'll never pick it up again." But he was not confined to admiring the genre of naturalism. He had nobility in his allegiance to authors as little popular as Mark Rutherford or Osbert Sitwell. He had some violent dislikes, of course, but it was hard to shake him when he liked anything. I tried to shake him, for example, on the subject of Dreiser's *American Tragedy*. It is my belief that there is a demagogue in Dreiser. The man who turned the limelight on the injured woman in *Jennie Gerhardt* is callously negligent of the far more injured woman in *An American Tragedy*. Dreiser's indictment of America for prosecuting the murderer is legal idiocy. So, at any rate, I urged on Bennett. He became very thoughtful, scrutinizing me with his grave eyes and saying nothing, but suddenly shaking his head and making a dogged reaffirmation of his faith.

Few men were more interesting to talk to, I imagine. Few men saw more sides of a question, few had more loyalty to the thing observed, few had so much emotional tenacity or were so initiated and shrewd. But he was English. He was slow to give himself. He would begin, subside, resume, make a point, break off. Like most gauche men, he suffered most from other people's shyness. He was extremely sensitive to moral and mental atmosphere and he was well aware that London and New York are whispering galleries.

Imperial Palace was a very natural culmination of his art. He had long since exhausted the Five Towns. He was far too loyal to life to write about writers, the novelist's confession that his arteries are hardening. He had ceased to be a provincial without acquiring London as second nature. He was intimate with War Lords, had done Lord Raingo, but was not sufficiently sociological to make Big Business his own. What then could give him the envelope he needed? He had become too prosperous to feel the poignancy of another *Riceyman Steps*. He was, in fact, saturated with the metropolis in which he lived—the world of audacious enterprise, of showmanship, of picture papers, of rewarded and thwarted ambition, of purchased luxury, of exterior glitter and speed and "swank." He inhaled this sort of thing and it intoxicated him. He was too honest, and too Machiavellian in his respect for experience, not to believe that this was Life. He thought of selecting Harrod's Stores, but Zola had done it in *Aux Bonheurs des Dames* and there was something more representative of his own joy in organization about a hotel. A great hotel—the climax of his lifelong admiration of workmanship. He had once described an Atlantic liner with gusto (the *Lusitania*, all except the steerage). But the hotel was as compact as a ship. Never, I think, had he such beautiful technique. *Imperial Palace* glides into its story like a great liner smoothly sliding from its moorings. With superb competence he manipulated both the machinery and the ostentation of it, the esprit de corps and the underlying ambition, its cosmopolitan men and especially its women. It was life, not as a spiritual experience but as an occupational experience. It was, in reality, a paean to power. But besides possessing himself of the body and soul of a hotel, in so far as it has a soul, Bennett gave a true, unsparing, audacious, and in some ways disillusioned portrait of himself as a hotel magnate. I found Bennett in every line. The book is a significant book, and a magnificent one.

But where was Bennett's sense of the *magnum mysterium?* When I finished this long volume, I felt at first a certain emptiness. Was this all? And then it dawned on me that the problem that Bennett's artistic life had always presented had been resolved by the triumph of the man of power. Expert in sensation, faithful to his libido, true to the Calvinism of commerce, Arnold Bennett had accepted himself as a captain of industry. The last words of his film *Piccadilly*, "life goes on," were essentially the last words of his novel. A remorseless agnosticism. Meanwhile, he really enjoyed luxury and sumptuousness, fame and money, and the integrity of balancing his accounts. He was there as an artist, but his art had become subordinate. And the love story, exterior to the drama of the hotel, was inherent in the story of power.

"Life goes on." The individual is a dimple in the stream, a whorl in running water. Yet memory also goes on, and judgment of values goes on. As I listened to the most ethereal choir I ever heard, the other night, the Palestrina Choir in Copenhagen, I kept thinking of Arnold Bennett in this new perspective of death. A friend of his had said, "He never quarreled with fate." But did he not allow the standards of one sort of integrity to encroach on the unity of his being as a writer? Did he not take too seriously the "average sensual man" in himself? A hotel, after all, is only a mud hut in another form. To take it as ultimate is to close out those rhythms that mount from Palestrina to the roof, and from the roof into spaces beyond. I accepted Bennett as he was, and I was proud of knowing him in his strong and rich English complexity. But there was something I wanted to hear from him in utmost candor, something of his own self and *miserere nobis*. A man with such a sense of romance and tragedy needed to ignore the exterior world, put off his armor and tell the story. . . . And now he is silent.

D. H. LAWRENCE

by Richard Aldington

A misunderstood genius, the first great writer of the real English working class, a man deprived of fame and fortune by the fanatical hatred and persecution of officials and critics in his own country —this is D. H. Lawrence as seen by his friend Richard Aldington, who offers a brilliant defense of the controversial writer.

JUNE 24, 1939

NEARLY TEN YEARS have passed since the death of D. H. Lawrence; and more than ten years since I last said goodbye to him, with no suspicion that I should never see him again. True, during the eight or nine weeks we had been together, he had been seriously ill; but then he had been ill so often, yet had always recovered. It seemed as if some mysteriously inner vitality triumphed over sickness. Actually there was a physical basis for this. Recently I talked with the doctor who attended Lawrence in his last illness. From him I learned that, although the lungs were badly scarred, there was still plenty of resistance, and he would have survived even then but for the psychological defeat which had destroyed his will to live.

I propose here only to relate the outline of this tragedy—the inner complexities need a long essay. Lawrence, it must be remembered, was a striking personality. The books published about him show the almost fanatical devotion he aroused in his own inner group. I have never been able to see why this was the occasion for so much sneering. On the other hand, little or nothing is said about the equally fanatical and far more extensive hatred developed against him. I have often been astonished by it, and still am. People who had never even seen Lawrence, to whom he had done no harm, who had merely listened to gossip and given a prejudiced glance to one or two of his books, united to disparage and thwart him in a way which virtually amounted to persecution. It is to Lawrence's credit that he never developed persecution mania, though he was aware of this hatred, deeply wounded by it, and naturally rather resentful.

It is a peculiar situation. Here was the son of a workingman who, through his mother's determination and self-sacrifice, received enough education to become an elementary-school teacher in a London suburb. Since his father could barely read and write, that was already an achievement. But from that he went on to make a world reputation as an imaginative writer, with no resources beyond what he could earn with his pen, and in spite of ever-growing opposition. Nothing very criminal in this, one would suppose.

From the beginning an odious class snobbery came into action. Lawrence was condescendingly patronized by the London intelligentsia as a worthy sort of inferior who ought to be glad to receive their superior instruction. His early books were handled pretty roughly by the London journalists while they praised forgotten mediocrities. There was some Pecksniffian grumbling about what was called his "eroticism," and this became virulent when he eloped with a married woman, who subsequently became his wife. In spite of or perhaps because of malicious gossip, his third book was a success. But in September 1915, a year after the outbreak of war, his fourth novel, *The Rainbow,* was successfully prosecuted for obscenity and ordered to be destroyed. The book contains one paragraph with a faint suggestion of female homosexuality (so faint that I didn't see it until it was pointed out to me) and several chapters expressing disapproval of war. British magistrates love to insult authors and artists, and the defendant never has the ghost of a chance. The so-called "trial" is invariably a farce, as the judge refuses to admit any witnesses for the defense.

A few weeks after this trial I was surprised to receive a copy of a report issued by the London "Public Morality Council," which among other activities sends old women to previews of films to shorten the kisses and cut out the underclothes. The Bishop of London was an active supporter. My subscription to this association of sex-starved spinsters was demanded on the grounds that they had been responsible for getting *The Rainbow* suppressed. These people know nothing about literature and are nothing more than smuthounds, but they still continue to function.

The Lawrences were ruined at a stroke by this. No royalties, naturally; and then no British publisher dared issue a novel by Lawrence until after the war. It would have been unpatriotic. The Lawrences took refuge in a tiny cottage on the north coast of Cornwall, for which they paid about a dollar a week and even then nearly starved. You would think they were harmless enough.

Lawrence was rejected by the army as totally unfit, and by way of doing what he could, worked on a farm. But Mrs. Lawrence was a German by birth; and sitting by the fire at night they sometimes sang German folk songs. Suddenly the military descended and searched the house, carrying off Lawrence's papers. All the papers were subsequently returned as harmless; but the Lawrences were ordered to leave Cornwall. Apparently they had been accused of showing lights to guide nonexistent German submarines into the Bristol Channel! Lawrence, who of course was utterly and entirely innocent, could never be made to see that mistakes like this do occur in wartime. Nor did he realize that the French at that moment had the jitters about spies, and had insisted that the British government take action against all suspicious characters.

Things did not rest here. Toward the end of 1917 the Lawrences stayed at the same house in London that I used. I had been back some months from the front and had just passed my final examinations as an officer-cadet. I came into the house alone at dusk one evening and found a strange man on the stairs. I asked him what he wanted, and to my amazement I found he was a detective sent to spy on Lawrence and probably to arrest him. I spent over an hour with this sinister dumbbell trying to persuade him of the absurdity of his suspicions. Thanks chiefly to the fact that I was in uniform, I think I succeeded for the moment. Naturally, I didn't tell Lawrence about it—with his capacity for moral indignation he might have done something rash. So far as I know, he was not further troubled by spy-hunters during the war.

Curiously enough, at exactly this time another Lawrence was actively employed as a British agent in Arabia—a strange coincidence.

In 1919 D. H. Lawrence left England and never returned except on brief visits. The official and unofficial persecution did not disappear, however. In 1922 the Lawrences were in Australia, and he wrote an autobiographical novel of their experiences called *Kangaroo*. In one chapter of that novel is a vivid description of Lawrence's fury and disgust when a hitherto friendly Australian turned up to inform him sneeringly that he was—a spy! Where had the man got this interesting information?

For the next three or four years the Lawrences were in America, and in no way troubled by this sort of thing. In 1926 on their return to Europe I saw them again, when they stayed in their home near Florence. In 1928 *Lady Chatterley's Lover* was printed in Florence and was immediately prosecuted. Opinions may differ as to the merit of that work, but I think any decent person would have been revolted by the columns and columns of swinish abuse of Lawrence published in the British press. I happened to be with Lawrence when these cuttings arrived and saw how outraged he was. The truth is that he never had the least intention of writing a pornographic book. He had lived so long away from ordinary people that he had half forgotten their prejudices. He felt he would soon die and wanted to leave a testament of beauty—he rewrote that book three times. With his narrowly passionate puritan nature and incredible naïveté, he saw himself as a crusader for a saner sex life. The foul abuse of the English press was as unexpected by him as it was shocking. I have a feeling that something died in him that night when we sat reading that malevolent trash before a log fire on the island of Port-Cros.

And this wasn't all. An exhibition of his pictures was closed by the police and several of them seized as obscene. Americans who have looked at the volume of colored reproductions will know how harmless they were—practically any modern art show has equally wicked examples of painting. The incredible thing is this. A few years later, long after Lawrence was dead, I happened to pick up a copy of an obscure and short-lived periodical containing an interview with Mr. Ernest Thesiger. In this interview he boasted that he and Sir John Squire had acted as common informers, and thus compelled the police to take action. I may add that this was not under the Bodkin regime. There was a Labor government in power, and Clynes was Home Secretary.

That makes the next stage even more amazing. As I have said, Lawrence was living with me in an old fort on the island of Port-Cros, which lies about twenty-five miles from the naval base of Toulon. The fort had been lent to me for two or three months by a French friend. It had a superb view, and French tourists occasionally asked to be allowed to see it. I invariably accompanied them, as Lawrence was very ill in bed—he had a terrible cough, and his lung had started to bleed again. One afternoon three French staff officers arrived and very politely made the usual request. I took them to the best viewpoint, and by the merest accident mentioned on the way that I had served in the war. We had the usual veterans' get-to-gether, and then they began asking about Lawrence. I explained that he was a very talented English author, but that the British didn't like him because he had published a book of a sexual nature. This tickled the Gallic sense of humor, and they laughed heartily, while we all got in some cracks about British prudery and hypocrisy.

Still they insisted politely but firmly that they must see Lawrence. I explained how ill he was. They went on insisting, and suddenly the ghastly truth came to me—somebody had been pitching that idiotic spy story to the French naval authorities in Toulon! Luckily, Mrs. Lawrence then arrived on the scene and talked in her frank, open way, which I am certain reassured them. At last they went away. It would have been fatal for Lawrence to see them at that moment. He hated men in uniform, and with his extreme quickness would have seen at once what they were after. His anger over the *Lady Chatterley* press clippings had started his lung bleeding again; and the shock of that interview might have killed him. The intention seems to have been to get him deported from France, and as soon as he reached England he would probably have been prosecuted for "uttering an obscene libel."

In any case mail from him to England was being opened by the police, which is quite contrary to law. An envelope containing the manuscript of *Pansies* was confiscated by the police during transit through the mails, and certain poems destroyed by them.

As a rule, when a man dies, his obituary notices are not stones thrown on his grave. Such was not the case with Lawrence. An obscure journalistic clown named Jimmie Douglas published two columns of illiterate abuse under the title *The End of Filth,* and Jack Squire contributed a stupid and venomous insult to the dead. There were a good many others.

This disparagement by England of one of the most original English authors of this century still continues. Every book about him has been sneered at. When Mrs. Lawrence published her memoirs, the newspapers quoted—with insulting banner headlines—anything which seemed to belittle him, but not a single word of the many passages showing the beauty and happiness of their lives together. Even his widow had to be insulted. More recently, the word has gone forth that Lawrence never amounted to anything and will soon be forgotten. It almost looks as if certain people *want* him to be forgotten. There is not even a birth plaque or memorial of any kind to him in his native town.

Meanwhile the other Lawrence has bloomed into a national hero and is commemorated by a public monument in St. Paul's Cathedral, London; and there is no end to the skillful publicity. It would be unfortunate if either of the two Lawrences were disparaged for the benefit of the other. Yet the process of making T. E. Lawrence into a national hero seems to include the belittling or the ignoring of D. H. Lawrence by quasi-official methods. I cannot recollect that any official or even influential person has ever said one word in favor of D. H. Lawrence, with the solitary exception of the Probate Judge who decided the intestacy case and referred to him as "a distinguished man." There are not so many great figures in twentieth-century England that it can afford to despise any of them, and they certainly may be proud of D. H. Lawrence. The prejudice against Shelley did not abate until a quarter of a century after his death (yet I have heard an old-fashioned Englishman say that Shelley was "a public scandal"!) and probably that period must elapse before D. H. Lawrence achieves his just fame in his own country.

I was never one of the Lawrence "inner group." I knew him in London in prewar days and saw him several times through Amy Lowell, who had a genuine admiration for his work and was anxious that the contributors to her anthology should be on good terms with one another. Thereafter my life crossed his from time to time almost by accident, and it was the merest coincidence that I was twice able to stave off official interference with him. I never told him, because I knew it would have a bad effect on him; though from passages in his letters I suspect he did learn from someone else. I know there was an inner tragedy in Lawrence's life which will one day be explained, but I can't help feeling that these exterior annoyances (not to overstate) contributed to his "psychological defeat."

The hostility of the smut-hounds in England needs no explanation. Americans are familiar with these disagreeable canines (so frequently of the female sex) though they are now pretty well muzzled here. But that prosecution in 1915 harmed Lawrence's reputation and finances seriously. The fact that he had been successfully prosecuted for obscenity was a powerful weapon in the hands of his literary enemies. (It must always be remembered that Lawrence was practically the first great writer of the genuine working class England has produced; that he proudly refused to truckle to his "social superiors"; and that this was an unforgivable offense.) On the financial side it hit him hard. Before the prosecution, he had received as much as one thousand five hundred dollars advance for the English rights alone of a novel. Until the *Lady Chatterley* scandal made him profitably notorious, I think he never got more than five hundred thereafter, and I have more than once heard him say that but for America he couldn't have lived. In the middle of 1918 the Lawrences were very near starving.

The origins of the "spy" nonsense are easier to understand than the persistence of the delusion in the official mind. Imagine a harassed Military Authority in 1917; the growing submarine campaign against merchantmen; the French insistence on stringent action against spy activities in England; a man with a German wife, who sings German songs, who is disliked by the suspicious Cornish, who is alleged to be an author of obscene and subversive tendencies. . . . In wartime there is no time to investigate queer exceptions. But after the war, it should have been obvious even to the official mind that the whole charge was a grotesque error. Yet so persistent was the official prejudice against him that until recently the British Broadcasting Company would not allow his name to be mentioned. There was a rumor at one time that a well-known English author resigned his position as book commentator rather than submit to this restriction on his liberty of speech. Since then I have listened to an attack on Lawrence's prose style by that master of creative and imaginative prose, Mr. Desmond MacCarthy; and I have heard Lawrence quoted in a broadcast without acknowledgment.

There seem to be many Americans who believe that Lawrence's work is on the way to oblivion, the fate so ardently desired for it in his own country. I don't believe it. The curve of every writer's reputation and influence fluctuates, and usually falls to a low before it begins gradually to rise to its true permanent level. For various reasons the Lawrence curve is low and may fall lower, but he will not be forgotten. His personality is too remarkable; his work, though uneven, too original and vivid, for such a fate. But it is a fact that nobody can form an accurate judgment of Lawrence's achievement by reading a few of his books at hazard. The only way to do that is to read the whole lot in chronological order with constant reference to the Letters. Only thus can a reader become fully acquainted with the strange and sometimes very beautiful spirit of the last of the individualists.

MEMORIES OF YEATS

by Mary M. Colum

In a land tormented by political contention, Irish poets, play-wrights, and authors found that their works were inevitably being judged in terms of nationalist issues instead of on their own merits.
William Butler Yeats, the mystic Hibernian, was in the midst of the turmoil. This sympathetic and exciting memoir was written after the poet's death by the wife of Padraic Colum. As Mary Maguire, she was a young student and admirer of Yeats in Dublin during the first years of this century. Later, as Mary M. Colum, she became famous as a writer and literary critic.

FEBRUARY 25, 1939

Cast a cold eye
On life, on death,
Horseman pass by.
> (Yeats's lines for his tombstone from his last poem)

THESE ARE STRANGE lines for the epitaph of a poet who never cast a cold eye on life or death. The last time I saw W. B. Yeats was in June 1938, in his house outside Dublin. He came into the room with his well-remembered, eager step, speaking in his well-remembered, eager voice. But he was changed. Old age that had left him so long untouched was making inroads on his physique. The old energy now came only in flashes. One of his eyes was covered with a black patch; it was blind, and he could use only one eye. "We are both changed," he said, examining me with his one eye. "You were once my ideal of a youthful nihilist." This was what he used to say to me in my student days when I was so delighted to be Yeats's ideal of anything that I didn't care what the word meant. Nihilism was the romantic form of revolt in Yeats's early days; his friend, Oscar Wilde, had made a first play about Vera, the girl nihilist. I think, vaguely, in his mind it represented a youthful fighting spirit that went with reading Russian novels, French Symbolist poetry, and Nietzsche. To attribute to anyone a fighting spirit was Yeats's most heartfelt compliment.

It was wonderful in those student days, after a day's listening to some minor professor treating literature as if it was sawdust, to go to one of the clubs where Yeats frequently held forth, and hear him talk of art and literature and life and read poetry, especially the poetry of the men he had known. "I am the last of a doomed generation," he was fond of saying. That doomed generation included the men of the nineties—in England, Dowson, Oscar Wilde, Lionel Johnson, Ernest Henley, Aubrey Beardsley, John Davidson; in France, it included Verlaine—not Mallarmé. Contrary to what I have seen in print several times in this country, Yeats never knew Mallarmé, never went to Mallarmé's Tuesday evenings; all the criticism of his poetry built on the notion that he took any part in the celebrated discussions of the Mallarmé group is unrelated to reality. He never knew any language except English and had no firsthand acquaintance with French literature—symbolist or any other species. But he had met and talked with Verlaine in English and has left a record of the meeting. He knew all the poets who had met a miserable end and he would repeat their poems—Dowson's, Johnson's, Wilde's, or he would repeat Blake or some Elizabethan like Nashe.

Sometimes he would give a formal lecture on poetry or drama. To look back on the situations he was in during those years convinces one that the life of the real artist is always a battle, particularly in the case of a great artist like Yeats, who tried to reform the literary and intellectual life of his country and his period. He was bitterly attacked in Dublin during the heyday of the literary movement; he was so different from other people in his ideas and even in his appearance that they were exasperated by him. Sunk in dreams, he would pass friends or acquaintances in the street with an unseeing eye; he did not consider that many people knew much about poetry, and his assumption of this in his numerous public speeches in the clubs and literary societies of the town got people's backs up. Then there were a number of older literary men who would get up and contradict him at every assembly and tell the audience that literature or poetry could wait—the main cause being the fight for freedom, and the business of literature was to advance the national aspirations.

Until Yeats made himself literary dictator, the subject of discussion at literary gatherings in Ireland was not literature but patriotic ideologies. When he informed us that lines like

> For thy hapless fate, dear
> Ireland,
> And sorrows of my own

were but conventional sentiment and could not move us deeply, when he became mocking about "Believe me if all those endearing young charms that I gaze on so fondly to-day" and similar effusions of the national poet, Tom Moore, he reduced over half of his audience to almost speechless rage. Somebody would recover sufficiently to say that Yeats was living in an ivory tower and all the other things men say when they are faced by somebody who takes the discipline of art seriously. At some of the societies and clubs where he spoke he would make an address so stirring intellectually and artistically that the ideas and the words became a lifetime's possession for some of us. But it would be some other speaker, who delivered himself of the humanitarian and political platitudes in fashion, who would be congratulated by the audience.

The newspapers were, nearly all of them, against him and his ideas; even often such an intelligent journal as Arthur Griffiths' *United Irishman* which later became *Sinn Fein*. Some of the critiques of his most lovely poems both in England and Ireland were ignorant and contemptuous. In Dublin, in the university groups, a few progressive-minded professors supported him; among the students, a group that were considered wild and eccentric were his followers. I was the president of a small Students' Literary Society which followed him around from one hall to another wherever he was to speak, and applauded with hands and feet. The plays in the Abbey Theatre were so sparsely attended that when the members of this Society entered in a body—we were about ten or twelve in number—the audience was appreciably augmented, and Yeats would cast a pleased eye on us. We could be depended on to listen ecstatically to every line of a verse play; we went, not only to all the plays, but to all the performances of them. Some of our professors a hundred and fifty years after Lessing were still talking about the rules of composition. When, in Synge's *Riders to the Sea*, the body of the drowned man was brought on the stage, certain professors pronounced this against all the rules of art, and one of the most enlightened of the political weeklies invariably referred to the play as "a corpse-curtain-raiser."

The country Yeats faced had had its intellectual life twisted awry with political and defensive preoccupations and its artistic life made anemic through the writers' making themselves mere auxiliaries of political leaders. When writers are too feeble to be able to give artistic statement to great human experiences, they are too likely to swim with the tide and indulge ineffectually in the social and political platitudes that are the fashion. There is nothing for an innovator to do but fight these: Yeats was a wonderful fighter—eager, sardonic, tireless—and he was at his very best when fighting for another man's work. The fight he put up for *The Playboy of the Western World* was an exhibition of fighting strategy, of immovable courage, of indifference to public hostility such as I have never seen anywhere in anybody else. At the opening night of *The Playboy* the first act went well, but as the performance went on the uproar began. The man near me who began the hissing was Francis Sheehy-Skeffington, and he was neither narrow-minded nor puritanical. Why did he hiss? Why did the theater in the end become a swaying mass of angry humanity? I never knew; it was something I could not understand. Yeats was lecturing in England on the opening night; he was telegraphed for, for he alone could handle the trouble and cope with the insistence for the withdrawal of the play. Back he came; he announced that the play would continue for the advertised number of performances; he lined the theater with police and forced a hearing for Synge's play. Synge himself, his face drawn and blenched, would from the front seats from time to time throw a furtive glance at the audience. The demand for withdrawal continued; Yeats announced—these were his words—that neither the house nor the race that bred him had given him a pliant knee, and he was not going to bend before the public. After the play's run had been completed, he told them, he would throw the theater open for discussion of the play.

On the night of the public discussion the streets near the Abbey were crowded with police and there was an excitement as if a revolution had started. A motley mixture of workmen, students, and bourgeoisie in evening dress filled the theater, most of them with denunciatory speeches ready to deliver. Yeats took the platform in full evening dress and faced the crowd. Step by step he interpreted the play, delivering in the process some of his most complex theories of art, one moment cowing the audience, the next shouted down by them. The author of the play, who was no fighter of this kind, stayed at home. When the usual speech about freedom, patriotism, came from somebody in the stalls, the audience cheered. But even

on the patriotics Yeats was equal to them. "The author of 'Cath-
leen ni Houlihan addresses you," he said. The audience, remembering that passionately patriotic play, forgot its antagonism for a few
minutes, and Yeats got his cheers. At one moment a student supporter of his took the platform beside Yeats and made a remark
which caused nearly all of the few women in the audience to walk
out. Myself and another girl student were the only members of the
female sex in sight: we were surrounded by a group of angry males
ordering us, if we were virtuous girls, to leave the theater. We stood
our ground, and Yeats, who, in spite of his well-publicized dimness
of vision, could always see when it suited him, saw our difficulties
from the platform and sent a couple of theater attendants to escort
us to the stalls among the men in evening dress, who, however, did
not regard us with a friendly eye, either. I never witnessed a human
being fight as Yeats fought that night, nor never knew another with
so many weapons in his armory. He was then in his forties, but he
looked under thirty, a fearless, dominating man in spite of, or perhaps because of, all his dreams and visions and esoteric philosophy.

In the end he won every battle, as men of unbending artistic and
intellectual integrity are likely to do. What was he battling for?
Perhaps only a few understood, perhaps it never could be completely stated. In one of his poems to the beautiful, stormy woman
—as great a fighter as himself—to whom his love poetry was written,
he cries:

> *My darling cannot understand*
> *What I have done, or what would do*
> *In this blind, bitter land.*

And yet a great poet of his type, an intellectual and artistic reformer, would certainly have more opposition in a larger country,
might have found such a place also a "blind and bitter land."

But all the fighting he had to do must have altered his personality, for the friends of his twenties would talk of the warmhearted,
affectionate, ingenuous boy, while the man we knew was hard,
strong, reserved, deliberately living behind a mask, that particular
mask which, as he has explained to us, all artists must find for
themselves. People who expected to find in him the ordinary simplicities or the ordinary complexities were disappointed and even
exasperated. He was very hard to understand; it was hard to cor-

relate the fighting man with the poet, the administrator with the
visionary, the "smiling public man" with the believer in astrology,
spiritism, in nonhuman presences, and in magic. But he was one of
those philosophers, adepts, or initiates who believe that all that
mankind has ever believed in was true and lasting, existing somewhere, in some realm of knowledge that could be entered.

He had the hard Irish memory for wrongs once done him; I
doubt if he ever forgot a friendly deed or forgave a wrong. I think
that if he loved or liked any person it was for always. The Greeks,
he sometimes said, thought it as great a virtue to hate your enemies
as to love your friends; he did both. Like the Greeks, too, he hated
old age, and through his later poems runs his resentment that the
great energy that was his in his strong manhood was flickering away
and could be less and less relied upon to support the tireless efforts
of his mind:

> *Consume my heart away; sick with desire*
> *And fastened to a dying animal*
> *It knows not what it is; and gather me*
> *Into the artifice of eternity.*

Like Swift, he has written his epitaph. That last poem which has
the epitaph for its conclusion—it appeared in *The Irish Independent* but has not yet been published here—is full of the old fighting
spirit:

> *Know that when all words are said*
> *And a man is fighting-mad,*
> *Something drops from eyes long blind,*
> *He completes his partial mind,*
> *For an instant stands at ease,*
> *Laughs aloud, his heart at peace,*
> *Even the wisest man grows tense*
> *With some sort of violence*
> *Before he can accomplish fate,*
> *Know his work or choose his mate.*
>
> *Irish poets, learn your trade,*
> *Sing whatever is well made,*
> *Scorn the sort now growing up*
> *All out of shape from toe to top,*

Their unremembering hearts and heads
Base-born products of base beds.

Cast your mind on other days
That we in coming days may be
Still the indomitable Irishry.

This, I think, is his last finished poem, his testament.

AMY LOWELL

by William Rose Benét

Poet, critic, biographer, "a firm friend and a frank opponent"—
Amy Lowell as remembered by a fellow poet.

MAY 23, 1925

THE SHOCK OF THE sudden death of Amy Lowell still numbs the
hearts of her friends. But it has thrust home the realization of her
greatness. In less than fifteen years she produced a body of work to
which she set the impressive seal in her recent two-volume life of
Keats. Her poetry now remains to us in many volumes, rich in variegated color, remarkable in variety of rhythm, superb in vigor and
originality. Two books of appreciation and criticism of French and
American poets illustrate her keen critical faculty and her absorbing
interest in her contemporary craftsmen both here and abroad. The
Keats demonstrates her power of penetration into the soul of the
literature of the ages, the thoroughness of her knowledge of the
past, her keenly discriminating faculty of appreciation of one great
literary age in terms of another.

It was Amy Lowell's thorough familiarity with the world's heritage of great English literature, coupled with the powerful originality of her creative imagination, that enabled her to pioneer successfully and advance the frontiers of poetry. Her work enlarges the
estates of the Muses. She cast new material into new molds. Her avid
intelligence seized upon the pictorial world about her and the great
store of untouched myth and legend in the past and created out of it
every kind of poetry, from the briefest fragments of vivid observation
to the most elaborate orchestration of glowing romance and grotesque myth. She touched the austere and delicate beauty of New
England with new magic, wrought startlingly in the *macabre,* dramatically in dialect, made banners crackle, armor clank, and satins
rustle audibly from the "storied past." She ransacked all epochs. She
adapted from the Chinese and Japanese. She ran the gamut of ono-
matopoeia, adventured in every possible effect of rhythm, and
created many new patterns of verse. She spread her palette with rain-

bow color, and juxtaposed hue and hue with spectacular brilliance.

Such generalizations about her work rise immediately to the mind of one who always rejoiced in her extraordinary versatility, in the gusto of her achievement as a painter with words. Never has there been a practitioner of a craft more worthy of the title of artist. Fortunate enough to be able to devote her entire life to labor in a chosen domain of art, she made that labor unremitting. She concentrated every faculty upon what she conceived to be the most perfect expression of what she had to say. And beside this she devoted herself whole-heartedly to the advancement of an aesthetic standard.

In the period during which she championed certain new poetic theories she proved herself by far the intellectual superior of the majority of her opponents, intrepid in her attack upon false values wherever she discovered them, a courageous foe of slackness and humbug. She restated forcibly and freshly eternal principles of art and was a tremendously energizing influence in contemporary poetry.

In what was to be her last work, she set herself an exhausting task of scholarship, for her mind was always on the march, ever contemplating the conquest of new territory. Even with the assistance of secretaries, the meticulous care, the assiduous research, the strenuous re-creative process that resulted in the world's definitive biography of Keats, were a heavy drain upon a constitution already undermined by illness. She brought her task to triumphant completion. Another age lived vividly in her pages. But its reconstruction had sapped her strength.

Amy Lowell was a firm friend and a frank opponent. Her feminine sensitiveness went masked by an almost masculine forthrightness, and beneath occasional abruptness and belligerency she concealed true and warm kindness of heart. She hated sham in every form, sham emotion, sham aesthetics, sham scholarship, sham opinions. She expressed herself forcibly but honestly. She was ever ready with aid and counsel for younger poets. She lived in a clean, clear world of the mind, rejoicing in the exercise of an unusual taste and an unusual intelligence. And yet she was also a dominating woman of the world with a natural executive and administrative gift that many men might have envied.

If to be American—aside from the thoroughly American lineage that was hers—should happen to mean to love spiritual freedom, to exercise inspired ingenuity, to constantly discriminate between code and mere convention, to exult in the abundant richness of life,

to fight for an unpopular principle, to go intrepidly forward, sur-
mounting obstacles in the search for new horizons, Amy Lowell was
in her art a great American. Intensely cultivated, she was also
properly eccentric (being possessed of genius) to the formal emptiness of much of the life around her. She gave and demanded constant
mental stimulus. She shouldered the responsibilities of the artist,
which may be other than the responsibilities of the average person,
but are (what the average person rarely understands) every whit as
onerous.

I admired and admire her because she always carried with her the
zest of intellectual conflict; my affection goes out to her in memory
because of many instances of graciousness. Benefactions of the spirit
are difficult to render or acknowledge. And sometimes we were far
enough from accepting each other's theories. Sometimes we were
both belligerent. But I acknowledge many benefactions, of rapier-
keen analysis, of priceless characterization, of sudden unexpected
blunt bits of praise that dwell in the memory.

That high-hearted, straight-gazing, often smilingly savage antagonist is gone. Private kindnesses in multitude she hid behind
seeming truculence. In the immediate past one grieved to see her
worn in constant service to her art, proceeding gallantly despite
sickness and ill-health. She had achieved a shrewd philosophy, without sentimentality, but full of charity. The little, brittle bickering
of the mere formalists and the pedants had long since impatiently
been brushed aside. All that mattered was to continue to create at
one's highest pitch.

And often, how courtly an antagonist! And, God, how she praised
this world! Has the world, that often made such a cheap and silly
mock of a few piquant eccentricities, any conception of how royally
her burning view of its cities, seas, clouds, flowers, sunsets, of its
history and lineage and legend repaid it? Well, her pictures have
durable color. They will remain to stimulate the observation and
inspire the technique of other generations. She knew the proper uses
of her pen. She rode a high horse on the King's Highway of Art. A
great lady, a great opponent, a great friend! Her head is still high,
her spirit is still riding.

GILBERT KEITH CHESTERTON

by Hilaire Belloc

*In his own country G. K. Chesterton was the center of a mild
storm of religious controversy when he became sympathetic with
Catholicism. He was converted in 1922 and thereafter wrote many
books in defense of the faith. Hilaire Belloc, historian, some of
whose books were illustrated by Chesterton, reflects bitterly on
the treatment his lifelong friend received at the hands of his coun-
trymen.*

JULY 4, 1936

GILBERT KEITH CHESTERTON was both a literary figure and a political influence of far greater stature than his somewhat bewildered
contemporaries in England today have as yet appreciated. I stood the
other day at his graveside, at the graveside of this, the last to die of
my intimate personal friends from the friendships formed in early
manhood—which are the strongest in the world—and I marveled at
the nature of the mourners there assembled. I marveled not at their
exiguity, for they were very many—nor at their lack of distinction,
for there was among them the greatest modern writer of English
prose, Max Beerbohm; one of the most famous of the modern
young men, Aldous Huxley; the chief of the Catholic communion
in England, the archbishop of Westminster, who officiated at the
Requiem and at the order of burial that followed. It was a great
and an impressive gathering. But it had not in it those who should
impersonally represent society as a whole. The only official representative of anything corporate was the High Commissioner for the
Irish Free State. What an irony that he alone should be there, of
official figures! He was indeed most worthily there, for Gilbert Chesterton had always been alive with understanding of the Irish people, he had stood in his later years overtly for that religion in the
defense of which they have almost perished but which they have

survived to defend, establish, and propagate throughout the world.

It would be, I think, to any visitor from the continent of Europe an incomprehensible thing that this very great Englishman should have been passing through the funeral rites which should be and commonly are of national moment when national figures pass, and that there should be no trace of national recognition.

We have in this country an official press, for everything that counts is with us official; we have in particular one daily paper, *The Times,* which is openly and by definition official. Its memorial upon the dead man omitted all that was of importance in him—I have elsewhere called it with justice negligible.

I have written thus at the beginning of what I have to say not from a passing surprise or indignation, not as a mere expression of detached emotion, but as a text for what the man was and will be. He was the most English of Englishmen; but because he stood on one side of a certain line of cleavage which runs through all modern Europe, and grows in distinction and profundity with every passing day, he was not officially recognized by his country. Though he was devoted to that country with a simple and permanent filial affection based on a complete comprehension of it, though he was typical of it in every function of his mind and in all his habits, it looked at him somewhat askance and it treated him as in some way exceptional or alien. The line of cleavage of which I speak is the line dividing not so much the Catholic faith as the Catholic culture from its opponents. Official England is strongly rooted in opposition to the Catholic culture, and because Gilbert Chesterton had stood during all his active life upon the one side of the hedge, in sympathy with the Catholic culture and with all its products, because he had in the last issue openly declared himself a member of the alien communion, therefore did official England pretend that he was something other than he was. That official neglect was a most memorable gesture, and one the more memorable because in England it has passed almost unperceived.

As I so watched the farewell given on his own soil to this very great man, I asked myself a question which many are asking who knew how great he was: What will the future of that name be?

There will be nothing of greater interest in our local world, over here at this moment, than to watch the development of that future fame. Not that I shall see it, I am too old; he was even four years younger than I; but my children will begin to see the thing at work, and my grandchildren will see it finally registered. He wrote in the

English tongue, and though that is now so widely spread, he wrote at first only for an English public, piercing later to English-speaking publics elsewhere. He wrote wholly for the purpose of being heard by that public of his fellow citizens with whom he was in such deep communion. It was this which made him so difficult to translate into any other language; and though the scale of the man was soon recognized upon the continent of Europe, notably in France, his idiom was always entirely that of his birth and surroundings, of his family tradition, and of that group of things which belongs wholly to England and cannot properly be known save to men of the English experience.

I knew him, I think, as well as any man ever knew another, not only from the depth of my affection, nor only for the intimacy and very long acquaintance of that intimacy—close on forty years—you may say the lifetime of a man, but most of all because so thoroughly did my mind jump with his, so fully did his answer meet the question my own soul was always asking, that his conclusions, the things he found and communicated, his solutions of the great riddles, his stamp of certitude, were soon part of myself. Therefore the testimony I bear to him is true.

There was in this communion between us something of heredity, and here I must be pardoned, against all modern convention, a personal note. I was brought up wholly by my mother, and in England: my father died before I can remember. Now, my mother derived directly from that English middle class of yeomen and liberal stock which in literature and the arts, in law and even in arms, in merchant enterprise, and, most of all, in metaphysical and religious speculation, has determined the character of England from the moment of the Puritan triumph three hundred years ago. We were millers and small landowners of Warwickshire—of the Midlands—Nonconformist, originally Puritan, later skeptical, ending in Unitarianism. It was almost more a corporation than a class, it prided itself most justly on its high culture, its possession of the classics, its pure breed, its intense nationalism. Such was my stock.

Well, that was just the social stock from which Gilbert Chesterton also came. From the years in which a man first begins to strengthen and grow roots, from the late twenties, when we first met each other, each knew that the other had in him that foundation. I had been born of a woman drawn from that same blood, and brought by sheer power of brain into the Catholic Church.

I was not when I first met him as alive to the strength of that word *Catholic* as I am today; I myself have gone through a pilgrim-age of approach, to a beginning at least of understanding in the matter; but it was never my good fortune to bear witness by the crossing of a frontier: a public act. Such good fortune was his. I was born within the walls of the City of God: he saw it, approached it, knew it, and entered. I know not which is for the run of men the better fate, but his was certainly of our two fates the better. Having said so much in this matter, I will leave it, for it is too personal and has been too prolonged.

Gilbert Chesterton spent his life not in the search for truth but in the continual extensive and additional discovery thereof. Truth had for him the immediate attraction of an appetite. He was hungry for reality. But what is much more, he could not conceive of him-self except as satisfying that hunger; it was not possible to him to hesitate in the acceptation of each new parcel of the truth; it was not possible for him to hold anything worth holding that was not con-nected with the truth as a whole. Hence that strange consistency, which had at once the simplicity of childhood and the complexity of the very wise, and which marked him throughout the whole of his life.

What was much more to his fellow beings even than this passion for what is, with the corresponding rejection, instinctive and total, of confusion almost as much as falsehood, was the driving power moving his spirit to disseminate what he knew.

To him should more fully apply than to any other of our con-temporaries the capital sentence "The business of a man is to dis-cover reality, and having discovered it to hand it on to his fellows." For this task he had happily been furnished with instruments of the most powerful kind, and it is to these that I would direct par-ticularly the attention of those who may read me here. I would so direct them particularly because among his sheaf of talents, corus-cating and gleaming with a multiple gleaming, there were those which might distract from the central thing. He played so much with the forms of the English language, he so much loved a jest, and that exuberant vitality of his was so passionately filled with the sense of adventure that the central thing in him—power of proof—may not be as apparent as it should be. For it was not only the cen-tral thing, it was the whole meaning of his work. I say of his work, not of his life. The whole meaning of his *life* was the discovery, the appreciation, of reality. But his *work* was made up of bequeathing to others the treasure of knowledge and certitude upon which he had come.

For it has been well and universally said by all those who knew him that side by side with and a product of that immense exuberance in happiness not only of himself but of all around, of that vital rejoicing not only in man but in every other work of God and in God Himself, the most conspicuous fruit was generosity.

One of his contemporaries writing in these very days, moved by his death, has said publicly this exceedingly true thing. "He squandered, because he was a millionaire." He gave of himself and all that he had, and there was so strongly gushing so high a spring within him that his generosity was continual and universal. He could write on all things because he was in the spirit of all things and from this central position he could explain, predicate, and give peace.

The possessions of his mind, literary, historical, political, domestic, and foreign, were not only those of the cultivated man in the society to which he was born, that English society which he understood so thoroughly and which he attempted to save; they were also possessions held in a certain balance, in a certain proportion, with certain values which made the whole body of them not only a living unity but a just unity. He exaggerated in nothing save in emphasis of expression when rhetoric demanded. In statement of truth he did not and could not exaggerate because truth, which was his sole concern, is of its nature absolute.

Nor was he an advocate—and what a thing it is to be able to say of any writer or speaker in England today that he does not advocate but tells. Nearly all that men say and write with us is mere advocacy. In our public life the thing has grown to be a universal disease. All is special pleading and special pleading undertaken as is the special pleading of the lawyer—that is, undertaken for personal gain. We attempt to obtain the truth on any matter, even on small practical matters, by the new strange process of reading contradictory falsehoods proffered by opposing brief-holders—commonly hired. We think that in a balance between the two unreal extremes we may grope at something approaching fact. In the midst of such a chaos Chesterton's voice and pen proclaimed not selected evidence but the thing that *was;* the thing that he saw and knew.

Since this was the leading passion of his mind, to discover, to prove, and to proclaim, it followed of necessity that gain was adventitious to the affair. Gain was necessarily present, for his audience grew larger and larger, continuing until the last hour and certainly destined to increase further and further yet as the years proceed. Such an output, such an audience, such a consequent circulation, meant, under our capitalistic production, gain for all those who undertook the mechanism of it and necessarily gain for himself. But gain could not be his motive. He was not capable of entertaining that motive side by side with the motive of expression. Save in the case of a few rich men, most of them futile, I know of no other among his contemporaries to which this judgment applies. We all work for our living; so did he, but the living came as a result of the work; the desire, or even the necessity for it, did not produce the work. Others also would now and then do work separate from their ordinary in order to feel for once free from economic necessity. The poets have for the most part withdrawn themselves from that necessity, and here and there some fastidious writer under the advantage of a private fortune has done the same. But this man was the extreme opposite of the fastidious. This man was never withdrawn from his fellows. This man spoke aloud in the market place and spoke continually and yet was not of the market.

So worked under such conditions and inspired by motives so singular to himself this high contemporary, living wholly in an air of freedom, acting only under his own will in a day when, particularly in the world of letters, wills have become so much enslaved that the very quality of freedom is forgotten.

When I consider the various manifestations of his spirit, how clear the central nature of that spirit becomes! His ceaseless setting down with the pencil of human character, for example. The sketches lie in profusion; scores of his friends can bring forward sets of them. They lie finished and half finished all around him as it were, scattered along the whole of that long path which he trod with such triumphant happiness from his beginning to his earthly end. The faces of every kind of man and woman in the wide world he knew, all characters, all absurdities, many virtues, not a few dignities of English life, fell from that pencil, as might verdure from a tree, without effort, part of himself perpetually produced—scattered at will and penetrating to the very roots of England.

I return to that theme which in writing of this man it is impossible to forget or to abandon, England. He knew her present peril, he knew the cause of her peril, he was tireless in exposing and correcting those causes. Nor is this unhappily today a passport to England's gratitude. Whenever was it a passport to the gratitude of a society that its peril should be emphasized, ridiculed, denounced with high rhetoric, checked or seared with scorn? Now Gilbert Chesterton throughout his life was on the side of those who at so much risk determined to reverse if reversed it could be the current of the time. All around him was a society which had determined upon the opposite and fatal course—hiding its weakness—and of erecting an imaginary world that should satisfy foreign critics and lull its own confidence in security. Against that official mask he pleaded and laughed continually. But alas, it was against a mask that he laughed, to the cardboard ears of a mask that he pleaded, and on the empty, scissor-slit eyes of a mask that he gazed. If any man could have reversed the current he could have done so; but there would seem to be a fatality in all this, and, evils having been entered into, it would seem that they must bear their fruit, unless indeed there should be repentance. What collective repentance has ever been known? Penance it would seem is for individuals, and happy indeed such individuals who can perform it, for the most part they must "dree their weird" and perhaps all nations will dree their weird more surely than individuals do.

I wonder whether in times to come men looking back upon the present crisis of our national fortunes will not see some connection between the moment through which we are passing in those fortunes and the loss at that moment of this great spirit. In two senses of course he is not lost, neither to the England which he so loved nor to ourselves: in the lesser sense that the living word is never lost he continues, in the greater sense that the living soul lives for ever and is secure he continues. And we are secure in that knowledge. But there goes through me some thrill of fatality when I think that this life ended, just in that phase of our society during which it has manifestly failed to redeem itself and has met that failure by nothing more than empty boasting and puerile falsehood.

O dear and sacred head! Companion, champion, and friend! The greatest master of the prose word among the pagans said:

> If there be some place of groves, as our fathers loved to imagine, wherein the spirits of the just may take their peace, there shall I find you.

But he and I were not pagans. I use no if. Whether I shall attain the permanent places I know not, nor does any man; but he has attained them.

EDNA ST. VINCENT MILLAY

by John Ciardi

One of the brightest stars of American poetry during the twenties died in 1950 at the age of fifty-eight. Although she had published relatively little during the later years of her life, more than a score of volumes of her verse remain in print, including Renascence, *which first won her a following, and* The Harp-Weaver, *which won her the Pulitzer Prize in 1923. Saturday Review Poetry Editor John Ciardi appraises the poetry, and the things it stood for, of Edna St. Vincent Millay, "a figure of passionate living."*

NOVEMBER 11, 1950

POLITICAL HISTORIANS remember 1917 as the year in which the United States went to war to make the world safe for democracy. Literary historians recall it as a time of great stirring in American poetry. Ezra Pound and his followers were beginning to imagize. T. S. Eliot stood between "Prufrock" and "The Waste Land." Baudelaire was becoming an excitement in advance circles. Yeats was at the point of his best writing. Hopkins was about to be published. Joyce and Gertrude Stein had already brought their techniques far enough forward for E. E. Cummings, as a Harvard undergraduate, to have written an extremely perceptive assessment of their experiments and aims. In short, The Age of the Manifesto was upon us. Schools and movements were everywhere. The next ten years were to see them flower and fade quarterly, leaving behind them stacks of unread little magazines.

Into all this excitement and search for a new way of writing stepped twenty-five-year-old Edna St. Vincent Millay, who had just been graduated from Vassar and had just published a volume of verse called *Renascence*. Miss Millay brought forth her ballad stanzas, her archaic embellishment, and her sonnets in the grand manner. Perhaps not surprisingly, even her traditionalism was

enough to excite a school into being. Edna St. Vincent Millay became a name for a kind of lyric to be imitated wherever the female
heart beat fast.

Her popularity, easily won, was to continue through all the
twenties and—perhaps a sign of dangerous limitation or perhaps a
sign of fundamental power—was to reach beyond the "literary" to
something resembling the "public." Her reading appearances were
to become triumphs of trailing gowns and far-flung gestures. The
legend of her loves was to illuminate dreams from Keokuk to Salt
Lick.

Now Edna Millay is dead, and somehow the twenties, when some
of you were very young and some of us were children, are suddenly
sent splintering into antiquity. What a long way back it is to yesterday when Edna St. Vincent Millay was The Village and The Village
was Edna St. Vincent Millay, and you went back and forth all night
on the ferry, and I, still in knickers, read about it in Medford, Massachusetts, and daydreamed the wonders of the life being lived just
off Washington Square.

Or else it was just silly and adolescent with shouting on street
corners, and dreary recitals by bearded poets, and a great deal of
very high level small-talk by flat-chested girls in excruciating dresses.
But, silly or not, it was a time of tremendous vitality, and certainly
no one lived it more passionately and beguilingly—or so at least it
seemed to me, and so it must have seemed to thousands of adoles-
cents like me—than Edna St. Vincent Millay.

There are always two of every poet: one a person, the other a
presence contrived by the poems. Whatever the person is, the presence is something else, an aspect of the person or a series of aspects.
The reader of Edna Millay is easily confused in this since the person and the presence seem so bound up together, the legend of her
living so much a part of the poems. One reads the poems and thinks
he could walk down the street and identify their author on sight.

It is impossible, of course, to say whether or not Edna Millay's
poems will "survive"—whatever that means—but in the very immediacy with which one makes a person of the presence may lie the best
testimony to a creative achievement. For it is not good enough
simply to dismiss the issue by saying that the poems are autobiographical. Or if it is, it is only good enough if one realizes that
autobiography is not transcribed so much as it is invented. No one
can write all of himself; he must select, and every selection invents.
Whatever powers and whatever limitations are to be found in the

poems, their achievement is that they invented Edna St. Vincent Millay.

Almost, one is tempted to say nostalgically, they invented a decade. One knows this is an absurdity and yet one half-thinks it. One may as well say the raccoon coat invented the plastic age. No, what I am thinking is that she invented it (or somehow brought it alive) to me and certainly to many of my generation busy at their first fumblings and exaggerations.

I must have been nearing fifteen, a happy prowler in the dark stacks of our public library, when I began to pull down poetry from the shelves. About all the poetry I had behind me was Kipling and I was not sure but what he was too "young"—by which I meant I had read him more than six months ago. Then I found "The Man with the Hoe." That was a wonderful discovery: "Who loosened and let down this brutal jaw?" I would demand of my sisters. *Spoon River* was another: "Seeds in a dry pod, tick, tick, tick."—it was enough to make me feel like a critic. Then one day I opened *The Harp-Weaver* and came on "The Goose Girl":

> *Spring rides no horses down the hill,*
> *But comes on foot, a goose girl still*
> *And all the loveliest things there be*
> *Come simply, so it seems to me.*
> *If ever I said, in grief or pride,*
> *I tired of honest things, I lied;*
> *And should be cursed forevermore*
> *With Love in laces, like a whore,*
> *And neighbours cold, and friends unsteady,*
> *And Spring on horseback like a lady!*

Now there was a thing you could really recite: grief, pride, curses, whores! This was life! I began to read Millay avidly, to spout her endlessly. "What lips my lips have kissed." Mine hadn't kissed anything but the cheeks of aunts, but wasn't that part of the drama? "Euclid alone has looked on Beauty bare." How rich that was!

> *Let all who prate of Beauty hold their peace,*
> *And lay them prone upon the earth, and cease . . .*

What a sudden sense of life they released! Even the too-muchness was right. In retrospect, of course, one knows that it was exactly the too-muchness that was right, but what an excitement it was then to curl up with it in a corner of the stacks and wait for the time when you could recite it to a girl with the moon beside you or, perhaps more accurately, to the moon with a girl beside you. Certainly the moon comes first.

"The Goose Girl" still strikes me as the most typical of Edna Millay's poems, of the kind of presence she sought to invent. Its measure is cut to absolute simplicity; one thinks immediately of Housman, whose hand has surely touched Edna Millay's first poems. And immediately one senses a difference in the simplicity. "The Goose Girl" bears many surface resemblances to Housman's "Cherry Trees." The meter, the kind of language, the easy flow of the symbols, the imagery, all have a great deal in common. Yet Housman's poem remains convincing, and somehow "The Goose Girl" does not.

The difference occurs not in the way of saying but in the attitude of the saying, a point Robert Frost once made especially well in speaking of "the way the poet takes his subject, the way the poet takes himself." One is finally forced to distrust the way Edna Millay takes herself in this poem. One can believe without reservation that Housman wanted to walk out quietly to observe the cherry trees. His feeling for the false bloom of snow upon them is evoked beyond question. But can one feel the same conviction in the evocation of spring as the Goose Girl and the Lady on Horseback, or is the author being consciously picturesque? And when we are told that

> . . . all the loveliest things there be
> Come simply, so it seems to me,

not only the archaic use of *be* but the knowledge of Miss Millay's archness in so many of her other poems makes us wonder if this is not simply another pose. We doubt, and immediately the poem confirms our doubt by the burst of rhetoric that fills up the next five lines. This is not an experience, we conclude; it is a pose.

And poem after poem confirms this experience: there is always that element of the overdramatic about them, a fabrication of the words rather than of the feeling, of a posture rather than of an experience. It is, one suspects, exactly this in the poems that once set twenty years of undergraduates to imitating them. Something in the overstatement of the poems fitted our own imbalance. Perhaps that explains why I fell violently in love as a sophomore at Bates College

with our local Edna, or, more precisely, with the best of our local
Ednas, for even at so small a school as Bates there were at least two
dozen of them. Certainly something powerfully suited to our needs
grew at that edge of bathos.

> *I screamed, and—lo!—Infinity*
> *Came down and settled over me.*

Or in the coy first hungering for great sophistication:

> *After all, my erstwhile dear,*
> *My no longer cherished,*
> *Need we say it was not love,*
> *Just because it perished?*

It swaggered with us like our first self-conscious cigarettes, an endless, very fine portrait of ourselves being very wise.

It seems impossible now that we could have been so moved by
such lines. Or is it simply that we can never again be so moved by
anything? Whatever the truth of it, we were moved, we were filled,
we were taken.

Then somehow it was all over. The twenties had ended even for
those of us who were too young to do more than overhear the tail
end of their legend. Symbolically, Edna Millay's power to thrill and
carry the reader seemed to end with them. For what made the
poems immediate was the passionate youngness of their author.
And suddenly it was years later and the youngness had fled. One
read Auden and Spender instead, and as each of the new Millay
books appeared—*Wine from These Grapes, Conversation at Midnight, Huntsman, What Quarry?*—one wondered what had happened to the breathlessness and carry that used to be in the poems.

The simple fact seems to be that, having outgrown her youth,
Edna Millay had outgrown the one subject she could make exciting.
Conversation at Midnight was her attempt at intellectual reportage
of an age, but it provided no subject for her gift. It seemed as if
she had stopped living in order to talk—to talk endlessly and dully
—about life. There is still here and there the intense preoccupation
with herself, her body, the pose of her body, but where once we
read of the body in love we now read:

> *Over the sound of flushing water, which*
> *For some strange reason, science having gone so far,*

Even in the houses of the extremely rich
Still roars in a room, and everybody knows where you are. . . .

Instead of bright children on MacDougall Street,
Sons-of-bitches at Hialeah
hacking their initials in the royal palms . . .

Instead of the endless energy of the girl, we are presented the matron posing before her dressmaker who turns her about and is made to cry: *"Que Madame est maigré."*

Then came the war, and the social consciousness that had first driven her to write some of her worst poetry in *Justice Denied in Massachusetts* (the Sacco-Vanzetti trial) betrayed her into such books as *Make Bright the Arrows.* These are tragic books from which the last vestige of gift has disappeared; nobly to be sure, for reasons that all men of good will must be tempted to condone. But finally poetry must be protected from even the highest motives. Perhaps especially from the highest motives. Moral indignation is no substitute for art. In these poems, unfortunately, only that substitution speaks: line after line of exhortations from the vocabulary of humanism, page after page of moral platitudes, but not a phrase of poetry. We agreed that there were no islands left, we wept for Lidice, but the poems could not find our feelings. The facts themselves were so desperately more moving.

But to enumerate a poet's failures is not to judge him. A writer must be judged by his best. Edna Millay's best came at a time when many needed her excitement. Whether her capture of that audience was a good or a bad thing for the course of poetry one cannot say with any conviction. Certainly her intimate treatment of the frankly sensuous was some part of an age's contribution toward broadening the range of subjects permissible to poetry. That much is surely good. Certainly, too, the kind of poetry she set herself to write has found no followers except among the dim mediocrities of the Poetry Societies. And that cannot be good. But neither merit nor lack of merit defined her position in the poetry of the twenties. It was not as a craftsman or as an influence, but as the creator of her own legend that she was most alive for us. Her success was as a figure of passionate living.

Unfortunately, passion is nonreflective. At its slightest her passion made her the mother of the O-God-the-pain! girls, of the O-world-I-cannot-hold-thee-close-enough! school. And even at its best it is not likely that her work can be popular so long as poetry continues its present development toward the ambivalent consciousness and the pessimistic intellect. Perhaps her poems must be forgotten. Or perhaps they will become like *The Rubáiyát* and the *Sonnets from the Portuguese,* poems that generation after generation of the young will be swept away by, gorgeously, overwhelmingly swept away by, and then outgrow.

But today none of that seems to matter. One finds himself less inclined to criticism than to nostalgia. At least it will be so for all of us who were very young and very merry and aren't exactly that any more, but who once long ago opened those little black books with their titles pasted to the binding, and suddenly found the wind blowing through everybody's hair and a wonderful girl running to us through the wind. *"Que Madame est maigré."* But what a whirling all-night time it was!

HARLEM LITERATI
IN THE TWENTIES

by Langston Hughes

A delightful description of the growing pains of the new Negro intellectuals of that time, by the traveler, author, poet, lecturer, lyricist, biographer, and jazz buff (not necessarily in order of importance or chronology), James Langston Hughes.

JUNE 22, 1940

IN THE EARLY DAYS of the New Negro Renaissance, one summer, that of 1926, I lived in a rooming house on 137th Street in Harlem where Wallace Thurman and Harcourt Tynes lived, also. Thurman was then managing editor of *The Messenger,* a Negro magazine that had a curious career. It began by being very radical, very racial, and sort of socialistic just after the war. Later it became a kind of Negro society magazine and a plugger for Negro business, with photographs of prominent colored ladies and their nice homes. A. Philip Randolph, now President of the Brotherhood of Sleeping Car Porters, Chandler Owen, and George S. Schuyler were connected with the magazine. Schuyler's editorials, à la Mencken, were the most interesting things in *The Messenger*—verbal, vigorous brickbats. I asked Thurman what kind of magazine *The Messenger* was, and he said it reflected the policy of whoever paid off best at the time.

Anyway, *The Messenger* bought my first short stories, for which they paid ten dollars each. Wallace Thurman wrote me that they were very bad short stories, but better than any others they could find, so he published them.

Thurman had recently come from California to New York. He was a strangely brilliant black boy who had read everything—and whose critical mind could find something wrong with everything he read. He would like a book and then find a million faults in it. He would get from the library a great pile of volumes, go through them in less than a week, reading eleven lines at a glance, and be able to discuss each one at great length with anybody. That was why, I suppose, he was later given a job as a reader at Macaulay's —the only Negro reader, so far as I know, to be employed by any of the larger publishing firms.

Later Thurman became a ghost writer for *True Story* magazine and other publications, writing under all sorts of fantastic names like Ethel Belle Mandrake or Patrick Casey. He turned out Irish and Jewish and Catholic "True Confessions." He collaborated with William Jordan Rapp on plays and novels. Later he ghosted books. It has been said that he wrote blond Peggy Hopkins Joyce's *Men, Women, and Checks.*

Wallace Thurman wanted to be a great writer, but none of his own work ever made him happy. *The Blacker the Berry,* his first book, was an important novel on a subject little dwelt upon in Negro fiction—the plight of the very dark Negro woman who encounters in some communities a double wall of color prejudice, within and without the race. His play, *Harlem,* considerably distorted for box-office purposes, was, nevertheless, a compelling study—and the only one in the theater—of the impact of Harlem on a Negro family fresh from the South. And his *Infants of the Spring* was a bitter, but superb, portrayal of the bohemian fringe of Harlem's literary and artistic life.

Yet none of these works pleased Thurman. He wanted to be a writer like Gorki or Thomas Mann, and felt that instead he was merely a journalist. His critical mind, comparing his work with that of Proust, Melville, Tolstoy, Galsworthy, Dostoevski, Henry James, Hemingway, Romain Rolland, found it vastly wanting. So he took to writing a great deal for money, laughing the while bitterly at his fabulously concocted "true stories," creating two bad motion pictures of the "Adults Only" type for Hollywood, drinking more and more gin, and then threatening to jump out of windows at parties and kill himself.

During the summer of 1926, Wallace Thurman, Zora Neale Hurston, Aaron Douglas, John P. Davis, Bruce Nugent, Gwendolyn Bennett, and I decided to publish "a Negro quarterly of the arts" to be called *Fire*—the idea being that it would burn up a lot of the old, dead conventional Negro-white ideas of the past, *épater les bourgeois* into a realization of the existence of the younger Negro writers and artists, and provide us with an outlet for publication not available in the limited pages of the small Negro magazines then existing, *The Crisis, Opportunity,* and *The Messenger*—the first two being house organs of interracial organizations, and the latter being God knows what.

We met on torrid summer evenings to plan *Fire.* Each of us agreed to give fifty dollars to finance the first issue. Thurman was to edit it, John P. Davis to handle the business end, and Bruce Nugent to take charge of distribution. The rest of us were to serve as an editorial board to collect material, contribute our own work, and act in any useful way that we could. October came before we were ready to go to press. I had to return to Lincoln, John Davis to law school at Harvard, and Zora Hurston to her studies at Barnard—whence she went about Harlem with an anthropologist's ruler measuring heads for Franz Boas. Only three of the seven had contributed the stipulated fifty dollars, but the others faithfully promised to send it out of tuition checks, wages, or begging. Thurman went on with the work of preparing the magazine. He got a printer. He planned the layout. It had to be on good paper, he said, worthy of the drawings of Aaron Douglas. It had to have beautiful type, worthy of the first Negro art quarterly. It had to be what we seven young Negroes dreamed our magazine would be—so in the end it cost almost a thousand dollars—and nobody could pay the bills.

I don't know how Thurman persuaded the printer to let us have all the copies to distribute, but he did. I think Alain Locke, among others, signed notes guaranteeing payments. But since Thurman was the only one of the seven of us with a regular job, for the next three or four years his checks were constantly being attached and his income seized to pay the printer's bill. And whenever I sold a poem, the money went there, too—to *Fire.*

None of the older Negro intellectuals would have anything to do with *Fire.* Dr. Du Bois in *The Crisis* roasted it. The Negro press called it all sorts of bad names, largely because of a green and purple story by Bruce Nugent in the Oscar Wilde tradition which we had included. Rean Graves, the critic for the Baltimore *Afro-American* began his review by saying, "I have just tossed the first issue of *Fire* into the fire." Commenting upon various of our contributors, he said:

> Aaron Douglas, who, in spite of himself and the meaningless grotesqueness of his creations, has gained a reputation as an artist, is permitted to spoil three perfectly good pages and a cover with his pen and ink hudge-pudge. Countee Cullen has written a beautiful poem in his "From a Dark

Tower," but tries his best to obscure the thought in superfluous sentences. Edward Silvera is guilty of two poems. Langston Hughes, in three poems, displays his usual ability to say nothing in many words, willfully violating all the rules of poetics and still calling his work poetry.

So *Fire* had plenty of cold water thrown on it by the colored critics. The white critics (except for an excellent editorial in *The Bookman* for November 1926) scarcely noticed it at all. We had no way of getting it distributed to bookstands or newsstands. Bruce Nugent took it around New York on foot, and some of the Greenwich Village bookshops put it on display and sold it for us. But then, Bruce, who had no job, would collect the money and eat it up before he got back to Harlem.

Finally, irony of ironies, several hundred copies of *Fire* were stored in the basement of an apartment where an actual fire occurred and the bulk of the whole issue was burned up. Even after that Thurman had to go on paying the printer. Now *Fire* is a collector's item, and very difficult to get, being mostly ashes.

That taught me a lesson about little magazines. But since white folks had them, we Negroes thought we could have one, too. But we didn't have the money.

Wallace Thurman laughed a long bitter laugh. He was a strange kind of fellow who liked to drink gin but *didn't* like to drink gin, who liked being a Negro but felt it a great handicap, and who adored bohemianism but thought it was wrong to be a Bohemian. He liked to waste a lot of time, but he always felt guilty wasting time. About the future of Negro literature Thurman was very pessimistic. He thought the Negro vogue had made us all too conscious of ourselves, had flattered us and spoiled us, and had provided too many easy opportunities for some of us to drink gin and more gin on which he thought we would always be drunk from then on. With his bitter sense of humor, he called the Harlem literati the "niggerati."

Of this "niggerati" Zora Neale Hurston was certainly the most amusing. Only to reach a wider audience, need she ever write books —because she is a perfect book of entertainment in herself. In her youth she was always getting scholarships and things from wealthy white people, some of whom simply paid her just to sit around and represent the Negro race for them, she did it in such a racy fashion. She was full of side-splitting anecdotes, humorous tales, and tragicomic stories remembered out of her life in the South as a daughter of a traveling minister of God. She could make you laugh one minute and cry the next. To many of her white friends, no doubt, she was a perfect "darkie" in the nice meaning they give the term— that is, a naïve, childlike, sweet, humorous, and highly colored Negro.

But Miss Hurston was clever, too—a student who didn't let college give her a broad *a* and who had great scorn for all pretensions, academic or otherwise. That is why she was such a fine folk-lore collector, able to go among the people and never behave as if she had been to school at all. Nobody could stop the average Harlemite on Lenox Avenue and measure his head with a strange-looking anthropological device and not get bawled out for the attempt, except Zora—who used to stop anybody in the street whose head looked interesting, and measure it.

When Miss Hurston was graduated from Barnard she took an apartment in West 66th Street near the Park in that row of Negro houses there. She moved in with no furniture at all and no money, but in a few days friends had given her everything from decorative silver birds and genuine etchings to a linen cabinet and a footstool. And on Saturday night, to christen the place, she had a *hand-chicken* dinner, since she had forgotten to say she needed forks. She seemed to know almost everybody in New York. She had been a secretary to Fannie Hurst, and had met dozens of celebrities whose friendship she retained. Yet she was always having terrific ups-and-downs about money.

Strange thing about that Negro Renaissance that boomed and bloomed in Harlem. Practically none of the Negroes taking part in it were Harlemites. Jessie Fauset was from Philadelphia, Charles S. Johnson from Virginia, Arna Bontemps from California, Countee Cullen from Kentucky, Aaron Douglas from Kansas, Wallace Thurman from Salt Lake City, Rudolph Fisher from Washington, Walter White from Atlanta, Paul Robeson from New Jersey, Ethel Waters from Philadelphia, Richmond Barthé from New Orleans.

But Harlem was like a great magnet for the Negro intellectual, pulling him from everywhere. Or perhaps the magnet was New York—but once in New York, he had to live in Harlem for rooms were hardly to be found elsewhere unless one could pass for white, or Mexican, or Eurasian, and perhaps live in the Village—which always seemed to me a very arty locale, in spite of the many real artists and writers who lived there. Only a few of the New Negroes lived in the Village, Harlem being their real stamping ground.

The wittiest of these New Negroes, the one whose tongue was flavored with the sharpest and saltiest humor, was Rudolph Fisher, whose stories appeared in *The Atlantic Monthly*. His novel, *Walls of Jericho*, captures but slightly the raciness of his own conversation. A doctor and X-ray specialist, who always frightened me a little because he could think of the most excessively clever things to say—and I could never think of anything to answer. He and Alain Locke together were great for intellectual wisecracking. The two would fling big and witty words about with such swift and punning innuendo that an ordinary mortal just sat and looked wary for fear of being caught in a net of clever witticisms.

IVAN BUNIN

by Essad Bey

*Exiled, the Russian poet and novelist Ivan Bunin underwent a
depressing, aimless, lonely existence in a foreign land. Yet he wrote
his finest work under these unhappy conditions. Essad Bey, who
was personally acquainted with Bunin, wrote several books on
Russia.*

DECEMBER 2, 1933

FOR THE FIRST TIME since its inception, the Nobel Prize, foremost of
all literary awards, has been tendered a Russian writer.

Both Tolstoy and Chekhov, as well as the still active Gorky, might
have been expected, at one time or another, to bring the award to
Russia. Instead, it has now gone to Ivan Alekseevich Bunin, who,
there is no doubt, is at present the most important of the contemporary Russian prose writers.

Ivan Bunin comes of an old and noble family. Several centuries
ago his ancestors migrated from the Tartaric steppe and settled in
the Government of Voronezh in Central Russia, where they acquired
vast land holdings and thousands of slaves. Their riches remained
virtually intact until well into the early days of the Revolution. Bunin today is sixty-three years old. The Nobel Prize for Literature,
which can hardly be said to be destined for youths, has in his case
rewarded four decades of assiduous literary activity.

Toward the close of the last century Bunin arrived in St. Petersburg as a young student. Russian literature was just then undergoing
a sort of renaissance; and among the creative talents of the period he
played a significant part. Inwardly attuned to the symbolism and the
decadent tendencies then prevalent, the young poet, better than
anyone else, understood the need for arraying the obsolescent tradition of Pushkin in the new garb. And goaded on by this understanding, he strove successfully to elevate his language to a plane of un-
surpassably beautiful, utter clarity. He explored his medium, language, as a physician explores the human anatomy. Those who knew
him at the time say that he would ponder over the cadence of a

sentence for hours at a stretch, to fathom the magical content of words.

The result of his painstaking labors was a book which for years thrilled lovers of poetry throughout Russia, a translation of *The Song of Hiawatha*. Only those who can appreciate the difficulty of transposing brief English sentences into long Slavic ones can realize what a gigantic task he accomplished. His translation is not only a great poetic achievement but an almost verbatim *Übersetzung* of the grandiose original of Longfellow. The Russian people took *The Song of Hiawatha* to their heart. Whole generations thrilled to the music and the heroic motif of the poem. Not a provincial town or a hamlet but knew and was stirred by the deeds of the faraway Indian demigod who, in this fashion, became kin to the heroes of Russian legendry.

Bunin was the first to bring American literature into the vast domain of Russia. Before him American literature had meant nothing even to the educated Russian. He it was who showed his compatriots that even Americans had vital things to offer in the realm of the written word. Thenceforward their interest in American writings has continued unabated.

At twenty-three, therefore, Bunin received the Pushkin Prize, the outstanding literary award of Russia, which the Imperial Russian Academy has only once bestowed outside its fold. This recognition shaped Bunin's future. Completing his university studies, he set out to make poetry both the task of his life and its content. His lyrics were soon famous. By the time he was thirty he was one of the leaders of the younger generation of poets, and among the literati was looked up to not alone as the master but as the brightest hope of contemporary literature.

With the years, however, Bunin's ways digressed so far from those of pure poetry that, in the story of Russian and of world literature, he will be remembered not so much as a poet as he will for his masterful prose. Every summer, when the streets of Moscow and St. Petersburg thinned of their moiling populations, Bunin deserted the literary salons and went back to his estates in the Government of Voronezh. There he came into intimate contact with the Russian peasant. At this time, it must be explained, there was a plenitude of peasant novels and stories, works notable primarily for their complete lack of understanding and truth concerning their subject matter. In them the peasant was depicted as the symbol of goodness. Justice, morality, and propriety existed only in the village and among the peasantry. If a man wanted to find himself he had to go to the village and to the peasant to redeem his soul.

This time-honored literary formula fitted in with the political ideology of the Russian intelligentsia who, clamoring for a democratization of the feudal aristocracy, saw in the peasant their hero. Bombs were thrown, czars murdered, and revolutions instigated— in the name of the peasant; young people of good family left home and hearth to join the peasant, to learn from them the Truth and the Right.

But precisely what this peasant was, what he was after and what he thought, and above all, what he did, the mundane scribes from Moscow did not know any more than did the impetuous revolutionists in St. Petersburg. Bunin, himself a member of the more liberal circles of the Russian intelligentsia, was the first one to discover the shocking lack of verisimilitude in these books and stories. Quite suddenly he changed horse and became a prose writer. His first books, collections of short stories, caused a veritable storm in his own circles. They had the effect of a slap in the face of public opinion. With consummate artistry Bunin portrayed the peasant as he was; not as a mythical God-seeker, but as a wild, robust, primitive man tormented and hedged in by cruel superstition. Life in the villages, the perpetually drunken peasants, the constantly abused women, the neglected children, formed the background of his numerous short stories written at that time. The psychic structure of the peasants was here shown in complete clarity. In the depth of their childish souls slumbered the most brutal, egotistic instincts—envy, hatred, and the lust to kill. Russian peasants, sons of slaves and descendants of the wild Tartar, were after all neither pietists nor philosophers.

Harsh tales of peasant life, tales that made the hair on the heads of liberal readers stand on end, filled the works of the erstwhile poet. Despite the prompt denunciations of his work by the critics, Bunin emerged victorious in this battle between fiction and truth. Not hatred, but sad and desperate love, dyed his pen. His work was not the malevolent criticism of a reactionary, but the bitter warning of a friend.

Beyond that, his tales were all of a high artistic order; his descriptions of nature were, artistically, simplicity itself—the single figures overwhelmingly plastic. It was not long before even the most adverse critics had to admit that such poetic genius could not be identified with blasphemous slander.

To know the whole truth about Russian peasants one has but to pick up a book of Bunin's. For he actually lived in their midst and knew these hundred and fifty million souls as the powdered and perfumed snobs of the major literary circles never could.

Even Tolstoy, who originally disliked Bunin, and whose perspective toward the people was diametrically opposite to his, finally had to concede the great, if tragic, talent of his unique rival. Years passed, and ever riper grew the demoniacal gift of this strange man. Poems and prose pieces of unimaginable verbal clarity and complete beauty, he wrote, along with never-ending appeals to Russian society. He, the dreamer, recognized, far better than did the provincial politicians, the imminent danger of the peasant revolution which would uproot and annihilate everything—the realm and the people, culture and mores. The shortsighted politicians wagged their heads at the time, but now no doubt recognize the intrinsic truth of his prophetic words.

The oft-prophesied uprising, which came in 1917, originated in the very depth of the people; and the true peasant tyro was a verbatim copy of those gruesome Bunin visions. When the realm went to pieces, when the peasant hordes roamed the country, when warm red blood stained the earth, Bunin, together with many other writers, scientists, and clergymen, left the capital. He moved to the sunny South, to the Crimea where the White Russian movement fought to preserve the last remnants of the state. Bunin, however, never believed that the peasant revolution, the concentrated hatred of hundreds of years, could be overcome by a small group of White Russian generals.

He stayed in Russia until the bitter end; with hands and feet he clung to the last little patch of Russian soil. For, true artist that he was, he knew how deeply his art was rooted in this soil. Only when the Red battalions penetrated into the South Russian cities, when even the last corner of Russian paradise, the Crimea, was about to drown in blood, when the Hungarian, Bela Kun, became head of the Cheka in the Crimea, did Bunin go. Swept off his feet by the avalanche of fugitives, he was carried away on a rotting iron ship, across the Black Sea to Constantinople. Of his earthly possessions he took very little along: a few manuscripts, a small satchel, and one worn suit. Nobody could have recognized the famous poet in this dilapidated, aging man.

Constantinople. Two million Russians passed through the Turkish metropolis in 1918 and 1919. They loitered on street corners, slept under bridges, lodged themselves a hundred to a room in the once magnificent reception chambers of the Czarist Russian embassy. Their former allies considered them the scum of the earth.

It is said that the bread of exile is bitter as gall. That isn't so. The bread of exile is neither bitter nor sweet. . . . The soil of exile is barren for the exile. . . .

Like other émigrés, Bunin lived in Constantinople, tattered, hungry, uncertain of the morrow. Months passed; nobody troubled to remember the renowned poet. Then suddenly, unexpected salvation came to Bunin and a number of other Russian writers from an unlooked-to quarter. Alexander, in far-off Belgrade, was crowned King. In August, 1914, when the Austrian army had passed the Serbian border, Alexander, then the Crown Prince, had wired the Czar: "Save our country in the name of our Slavic brotherhood!" That telegram had been the outward cause of Russian intervention in the war. At the end of the war Serbia emerged big and powerful while Imperial Russia was crushed. The human flotsam of the Czar's realm clung like barnacles to the Bosphorus. Now King Alexander remembered the tragic days of August, 1914. He himself at one time had been an exile in St. Petersburg and knew well what exile meant.

Thus it came to pass that Bunin and a goodly number of other Russian writers one day received a brief notice from the Yugoslavian Embassy. It read: "His Majesty, the King of Yugoslavia, has resolved to subsidize the most important of the Russian intelligentsia. Thus you will receive a pension of——francs." This pension granted by King Alexander saved the vestiges of Czarist culture from complete and final oblivion. Bunin went to Serbia and from there to Paris, where most of the Russian emigrants finally congregated.

After long interruption he began again to write creatively. Exile alters people's views. Clergymen preach bloody revolution, humanitarians demand the annihilation of human beings, pacifists press for war—and lyric poets write odes full of venom. Indeed the poet Bunin, author of the sinister and apocalyptic book, *The Village,* and of countless short stories depicting the baser instincts in human beings, potentially the leader of Neo-realism, could readily have fallen prey to this pessimism! Instead, an extraordinary thing happened. The daring, merciless portrayer of human characters wrote the unexpected *Mitjas Love.* Exile, bloodshed, and civil war had failed to embitter him. His dark prophecies having materialized, it was as if the nightmare had gone from him, never to return.

Mitjas Love is a work of sheer delicate, lyrical tenderness, bursting with a love of nature and man unequaled in literature. The story of a brief life, young Misha's, his burning love and his tragic end, is easily the finest-wrought book, stylistically, of contemporary Russian literature. It made a sensation. Once again the poet Bunin had given the world a glimpse of the wealth of variations that lay buried in his soul. Next to *The Gentleman from San Francisco* and *The Village, Mitjas Love* is the apogee of his artistic endeavors.

Years passed, and in exile Bunin fashioned his three-volume novel, *The Life of Arsenjenv*, essentially autobiographical. In exile, too, many fragments emerged from under his pen, later to be collected and published between covers. Fifteen years had gone by since the poet Bunin had had to leave his homeland. In that time he had grown ever more tranquil, residing in some provincial town south of Paris, while it became increasingly difficult to adjust himself to an alien world. Financial difficulties again and again forced the King of Yugoslavia to cut his largess to the exiled Russian writers, and Bunin's existence grew lonelier and more abject. Only rarely did he show himself at the salons of the émigrés in Paris. His pension at last no longer sufficed for the barest necessities, not even to provide heat in his humble cottage. Together with his wife, the poetess Golina Kusnjezowava, he struggled along one step removed from pauperdom.

To be sure, the Soviet Publishing House still issued his books, the editions of which reached into hundreds of thousands. Even among the rising Communistic generation he was, and still is, considered the peerless master of the word. But these honors were bestowed only upon the abstract figure of the poet. The Soviet Publishing House never paid him a penny.

A few years ago I visited an emigrants' gathering in Paris on the occasion of the anniversary of Pushkin's birth. The leading members of exiled Russia were there. Suddenly word went around that Bunin had arrived; he was, in fact, in a far corner of the hall, leaning against the wall—an emaciated man of sixty. His face was gray, his cheeks were sunken, his hair was white; his oblong head was ennobled by cavernous, attentive, kindly eyes.

I approached him and he greeted me. He told me he was writing a new book, as yet untitled, whose content was still confused. He was working day and night. "It is difficult to work here," he said, rubbing the slender fingers of his left hand with his right. Then he stared fixedly into space and added quietly, "Probably I shall be buried in French soil." Unexpectedly his face flashed in a smile as he held out his delicate brown hands. "After all, I do have beautiful hands; they too will have to rot." Again he stared moodily over the hall and at the host of people. Russian émigrés surrounded him and old acquaintances shook his hand. But he spoke little and obviously longed for the refuge of his small, dark room with its table full of manuscripts.

Ivan Bunin's attainment of the coveted Nobel Prize must certainly cause surprise and controversy in Europe. When one mentions the most famous Russian poet in Europe, one invariably names Gorky. Bunin's fame has not penetrated beyond the boundaries of his native country. Few translators would be capable of re-creating Bunin's marvelous lyric quality.

Outside of intimate literary circles, translations of Bunin's works find but scant attention. Nevertheless, the prize has not gone to one who is unworthy of it; the masterful productions of this poet altogether justify the unanticipated choice of the Selection Committee.

FANNIE HURST

by Zora Neale Hurston

The writer of this little piece was for many years Miss Hurst's amanuensis. Here are some interesting anecdotes that help explain what kind of job that was.

OCTOBER 9, 1937

SOMEBODY SAID one day in writing that Fannie Hurst was the only woman writer in America who looked like what she was. Right away I knew what he meant. It is true that she is a stunning wench, but that was not all that he saw with his eyes. He meant that she had something more to show than a head, two legs, two arms, and what holds them together. He was saying that she looked like a Somebody to him. And that is right. She does.

It is not just her grooming either, though she knows very well what to do with those eyes and her white skin and black hair. She knows what black and white and red can do for her looks and she does it. She and the Queen of Sheba both know what to look like when calling on the king. She has got something else besides clothes that sprangles out from her when she moves. It is something like a rainbow wrapped and tied around her shoulder that glints and gleams.

And if you stay around Fannie Hurst you are not going to take a good look at her and go on off to sleep either. No, you will hop from one emotion to the other so fast that not one suspicion of sleep will dim your eyes. She is apt to wring you dry and be bored with you long before you are through with her. You will pay attention, for Fannie Hurst is a person of the most contradictory moods and statements of anyone in public life. But if you study her out, she is the very essence of consistency. She is the repository of talents and not the usual assembly of female parts and thoughts. What the gods within her direct today may be absolutely repudiated by what they dictate tomorrow, and that is as it should be. So it is ridiculous to go and get your mob-size measure and attempt to take her size.

She is a writer because she had to be one. She had money when she was born, so she did not need to try for that. She had looks and sex appeal so she did not need a career as a mating device. She had place in the social scheme. She writes because she must. But that must is inside of her, and has nothing to do with a publisher's order. If everything she writes is not a *Humoresque, Back Street,* a *Lummox,* or a *Vertical City,* it is not a play to the gallery. It is because the gods inside have failed her for the moment.

Personally, Fannie Hurst is a little girl who is tall for her age. You can just see her playing dollhouse with grown-up tools. One moment a serious worker controlled by her genii; the next instant playing make-believe with all her heart. Playing it so that it is impossible for you to doubt that for her it is true while it lasts. Then you can understand her. You can just see the child in St. Louis wandering around in the big house with no other children to play with. She could not run loose in the streets because her people were never poor. There were too many good carpets and lace curtains in her house for it to be overrun with just anybody's children, either. She did not even have a cousin near her own age. She had her little life all to herself. She was the little girl with the long curls who looked out of the big window until she got tired. Then she would fiddle with the lace curtains until she was told to stop. She put up with adult company as long as she could stand it, and you can see her when she hit upon the glorious device of making up her playmates out of her own head.

She did not feel any great yearning for degrees, but she went to college anyway. She took her bachelor's degree at a college in St. Louis, but prefers to think of Columbia University as her Alma Mater because there she felt a spiritual tie that she never felt in St. Louis. By the time she entered college she was putting her fancies on paper. She sent things out to the publications, but had no success to speak of in those days when she was learning to use her tools, so she decided to come East and fight it out with these editor-people at close range. That brought her to New York and to Jacques Danielson. Not before she had tried briefly the career of waitress, elevator operator, and a few other odd jobs like that to gain experience. That period was short because she met Jacques Danielson, and that sensitive musician wanted to take her under a roof that he paid for and keep her. But at the same time he understood her dreams and agreed to the separate domiciles that the writer might not be destroyed by the musician and vice versa. So they made that agreement of three nights a week together which has been given so much publicity

However, I have known him to sneak up the back stairs to spend
some extra evenings with his wife and I have never seen her make
the first move to drive him off.

She had his full sympathy and co-operation in trying her wings in
literature. She tried and failed and tried again and he was always
full of encouragement and faith. He told her she had genius over
and over, and after *Humoresque* there was no doubt in the minds
of the critics that she was among the unforgettables. The short story
or the book-length piece were all one to her. The length had
nothing to do with her creation. She had learned to write prose. She
was asked why she never attempted a play and she said that the
drama was life in high relief and she preferred to work in the round.

Miss Hurst loves beauty. You can tell that the moment you enter
her cathedral-like studio apartment. There is the air of the Medicis
about. There are beautiful bits of this and that from here and there
in the world, but mostly from Italy and Italy of the great art period.
She might seek here and there for a bargain in soda biscuits to eat
with cheese, and then pay an enormous sum for a beautiful plate to
eat it from.

But to go back to the little girl in Fannie Hurst. She is extremely
intelligent and nobody's fool in business. I have heard some editor
or publisher call her up and try a little strong-arm stuff. Try to sort
of push and shove her around a bit. Just so much of that and The
Fannie is all over him like gravy over rice. Then I have seen her,
annoyed by some petty incident, drop everything and rush to the
telephone to tell her husband all about it. And the way she says
"Jack" it is the most helpless sound in the whole world. "Jack, they
did this and thus to me. What must I do now, Jack? When are you
coming home, Jack?" You can just hear him on the other end of the
wire figuratively patting her curls and wiping her eyes, and she is all
mollified again. She returns to her desk with the air of, "There now!
I told Jack on you and I bet he'll fix you *good*. Goody, goody,
goody!" It is like the cave woman who probably took a rock and
beat a saber-toothed tiger to death for sticking his head in her cave.
Then when her big hairy husband came home from the hunt, he
found her crying in fright over a mouse.

Once I saw her playing at the little girl who runs away from home.
She said to me perfectly sober sounding, "Come on, Zora, with your
car and let's you and I go on a trip." That was good because I love
to go on trips. "Elizabeth Marbury," she went on, "is up at her summer home at Belgrade Lakes, Maine. She wrote me that she wants

to see me at once and have a talk. It is something important and I really *must* go to her. Can we start tomorrow?"

So the next morning bright and soon I had the little Chevrolet all serviced and at the door. Miss Hurst came down with her mouth all set like a Christmas present and got in the car. And in no time at all I was going up the Boston Post Road washing my foot in the gas tank. Early that afternoon we were in Saratoga Springs. Miss Hurst told me to stop.

"We must stop here awhile. For one thing you have never tasted this spring water here and it just does wonders for people. I'd feel guilty if I didn't give you a chance to drink some of this water. Besides, Lummie needs to stretch his legs." (Lummox was Miss Hurst's two-pound-size Pekingese.)

We stopped in front of the United States Hotel and gave Lummox a brisk walk of about five feet. Then I went over in the park where I saw water that didn't look too private spouting up from a fountain and took a drink. By that time Miss Hurst had come back from the telephone and we all got back in the car. Miss Hurst had that look in her eyes that a child has when it is about to tell its mother that it has seen a fairy.

"Zora, your getting that drink of water reminds me to ask you if you have ever seen Niagara Falls?"

"No, I never have, Miss Hurst, but I have always meant to see it someday."

"Oh, well then, you might just as well see it now. Everybody ought to see Niagara Falls as soon as possible. Suppose we go there right now?"

"Fine, but what about Miss Marbury?"

"Oh, she can wait. I couldn't think of letting *you* go back to New York without seeing the Falls."

So we pointed the nose of the Chevrolet due West with my foot on the gas splitting the wind for Buffalo. And next afternoon we were there before sundown.

We parked the car, and Miss Hurst stood by the car because she had seen the Falls many times. You know those falls are a great big thing, so I went right up to the rail to stand there and look. It is monstropolous. It looks like the Pacific Ocean rushing over the edge of the world. But before I could really conceive of the thing, Miss Hurst called me. Mouth all primped up again.

"Zora, you must see this thing from the Canadian side. Let's go over there and get the view. They light it up at night, you know."

In five minutes we had crossed the international bridge and I had to go into a little building right close there to register the car. When I came out, Miss Hurst was almost dancing up and down like a six-year-old putting something over on its elders.

"Get in the car, quick, Zora. I think we can make Hamilton before dark!"

So we saw Hamilton, and Kitchener, and Gault, and many another town in Ontario. It took us two weeks, not a minute of which was dull. I cannot remember in which town it was, but in some town in that part of Canada we saw a big sign that said that Vilhjalmur Stefansson, the great Arctic explorer and lecturer, was speaking on the Chautauqua. So we hunted him up and he gave us free passes to the lectures and they were fine. All about mosquitoes practically eating up dogs beyond the Arctic circle, and how wolves *don't* go in packs.

Then one night Miss Hurst began to make notes and look very studious, and the next morning we were headed for New York state and the city on the Sound. The little girl who had run off to the horizon to hide from her complicated existence was grown up again. The artist was about to birth a book. She had had the fun of running away (who among us has not planned to do that same thing ever since we took off our diapers!) and she had had the fun of fooling me off to go along with her.

Fannie Hurst is a blend of woman and author. You can't separate the two things in her case. Nature must have meant it to be that way. Most career women are different. Their profession is like oil on water. You can see where one stops and the other begins. And then again some women writers are writers and some of them are women. Anytime, day or night, you run across Fannie Hurst you can see and feel her womanhood. And if you read her, you are going to find out that she is an author.

FRANK CROWNINSHIELD

by Geoffrey T. Hellman

Friend and editor to most of the notables on the American literary scene for half a century, "Crownie", was lively and sophisticated. His reputation for charm is matched only by that he earned as editor of Vanity Fair, *a position he held for the entire period of its existence, 1914-1935. They still talk about it as a classic example of magazine publishing and editing, a monument to the name of Frank Crowninshield.*

APRIL 10, 1954

AMONG OTHER ATTRACTIONS, Frank Crowninshield was one of the most graceful speakers around. He was an urbane and lively toastmaster, with a sure wit, often exercised, and he was also a rather unscrupulous one. Over a period of something like fifty years, he publicly proposed toasts and ostensibly drank to the health of everyone from Teddy Roosevelt to Gypsy Rose Lee, but no drop of alcohol ever sullied his throat. He took the pledge when he was ten, out of politeness. His maternal grandmother had taken him to a prohibition rally in Boston where the chief speaker asked people who would undertake never to swallow a drink the rest of their lives to stand up. Frank's grandmother got up, and the lad, who had been taught never to remain seated in the presence of a standing lady, rose automatically. He was later ribbed for his stand, and he resolved to stick to it when he reached man's estate. For half a century, at the banquets which he rescued from boredom with his presence, he simply raised the glass to his lips, assumed a genial expression, and sardonically watched his fellow guests trifle with their health. He never preached what he practiced. He served liquor to his friends, and he even went so far as to write forewords to books on food and wine in which he knowingly proclaimed the superiority of burgundy to Scotch, and the unbeatable quality of French champagnes, none of which he ever touched.

Crowninshield had a gift for friendship and he had an enormous number of friends of all ages and sizes. He was for the entire

225

twenty-two years of its existence the editor of *Vanity Fair,* and after that a major contributor to *Vogue,* so many of his friends were writers and artists, but he also tolerated bankers, publishers, lawyers, architects, cotillion leaders, and daughters of the original Commodore Vanderbilt. He and Condé Nast, with whom he shared an apartment for several years, used to mix up various categories of people at parties they gave in the twenties. This was the beginning of café society, which has since degenerated. Crowninshield was a pioneering editor. He attracted to *Vanity Fair* many young writers who later became famous. His magazine was the first to publish Robert Benchley, Robert Sherwood, Dorothy Parker, Corey Ford, Donald Ogden Stewart, Thomas Beer, Carl Carmer, Thomas Wolfe, and Edmund Wilson. He was the first to bring to American magazine readers Aldous Huxley, Noel Coward, P. G. Wodehouse, William Bolitho, Ferenc Molnár, and Colette. He was also the first American to publish reproductions of Picasso, Van Gogh, Matisse, Gauguin, Rouault, and a whole bunch of others, at a time when they were not well known. "Crownie discovers people before they discover themselves," Nast once said.

I talked to a lot of Crowninshield's friends one time when I was doing a piece on him, and read what they and others had had to say about him, and I will therefore produce, or adduce, a few exhibits.

Clare Luce, who was one of his managing editors on *Vanity Fair,* wrote: "Crownie, Frank, or Uncle Frank, as he is known in his various incarnations, is somebody I dearly like to talk about. The one scene above all I yearn to describe is the drama that was enacted weekly in the offices of *Vanity Fair* when a smooth but obdurate Mr. Crowninshield tried to sell a ruffled but equally obdurate Mr. Nast on his latest Modigliani or Chirico which he wanted to publish in four colors in *Vanity Fair.* The technique of the sale, which Crownie generally made, was as graceful and as enchanting and as mysterious to the onlooker as magician Mulholland's canary-cage trick. And, incidentally, Mulholland was a great Crowninshield crony. He used to come to office luncheons where he did card tricks while Crownie passed around his African sculptures between the scrambled eggs and the ice cream. Twixt card tricks and African sculpture, Mr. Crowninshield laid glibly before the editors, for their distracted consideration, the serious articles on labor, politics, and science which Mr. Nast was then ordering from Jay Franklin, Walter Lippmann, and Matthew Woll, in the days when not only

Vanity Fair was dying, but the very world it stood for. Mr. Crown-inshield, alas, was not the man to outflank the world of Mrs. Astor and Mrs. Van Rensselaer, even with the help of Matthew Woll. He was spiritually, if not intellectually, too much a part of that world. "For the rest, he is the most thoughtful, punctilious, and at the same time whimsical man who ever lived. He is the last and probably the greatest of a species which is rapidly disappearing all over the world known as 'the gentleman.' "

The next memorandum is from Mr. Nast: "A trait in F.C. which has always struck me is his concern over the aged, the sick, the underprivileged, and forlorn. (His friendships with servants seem always as close as those he maintains with their employers.) He has a remarkable way of continuing an active contact with old friends. A happy result, for our publishing organization, has been that if a friendly contact had to be established he seemed certain either to know the men and women we were after, or to sense, exactly, how to bring them into line. It was always, for example, easy for him to persuade Joseph H. Choate to write for us, or Irene Castle to pose for photographs, or John Sargent to permit our use of his sketches, or Joe Louis to pass an hour or two before the cameras in our studio, or persuade August Belmont and Harry Payne Whitney to co-operate in photographing their horses in their stables, or Isadora Duncan to help in a benefit dance recital, or Geraldine Farrar to do us any order of favor."

Crowninshield was an indefatigable and ruthless golfer, and in this connection Benchley once wrote: "The same freedom from convention and restraint which has marked his editorial products is a noticeable feature of his golf game, and the reaction of a golf ball to his singular personality is considered nothing short of re-markable. He can, without the aid of an assistant, cause a golf ball to wound birds on the wing, sail through open windows, disappear absolutely on level stretches of green, fly backward, and break into four equal parts."

Benchley also wrote, of another side of Crowninshield: "At the risk of being exiled to Lake Mahopac when the great proletarian revolution breaks, he still maintains a certain touching faith in the—so to speak—aristocracy of America. If a rich man has good taste, he is just as worthy, in the eyes of Frank Crowninshield, as a man who has no money at all. He is like that in everything—broad-minded."

Robert Simon, the publisher, said, "He can order a can of sardines and give you the impression that it is a distinguished and festive thing to do."

Mrs. Edna Woolman Chase, when she was editor of *Vogue:* "He hated fountain pens and never listened to the radio. He'd reach back into a rich background of friendships and information and always pull out the right answer for you. He'd sign acceptances to dinner parties 'Vishinsky' and write, 'Please submit the names of your other guests and the seating arrangements.' He'd step on my toes in a crowded elevator and say loudly, 'Give me back my latch-key, you wicked woman.'"

Miss Caroline Duer: "He pretended to drink at Mamie Fish's dinners. He is fearless in his opinions, and always willing to listen."

A girl in Crowninshield's office: "He'd bring ghastly African masks to the office, and the girls had to put them on. Oh, the things I've had to admire there! He was always bringing in paintings and books. He was sort of cold if you didn't react right. But it was fun working there—we laughed all day long, the work wasn't hard, every-one was witty, and Crowninshield was the core of it."

Westbrook Pegler, in the days when he was feeling more cheerful: "There are two men in New York who are recognized as the nicest, politest, most gentlemanly gentlemen in town. You could run them through a wringer and analyze the juice and never find a drop of dirt, vulgarity, or poison. The other one is Mr. Walter Trumbull. . . . If you have never seen Mr. Crowninshield and Mr. Trumbull in action, in the finals of a politeness tournament in somebody's penthouse, then all you have seen in the way of manners is at best merely the rough-and-tumble deportment of a lot of bums. They are that far in front of the next man. It is Moody and Jacobs, McLar-nin and Ross when Mr. Crowninshield and Mr. Trumbull come down to the championship, with first Mr. Crowninshield winning by a mere inflection, then Mr. Trumbull taking back the title by beating him to it in lighting a match for his opponent's cigarette."

As a matter of fact, Crowninshield didn't smoke. Young people often came to him with their troubles, ranging from financial to matrimonial, and he would generally ascribe these, reprovingly, to the use of tobacco. As another matter of fact, Crowninshield's politeness covered a lot of iron. "I am not as genial as I seem," he once said to a friend. He had an enormous amount of energy, and he was an extraordinarily meticulous editor. He edited his own letters, sometimes crossing out adjective after adjective, and sub-stituting others, until he came back to the original one. He used to smell his mail before opening it. "This is from a chorus girl," he would sniff, "and this is from a lady."

Crowninshield was one of the four founders—and what Harrie Lindeberg, the architect, calls the Mother Superior—of the Coffee House, which opened its doors, or door, a little over thirty-eight years ago. He had just written an article for the *Sun* which shows what he *wasn't* aiming at in the way of a club. "When I think of the clubs which I have joined (or visited)," he wrote, "a strange lassitude and weariness lay hold of me—a feeling of mild but abject despair, for it is a saddening truth that the essence of club life is to be bored. Now if women were only admitted to membership! As at present arranged, club life compels us to listen to endless arguments and needless complaints; to be waited upon impersonally and apathetically by dejected and cuffless waiters; to listen to lugubrious moralizings upon life, love, liquor, and the ladies; to wash and rewash our hands; to fight off the grim and ever-threatening figure of ennui; to discuss the morbid condition of the liver and the stock market; to bicker and quarrel at auction; to find fault with the sauce on the fish or the temperature of the claret; and, finally, to fly the place in despair because of the untoward and disheartening entrance of some worthy but defatigating member." None of these things, of course, ever happened at Crowninshield's favorite club.

This isn't a very chronological report, and I will now, as I approach its conclusion, state that Crowninshield, whose parents lived abroad a good deal, was born in the Pavillon de Rohan, a small Paris hotel later torn down to make way for the Louvre department store. He liked to take friends to the second floor of the store, point to the corset department, and tell them he was born there. His first job was with Putnam's in 1890, when he was eighteen. He got it on a recommendation from William Dean Howells. I have two letters which Howells wrote him. The first, dated August 4, 1889, contains the kind of professional advice that Crowninshield himself later dispensed to young people looking for jobs:

MY DEAR FRANK:

Between Appletons and Harpers, I think I should choose Appletons. My own experience of the Harpers is an ideally friendly and cordial one; I have the greatest regard for them; and I merely fancy, without knowing why, that the chances of promotion would be greater with another house. For another reason, I should prefer Putnams to Appletons, Holt to Putnams, and Stokes to Holt; and that is, a younger house,

with a less fixed tradition, will be apt to do a more various
business and give you the range of the trade quicker. You
ought to look forward to an interest, and with a small house
you could do this more hopefully than with a large one,
where you would have more competitors. There's no secret
of the business that isn't known to all the publishers alike.
In a small house you would meet authors and artists more,
and be thrown with the young fellows destined to do the work
you would someday publish. An old house is more apt to
publish old established authors. When you've made up your
mind, I'll be glad to give you a "character."

With the family regards to all,

Your friend,

W. D. HOWELLS

Howells's second letter, dated February 20, 1896, and written at
a time when Frank had left Putnam's to become editor of *The
Bookman* for Dodd, Mead, runs as follows:

MY DEAR FRANK:

I am heartily glad of what seems a forward step for you,
and I know you will make it an advantage to others as well
as yourself. It is always pleasant to think of you, because
you have not only a good head, but what is much rarer, a
good heart; and your life is the daily effect of right feeling
and right thinking in a world where there is so much of
neither.

Yours cordially,

W. D. HOWELLS

Howells's estimate stood up pretty well for the remaining fifty-
one years of Crowninshield's life. He died three days after Christmas six years ago, and two weeks before this, in the hospital, when
he knew what was up, he directed the sending of innumerable tele-
grams, fifteen hundred Christmas cards, and forty presents to his
friends. What he said of his brother Edward, who predeceased him
by nine years, was equally true of himself—"Although dying, he
could brighten up a room."

THE SAUK-CENTRICITIES
OF SINCLAIR LEWIS

by Charles Breasted

Few writers in the long history of literature have been more color-
ful in their personal behavior than Sinclair Lewis—which accounts
for the spate of reminiscences that have been written about him
since his death in January 1951. This memoir by Charles Breasted
covers the period from 1922-1926—from Babbitt to Elmer Gantry—
and reveals that behind the eccentricities, exhibitionism, and bom-
bast there was a fundamentally humane man who lived, as he died,
in ultimate loneliness.

AUGUST 14, 1954

I FIRST MET Sinclair Lewis in the United States, when he was capitalizing on the success of *Main Street* by lecturing far and wide; but our real acquaintance and eventual friendship dated from a February afternoon in 1922, when we both happened simultaneously to converge upon the American Consulate General in London to have our passports extended. Lewis was then completing *Babbitt* in a bare-walled, single-windowed room, furnished with a table and two chairs, which he had rented in the Middle Temple in London. During those days he used to join me periodically for dinners and simple soirées at the homes of old friends in the Holland Park and Camden Hill sections of London, where we met such diverse personalities as George Peabody Gooch, the English historian; Hermann Gollancz, the Semitist; Maxwell Armfield, the sadly crippled yet extraordinarily active artist; Cyril Scott, the composer; Edmund Dulac, the illustrator; and many others. Lewis had already struck up a warm friendship with H. G. Wells (which was to prove sadly short-lived), and had met Galsworthy, Claude Lovat Fraser, Barrie (his historic visit with Conrad, which Wolfe so witheringly described in *The Web and the Rock,* came much later), and other leading figures of the day. He was greatly impressed with what seemed to him their un-British easy informality, and with the fact that their social gatherings included every age level and that the young people in their teens seemed genuinely to enjoy such association with their elders. He would always compliment his hosts especially on this latter aspect of their social life, which was in such contrast to the separation between generations in the United States. This in turn would lead him to expound upon the foibles and fortes of life in America. If the occasion included games, he was likely to be in the middle of them, usually on the floor; and as often as not he would end up by teaching a group of guests, including the prettiest girl present, the subtleties of poker.

One evening when we were on our way in a taxi to some such gathering I asked Lewis if *Main Street* wasn't largely autobiographical. He answered that of course Doc Kennicott was a portrait of his father. Then I said, "What about Carol Kennicott—isn't she a portrait of you?" He seemed startled and said that only a very few people had guessed her identity. "Yes," he added, "Carol is 'Red' Lewis: always groping for something she isn't capable of attaining, always dissatisfied, always restlessly straining to see what lies just over the horizon, intolerant of her surroundings, yet lacking any clearly defined vision of what she really wants to do or to be."

For a number of years during which my work involved much travel to the Middle East, I saw Lewis often as I moved back and forth. Wherever it might be, he was always a magnet for a heterogeneous agglomeration of personalities who at all hours of the day, and more especially of the night, trooped through his current domicile. While they flattered his ego, they primarily reflected his inexhaustible interest in people, among whom young writers were always the objects of his special solicitude, encouragement, and, very frequently, financial assistance. Somehow, despite his own work and crowded off-hours, he always managed to find the time for reading, or at least tentatively appraising, most of the manuscripts which he continually received from eager young hopefuls. He was genuinely delighted whenever this stream of bathos and mediocrity yielded anything of even modest promise, and felt supremely rewarded when—as in one instance which I have never forgotten—he came upon a pearl of great price.

One morning in the spring of 1928, when he was again keeping bachelor quarters in London at No. 10 Bury Street, I happened in, en route home from Egypt, and found him completely enthralled by a typescript, about which in his overwhelming enthusiasm he was for once almost inarticulate. "If this isn't it," he burst out, "I predict that the young giant who wrote it *will* eventually produce *the* American novel, and anyway some of the finest work of our generation! His name's Tom Wolfe, and he's absolutely superb! I want you to meet him—he's dropping in tonight about two A.M."

When I returned late that evening "Hal" Lewis (as he was known to his older friends) was still sitting amongst the typescript of *Look Homeward, Angel.* He continued to expatiate upon it and toward two o'clock glanced at his watch and remarked that Tom should be along any minute now. "He'll announce himself long before he gets here," Hal said. He had hardly spoken when from the far end of Bury Street the stillness was shattered by an unholy clatter as of ash and refuse cans being dragged across sidewalks, emptied into the gutter, and tossed high into the air, to roll booming and clanging down toward St. James's. From the speed with which the cacophony was approaching, it was evident that more than one man was at work. We leaned out of a window and watched the methodical, efficient Halloween rampage of a pair of young Americans, one of whom, in the light of the street lamps, looked like a titan. When they reached No. 10 they dusted each other off and, leaving Bury Street looking like a prophecy of a future "blitz," started upstairs in the lift, which they insisted on operating themselves.

"After midnight," Hal said, "Tom upsets ash cans all over London, and the bobbies on the beat always politely look the other way!"

Tom Wolfe and the other marauder, a young American musical-comedy librettist, appeared at Hal's door, greeted him cordially, apologized for being so late—"We had to work our way over from Leicester Square," Tom explained—and after washing up, poured themselves double drinks and settled in for some of the best talk I had ever heard. They were still going strong toward five in the morning when I finally left my first, and only, meeting with Tom Wolfe.

Two years prior to this encounter, in the summer of 1926, Hal and I had unexpectedly met again, as fellow guests at a houseparty on one of the ten thousand islands in Rainy Lake, Minnesota. He was at work on *Elmer Gantry.* His father, old Doc Kennicott of *Main Street,* was at the moment gravely ill, and one night Hal's almost feminine intuition suddenly warned him that the coming morning might bring news from Sauk Center of the old doctor's death. He was unable to sleep, and so came and roused me and asked me to sit with him in the dressing room of our guest house and talk—which for me meant listening. We sat on a bench, he with his knees drawn up and his arms resting on them as he smoked incessantly.

"My father has never forgiven me for *Main Street*," he said. "When I saw him a few weeks ago, we shook hands—but he can't comprehend the book, much less grasp that it's the greatest tribute I knew how to pay him. He felt that I should have served an honored profession by becoming a doctor myself, insteading of derogating and besmirching it in a book libeling my own birthplace. *Main Street* condemned me in his eyes as a traitor to my heritage— whereas the truth is, I shall never shed the little, indelible 'Sauk-centricities' that enabled me to write it—that make the unbridgeable difference between me and my son Wells!"

Suddenly he rose, went to a mirror, and, turning his head from side to side, studied his face for some time. Then he said quietly, "You know, as the fire dies down inside of me and I grow old, I shall resemble somewhat a dignified old gentleman of the old school, but actually I shan't be. It takes three generations, and I'm only the second. My son Wells is the third. I think he *is* a gentleman, and perhaps he may create literature—as I have not. I've already done my best work, and of that *Babbitt* will probably be rated my best book—though my own favorite will always be *Arrowsmith* and, incidentally, my favorite character will always be old Max Gottlieb. Oh, in the future a book of mine will probably always be good for a sale of fifty thousand—but neither the critics nor the author will be fooled. The best of what I'll ever have produced will bear the same relation to true literary achievement that a jacket blurb does to the text of a really great book."

The next morning a speedboat brought a telegram: even as we had sat talking in the night Old Doc Kennicott had died. The same boat took us back to the mainland, where we parted, and Hal turned southward to bury the stranger who had sired him in Sauk Center.

A fortnight later I saw him in Chicago on his way to Washington, D. C., where for reasons I cannot now recall he had asked Gracie, his first wife, to rent a house in which he would finish *Gantry*. His father's death, and the entire Sauk Center community's heart beating as one at the funeral services, had moved Hal profoundly, and left him for the moment again in a subdued mood of clear self-perspective and genuine humility. Just as on the island on that last night, he spoke of his best work as already accomplished, and he seemed unimpressed by the prospect of whatever he might produce during his remaining years. Although he began to regain some of his natural buoyancy, it was in this mood of unaccustomed gravity that he had left Chicago for Washington.

Business shortly took me to New York and Washington, where I spent a day with Hal and Gracie. They were trying valiantly, actually quite desperately, to carry on together, but the futility of their effort was continually betrayed by the underlying tension of their badinage. When we were alone together for a moment Hal told me I might soon be seeing him in New York; and when Gracie drove me to the station she said, without breaking her tone of feigned gaiety, that the future of her relation to Hal appeared at the moment even more problematical than ever before. It was their last attempt, and the cumulative bitterness their incompatibility had engendered was to find vent, respectively, in his *Elmer Gantry* and in her book *Half a Loaf*.

Not long afterward, in New York, I received a telephone call from him, urging me to come to his room at the Hotel Shelton. I found him in a bleak, gray tower room, in a state of abysmal depression and near-collapse. After a final flare-up, he had rushed away from Washington with virtually nothing save his current manuscript. The only other personal effects I noted were three brandy bottles, two of them empty.

I asked him if he had any definite plans. Only to complete *Gantry*, he answered, a matter of three or four months. He expected to leave for Europe before its publication because he was certain that once it had appeared he would be thrown out if he didn't leave voluntarily! At this point I asked him if he would care to share my bachelor apartment in lower Fifth Avenue while he finished the book. For some reason this sent him rather to pieces, and it was several minutes before he tried to speak. Finally he said that this seemed a very kind proposal, which he would probably accept, but he would like a few days in which to think it over.

Considering his general condition at the moment, I wondered whether he would even remember this proposed arrangement. To my surprise, he not only did, but decided that in order to be really fit for this last lap of his latest job he would attend some famous health camp or other, up the Hudson. Then, just as he was departing for the latter, he startled me still more by asking me to agree that we should have no alcohol whatsoever in the apartment and should, furthermore, entertain as few people as possible!

He returned ten days later, looking healthier and more relaxed than I had ever seen him. During that time he had, of course, been forbidden tobacco and alcohol, been made to exercise all day long, and to be in bed and asleep by nine o'clock each night. He felt so exuberantly well that even before unpacking his bag he telephoned his bootlegger and gave him a sizable order. And within a few days the familiar procession of people began milling through our living room at any hour between two P. M. and three A. M., almost never between seven-thirty A. M. and midday, for during those hours, no matter when he had gotten to bed, the writer Sinclair Lewis kept extraordinarily faithful tryst with his work.

He now began to indulge his love of books, and seldom returned from a walk or a trip uptown without an armful of them, or without there appearing messengers in his wake laden with parcels of two or three books at a time. He never took a book from such parcels without also removing the dust jacket. I had always been in the habit of preserving book jackets, partly for the brightness they gave to a bookshelf, but largely because of the interesting and illuminating data they usually contained about the author; and I was the more distressed when he removed all the jackets from my own little library, insisting that they made a book look unread. Books were to him as much a necessity as food—and, alas, drink—and his continual purchase of them did not, therefore, make him conscious of his comparatively recent economic emancipation. But when he came home one afternoon with a parcel filled with new shirts, socks, and numerous neckties there was a curious, almost boyish pleasure in his face as he contemplated the neckties, and said to me, "You know, I can't get over the strange feeling and the sense of unaccustomed freedom it gives me to be able to *afford* to go in and *buy* some good-looking neckties I've seen in a shop window, and to do it without a sense of worry about the money, and without the feeling that I was depriving Gracie of something I ought to have bought for her instead!"

During the first month or two Lewis seemed to take great pleasure in our living arrangements. We took frequent walks together and saw many of our old mutual friends of evenings. Later at night he liked occasionally to revisit the Greenwich Village cafés and speakeasies he used to frequent in his pre-success days, even though he knew he would be plagued with requests for "loans" by the same down-and-out habitués who were there in his day, like Maxwell Bodenheim, whose nauseatingly unctuous flattery never failed to arouse Lewis's pity to the tune of a generous sum.

At this time I was an "associate" in the office of the already legendary dean of public-relations counsellors, an order destined to pullulate indefinitely in more or less his own image. There were definite reasons why I wanted to become familiar with public-relations techniques, but they were unapparent to Hal, who said I was dissipating the best years of my life and that I should concentrate on creative writing.

"It's utterly true that to learn to write," he would say, "one has to write and write and write and *write!* And if you can possibly avoid it, don't waste your energies on short stories and stuff for ephemeral publication. Write *books*. Be known as the author of 'Such-and-Such.' No matter what else you're doing, write at least eight hundred words a day, if possible a thousand—work in a bare room with nothing in it but a table, a chair, and a typewriter, and enough light—but *no view!* I wrote *Our Mr. Wrenn* while commuting on Long Island Railroad trains to my blurb-writing job at Doubleday, Doran's. One competent full-length book will do more to establish the prestige of a potential writer than a flood of short pieces."

In this connection, Lewis put up to me time and again—partly with the idea that in my case it might serve as excellent training and experience—his plan for gathering the research material for his long projected novel about labor. I suppose there was no younger man in whom he had seen the slightest literary promise who had escaped this proposal to join him in a Model A Ford tour of most of the leading industrial centers of the United States, and while he himself would engage typical working men in presumably revealing conversations, his younger collaborator was to take careful notes of the gist of each such encounter. I was still too unfamiliar with Lewis's major vagaries, and with the extent to which he had made the same offer to others, not to have been at the outset rather flattered by this repeated proposal; but instinct led me not to commit myself. I believe that in one or two instances he actually initiated such a tour; but, as might have been expected, they foundered almost at the outset. So far as I am aware, he never produced even a portion of a novel primarily concerned with labor.

Even had I then been free to follow Lewis's advice to devote myself exclusively to creative writing, there were at the moment certain obstacles which he was inclined to ignore. For after a full day in lower Broadway, capped with a final pummeling in the subway, there was no telling what I might find in our living room. More likely than not, Lewis would be surrounded by a welter of hopeful artistic strays from neighboring Greenwhich Village, some of whom were certain to touch him for loans; girls who ran basement bookshops; undergraduates from here and there, ostensibly doing research for English term papers, trying to look at ease in an atmosphere which left them puzzled and incredulous; a foreign correspondent or two, and at least one professional adventurer; and always a number of what Alf Harcourt described as "recurrent bevies of human alley cats and queers," odds and ends of humanity Lewis had met somewhere in his travels and had urged to be sure to look him up in New York, and who now, out of context, appeared lost and unassimilable.

To the least of these Lewis would listen with genuine deference— or more likely he would use the entire roomful as an audience for his clowning or his speeches in dialect—striving endlessly to stimulate a lively give-and-take, too often achieving no more than a rather hollow and specious kind of camaraderie.

Then again, by way of an enchanting interlude, one might find Elinor Wylie (whom he adored, and I shall never forget), peacefully having tea. Or of an evening there would gather, at one time or another, Rebecca West, the Van Dorens, Bill Benét, Hugh Walpole, George Jean Nathan, Osbert Sitwell, Laurence Stallings, Lewis Browne, William Seabrook, old Bill Woodward, Arthur Hopkins— and many, many others I can't now recall. In the presence of these Lewis usually restrained his histrionics and made a definite effort to entice his guests to lead the conversation. For these were individuals whom he respected either for certain skills or attributes, or because they had something to teach him—for, with all his egotism and occasional arrogance in other directions, I was always impressed by his open-mindedness and readiness to learn about his craft.

Although so frequently at the price of sleep, the general talk, critical opinions, and discussions of their various professions which such personalities exchanged when they thus gathered informally together were, of course, tremendously stimulating and instructive to a young man with tacit hopes and visions. In addition, at every opportunity when he was in the mood, I asked Lewis technical questions about his own methods and findings. He always answered most willingly and with great clarity, usually citing exceedingly apt examples from his enormously wide reading to illustrate his meaning. As he was drawing within sight of the completion of *Gantry*, I asked him what he regarded as some of the most difficult and arduous technical problems of writing a novel.

He answered at once: "In my own experience, one of the toughest and stubbornest problems is to evolve natural, smooth 'connective tissue' between the incidents, sequences, and divisions of my story, so that the reader will follow its transitions without being conscious of them. Another phase which frequently involves some of the hardest work is to dress characters, rooms, and scenes accurately and convincingly, and at the same time to make the process interesting enough to hold the reader's attention. Then there's the fundamentally important matter of unobtrusively familiarizing the reader with the locale of the story, so that, ideally speaking, he unconsciously acquires a sense of eye-witness, *living* participation in it. I've always made detailed maps of the more important fictional towns in my stories—let me show you the ones I made of Gopher Prairie, Minnesota, and of Zenith and Elk Mills in the State of Winnemac, and of a whole atlas-and-gazetteer-ful of places!" From his file he brought out a folder full of maps, all of which he had drawn, becoming progressively more detailed as this atlas of his Middle Western world expanded. Here were the towns in *Our Mr. Wrenn, The Trail of the Hawk, The Job, The Innocents,* and *Free Air.* Between Gopher Prairie and Zenith the detail increased until it was almost like an annotated commercial map, as for instance the ones of the business district, and of Floral Heights, the residential district of Zenith, whose outer fringes marked the horizon of Babbitt's daily life. By this folder full of maps Lewis had translated the world of his imagination and experience into something so close to reality that in listening to him one promptly became wholly convinced of their actuality. He was very proud of this distillation of his years of roaming and of photographic observation in every corner of the Middle West and in much of the rest of the United States; it was as real to him as *Bartholomew's World Atlas.*

I have always felt that nothing which happened during those months more accurately illumined Lewis's development from prairie boyhood to a place in the creative literature of his country than his first meeting with my father, which occurred when the latter paid me a few days' visit just as *Gantry* was being completed.

It will be recalled that Carol Kennicott wanted to study art. Lewis confessed to my father that during the period of his own adolescent struggle in Sauk Center to find his proper metier he had often considered studying Egyptology under young James Henry Breasted at the then almost equally young University of Chicago. One morning my father was working at my desk when Lewis, in faded pajamas and a battered dressing gown, stalked in, holding a sheet of manuscript. "It's the last page of *Elmer!*" he announced, as he handed it over, and genially draped himself at right angles across a chair.

My father laid the sheet on the desk and turned toward him. "You know, Hal," he said with twinkling-eyed solemnity, "I've had a bone to pick with you ever since I read *Main Street*, in which you are guilty of an omission tantamount to an untruth!"

Lewis peered expectantly over his horn-rimmed glasses.

"The book interested me enormously, and moved me as one is bound to be by the powerful portrayal of the stuff of which one's own life is made. I read it with peculiar sympathy and appreciation, and regard it as a remarkable achievement. I should think it would gain for itself the same lasting place in our American literature accorded to those comparatively few books which have captured the spirit of our vanished frontiers, and the significant moods and phases of our maturing national development. The historian delineates the bones and sinews of a nation's being. The *great* novelist clothes them with the flesh and blood of contemporary actuality, the human fabric of social background. *That* is an inspiring and very personal art. I envy you—and you'll smile when I confess that I would have considered myself really successful if I could have written a book about my own bailiwick like Kingsley's *Hypatia!*"

"I'm very flattered and touched, Doctor," said Lewis. "But what bone have I inadvertently left 'unclothed' for you to pick with me?"

"This: *you and I both* came from Main Street. We aren't geniuses, but we've had our creative impulses and the courage to pursue them —far beyond Main Street. Judging ourselves by our own standards, we know we aren't great—and we know we're not failures. We're solid and honest and eager and imbued with a modicum of vision, and in our small way we're a hopeful sign. The roster of American men and women of achievement in every field is filled with Main

Street kids. But *nowhere* in your book did you give Main Street credit for contributing such people to the national community or to the world. Your picture is barren and sterile of all that we and our kind represent. Such an omission is a misrepresentation: it is as if you'd held up to Main Street one of the distorting mirrors we used to see in country circus and county fair side shows. I believe you would have strengthened your case, Hal, by making at least a slight concession to these facts. Magnanimity is sometimes more effective than annihilation. Well, *that* was the friendly bone I've wanted to pick with you, ever since reading *Main Street.* I hope I haven't hurt your feelings!"

Lewis uncoiled himself from his chair, walked over, and laid his hand affectionately on the older man's shoulder.

"You're quite right," he said quietly. "I was younger then and terribly anxious to make a mark with my first major book. I *did* exaggerate to make my point."

He lighted a cigarette, picked up the sheet of manuscript, and looking at it thoughtfully as he moved toward the door, added almost to himself, "I suspect I might have been a more humane novelist had I studied Egyptology under Breasted!"

It happened that while my father was still staying with us, a young artist named Hoffman was sent up by the editor of *The New York Times Book Review* to do a portrait sketch of Lewis in anticipation of their lead review of his forthcoming book. Noticing that the young man looked quite gaunt and unwell, Lewis quickly ferreted out his personal history and that he had been and was still almost starving to death.

In another day or so my father left, ending his only meeting with Lewis. Sheaves of galleys began arriving by messenger, and—as always at this stage—Lewis worked night and day while shifts of male stenographers with court reporters' training worked in our living room around the clock, copying drastic revisions and rushing them off to the publisher, until the day came when all this was finished and he was to sail that night.

When I returned home late that afternoon he met me at the door and with a particularly gay manner said that he wanted my opinion of a portrait of himself which he had commissioned Hoffman to do as a surprise goodbye gift to his son Wells. He ordered me to face the other way while he set it up properly. "Now," he said, "turn and look at it!"

It was an oil portrait of my father, done rapidly but with such skill that it had caught the lovely quality of his complete absorption in his work of the moment, wholly unaware that he was posing for young Hoffman. Lewis's eyes were very expressive as he said simply. "I thought you might like it—as a reminder!"

It hangs on the study wall just above me as this is written.

NOBEL THE PRIZE-GIVER

by Harland Manchester

The irony has often been noted: A prize for peace was established by the inventor of dynamite, a man who believed that high explosives, because of the terrible destruction they could cause, would put an end to war. In this account Harland Manchester elaborates on such twists of fate in the life of the strange Swede, Alfred Nobel. A would-be writer, he had little talent for writing. In his forties he was rich, lonely, and bothered by stomach trouble and an unhappy love affair. As a final ignominy, even the famous prizes are not being awarded in the manner he intended.

JUNE 17, 1939

ONE DAY IN 1861 a group of Paris bankers gave impatient audience to a young man who said he had a big idea. Neither he nor his hearers connected his idea with an annual accolade to distinguished writers, yet today his name looms large in the field of literature. He was a Swede; a thin, sickly, nervous chap, with penetrating blue eyes and plenty of assurance.

"Messieurs," he announced dramatically, "I have an oil that will blow up the globe!"

The bankers jumped, but he produced no infernal machine, and calmly went on to explain his new explosive. Shortly his hearers cut him off. The whole thing was impossible, and anyway, who wanted the globe blown up?

When Napoleon III heard about the young Swede, however, he spoke to a financier, and Alfred Nobel went back to Stockholm with a draft for 100,000 francs. Within a year, he and his father were manufacturing nitroglycerin for commercial use. Soon the world was startled by a new word: dynamite. And the foundation was laid for the Nobel fortune, the income of which is now distributed annually to workers for peace, to scientists, and to gifted writers.

To Alfred Nobel, there was nothing sinister about powerful explosives. His father, Emmanuel Nobel, an architect turned in-

243

ventor, has been tinkering with them for years, and had invented a naval mine used by Russia in the Crimean War.

Emmanuel's income varied as much as his ideas. Despite the patient efforts of Mrs. Nobel, the family was often in hot water. They moved a great deal, and not by choice. When the landlord wanted cash, Emmanuel showed him blueprints. His enthusiasm was contagious, and sometimes the landlord forgot that the sketches were not legal tender. The year Alfred was born—1833—was one of those times when his father couldn't pay the rent. This time the creditors were not beguiled, and Emmanuel was thrown into bankruptcy.

Alfred was the third of four brothers, and the puniest of the lot. As a baby, he had convulsions, and for years his mother fought a constant battle to keep him alive. He had a weak spine, and when other children were playing, he sat on the sidelines and envied them. He had nervous headaches and a poor digestion, and was extremely sensitive to criticism.

Ludwig, the second son, was the apple of the old man's eye. Ludwig had genius, said Emmanuel, but Alfred worked harder. This talk got under Alfred's skin when at the age of seventeen his father sent him to New York to study a new heat engine invented by John Ericsson, who had migrated to New York and who was soon to revolutionize the world's navies with his ironclad *Monitor.* He sailed willingly, but no one knows how long he stayed in the United States or what he did. Soon he was back in Europe, rambling aimlessly here and there. He explored Paris night life, turned from it in disgust, and met a young girl with whom he fell desperately in love. She died, and he walked the streets all night, saw the sun rise, and wrote a long, introspective poem which he was to treasure all his life and to read to people who seemed sympathetic.

At the age of twenty-one the prodigal returned to his father's factory. Bitter, disillusioned, and hardened, but cherishing secret ideals which seemed impossible of realization, he went resolutely to work, for work, he decided, was all that life held for him.

Emmanuel Nobel was already convinced that nitroglycerin had great possibilities as an explosive, though it was used then chiefly as a stimulant in heart ailments. Under certain conditions it would explode, but no one knew just what these conditions were. Sometimes a container of the stuff would fall to the ground with a thud, and nothing would happen; sometimes a small jolt would cause a shattering explosion.

Some time during Alfred's four unexplained years, he had picked up a good working knowledge of chemistry, draftsmanship, and mechanical engineering. Gradually he took the lead in the experiments and arrived at the theory that the only sure way of exploding this soupish liquid was to confine it in a stout container and set it off with a sharp primary explosion. A match wouldn't explode nitroglycerin; it took force. He evolved the blasting cap—an invention still the basis of the whole nitroglycerin and dynamite industry.

After securing Louis Napoleon's help, Alfred and his father went hopefully to work, but nitroglycerin still would not behave. Neither Emmanuel nor Alfred was in the shop one morning in May 1864. The youngest son, Emil, and four workmen were there. An explosion killed everyone in the room instantly. Old Emmanuel was prostrated; he had a paralytic stroke from which he never recovered. He lingered for years, and from his bed or wheelchair continued to turn out "inventions," which Mrs. Nobel faithfully recorded. Stockholm shook with terror at the news of the explosion. The Nobels had no permit to work with explosives, and the authorities cracked down. But meanwhile, engineers and miners everywhere heard of the new time-saving, money-saving blasting oil. Orders and inquiries came in from all over the world.

Alfred Nobel moved his plant to a barge moored in a lake. Within a year he had launched manufacturing companies in Sweden, Finland, Norway, and Germany, and the Swedish government was using his "soup" to blast a terminal railway tunnel under Stockholm. Chemist, manufacturer, bookkeeper, and salesman all in one, he hardly took time to eat, and succeeded in ruining his digestion for life. Men with money to invest wanted demonstrations. Handling nitroglycerin often gives people headaches, and it affected Nobel violently, but he would allow no one else to run the risk. He would show them, he said, that his blasting oil was safe.

He was too optimistic; nitroglycerin's reign of terror was about to begin. One morning in November 1865, a Westphalian miner went to a store and asked for two pounds of blasting oil. The clerk started to pour it out, and that was the last of the clerk, the miner, and the store. At about the same time, Nobel's nitroglycerin plant in Norway soared skyward. A few weeks later, a railroad worker in Silesia tried to cut frozen blasting oil with an ax. They found his legs half a mile away.

The next April, nitroglycerin blew up aboard a ship docked in

Panama. Even the wharf and freight house near by were wrecked, and another ship badly disabled. Sixty people were killed, and the damage came to $1,000,000. Seventy cases of the stuff, marked for San Francisco, had blown up in the *European's* hold.

A few days later a freight wagon, bearing several oil-stained wooden boxes, drew up before the express office in San Francisco. The driver said, "Whoa!" and that was his farewell to life. Fifteen persons were killed, many were injured, and a $200,000 block of buildings was wrecked. The shipment of nitroglycerin was traced to Nobel's New York agents. Other nitroglycerin catastrophes followed.

Alfred Nobel arrived in New York on a business trip a few days after the San Francisco blast, bearing some boxes of "soup." He was about as welcome as the plague. The newspapers had aroused the public, and Fire Marshal Baker was chasing down rumors that parcels of the "murderous compound" were stored in lofts and warehouses. People avoided Nobel, and hotels turned him away. When he announced that he would give a public demonstration at a quarry on Eighty-third Street, only about twenty men came to see the fireworks, and even they kept their distance. Nobel brought out a flat piece of iron and laid it on a rock. He poured a little of the terrible oil on the iron, and then raised a hammer. The spectators ducked for cover as the hammer descended. There was a sharp report, but Nobel was unharmed. He coaxed them nearer, and in a dry, scientific manner explained that only the oil struck by the hammer exploded. There was the rest of the puddle, undisturbed. You couldn't blow off the lot, he said, without confining it. Then he touched a match to the puddle. It burned, but didn't explode.

For two hours Nobel put the mysterious giant through its paces. He finished the performance with some real blasts, to show what the giant would do when you gave him his head. The crowd went away convinced.

But governments were not convinced, and neither were transportation companies. Although Nobel's office was swamped with orders and a fortune was within his reach, he almost failed that year. Several countries passed laws forbidding the use of Nobel's "soup," and ships refused to carry it. A safe nitroglycerin had to be invented. So Alfred Nobel invented it, though some say it was an accident. In Northern Germany there is a light, absorbent earth called *Kieselguhr*. Nobel's workers ran out of sawdust and used it in packing nitroglycerin cans. The story is that one of the cans leaked, and Nobel noticed that the *Kieselguhr* drank it up like blotting paper.

He mixed three parts of "soup" with one part of *Kieselguhr* and his prayers were answered. The stuff could be kneaded like putty and packed in cartridges, it could be exploded with a blasting cap, and it was safe to chip. Nobel called it dynamite. Within a decade, fifteen Nobel plants were turning out six million pounds annually of the new explosive.

At forty, Alfred Nobel found himself a lonely, exhausted, melancholy man, with no interests outside his work, and few acquaintances outside his companies. He had money enough to satisfy any taste, but he couldn's relax and didn't know how to go about enjoying himself. He didn't even have a home. They called him "the richest vagabond in Europe."

He tried to make himself over. He bought a fine house in Paris and lived there most of the time. There were few things he could eat because of his stomach trouble, but he installed a good cook, began to entertain, and took great pride in his cellar and his table appointments. He returned to Shelley, the god of his boyhood, and had an idea of writing something worth while. But he was equally at home in six languages and never could make up his mind which to use. Even in conversation he wandered from one to another, unconsciously slipping into the language which the topic suggested.

He had written great quantities of blank verse in his youth, but late in life he burned the lot, except for the gloomy, introspective, autobiographical poem, a hundred pages long, in which he had traced his life from infancy through his unhappy love affair, concluding in a tone of self-dedication to a life of work. He wrote the poem in English, later translating it into Swedish.

Nobel was a prodigious reader, not only of technical books but of poetry, philosophy, and, in general, what he called "ideal literature." He sternly disapproved of Zola and the realists, and greatly admired the work of Bjørnson and Selma Lagerlöf (who were both to receive the Nobel prize in literature) and the Swedish poet, Viktor Rydberg, romantic idealist. Many of his letters—he often wrote fifty a day—were exhaustive discussions of new novels, plays, and books of verse. He liked those writers who bolstered his belief in the constant progress of humanity. He had a lofty vision of a time when "people would come into the world with better-developed brains." Yet, paradoxically, he scoffed at man's meanness and insignificance, and called himself a "benevolent misanthrope."

For a time Nobel frequented the salon of Madame Juliette Adam, editor of the *Nouvelle Revue,* whose influence on politics and literature was considerable. Authors read from their books there, and actresses recited poems. He also went occasionally to Victor Hugo's house. These meetings spurred him to resume writing, and two unfinished novels resulted. *Brothers and Sisters* dealt skeptically with religion; *In Lightest Africa* was not a travel book but a vehicle for Nobel's political attitude, which may be described as a kind of socialism modified by distrust of the mass mind. In both attempts, the characters are mere mouthpieces, and there are long, involved dialogues suggestive of duller passages of Ibsen or Shaw.

He also tried playwriting. Bitter at the loss of a patent suit in England, he wrote a satirical play about it which could interest no one except those involved in the litigation, and he worked for a time at a trivial domestic comedy which he called *A Victim of Imagination*. The year of his death, he turned out a four-act tragedy, in which he became completely absorbed. He went to London for a business conference, talked business for five minutes, then brought out his play and read it.

The play was called *Nemesis,* and it was based upon the same theme as Shelley's tragedy, *The Cenci*. It was full of tedious declamation and was too close to Shelley for comfort. Nobel's writing friends suggested changes, but he refused to alter a word, saying that he would rather "flutter with his own wings than fly with those of others." The play was about to be published when he died. His executors looked it over and thought it best to burn the edition, saving only three copies for the files. They said that the memory of a great man should not be dimmed by a poor play.

It would have pleased Nobel to make his house a meeting place for intellectuals; and because he wanted to entertain, he considered marriage, but since his early love affair he hadn't met a woman he thought he could get along with. He made cynical remarks about women, for he was desperately shy and believed himself so repulsive that no woman would marry him except for his money. Yet he could be very entertaining, and whenever an attractive woman made a determined attempt to be nice to him, he opened up like a peony.

It was his loneliness, in fact, that led to the establishment of the prizes. In his study there was a secretary's desk, but it was usually vacant. His correspondence was in six languages, and it was not easy to find a good secretary and an accomplished linguist in one person. He knew that he was asking a lot and got so that he hated to hire secretaries because he dreaded dismissing them.

In 1876 he tried once more, with this notice: "A very wealthy, cultured, elderly gentleman desires to find a lady also of mature years, familiar with languages, as secretary and manager of his household." He probably thought it discreet to call himself "elderly." He was only forty-three.

Bertha Kinsky, a Bohemian countess, answered this advertisement. She was an attractive woman of thirty, well educated, charming in manner, and a good listener. Nobel's gloomy, kindly, and occasionally sarcastic manner appealed to her. He, in turn, was much impressed, but before she had actually entered upon her duties, she eloped with young Baron von Suttner.

The young couple worked for the Red Cross during the Russo-Turkish War. The Baroness came back appalled by what she had seen and wrote a passionate antiwar novel. Soon she was a recognized leader in the peace movement. The Baroness and Alfred Nobel had remained firm friends, and now she appealed to him to help in the movement. He was skeptical, but asked her to send him reading matter and keep him informed. She bombarded him with pamphlets, and they had long debates.

The Baroness had approached Nobel at exactly the right time. With leisure to think, he had made up his mind that many things needed changing. He became opposed to the inheritance of large fortunes. He provided for his mother handsomely but told the rest of the family not to expect anything when he died.

Nobel was undoubtedly moved by Bertha von Suttner's enthusiasm, although he sometimes poked a little fun at her. What she needed was not money, he told her, but a workable plan. There were too many "gas bags" in the movement, he told her, and some of their schemes were ridiculous. He predicted that his high explosives would put an end to war sooner than her peace meetings, because as military weapons became more deadly, horrified nations would disband their troops.

In spite of his doubts, Nobel made up his mind that he would leave his fortune—which amounted to about nine million dollars at his death—to found a prize for distinguished peace workers. Later he included the prizes for science and literature. It is interesting that he intended these money awards not as crowns for the eminent and successful but as lifebelts for sinking geniuses, which would save them from financial anxiety while they went on to new achievements. He said that he wished to help dreamers who have a hard time getting a living, and once, when asked to contribute to a Rydberg memorial, he said he preferred "to consider the bellies of the living." Yet the terms of his loosely drawn will have made it impossible for the award committees to consider the financial status of the recipients.

All this was not exactly what the Baroness had in mind, but her part in bringing it about was widely recognized. When the first Nobel Peace Prize was awarded in 1901, Henri Dunant, co-winner, wrote to thank Bertha von Suttner. The prize was her work, he said. It seems fitting that four years later the peace prize went to the Baroness herself.

Alfred Nobel ended his days in austere solitude in his luxurious villa at San Remo, Italy. He had turned his back on Paris when the French government, alarmed because he had sold his smokeless powder to Italy, placed restrictions upon his work. When his brother Ludwig, who had made a fortune in oil, died, the French papers thought it was Alfred; and he had the peculiar satisfaction of reading his own obituaries. They were not complimentary.

At San Remo he spent most of the time in his laboratory working on synthetic rubber and artificial silk. His heart began to give out, and he went to specialists. He laughed when they prescribed nitroglycerin. He bought a sphygmograph, watched the line which showed the irregularity of his pulse, and pointed out to friends the degree of variation that would kill him. On December 10, 1896 he died.

Before his death Alfred Nobel abandoned the idea that more powerful killing agents would frighten the nations into peace. He pinned his faith on something very much like the League of Nations. "The only true solution," he wrote, "would be a convention under which all the governments would bind themselves to defend collectively any country that was attacked."

At first, Nobel did not intend to found a perpetual peace prize. He suggested that it be discontinued at the end of thirty years, for he believed that if international peace were not assured by then, the world would relapse into barbarism. He said that in 1893. It was just thirty years later that an Austrian house painter led a *Putsch* in Munich.

THE JOYCE I KNEW

by Oliver St. John Gogarty

Nobody could ask for more intimate, revealing, shocking, or amusing anecdotes about James Joyce than these by his close friend, Oliver Gogarty. And perhaps one could not ask for a more scathing blast at Joyce and his great work than this one from the man who is supposed to have been the Buck Mulligan of Ulysses. *The distinguished Irish literary figure—an ex-surgeon—draws his scalpel across the abdomen of Joyce in this piece and the one that follows, and performs an autopsy the like of which we shall not see again for many a day.*

JANUARY 25, 1941

THE NATIONAL LIBRARY stands in a little park off Kildare St., Dublin. It is a domed structure and faces a similar building, the National Museum. Both are surrounded by a pillared circular portico. Between these a seated figure of Queen Victoria holding a scepter, on a high pedestal of white stone, adorns the lawn.

This library was used chiefly by students who found it most beneficial. It enabled "medicals" to pawn the expensive books their parents provided and to spend the money in counteracting the results which their soberer studies might be expected to produce on their spirits. Law and engineering students and a few "lady medicals" with one or two "queer" characters made up the attendance. The sporting fraternity and city idlers found no appropriate reading matter in the National Library because by order of the Director, Dr. Lyster, all reports of horse races and such items had been blotted out from the daily newspapers.

The atmosphere of the place was friendly, for the readers were all more or less known to each other. The service was prompt and it took only a minute or two to obtain any book or books, listed on one of the slips provided at the desk.

The large round room, which was rarely ever full, was furnished by oak tables and chairs. The tables held from six to ten readers each. On each a notice, "Silence Please," stood.

251

With his back toward the center of the room a slim figure was seated in front of a large map. He was wielding a compass in his computations. He wore—which was rather remarkable—a white yachting cap. Frayed white rubber shoes matched the cap. His trousers of dark gray cloth were worn and ran into little torn tassels at the heels.

Filled with curiosity, I took a seat beside him. I was astonished to discover that the shy youth was an acquaintance I had made some months before with Vincent Cosgrave, a common friend, who was what was known as a "chronic medical"—that is, one who had taken lectures, walked the hospitals, but had failed to keep pace with the examinations. The shy youth was carrying two volumes (won as a prize for English literature) of Paracelsus, bound in red morocco, to the pawnbroker.

I said, "Hello, Joyce."

Gravely the nearsighted blue eyes with their broad, curved, light brown lashes saluted me. Without preamble, he said, "From Ushant to Scilly is more than thirty-five leagues." I observed that the map spread in front of him was a map of the English Channel.

Although he saw that his remark had failed to convey all his meaning, he did nothing to enlighten me. This, I was to find later, was a mannerism. Instead he sang in a low, sweet voice.

> *Farewell and adieu to you, Spanish Ladies,*
> *Farewell and adieu to you, Ladies of Spain:*
> *For we've received orders to sail for Old England*
> *But we hope that we one day may meet you again.*

Then with his voice filling and his finger beating time and, as it were, admonishing me, he continued:

> *We'll rant and we'll roar, like true British sailors;*
> *We'll rant and we'll roar across the salt seas,*
> *Until we strike soundings in the Channel of England;*
> *From Ushant to Scilly is thirty-five leagues.*

> *It's forty.*

Suddenly from the opposite side of the table a clergyman with a broad red face shouted, "Silence, please," and pushed roughly toward us the wooden notice on which the words were written.

With strange gravity James Augustine Joyce bowed his head

toward the priest and continued to point out to me the beauties of the old sea chanty with its assonantal rhyme "seas" with "leagues."

The priest rose with a snort and made for the door. James Augustine Joyce picked up from the floor an ash plant which he used as a walking stick and made after him. He walked silently in his white rubber shoes with a loping stride. At the door he overtook Fr. O'Driscoll.

"Might I ask, Father, are you a parish priest?"

"No. Why do you ask?"

"Because you have the manners of one."

I wondered at the time what had been the cause of such bias against the Church. Later I learned.

He came from the lower-middle-class society, as that social stratum was dubbed in Victoria's day. His father had some little income of about $250 a year. This he spent on drink and good fellowship while his wife, who was delicately nurtured, was left to feed her starving sons and daughters as best she could. There are stories still current about "auld Joyce," with his smattering of law probably derived from his brother, James's uncle, who worked in an attorney's office and was what was known as a solicitor's clerk. Old Joyce was said to have been paid by many a landlord to take himself and his family out of the house.

Joyce was deeply attached to his mother. He described how he had seen her with her delicate fingers red from the lice she had killed on the bodies of his starving sisters. From such a home did Joyce when he was at the impressionable age of eleven come to that class in a Jesuit school to hear the sermon on eternity which he describes as timed for one hour by the clergyman's watch. It was a turning point for Joyce. For from the psychic trauma of that sermon I believe he never recovered. Coming famished from such a house at that moment the child's mind was filled with terror that later was to turn impotently to rage against the Word which is God and by making it, the Word, maudlin, to rid himself of responsibility to the God of his childhood and the heritage of eternal punishment.

This Hound of Heaven pursued him relentlessly to the end. There is no doubt about the *Prius dementat*. But there is another factor which arises from the character of the nation and the spirit abroad at the time which AE has touched upon and which will be referred to later on.

He won a second-class prize of twenty pounds in the Intermediate examinations. Most of this he gave to his mother, but he kept eight pounds to pay one year's rent of one of those fortresses with which the British Government dotted the east coast of Ireland after the threat of a French invasion during the Napoleonic wars.

This is the Tower mentioned in the first lines of *Ulysses* from the stairs of which a figure with smoke-blue eyes and glistening teeth emerges carrying shaving materials preparatory to going out to swim. The person so described is said to be myself, as it well may be, so alien is that gay, water-loving character who moved not sullen in the sweet air to all the thwarted, mad, miserable phantoms of the rest of that terrible exposition of indignation and revolt.

The first day we got the tower, Joyce, with inherited learning in such matters, "took possession" by depositing in it a bundle of sweet and simple poems. They were written in his beautiful and learned handwriting, each on a large separate sheet of paper. He took pains to explain that, as we had left in it private property, the bargain was ratified.

We had possession of a secure house. The next thing necessary was furniture. This I provided from the maternal home in Rutland Square.

For two years we lived off and on in this impregnable place. Whoever was likely to be home first bore the key, which was a foot and a half in length.

"You'd be a long time hitting a man with that before you'd make him laugh," said the Stationmaster at Sandycove when he saw it in my hand. We were warm, comfortable, and secure. And both our parents were spared anxiety on account of the vertiginous and variegated paths that those who would climb the hoofy hill must follow.

One morning in pursuance of certain bylaws of the railway and tram companies, discouraging to those who have no tickets, we decided to walk to the city. On the way Joyce told me that he could easily do the distance, that he had been fancied as a long-distance runner by his uncle. I thought that his uncle could have been but a poor judge of stamina if he expected it from the lean and undernourished body of his nephew.

On the way we met old Yeats, the father of the poet. He came on, walking rapidly toward us on the narrow sideway. He looked erect and tall and energetic. His black eyes burned brightly in spite of his years and his white beard and thick, whitening hair showed the vigor of the man.

I told Joyce who the pedestrian was.

"The father of the bard! Touch him!" he directed.

This I refused to do. Joyce stopped him with, "Good morning, Mr. Yeats."

After a little conversation with which I did not care to be associated, knowing its import, I heard the old man exclaim indignantly, "Ten pence? Certainly not! I have not the least intention of encouraging drunkards."

Joyce wrote to me saying that it was necessary for him to get a suit of clothes in order to sing at parties. He planned to get Dolmetsch to make a lute for him to which to sing in the south coast towns of England old catches, songs, and ballads which had for centuries fallen out of mind.

I remember one he loved. He sang it with his clarion-clear tenor voice, which sounded more like an instrument than mortal vocal cords.

> *Fresh a coom from Sandwith Street*
> *Dollie, Dollie*
> *My best friends here for to meet*
> *Dollie, Ah!*
> *Dollie de dil, and do,*
> *Dollie, Dollie*
> *Dollie de dil, and do,*
> *Dollie Ah!*
> *The Green Cuffs is coomin' in*
> *Dollie, Dollie*
> *That will make the lasses sing,*
> *Dollie Ah!*

Then turning to me, with serious brow and forefinger beating time, he would announce,

> *Dollie Coxon's pawned her shirt*
> *To ride upon the baggage cart.*
> *Dollie Ah!*

I never heard a voice to compare with his. Had sight singing, that is reading from the score, not been a *sine qua non* of the Feis competition, he would have borne off the gold medal and have been perhaps an unbodied John McCormack; but his voice, though as sensitive, had no more feeling than a manometric flame. He won the bronze medal but he threw it away in contempt for the judges.

No man had more erudition at so early an age. Though myopic, he wore no glasses, possibly because he could not afford them; but his reading must have been as prodigious as his memory was. "Memory, Mother of the Muses."

I thought of bringing him over to Oxford but regard for its conventions (snobbish reasons we would call them now) prevented me. I was competing for the Newdigate and I wished to try his method of punctuation, which seemed to me unique. I tried it unaided and astonished, to my cost, the examiners with the result—I will not say the result—for the now Bishop of Chichester's winning poem was more classical and austere—that I only achieved a *proxime accessit*. Had there been a medal, I should not have thrown it away.

From Oxford I invited to the Tower Samuel Trench, one of those Irish men of Cromwellian stock who had become "more Irish than the Irish themselves." In his rooms at Holywell and in Balliol he taught Gaelic long before it became the vogue. He refused to use boot polish unless it was Irish and he even thought of breaking the lampshades until they came to be produced in the country.

In the Tower I introduced him to Joyce. He was no snob; but Joyce had so much of that worship that he allowed it to appear in his implied inferiority to the Englishman Haines, whom Trench became in *Ulysses*.

Trench slept in a narrow bed to the right of the door which we kept ever open for light and air. I slept on the other side to the left. Joyce was away to the right at three o'clock on a dial under the shelves on which fish kettles and pots and pans and tin plates were stacked high. We used tin plates because they would stand being made red hot in the fire, a method by which we used to solve the grease problem.

For months all went well. Trench got a job among that Lorenzo il Magnifico of Dublin, Sir Horace Plunkett's, "home brighteners," Oxford youths and highborn maidens who were intended to go among the peasantry and show them how to raise, through the Arts, their standard of living. The Gaelic League was growing: the Irish Literary Renaissance was being born. Yeats kept on founding the National Theatre whenever anyone likely to endow it appeared. Lady Gregory was enticing over from Liverpool a Miss Horniman, who founded the Abbey Theatre and was then cast out.

If Joyce's social status or the lack of it precluded him from the company of Home Brighteners, his effrontery to Yeats shut him out of the band of geniuses for which Lady Gregory was advertising for the Abbey.

When Yeats reached his fortieth birthday, it was proposed that a sum should be collected to present him with a Kelmscott Chaucer imprinted at the press of his friend and (at the time) master, William Morris.

Yeats was staying at the Cavendish Hotel, the first house from Rutland Square in Cavendish Row.

One evening Joyce sought audience with Yeats and obtained it because Yeats happened to answer the ring at the door.

It opened on Joyce.

"How old are you, Mr. Yeats?"

Taken by surprise, Yeats answered, "I am forty years old today."

"I am sorry. You are too old for me to help you."

The door was slowly closed in his face.

He recited this incident without comment to me just after it had happened.

And that was about six o'clock. It must have been winter for we were in a tram and the evening was dark.

To this attitude and recoil from the world of beauty which Yeats was creating, like the ancient Thebes from song, George Russell refers somewhere.

As far as I remember, the gist of his comment was that it was inevitable that there should be a recoil in such a breast as Joyce's from the poet's ordered imagination and at a time, too, when the national spirit was re-creating itself through the art of Yeats. With savage indignation against all that was bad form and was holy, Joyce, a disheveled harbinger of the Bolshevik revolution, flung himself away from beauty and harmony to howl outcast for the rest of his life through the dark recesses of the soul.

The obstinate courage which enabled him for twenty years to keep on writing, all in longhand, a work of over a thousand pages without hope of a publisher is an outstanding proof of that unswerving belief in himself and his self-expression, which made him anything but a genial companion. He was a Dante who lost the key to his own Inferno. He never, though all his life was a purgatory, passed through it to make the ascent to Paradise.

The lovely, simple notes of pure lyricism which are to be found in *Chamber Music* (named in mockery after the sound he made by kicking accidentally a night jar) died away and maniacal rage against all things established took their place in a brothel in his lacerated heart.

His unyielding, unconceding opinion of himself was to my mind hardly consistent with sanity. But then who can rage against the Divine Word or Reason and be sane?

I do not know what went on during his interview with Lady Gregory. Before he went to see her he assured me that "they" had plenty of money and that a new movement was starting to form a National Theatre. He intended not to let the opportunity slip. What the opportunity was he did not reveal. But it was obvious when he came from his visit to her that the "Old Lady Says No" was all too true, even then.

I inquired how he had got on. With bent head and beating finger he recited his limerick gravely:

> *There was a kind Lady called Gregory,*
> *Who said, "Come to me poets in beggary";*
> *But found her imprudence*
> *When thousands of students*
> *Cried, "All we are in that category."*

When he first left Dublin about 1905 he went to Flushing to teach English in a Berlitz school. He was a linguist and could teach Italian or French. He had a picture post card printed. It showed him in a long overcoat muffled to the throat. It was in imitation of the French poet Rimbaud, whom he admired. Two poems on what looked like galley sheets followed. One was "Gas from a Burner." I forget what he called the other. They were both defiant, mocking, and satirical. They summed up all the Dublin coterie. He compared himself to a stag at bay. I came in for some disapprobation:

> *And one whose conduct seems to own*
> *A preference for a man of tone.*

This was a reference to the fact that Trench had outstayed him as my guest. And though he thought that Trench had fired at his bed it was I who got the blame. True, I had more in common with Trench, but then Joyce would never expand. He expected to be taken blindly at an undisclosed but apparently unlimited valuation while suffering from his own imagined inferiority. There is still something to be said for men of tone. You know where you are with them. They can die for the Ideal. They do not think it incumbent on them to demonstrate their own superiority by smashing down Idealism and merging it with the primeval slime.

I hope that the adulation, even though it may have been undiscriminating, of the literary dilettantes of Paris soothed his heart insatiable for fame. He certainly left himself at the mercy of a world which is miserly in its praise, yet, when it gives it, is rarely wrong. It must have seemed to him that acclaim if sufficiently voluminous was an assurance of immortality. So long as he was convinced of his immortality he must have been acidulously happy. He certainly attained an eternity different to that with which he was threatened by the Jansenistic Jesuit when he was "but and a little tiny boy."

I was able to like the man largely because I was able to dispense with reciprocation. And we were friends at a madcap, careless time. For his work he drew on all literature. Gertrude Stein, with her *Portrait of Mabel Dodge at the Villa Curona,* had begun the trick of shuffling sentences and expecting them to give more suggestion that way than if they made sense. But her nonsense was only superficial. She had not thought of intussuscepting words or of making them keep the jingle and suggestion of near words such as thieves use in their argot when they say I was "elephants," meaning that they were drunk: drunk, elephant's trunk: elephants.

Joyce went further than this.

In a rhyme in English argot of about 1705, the second stanza of which he quotes, you will see one of the springs of his idea. Far away from references as I am, I remember only the first stanza:

> *Doxy, oh, thy glaziers are*
> *As glimmer by the Salomon.*
> *No gentry mort has prats like thine*
> *No cove e'er wapt with such a one.*

Which might be taken to mean Doxy, thine eyes are as stars; by my solemn oath no lady had parts like thine; No cove ever was warped with such a one. I am told that here prats means buttocks; but what does it matter?

In *Anna Livia Plurabelle* his experiment is at its best. Here there is intelligible evidence of that for which he was striving, and that was to make words in a surrealistic way show roots as well as blossoms. His stupendous erudition is evident in every word. I don't know exactly how many names of rivers are suggested in the description of the Liffey's woven waves that drown the reader until the sense is submerged only to give him a moment's breathing space and a glimpse of it again. The history of Dublin, that city which for all his traveling he never left, is in it too and his mockery when he makes the two washerwomen who later become, one, a tree and the other a stone, wash the dirty linen of the Church. The oncoming of twilight is suggested by sentences that waver abruptly on the wing like bats. *Finnegans Wake* may mean, among many other themes, the death of Finn, the central figure of Ireland's Heroic Age which Yeats revived. Joyce must have found satisfaction at the national disillusionment which followed the entry of the Republicans to power in the Irish Free State. Even so a page or two should have been enough. Joyce was a great repudiator: he repudiated Ireland, he repudiated the Church, he repudiated the Classics and his more intelligible self.

When all is said, the choice between the Logos, the Divine Word, "this godlike Reason," and the large discourse and senseless mutterings of the subliminal mind's low delirium, yet remains to be taken.

There is room in this world of ours for every form of literature. But those whose gaze is clear and undimmed and steadfastly fixed on the Vision Beautiful, as Yeats's was, must see what a waste of ingenuity and what nonsense this vast concordance represents.

To me it is like a shattered cathedral through the ruins of which, buried deep and muted under the debris, the organ still sounds with all its stops pulled out at once.

THEY THINK THEY
KNOW JOYCE

by Oliver St. John Gogarty

*Continuing his analysis of Joyce, Dr. Gogarty theorizes on the
origin of the language in* Ulysses *and tells what he thinks of it.*

MARCH 18, 1950

WE WERE YOUNG, we were merry in our salad days in Dublin. There
were James Joyce, John Elwood (we called him "the Citizen," an
ebullient, tangential fellow with quizzical, dancing eyes and a lovely
mouth, whose favorite adjective was "terrific!"), and myself.

Opposite the National Library, where we met, was the National
Museum with a curved colonnade. Its hall was circular and decorated by nude plaster casts, somewhat larger than life, of the famous
statues of antiquity. One afternoon Joyce confronted Elwood as we
gathered at our usual meeting place. He assumed an air of very great
gravity as he was wont to do when about to perpetrate a joke.

"It has come to my notice, Citizen," he said solemnly, "that this
morning between the hours of ten-thirty and eleven you inscribed
your name in lead pencil on the backside of the Venus of Cnidus.
Are there any extenuating reasons that may be cited in your defense?"

"He's terrific," said the Citizen when we talked about it afterward.
"He's a great artist. Terrific."

In the Dublin use of the word *artist* lies the key to James Joyce:
the explanation of how this contradictory character, who in his early
days knew beauty so well, became chief of the apostles of confusion
and ugliness, the leader of the decadents.

In Dublin *artist* does not denote one who is devoted to painting
or any of the arts. In Dublin an artist is a merry droll, a player of
hoaxes. In Dublin if you went to a fancy-dress ball attired as a bird
and laid an egg that exploded, you would be an artist; if you bought
a ham in the morning, paid for it, left it hanging outside the store

until the rush hour, and then ran off, carrying it under your arm, with the police in hot pursuit, you would be an artist of the first category.

I wonder what all the worshipers of Joyce would say if they realized that they had become the victims of a gigantic hoax, of one of the most enormous leg-pulls in history.

Floods of nonsense have been poured on James Joyce by those who know nothing about Dublin. The authors of these learned treatises see significances and palimpsests, connections with the nine months' gestation of the human embryo and the development of the earth, as well as parodies of authors appropriate to the theme.

I think with sorrow of the Joyce worshipers. Perhaps when we consider that their enthusiasm is the measure of their ignorance it would be folly to try to enlighten them. But when they pretend that Joyce and they are inventors of something new and unprecedented in literature, "a new speech dimension," as one gentleman, C. Giedion-Welcker, calls it, our indulgence ceases. Here is a specimen of what Mr. Giedion-Welcker so admires in Joyce: "He had already woven various word jokes about Zurich into the section concerning 'Anna Livia Plurabelle.' 'Well, that's the Limmat' (for limit), 'You don't say the silly-post?' (for Sihlpost), and 'legging a jig or so on the sihl. . . . There's the bell for Sexaloitez. . . .' " A new speech dimension? It is infantile. Mairzy Doats! As Jung put it:

> [I] read it [*Ulysses*] from the end backwards. This proved to be as good a way as the usual one, for it has no forwards and no backwards, no top and no bottom. Everything could as well have been so before, or might easily still become so in the future . . . the entire work reminds us of the bisected worm that can grow a new tail and a new head where they are needed. We are in doubt whether we are dealing with a physical or with a transcendental tapeworm. In itself the tapeworm is a whole living cosmos—and it is fabulously procreative. This, it seems to me, is an unbeautiful though hardly an unfitting comparison for Joyce's chapters. It is true that the tapeworm can produce nothing but other tapeworms, yet it can produce them in inexhaustive quantities.

When we think of anyone's hailing *Ulysses* and *Finnegans Wake* as all the world's erudition in disguise, the question of the sanity, or even of the literacy, of the Joyce enthusiast arises. It is said that there are only 600 in a generation whom Nature has equipped with the necessary apparatus for perceiving the beauty of poetry. Joyce was pre-eminently equipped. He had a "nose like a rhinoceros for litera-ture," as Juvenal said about the long-haired boys in Rome. His repertory was prodigious; he was familiar with every line of the masters of English poetry and prose. His love of beauty, his capa-bility, and his unerring taste resulted in his little book of poems *Chamber Music,* composed when he was about nineteen, which con-tains all that he wished to keep of his visions of youth and loveliness.

What happened to cause him to produce *Ulysses,* a triumph of ug-liness and chaos and ineffectuality?

There was a small publishing firm in Dublin whose manager burned a whole edition of *Dubliners*—all but one copy, which he al-lowed Joyce to take with him to the Continent. He claimed that *Dubliners* contained an offensive reference to the King, which was unlikely, seeing that Joyce received a grant from the King's Privy Purse long before he established a place for himself in literature. This was the unkindest cut of all, coming on the top of failure to obtain employment or even food. The persecution complex was supplied. Something broke in Joyce: to Maunsell's firm and to the slum-stricken town he said, "A pox on both your houses." He fled to Flushing in Holland, whence he sent two abusive poems to his ac-quaintances. He admitted no one to his friendship. Henceforth it was to be James Augustine Joyce against the world.

He had come to consider all Dubliners his enemies. The last time he visited that city he called on me in Ely Place. He looked out at my garden, which was in all the beauty of blossom.

"Is this your revenge?" he asked.

"Revenge on whom?" I inquired.

"The public, of course," he said.

He was the most predamned soul I have ever encountered.

From Flushing I received a post card with a photograph of Joyce dressed to resemble Arthur Rimbaud. Rimbaud's revolution against established canons made him a god to Joyce. We must not leave Rimbaud out of the reckoning; if we do, we will fail to understand the influences that fashioned Joyce. Rimbaud, disgusted with man-kind, had withdrawn from the world. The logical end was for him to withdraw from all authorship because his kind of private writing would lead only to talking to himself. Joyce did not withdraw, so he ended by listening to himself talking in his sleep—*Finnegans Wake.* The Greeks have a name for such private persons—*idiotes.*

Dublin had proved itself to be sterile: his publishing ventures had been disastrous. With his persecution complex now uppermost, he decided he would put down all that he felt about the futility of life, the meaningless days of Everyman, all the ugliness of human existence. Above all, he would record the boredom of life in the cracked mirror of *Ulysses,* with its preposterous and factitious parallel to Homer's fairy tale. He would depict a world open at both ends wherein nothing happened, though everything was just about to happen, and all would hurry on in a senseless, chaotic cataract. He would hold up a mirror to a Dublin that had come to nothing.

In future he would give the world the obverse side of the medal, the gargoyle and the grotesque, instead of anything that might exalt and beautify life. He would write so that all who run might read all that Dublin offered to him. On the backside of beauty he would inscribe his name. If the writing proved to be indelible, all the better.

About this time the obscene bulk of Gertrude Stein appeared. She began making nonsense of the language and presenting the potpourri to a public which could be reached by people of her sort who controlled the avenues of publicity. *A Portrait of Mabel Dodge at the Villa Curona* appeared about 1907. It stated among other messages that "blankets are warmer in the summer: the explicit visit: there has been William."

Joyce moved to Trieste. Here for a dozen years he labored at *Ulysses* without any hope of its ever seeing the light. From what used to be thieves' argot—"elephant's trunk" for "drunk" and then for "drunk" simply "elephants"—he evolved the extraordinary amalgam of correlatives, echoes, parodies, and caricatures which is one of the most depressing things that has ever come out of literature: *Ulysses.*

Joyce was educated as a "Schoolman." According to his brother, who has written the most presentable account of him, he very nearly became a Jesuit. He never could be said to have left the order, for he was never received in it. But he never left the Middle Ages. He was "trained in the school of old Aquinas," he once said of himself.

Therefore it should not come as a surprise when we read that the Schoolmen of the Middle Ages, the very early Middle Ages, were in the habit of playing tricks with words. Here is a quotation from *The Gateway of the Middle Ages,* by Eleanor Shipley Duckett, with reference to *The Hesperica Famina, the Western Sayings:* "This is a collection of texts on various subjects composed in a bizarre and artificial style that seems to have been a vogue among cultured writers of Britain and Ireland in the fifth, sixth, and seventh centuries. . . . It seems as if the devotees of some literary cult had used all their ingenuity to pick out from the glossaries and all recondite and mysterious sources a language of their own foreign to the writing of the time."

Joyce had taught for a time at the Berlitz language school in Paris. What greater glossary could he have at hand than all the languages of the Berlitz schools?

I, who knew Joyce and the Dublin in which he lived and the way it treated him, find amusement here and there in *Ulysses,* even in the fact that Ulysses never comes into the book. Ulysses is the author, Joyce himself, seeking his true home in gaunt Ithaca. I personally can find here and there some pay dirt in *Ulysses,* for there are sparks to be glimpsed of bawdiness and argot. But these must pass completely unrecognized by anyone not well informed about the randy songs of the old city, with its despairing degradation of human life.

Ulysses was published at last. I have once been called "an accessory before the act" of Joyce's *Ulysses.* The United States may be called with more justice "an accessory after the act." Had it not been for Sylvia Beach, who published *Ulysses,* and Miss Wearing, who endowed Joyce with a liberal allowance, which enabled him to live in comfort for the first time in his life, there might have been neither *Ulysses* nor what followed.

Suddenly Joyce found that his leg-pull had acquired an international audience. Suddenly he discovered that to write his name on the backside of beauty was the most significant action of his life. He dared not retract; money and fame were at stake. He dared not let anyone into a joke that had gone too far and had been taken too seriously. I wonder what he thought when he found himself taken seriously so far from the only place where he could count on understanding. He could not let down his followers or his fans. His thin lips could not for one moment relax in a grim smile. The seriousness which he assumed when perpetrating a joke had overwhelmed him. Mockery was catching. What an "artist" he had become!

We must not blame Joyce's admirers too much if they are unaware of what happened in the monasteries and the schools of Ireland in the fifth and sixth centuries. In large part his admirers are internationalists whose mother tongue is any language but English. How should they know of this medieval gibberish?

But a stern protest becomes due when tribes of the inept but intellectually arrogant failures in literature, such as Gertrude Stein, seize on the opportunity of imitating *Ulysses* in presenting boredom, dirt, and despair as fitting subjects for poetry and prose. They ask us to bow down before all followers of "The Master," to hail them as innovators and immortal geniuses. The only thing about them that is immortal is their ineptitude. They ask us to join them in hailing the loss of human dignity, the degradation and disgrace of Man.

In the Polynesian group are certain islands where the demented are worshiped, and there is an island where to be happy is taboo. Joyce was far from demented. He had deliberation, persistence, and fortitude; *Ulysses,* his stink bomb for Dublin, had long, careful preparation. Like the unfortunate Polynesians, the Joyce worshipers reverence the topsy-turvy; by dwelling on the ugliness and misery of things they make themselves miserable and then expect us to share their wretchedness. In literature as in life their practice is the same. False contrasts, strangulated adjectives, pettiness, and rhythmless platitudes are all they can offer in the place of poetry. *Ulysses* was an example of making ineffectuality the subject of a novel. What a chance this presented for cashing in on their incompetence. Beards for the chinless!

Joyce's power of construction was weak, hence the obscene conjunction of *Ulysses* with the Homeric poem. As in the case of the so-called modern poets, Joyce's inheritors, a dislocated world demands a dislocated poem to describe it. But the business of the poet is to build anew and magnify, not to photograph or to hold a cracked mirror up to nature. It would be as logical to submit that you must talk broken English if you have a broken leg.

This mere conglomeration without sequence has been excused by reviewers calling it the adventures of the subconscious or, contradictorily, the stream of consciousness. All an effort to give significance where there is none, and where none was intended. The fatuousness of life was what Joyce wished to convey and this he accomplished. We are told that Mrs. Bloom, for instance, means the blossoming earth. If so, why not say it, and sweetly without stench?

This decadence might have been all harmless if it had remained on the Left Bank of the Seine. But, unfortunately, it has become in its most pronounced phases associated with America. Decadence and America! One would think they were antipodes. Whatever excuse there might be for the failure of the vital spirit in Europe, there is none for it in the New World. In England no one takes Joyce as a Colossus. In Dublin there are many unfamed (I will not say "infamous") "artists" of his ilk.

According to the *James Joyce Year Book,* the following is from the pen of a London critic:

> The reader who returns to *Ulysses* today finds it, first and foremost, a child of its age. The tens of thousands of capital letters and punctuation marks massacred on the Left Bank of the Seine by earnest disciples bear witness to the novel's effect on American expatriates. France and Germany have produced commentaries on it. But even in America itself, where Joyce's momentum was felt far more strongly than in England, one would say that the Joycean influence has been chiefly on writers not of the first rank.

Notice the "not of the first rank." Could there be a better example of understatement?

When I read those who although they have never been in Dublin set themselves up as "guides to Joyce" or as masters of "The Master," I feel sorrow for their ignorance and then anger at their presumption. I know how Joyce, who used a grim attitude long sustained when he was acting rather than "making" a joke, would laugh at these "fans" of his—and his dupes.

How does it happen that America should have become the chief infirmary for Joyceans? The answer is because America is the country *par excellence* of the detective story, the crossword puzzle, and the smoke signal. All these are supplied by *Ulysses.* Here, too, where mental homes are numerous, are to be found that unique class who think that the unraveling of an enigma or a puzzle is the height of poetry. The snake pits have become vocal.

Are we to take our values from the insane no matter how atrophied their taste has become, and no matter how arrogant their claim to be arbiters? When they can prove to us that poetry can be without rhythm and prose can be without sense, I will be happy to join them. Meanwhile, I think that poetry is powerful enough to survive even as Gulliver survived all the indignities of Lilliput, though even there the king issued no edicts on matters of taste. Joyce is said to have told a reader that he expected him to devote his whole life to the study of *Finnegans Wake.* What a puzzle that would be.

Language is meant to convey ideas, emotions, and messages. If a messenger boy spent his time in handsprings, wheels, and back somersaults instead of delivering the message, and defended himself with the plea that he had superseded and enhanced it, we would have a parallel to what Joyce has done with the language. He has (to change the metaphor) substituted the lampshade for the light.

Two castastrophic wars have destroyed our values. The world is filled with the rubble of these wars, until rubble seems to the slum-dwellers of literature to be more normal than a city. Hence the cult of fragments in vogue today. Loot was everywhere; the art dealers' stores became junk shops until the trash took the place of the art. Bad artists were promoted; the taste, the discrimination of the public was deliberately debauched.

Lately an art dealer (notice the "dealer") said, "Thank God we have got rid of beauty."

Men as robust and as creative as Aeschylus, Cervantes, Ben Jonson, and a host of others were off at the wars. During their absence the toads crept up the stairs and began to croak. The atmosphere turned miasmic, and "brek-e-kek-kek-kek-kek-koax" became the sole medium of intellectual exchange.

But all this is nothing new. The islander Greeks suffered from trespassers on Parnassus. I have faith in the intelligence of the human race, in the necessity for beauty and poetry to light and lighten our days. There is no need for violence to cleanse the literary stables; all we need do is to turn into them the stream of decency and sense. And healthy laughter. For when laughter comes it is a sign of a return of sanity. And impostors must run away.

"DES IMAGISTES"

by Richard Aldington

In the years just before World War I an odd assortment of gifted young poets formed the school known as Imagists. This is a good-natured, sometimes tongue-in-cheek account of what happened to this "bunch of young American and English writers." Of especial interest is the amusing explanation for the name given the school. Poet and novelist Aldington was close enough to the Imagists to have married one of them, H.D. (Hilda Doolittle).

MARCH 16, 1940

IMAGISM IS ANCIENT HISTORY, but it occurs to me that none of the English members of the group or tribe has yet told his tale of transactions which had some effect on the course of American poetry. What did the Imagists achieve in 1912? Well, they did some useful pioneering work. They dealt a fatal blow at the post-Victorian magazine poets, whose unappeased shades still clamor for Imagist blood. They livened things up a lot. They introduced free verse and an exacting if narrow standard of style in poetry. As a purely personal opinion, I may add that I think Ezra Pound, H.D., Lawrence, and Ford will continue to be read by anybody interested in modern poetry.

It will doubtless be an instant relief to the reader to be told that I don't claim to be the Fuehrer of the Imagists. I was five years younger than the next youngest member of the group, and when the first Imagist poems appeared I was all of twenty. The fame or otherwise of leadership must go to Ezra, who invented the movement; and to Amy Lowell, who put it over. That I can swear to, but I wouldn't take an affidavit that I remember exactly what happened and just what was said. I have only more or less vague memories.

I came across Ezra and H.D. almost at the same time, through an English friend who then collected poets. That was either at the end of 1911 or beginning of 1912—you see how poor my memory is. In those days Ezra was great fun, a small but persistent volcano in the dim levels of London literary society. He had vitality and charm, a

knowledge of European poetry which was almost as extensive as it
was inaccurate, and a generous wish to help other poets along. London was interested and amused by him. The evening papers carried
full-page interviews and a picture; and even *Punch* had to notice
the existence of a Mr. Ezekiel Ton, who had achieved a new syn-
thesis of Wardour Street and the wild and woolly West.

Unfortunately, Ezra had read Whistler's *Gentle Art of Making
Enemies,* which he practiced without the "gentle." Consequently, in
spite of his endearing qualities, Ezra does not inhabit The White
House in Chelsea, keeping one half of London perpetually irritated
and the other half perpetually delighted with barbed jibes. He is a
Rapallo troglodyte, suffering from the mental indigestion following
on a feast of fascism plus the too, too solid hokum of Douglas Credit.
Alas, poor Ezra! I wish him well. May he flourish.

Like other expatriates, Ezra and H.D. developed an almost insane
relish for English afternoon tea, a meal with which I can most willingly dispense. Moreover, they insisted on going to the most fashionable and expensive teashops (which I thought a sad waste of money)
not only in London but in Paris, and even in Rome and Venice.
Being merely an oppressed minority, I had to yield. Thus it came
about that our meetings nearly always occurred in some infernal
bunshop full of English spinsters. No doubt we all got off some
splendid cracks, but for the life of me I can't remember one of
them. I suspect that the cream of the wit lay in the fact that we were
young and happy and having a glorious time just being alive.

Naturally, the Imagist movement was born in a teashop, in the
Royal Borough of Kensington. For some time Ezra had been super-
vising our studies and poems, with alternate encouragements and
blue-pencilings. H.D. produced some poems which I thought excellent, and she either handed or mailed them to Ezra. Presently
each of us received a ukase to attend the Kensington bunshop, which
we accordingly did. Ezra was so worked up that he removed his
pince-nez and informed us we were Imagists.

Now here is where my faulty memory is such a nuisance. Was this
the first time I had heard of Imagism? I don't know. According to
the record, Ezra swiped the word from the English philosopher,
T. E. Hulme, and anyone can read in an appendix to one of Ezra's
books the five or six poems Hulme wrote to illustrate his theories.
They're pretty good, especially the one about the moon like a red-
faced farmer looking over a gate. Ezra's note on Hulme's poems
contains the ominous words: "As to the future, that is in the hands

of the Imagists." My own belief is that the name took his fancy and he kept it *in petto* for a time. If there were no Imagists, obviously they would have to be invented. Whenever Ezra has founded a new movement, he has never had any difficulty about finding members.

I can't remember anything that was said at that bunshop that afternoon. I do remember how pleased H.D. looked at the praise Ezra gave her poems. But I don't think she liked the idea of having them signed: "H.D. Imagist," and I don't think I did either. But Ezra was a bit of a Czar in a small but irritating way, and he had the bulge on us, because it was only through him that we could get our poems into Harriet Monroe's *Poetry,* and nobody else would look at them. So we had to give in. My own impression is that these poems of H.D.'s were the first to appear with the Imagist label, and that two or three of mine appeared in *Poetry* a month or two before without the label though they were afterward included in Ezra's *Des Imagistes.* I think this fact (which can easily be established by looking through the early files of *Poetry*) lends support to those who say the Imagist movement was H.D., and H.D. the Imagist movement.

I believe—though I won't swear—that at this same momentous tea fight Ezra proposed that the three of us should publish a book together. I believe H.D. and I were in favor of this, because it seemed the sort of thing the three musketeers would have done. But Ezra later changed his mind. He gravely pointed out to us that he already had a wide international reputation while we were miserable unknowns, and that consequently the whole attention of the world's reviewers would go to his poems and ours would not even be noticed. Evidently Ezra was having a good time extending the movement and compelling them to come in. With Fletcher he discovered a remarkable poet whom we were glad to welcome, and we didn't object to Flint, although the most imagistic things he had done so far were to read masses of young French poets and imitate Verlaine in English. Ford Madox Ford (then Hueffer) was a well-established author and we liked his poems, though until he began to imitate H.D. they were not strikingly Imagist. We were also glad to have our old friend, John Cournos, who afterward wrote some very good novels. But we did object to Allen Upward, Skipwith Cannell, and Amy Lowell.

This was in 1913. In February 1914, Ezra's Imagist anthology appeared in New York under the fantastic title *Des Imagistes.* What Ezra thought that meant remains a mystery. Amy's anthologies were called *Some Imagist Poets,* so she evidently assumed that Ezra thought *Des Imagistes* meant *Quelques Imagistes.* But why a French title for a collection of poems by a bunch of young American and English writers? Search me. Ezra liked pretentious and foreign titles. His first book was called *A Lume Spento;* another was called *Personae;* and where other people would have written a preface Ezra indited Prolegomena. It was rumored later that he was responsible for making T. S. Eliot use the title *Ara vus prec,* a snippet of medieval Provençal which I imagine is unintelligible to most people. It seems a rather childish form of high-hatting.

Under that ridiculous ensign our little boatful of poets started off, only to come at once under fire from apparently the whole American fleet of critics. I say "apparently" because we didn't bother about press clippings and only saw a few abusive ones which kind friends cut out and sent us. Columnists parodied the poems or reproduced them with derisive remarks. I seem to remember that the poem which gave most offense was a lovely little epigraph by H.D. which revolted the journalists by its sobriety and perfection of taste. Evidently we were a *succès de scandale.* The edition sold out.

Very likely some of the sales were to the kind of people who will always pay two bits to see a bunch of freaks. The serious part of the success was very largely due to H.D. Of course, the majority of poetry readers have little real judgment and practically no flair for good new work. But genuine obtuseness to art, such as is requisite in a successful journalist, was needed to overlook the fact that H.D., even in those first poems, showed an original and sensitive mind and an almost faultless craftsmanship. Version after version of a poem was discarded by her in the search for perfection, and the pruning was ruthless. I thought I was fairly exacting, but I was staggered by this relentless artistic conscience. The fervor with which ten generations of Puritan ancestors had sought moral righteousness was here devoted to aesthetic righteousness. I think it significant that H.D. was a close student of the epistles of St. Paul, but obviously her version ran: "Though I speak with the tongue of men and of angels and have not *style. . . .*"

In the summer of 1914 Amy was again in London, occupying her usual suite in the Berkeley with its view across Piccadilly to the Green Park. With her wonderful energy and vivacity Amy had been battling valiantly for us, but she was fed up with Ezra. So were others. I have a notion that Fletcher was particularly restive. Moreover, Ezra was now attaching himself to the *Blast* group and busy patenting a new movement, Vorticism, whatever that may have been. The first number of *Blast* was a brilliant production, but most of the brilliance was due to the editor, P. Wyndham Lewis, and the rest to a short story which I think one of the best ever produced by that gifted writer, Rebecca West. But *Blast* didn't seem quite the right medium for us.

Amy arrived with certain proposals, to which she had evidently given a good deal of thought. She proposed a Boston Tea Party for Ezra, the immediate abolition of his despotism, and the substitution of a pure democracy. There was to be no more of the Duce business, with arbitrary inclusions and exclusions, and a capricious censorship. We were to publish quietly and modestly as a little group of friends with similar tendencies rather than watertight principles. Each poet was to choose himself what he considered the best of his year's output, and the anthology would be annual. To preserve democratic equality names would appear in alphabetical order. Amy undertook to do all the practical work, to get the books published in Boston and London, and to account to us for the royalties. And well and loyally she discharged that task, which involved a good deal of work and correspondence.

On these terms Ezra was invited to contribute, but refused. There is said to have been a row between Amy and Ezra, but I certainly knew nothing about it. I seem to remember that H.D. and I pleaded with Ezra to stay in, but he refused to play ball. Obviously the odor of democracy was already growing offensive to fascist nostrils. But if we lost Ezra, we gained a much greater writer, D. H. Lawrence. The whole credit for this is due to Amy, who suggested that we should ask him to join us. As Lawrence was already publishing in the Georgian anthologies, the situation looked delicate. Most fortunately Lawrence was such an individualist that he didn't care a hoot about groups and their principles. I daresay he thought it was all poppycock.

I have one or two vivid memories of that evening when I first met Lawrence. It was the end of a sunny tranquil July day, and if we had only known, the end of tranquility in Europe for many a long and bitter year. There were several people in Amy's large private sitting room, where the Austrian waiters (already called to the colors) were setting out an elaborate dinner table with an ominously quiet deftness. For some reason I sat apart at an open window, looking down on the endless traffic of Piccadilly and the warm, golden light over the park. At the corner of the Ritz just opposite was a newspaper stand with a flaring placard: "Germany and Russia at War, Official." As I sat there men and boys came rushing along Piccadilly with hoarse shouts: "Special Edition. Extra." Someone tossed a bundle of papers and posters to the news man. The placard read: "British Army Mobilized."

Until that moment I had felt certain that England would not be involved in these senseless European squabbles. What on earth had they to do with us? But that mobilization poster was a first stab of doubt. I looked back at the room where friendly people were talking unhurriedly of civilized things—French poetry, the Russian ballets, Stravinski. At that moment the door opened, and a tall, slim young man, with bright red hair and the most brilliant blue eyes, came in with a lithe-springing step. As a rule I don't remember peoples' eyes, but I shall not forget Lawrence's—they were such startling evidence of a vivid, flamelike spirit. Before Amy could start the introductions he said quickly, "I say, I've just been talking to Eddie Marsh, and he's most depressing. He says we shall be in the war."

Eddie was then private secretary either to the Prime Minister or to Winston Churchill, I forget which, but he was certainly in a position to have real knowledge. There was a slight pause, and then somebody said, "Oh, nonsense." We all said it was nonsense. Did we all believe that? I know I had a sickening feeling of doubt. But a few minutes later dinner began, and we forgot all about war.

The sales of the new Imagist anthologies greatly exceeded our hopes. If I ever knew, I've forgotten what they were. But I do remember one unexpectedly large check representing my sixth share, and it seems to me that we must have sold about twenty thousand copies of the first two. I may be wrong in my calculations, but anyway the anthologies were widely read, and Amy kept the publicity going with superb generalship. But she did one thing I can't approve. She published her *Critical Fable* anonymously and then broadly insinuated that it was in fact written by Leonard Bacon. This was putting a gentleman on the spot with a vengeance, especially since Mr. Bacon highly disapproved of the Imagists. He either had to prove the lady a liar or labor under the imputation of denying his most cherished principles. It would have served Amy right if he had walked up and down outside her home in Brookline with a striker's placard: "Amy Lowell Unfair to Leonard Bacon."

By way of insinuating that the Imagists were merely an unimportant clique, Ezra raked together a number of easily forgotten poets in a Catholic anthology. Apart from causing astonishment and consternation to a few pious people, this compilation achieved nothing in particular. When America came into the war in 1917, Amy decided that we had better quit and each go his own way. The Imagist "movement" ended then, and it was left to others to carry on.

In 1929 my modern young friend, Walter Lowenfels, suggested to me in Paris that I ought to get out another Imagist anthology. Of course, I knew Walter thought the Imagists were dead as mutton and that his suggestion was ironical. I promptly took a taxi to the cable office, and as I had just published a novel which was a best seller I had no difficulty in selling the nonexistent book in New York and London within two days. I confess I felt a little perturbed at what I had done. However, I got to work; Ford and H.D. labored nobly; and *The Imagist Anthology, 1930* contained poems from everyone who had ever contributed before, except poor Amy, who was no longer with us, Skipwith Cannell, whom we couldn't trace, and Ezra, who was sulky. Ford wrote one of his genial introductions, and we sold several thousand copies between the two countries.

And that, I fancy, was the original and unforgivable sin of Imagist poetry—people bought it.

WATCH OUT FOR
MR. O'HARA

by Wolcott Gibbs

The discussion and controversy over the work of John O'Hara not only goes forward but, in this case, backward. Written some twenty years ago by the late drama critic of The New Yorker, *this appraisal of the young man adds an extremely appropriate chapter to the O'Hara saga. Presumably the laundry situation has improved since 1938.*

FEBRUARY 19, 1938

IN APRIL 1929, John O'Hara began to report the meetings of the Orange County Afternoon Delphian Society for *The New Yorker*. This series, dealing with the ruthless determination of the club ladies to make the cultural life in their little community a finer, braver thing, was purely an exercise in dialect. Unlike Sinclair Lewis, who has never hesitated to heighten or distort the idiom to suit his literary purposes, Mr. O'Hara reported almost exactly what he heard. Such austerity, though impressive, had its drawbacks from an editorial point of view. The first two or three of his pieces filled the reader with admiration for the beautiful precision of Mr. O'Hara's ear; from the fourth on, however, the sensation was uncomfortably like being actually trapped among the ladies while they talked. Mr. O'Hara's reporting was close to perfection, but cumulatively it may have been a little depressing. Jed Harris, who has a marked talent for omniscience after the fact, told me recently that he was no more than halfway through the first of the Delphian stories when he realized that an astonishing new talent had appeared in American letters.

"I knew that he was the greatest natural playwright in America," said Mr. Harris with what for him amounts to icy detachment.

It was intelligent of Mr. Harris to deduce so much from such fragmentary evidence, but on the whole it was an isolated reaction.

276

The Delphians, and a series about the employees of a paint company which alternated with them, were a success among such serious students of the idiom as F. P. A., to whose "Conning Tower" Mr. O'Hara had been a frequent and valuable contributor. For the casual reader, however, they were art in too pure a form, and apparently affected him with the same respectful apathy he might have felt if given a portfolio of perfect lithographs of Brooklyn Bridge.

Mr. O'Hara knew this as well as anybody else. He was, in fact, bored to madness with the Delphians long before he got through with them, and continued to write about them only when he needed money, which, in those precarious days, was practically all the time. Even while he was turning out Delphians as briskly as a doughnut machine, he was meditating the next step, and presently a different kind of story began to appear. These were very short stories in form, but the treatment was novel and often puzzling. Some of them seemed to have been written for the sole purpose of putting into print some dislocation of the language that had come to haunt their writer; others were cryptic, the end of the story concealed in what seemed to be a gratuitously irrelevant sentence (it was not unusual for the troubled editors to turn up with three contradictory ideas about what Mr. O'Hara was getting at); some of them were startlingly good.

In their technical aspect, as an example of a strongly original talent, advancing painstakingly through trial and error, they were all interesting and frequently exciting. Unfortunately, not many of them could be printed in a magazine whose readers had no special interest in experimental prose, and consequently these were rather thin days for the author. Gradually, however, the stories acquired substance and discipline and Mr. O'Hara lost much, though by no means all, of his earlier passion for indirection. One recent story, for instance, ended with its protagonist leaving the room with the bow on his hat on the wrong side of his head, and, while it was abundantly clear to Mr. O'Hara that this indicated great spiritual turmoil, it conveyed precisely nothing to many readers, who wrote in irritably. On the whole, though, he wrote a great deal less, but far more successfully, and nine times out of ten these days he accomplishes exactly what he intended to do. When he does, the result is worth any amount of earlier pain. In fact, two of his later stories in *The New Yorker*, "In the Morning Sun" and "Over the River and Through the Wood," and the title piece in *The Doctor's*

Son, seemed to me as honestly moving and as brilliantly executed
as anything of their genre, while *Appointment in Samarra* proved
that he was capable of sustaining these qualities throughout a novel.
In spite of the publisher's blurb on his new book, *Hope of Heaven,*
which with a sure instinct for the original phrase speaks of his
"meteoric rise," none of this has been easy or especially swift, and
his private desperation, I know, has often been about as much as
he could bear.

John O'Hara came into my life, with some of the accumulating
violence of a hurricane, some time in 1928. That, of course, was
during the middle years of prohibition, and I saw him mostly in
the speakeasies in the Fifties—Matt Winkel's, Tony's, Mino's, Michel's, "21," and many others, gone and forgotten. It was a queer
time—the fact that everybody was part of the same general conspiracy against a silly law broke down many barriers so that it was hard
to tell what might happen before any night was over—and the things
I remember about it are queer. I recall John complaining in a puzzled way because a lady had taken away his coat and mandolin—
God knows what he was doing with a mandolin—and given them
to her janitor. And there was the time *The New Yorker* sent him
up in an airplane to fly over the city and then write a story about
it. It turned out that John, nervous about airsickness, had taken
sensible precautions against it, so that when he came down, he was
in a state of mild confusion, and when the plane started to taxi
away across the landing field, he somehow got the impression that
there was no pilot in it and broke a window with the heroic intention of climbing in and shutting off the motor before somebody
got hurt. There was also the odd affair of the cheese knives. This
was when John, grimly determined to assassinate a man who had
brought him to the end of his negligible patience, secured for the
purpose a long, deadly blade from the free lunch counter. Alert
friends, however, took the knife away, and in a little while everybody in the bar, including John and the potential corpse, wandered
off amiably to Childs for a cup of coffee. Everything went quietly
until they got up to go, when a second and totally unsuspected
cheese knife fell from somewhere onto the floor. John, it appeared,
had simply decided to be prepared in case any further unpleasant-
ness came up. Finally there was the Italian voice, inexplicable but
menacing, which at exactly four o'clock every afternoon for about
a week, came over the telephone in his hotel room.

"All right, O'Hara," it would say softly, darkly. "Just watch out, that's all."

This horrible warning so unnerved him at last that he fled by night to another hotel, changing from one taxi to another on the way as adroitly as any Pinkerton. The voice desisted, but it was never explained and he still thinks about it a little uneasily from time to time.

While these odd things went on, I was gradually coming to learn a little about his earlier life, which was rather like one of those capsule biographies of the author that sometimes appear on the jackets of detective stories—a succession of unrelated and mildly implausible occupations. His father was a doctor in Pottsville, Pennsylvania, where John was born in January 1905. He had five brothers and two sisters, all younger than he. He went to Fordham Prep, The Keystone State Normal School, and Niagara Preparatory School, and was fired from all of them. After that, a college career seemed more or less impracticable, so he went to work. He was an evaluating engineer (whatever that may be), a steward on a boat, the secretary in a briquetting plant, a call boy and freight clerk on the Pennsylvania Railroad, a soda jerker, a reader of gas meters, a guard in an amusement park, a laborer in a steel mill, a press agent for the moving pictures, and a secretary to Heywood Broun, who was at the moment toying with philanthropy. Off and on, during the same period, he worked as a reporter, rewrite man, motion-picture critic, religious editor, and sports writer on such various publications as the Pottsville *Journal*, the Tamaqua (Pennsylvania) *Courier*, *Time*, *Editor & Publisher*, the *Mirror*, the *Morning Telegraph*, the *Herald Tribune*, and the Pittsburgh *Bulletin-Index*, of which, for a short space of glory, he was editor-in-chief. All these careers were fairly brief. In addition to the fact that he was agreeably disposed to drink anything with anybody at any time at all, he had a strong distaste for sunlight and preferred to stay in bed until the worst of it was over. Henry Robinson Luce, brilliant young assassin of the mother tongue, fired him from *Time* with the virtuous comment that the Luce publications had no use for a man who lolled in bed after nine o'clock in the morning, and that was the general complaint against him for he was unquestionably an able reporter. He went out to Hollywood twice and loathed it, although he never degraded himself by writing a script for them. His image, however, was preserved for posterity when he appeared for a split second as a reporter in a film called *The General Died at Dawn.*

John's domestic life, during the years I saw most of him, was also haphazard. He moved frequently and abruptly, and each place, even while he still lived in it, had an air of having been hastily abandoned in the face of a tornado. The laundry collected on the floor of the closet until there were no more clean things to put on, and at least twice I remember that he was driven to the unfashionable extremity of wearing a dress shirt in the daytime; the ghosts of old meals haunted the sink; the bed was usually unmade because of the circumstance that Mr. O'Hara was still in it. During his first marriage, which dissolved amiably after two years, there was a measure of order, but on the whole he was as disorganized and impermanent as a magpie. His social life was much the same. Making a date to have lunch with John was a risk only to be undertaken by a desperate gambler. Usually half past one came, or even two, and with it a telephone call and John's voice, scratchy with sleep, explaining he'd just waked up and would be along as soon as he was able to put himself together. On the other hand, he was more than likely to telephone or even appear in person at four o'clock in the morning with a cheerful suggestion that it seemed the best possible time to go out somewhere and get a bite to eat.

Last December he married again, and there are indications that this will mean another revision of his life, in the direction of quiet and order. The most arresting symptom of what may be expected to come is the fact that for the first time his name appears in the *Social Register,* a volume for which he once professed an unrelenting hostility. He regarded it and its clients so bitterly indeed that once when a friend, who also wrote, turned up unexpectedly in its pages, he received the news with melancholy scorn.

"The poor bastard is through," he said. "He's got himself in the *Social Register.*"

There has been, I suppose, a certain amount of nervous strain connected with knowing John, but nevertheless it has been an experience that I value. He reacts to criticism as violently and irrationally as a bull in the arena. I remember once hearing him stripping a critic not only of professional honor but also of private virtue, equipping him in fact with a past that would have fascinated the Jukes family. Did he actually know these things?

"Well, no," he said in what he must have imagined was a reasonable manner, "but the damn fool didn't like my book."

On the other hand, he is obstinately loyal to his friends and insists upon seeing virtues and talents in them which they would be the first to disclaim. He is, for instance, convinced that I am a formidable authority on poetry and, although my knowledge doesn't go much beyond the number of lines in a sonnet, he will probably have that impression till he dies.

He is, I think, preoccupied with a great many things that are trivial and not easy to reconcile with a mind that is adult enough in other respects. The fact that he didn't go to college, for instance, seems to me to have led him to invest those missing years with a warmth and wonder that they could never possibly have had. F. Scott Fitzgerald's *This Side of Paradise* has been a sort of textbook for him, to be reread at intervals, and he is more exhaustively informed on college clubs, traditions, and mores in general than all but the exceptional alumnus. Even his clothes—soft white shirts with the collars buttoned down at the corners, and loose, high-buttoned suits on the celebrated old Brooks Brothers model—belong to that lost though voluble generation. His books often recite long catalogues of high-class gents' haberdashery. On the other hand again, he is inclined to underestimate his remarkable knowledge of far more vital and important things—the broken and inconsecutive rhythms of living speech, the shrewd detail (over and over again in his work) that suggests the whole.

Focusing intensely on people, their physical surroundings and actual conduct, he is, I think, too biased emotionally and too impatient with anything except the taut realism that he admires (to him Hemingway is still the greatest American writer though given to chasing dubious goddesses) to be an especially good critic. When he talks about the things he knows from his own peculiar experience, however, he can talk as well as his best writing. He never forgets anything he sees or hears, and in telling you about it, he is remarkably graphic, almost disastrously acute. He can also be as funny as anybody I know, though somewhat inclined to be scurrilous.

It is conventional, in ending such fugitive biographies as this, to speculate cautiously about what the future holds for the victim. In Mr. O'Hara's case, this is a difficult assignment, as difficult as it would be for me to explain his occasional and apparently gratuitous physiological references which are denounced with so strange a mixture of shock and rapture by the lady patrons of the lending libraries. It is necessary, in fact, to approach him in a singularly glum and calvinistic spirit, very depressing to the reader and certainly maddening to Mr. O'Hara himself, because he is essentially a moral problem, there being no question of his brilliant technical equipment and sheer ability as a storyteller.

If he should decide (as a great many critics seemed to feel he did in *Butterfield 8*) to write skillful, rather melodramatic novels about people whose inevitable tragedies take place in a moral vacuum and are therefore not tragic or moving in any final sense, he will still be successful, but it won't be what his friends want from him, and I'm sure it won't be what he wants for himself either. If, on the other hand, he can contrive to write about the things he authentically hates—waste and hypocrisy and the sadness of potentially valuable lives failing, but not without some dignity, because they were not born quite strong enough for the circumstances they had to meet—and if he can write about them with the honesty and understanding which he possesses in as great a measure as anyone writing today, then he will certainly be one of our most important novelists. For my part I have every confidence that that is what is going to happen to him. It might even be that in the end he will write about someone *not* ruthlessly preordained to defeat, although that is probably asking too much of any young novelist in these disjointed times.

GBS, HEADMASTER TO THE UNIVERSE

by John Mason Brown

The Saturday Review's *Editor-at-Large assigns a place in history to George Bernard Shaw.*

NOVEMBER 18, 1950

OF COURSE, *Pygmalion* had a preface—even on the screen. Otherwise it would not have been Shaw's. There was the Old Gentleman himself, reading it as only the world's best actor could. There he was, looking like that most unlikely of mortals, a prophet with a sense of humor. There he was, exuding the charm which is held to be Irish and was known to be his. As usual, he was smiling his way through immodesties and overstatements calculated to win attention and laughter. No less characteristically, he was distributing insults as if they were cookies, and persuading people to gobble them up as such.

And what was he saying in his role of self-appointed headmaster to the universe? "You will have to make up your mind that you will lose me presently, and then heaven only knows what will become of America. I have to educate all the nations. I have to educate England. Several Continental nations require a little educating, but America most of all. And I shall die before I have educated America properly, but I am making a beginning."

All this was in 1938, a short-long twelve years ago, when Shaw was a mere stripling of eighty-two. Now we have lost him, and for many of us there is a kind of emptiness in the world. How the citizens of Rhodes felt when an earthquake toppled over the Colossus in their harbor, we do not know. But we do know the incredulity with which we face a universe without Shaw. In spite of increasing signs of his fatigue and warnings that he, too, must die, we had come to take his being here for granted. He was so palpably a natural phenomenon that we are bound to feel just now as if Niagara had dried up or Old Faithful had ceased to erupt.

283

When Mr. Roosevelt died, there were American teen-agers who, never having known any other President, could not imagine one. There are plenty of grandparents the globe over who, since their teens, have no memory of the literary scene when Shaw was not among the most towering of its landmarks. Longevity was one of his preachings which he practiced. He practiced it not only by keeping dazzlingly alive himself but by making this planet a far livelier —and different—place during those sixty years in which he functioned superbly as the challenger of every orthodoxy and the embodiment of his own Superman.

No one under seventy can pretend to have experienced the full detonating impact of Shaw when first he released the armory of his audacities against Victorianism in its every form. Those septuagenarians find it difficult even now to describe the heady delight and happy amazement with which they read him in their youth. They followed him gladly, not quite understanding or daring to understand, but with the joy of the emancipated. Although we, their children, got there later, there were plenty of wonders left and countless surprises.

We, too, knew the excitement of having him snatch the bandages from our eyes and lead us out of the shadows into a realm of sunlight. He pricked our consciences, routed our smugness, jostled us into thoughts undreamed of. He gave us a new boldness, and an unbelievable illusion of freedom, all the while that he was providing us with pleasures fresh and to this day unequaled.

Since nothing is deader than an idea or a cause which no longer needs to be fought for, younger people encountering Shaw at present are bound to find some of his audacities tame and some of his arguments superfluous. They cannot be expected to know how much of what they assume has become accepted only because his fighting helped to make it so. Take the "New Woman" he so ardently championed. Certainly she has lost her youth and grown into a very, very old lady. But they fool themselves, these young people (in the manner of their elders), if they think they have caught up with Shaw. To the end he remained almost as far ahead of them as he was of their grandparents. The likelihood is that their great-great-grandchildren will follow his circuitous trail, panting and outdistanced.

In *Sixteen Self Sketches* Shaw's explanation of why he had never written a complete autobiography was that "things have not happened to me: on the contrary it is I who have happened to them."

This was a statement, however unshrinking, of a truth from which no one can shrink. Shaw was not only a genius; he was an event. Someone likened him to a centipede with a foot in every cause. The range of his curiosities was so prodigious that the sun never set on his interests. From economics to religion, from government to painting, from history to music, drama to medicine, vivisection to literature, phonetics to Communism, the causes of war to the difficulties of peace, or yesterday's news to creative evolution, his mind leapt untiringly and with an athlete's prowess.

It was an extraordinary mind put to extraordinary uses. No one can read a page of Shaw's prefaces, his journalism, his letters, or his better plays without feeling its lunge, its force, magnificence, sparkle, and originality. It was an intellect giant-sized yet agile. In the field of letters only Voltaire's has been comparable with it in its mixture of lightness and vigor. It worked overtime and hummed like a dynamo. It was an ebullient mind as sudden in its contradictions as it was constant in its brilliance. If it borrowed freely and unashamedly the coinage of other men's thinking, it nonetheless managed to melt down what it had appropriated and remint it into a currency glitteringly golden and unmistakably Shavian. Its lacks were plain enough, but its virtues were plainer still. It spoke for a man who had the courage to say what he felt instead of what he ought to have felt, and who possessed to a supreme degree a genius for illumination, stimulation, revelation, and provocation.

No subject daunted Shaw, and few were touched upon by him without at least having been made the more interesting. Was his Caesar in his apostrophe to the Sphinx convinced, without ever giving her a chance to speak, that he had read her riddle? Shaw himself was always ventriloquizing for the Sphinx, expecting her to be as quiet as a dream-wife while he spewed forth answers to all the problems known to men and gods. The fact that he was childless no more deterred him from pontificating (hilariously and quite sensibly) as the final authority on parenthood than the fact that he was a Socialist prevented him from marrying a millionairess and emitting angry cries of outrage when, as a millionaire himself, his taxes were mercilessly increased by a Labor Government.

Any Shavian can point out the inconsistencies in Shaw, and a lot of dullards as well as bright people have. But the Ph.D.s in economics or government who will haunt his ghost in the years to come, sniffing and tracking down his deviations from himself, will always present the sorry picture of Lilliputians trying to take the measurements of a Brobdingnagian. Although they may, as the Bardolaters do, buy Bendixes at the expense of the man who is involuntarily their prey, they will only prove their own stature by trying to reduce his.

Even a literate student in a school of education must be aware that Shaw is as apt to disagree with himself as he is to disagree with everyone else. Everyone knows that Henry George changed Shaw's life. Everyone knows that William Archer came across him in the British Museum (Shaw's university) with Marx's *Das Kapital* on one side of his desk and Wagner's score for the Nibelungen Ring on the other. And everyone who is not a citizen of Dogpatch must also know that Shaw, throughout his many teetotaling years, swerved like a drunken driver in his allegiances. By his own proud admission he was a crow who had followed many plows.

He was an Irishman who preferred England. He was a Fabian who became a capitalist. He was a defender of the people, indeed a soapbox orator, whose questionable gods at one time were Napoleon and Caesar. He was a champion of the downtrodden who flirted, briefly and dangerously, with the dictator-principle in terms of Mussolini, Hitler, and Stalin.

As Bartlett will remind those who have never read his essay on "Self-Reliance," Emerson held a foolish consistency to be the hobgoblin of little minds, adored by little statesmen and philosophers and divines. Not even the fools who parade this world as wise men have accused Shaw of having a little mind. The dimensions of his mind can in a way be measured by its inconsistencies and perversities. "It is an instinct with me," he once boasted, "to attack every idea which has been full grown for ten years, especially if it claims to be the foundation of all human society." This explains why his thinking wavered over the decades. This is why his opinions were subject to change without notice and beyond anticipation. His variability was a part of his irreplaceable value. His surprises were unceasing. What mattered most in Shaw was not what he thought but that he made others think.

In the essay already referred to, Emerson, who included among his gifts a talent for freshening the wilted lettuce of bromides, observed that to be great is to be misunderstood. No great man has, I will wager, embarked upon such a far-flung, deliberate, and successful conspiracy to be misunderstood as Shaw. To most of the pygmies (meaning you and me) who are not only well-mannered enough but sufficiently realistic to realize how pint-sized are whatever talents they may possess, Shaw has seemed a titanic egotist.

Take, for example, his assertion, "I should have been a clerk still if I had not broken loose in defiance of all prudence and become a professional man of genius—a resource not open to every clerk." Or his famous explosion, "With the exception of Homer, there is no eminent writer, not even Sir Walter Scott, whom I can despise so entirely as I despise Shakespeare when I measure my mind against his." Or his claim, "I know a great deal more about economics and politics than Jesus did and can do things he could not do."

These were utterances of which no finishing-school graduate would have been guilty. Although they were shockers, planned with gleeful care, they were not meant to be blasphemous or even self-doting. On the subject of Jesus, about whom he has written beautifully, Shaw's only purpose was to point out the facts of economic and political change over the centuries. So far as Shakespeare was concerned, he was (from his deep love and profound understanding of Shakespeare's merits) merely trying to make "a fellow creature" out of the Bard who had been "a divinity" and "a bore." He was doing this even while waging his usual warfare against Henry Irving and for "the drama of ideas" Ibsen had inaugurated. When it comes to Shaw's reference to himself as "a professional man of genius," he would have been a liar had he described himself in any other terms.

By temperament and habit Shaw was an honest man. The truth as he saw it, which was the truth as very few others had seen it or could bear to face or state it, always mattered more to him than such manners as the world expected. If, as he put it, he could not respond to the "demand for mock-modesty," neither was he ever guilty of mock-conceit. No one capable of writing and thinking as Shaw did could have failed to realize that when he wrote he was outwriting and outthinking other men.

Said he in 1944, "When I contemplate what I know and have done (not that I ever do) I have a high opinion of myself. When I contemplate what I don't know and cannot do (which I am often forced to do) I feel as a worm might if it knew how big the world is." He was equally candid when, in a passage dashed off nearly a half century earlier, he wrote, "I am ashamed neither of my work nor of the way it is done. I like explaining its merits to the huge majority who don't know good work from bad. It does them good;

and it does me good, curing me of nervousness, laziness, and snobbishness. . . . I leave the delicacies of retirement to those who are gentlemen first and literary workmen afterward. The cart and trumpet for me."

Shaw never ceased being one of GBS's favorite subjects, and he made him a favorite subject throughout the world. No one has ever written about him so well as he has, and no one ever will. He was his own advance man to his own circus; his Dexter Fellowes to what beyond question was the Greatest Show on Earth.

As he phrased it, "Half my time is spent in telling people what a clever man I am. It is no use merely doing clever things in England. The English do not know what to think until they are coached, laboriously and insistently for years, in the proper and becoming opinion. For ten years past, with an unprecedented pertinacity and obstination, I have been dinning into the public head that I am an extraordinarily witty, brilliant, and clever man. That is now part of the public opinion of England and no power in heaven or on earth will ever change it. I may dodder and dote; I may potboil and platitudinize; I may become the butt and chopping block of all the bright, original spirits of the rising generation; but my reptutation shall not suffer: it is built up fast and solid, like Shakespeare's, on an impregnable basis of dogmatic reiteration." This was way back in 1898 and must be hailed as one of Shaw's more accurate prophecies.

Plato got along very nicely by contenting himself with being Plato. But Shaw was a modern Plato who could not resist also being Puck and Pantaloon. When it comes to clowning, Grock and the Fratellinis were amateurs compared with him. He could be downright silly. The gags he got off for the benefit of the wire services were often feeble, sometimes in questionable taste, and never dignified. If Shaw dispensed with dignity, however, it was not only because it was alien to his nature but because he did not need it. He had something far rarer and finer to offer. He had grandeur.

His wit delighted the public but misled it. Conventional people were confused by a man who said grave things gaily. Their belief was that men who are to be taken seriously must be dreary sobersides incapable of smiling. They found it easier to pigeonhole him as a humorist when he pleased them and as a buffoon when he shocked them. Shaw was well aware of the dangers he invited by laughing. "I have got the tragedian and I have got the clown in me," he once confessed, "and the clown trips me up in the most dreadful way." He explained this by saying that, like his father before him, he was in the grip of a humorous sense of anticlimax.

As a prophet, an economist, propagandist, and social reformer, Shaw realized that his inconsistencies no less than his wit blurred the effects he had hoped to achieve. The world has been guilty of the sorry, if understandable, error of mistaking the paradoxes of GBS for his purpose. Far more important than the polemicist, however, was the artist. The specific causes for which he fought have been or may be forgotten, but the artist will always be remembered and treasured. Eric Bentley once contended that the final paradox of Shaw's paradoxical career was that "by not saving the world [he] saved his dramas as art and, therefore, as teaching."

Like Molière's doctor, Shaw was an artist in spite of himself. He was the best, the sprightliest, the most deathless critic ever to have reviewed plays. He was no less lively on the subjects of painting and music. As *Pen Portraits and Reviews* makes blindingly clear, he was a journalist with Promethean powers of firing a reader's interest. Perhaps the final proofs of an instinctive writer's gifts are his letters. Shaw's letters and post cards are miracles of invention, perception, gaiety, and fluency. We already have many samples of his superiority as a correspondent. We shall have more. Indeed, one of the greatest and most fascinating literary adventures the future will know is bound to be those many, many volumes of Shaw's letters which will someday be published, even as the Walpole and the Boswell papers are now being issued.

Certainly *The Intelligent Woman's Guide to Socialism and Capitalism,* printed when Shaw was seventy-two, is one of the finest examples of expository writing on the subject of politics and economics known to any library. Then, of course, there are the plays—and the prefaces. Some of the plays are trifles. Others are dated. No one can say with any certainty which ones will speak most directly to unborn generations. But I, at least, would have only pity for a world which could not be touched by *Candida,* melted by *Androcles and the Lion,* amused by *Man and Superman* (including its scintillating interlude in Hell), quickened by *Caesar and Cleopatra,* and stirred by *Saint Joan.* Better than Shakespeare Shaw may not have been. Different he palpably was. Yet that his was the most fecund genius to have turned to the theater since Shakespeare's time seems safe from challenge.

Shaw explained that he wrote prefaces, as Dryden did, "because I can." I do not mean to subtract from the enrichment Dryden made to English prose when he was in a prefatory mood. I must insist, however, that Shaw's prefaces are in a class of their own. They are sizable additions to the gaiety of nations and the joys of reading. Prolix they may be; yet, if they tire, it is only because in them Shaw gives us no rest from his own untiring brilliance.

"Effectiveness of assertion," he contended, "is the alpha and omega of style. He who has nothing to assert has no style and can have none." Shaw never lacked something to say and always said it with incredible vitality and apparently without effort. His sentences, as Winston Churchill (himself no mean stylist) observed, are colored with "a debating tinge."

The two vital qualities Shaw demanded of literature were "light and heat." Both of these his writing possessed to an unmatched degree. He did not believe, as many now seem to, that a great writer uses his skill to conceal his meaning. Although he did not object to writing for profit, he seldom wrote without a purpose. He had only contempt for "art for art's sake." However gay his words or bold his overstatements, Shaw's intentions were apt to be serious. He may have been the born mountebank he described himself as being, but he was also a puritan.

He was an author who, as a boy, had been brought up in a musical household. This training was not wasted on him. His prose has the dancing lightness and the shining precision of Mozart. It is also capable of deeper Wagnerian sonorities. Hazlitt described wit as "the eloquence of indifference." Shaw, however, was witty not because he did not care but because he did. He could also rise to passages of great melodic beauty. His plays are studded with speeches quivering with a prophet's fervor and with sentences which literally sing themselves. Although not written in verse, they make most contemporary dramatic speeches written as poetry seem like the most meager and muffled of prose.

In spite of the multiplicity of his interests and his talents, the often ignored source of Shaw's greatness lay in the dimensions of his spirit. As surely as there was nothing little about his thinking, there was nothing little about his feeling. He never waged war on individuals. He waged war on the ideas for which they stood. His gift for forgiveness was even greater than his need at times to be forgiven. He was essentially good, kindly, clean, and gentle. His spiritual largeness explains why he, the supposed clown and acknowledged wit, was able to understand the dilemmas of such a man of action as Caesar, and to write in *Androcles and the Lion* and

Saint Joan the two most beautiful religious plays to have come out of the modern theater.

Although Shaw, the iconoclast, saw through men and institutions, he never lost his hope for what men might become if only they resolved to live up to their potentialities and outgrow their present limitations. The Life-Force, about which he wrote, was a potent factor in his own living. His plea was for progress. He loathed the shirkers, the loafers, the talent-squanderers, and time-wasters who deny themselves "the true joy in life" by not being used for a purpose they recognize "as a mighty one." The demands he made on himself were as unrelenting as those he made on others. Yes, and on God, too.

It is something to have lived on this planet as the contemporary of such a titan as George Bernard Shaw. Although he was mortal enough to die, we have not lost him. Of him it can be truly said, as he said of William Morris, "You can lose a man like that by your own death, but not by his."

TILLEY THE TOILER

by Russell Maloney

*Few publications have created such a unique place for themselves
in the minds of their public as* The New Yorker. *Possibly an even
greater financial success than literary, the magazine's idiosyncrasies
have not been limited to its printed pages. Behind the scenes all
sorts of characters come and go, either creating legend or carefully
nourishing it. At the top of the pile was Harold Ross, the brilliant
man who was* The New Yorker. *All this has been the subject of
much conjecture, but one of the first "profiles" of the magazine was
done in* The Saturday Review *by Russell Maloney, who was on the
staff of* The New Yorker *for many years. This article provides some
revealing information about some myths and misconceptions that
still persist today.*

AUGUST 30, 1947

THIS ARTICLE IS the work of a man who spent just under eleven
years on the staff of *The New Yorker* magazine, wrote two million
words for it, more or less, went through five hundred and seventy-odd
weekly deadlines, and resigned at last because he felt rather middle-
aged and pooped.

Once a year, on the anniversary of the first issue of *The New
Yorker,* there appears on its cover a portrait by Rea Irvin, the
magazine's first art editor, of the mythical character known around
the office as Eustace Tilley. Tilley, who is represented as scrutinizing
a butterfly through a single eyeglass, is a supercilious fellow dressed
in the height of Regency foppishness, complete with beaver hat and
high stock. He is the embodiment of *The New Yorker* legend, which
is surely the most voluminous body of fact, fiction, and conjecture
ever attached to any enterprise, let alone the relatively simple one of
publishing a twenty-cent weekly magazine.

Next February Tilley will make his twenty-third appearance on
The New Yorker's cover. His survival is symbolic of the fact that the
editorial staff has always worked as hard at being legendary as at the

routine chores of writing and editing. The faithful subscriber, who follows the gossip columns and reads the pieces about *The New Yorker* that have appeared occasionally in other periodicals, can recite all the classic *New Yorker* stories in detail: for instance, Thurber tipping over the telephone booth in the reception room, powdering his face, lying down in the booth, and pretending to be a corpse; or the card-index system, keyed to a series of colored tabs, which was prepared for the benefit of a new managing editor who turned out to be color-blind.

Aside from the legend, the actual accomplishments of the actual *New Yorker* magazine are impressive. The current idiom of American humor derives directly from *The New Yorker*. The illustrated he-and-she joke, which was once sold in quantities to the readers of *Judge* and the old pre-Luce *Life*, has been replaced by the one-line cartoon gag, in which picture and text are equally important. Further, these pictures are based on real current events or observation of human character, and not on the hack humorist's dreary world, in which Dusty Rhodes, the tramp, knocks on the door and asks for a piece of pie, in which Little Willie tearfully rebels against his Saturday-night bath, or plays hookey from the little red schoolhouse to go fishin' with a bent pin.

To the generally barren field of day-to-day journalism, *The New Yorker* brought a fresh style and enthusiasm. The mannered but severely accurate Talk of the Town reported little happenings unnoticed by the newspapers. Prominent or notorious citizens were the subjects of Profiles—a word that has become part of the language, despite occasional screams from *The New Yorker's* lawyers about copyright. The Reporter at Large series gave scope to writers with a story too big to be handled in Talk. Talk very soon in *The New Yorker's* career was taken over by James Thurber and E. B. White. By ordinary city-editor standards, both were very bad reporters, and they had actually proved this by working on newspapers—White in Seattle and Thurber in New York. Their contribution to Talk, however, did much to revive the moribund art form known in city rooms as the feature story. Before long, examples of their work were being reprinted in textbooks and were solemnly analyzed by professors of journalism. Reporters on other publications were stirred to emulation. Journalism began to look up.

Meanwhile, E. B. White, in the Notes and Comments department, was setting *The New Yorker's* editorial style—editorial policy would be too strong a term. Comment, through an inspired piece of bad make-up, has always appeared under the Talk of the Town heading, although it is a separate enterprise. Comment occupies the first page, Talk the second, third, fourth, and fifth pages. Except for a five-year hegira, from 1938 to 1942, when he lived on a farm on the Maine coast and contributed a monthly department to *Harper's* magazine, White has always been the leading Comment writer, accepting odd thoughts or bits of information from staff men or readers, combining them with his own observations, and blending the whole into a mellow and stylistically impeccable page. Before Hitler became an active menace, *The New Yorker's* editorial stand, as defined by White, was simple and, theoretically, not impossible to put into action. *The New Yorker* was on record as being against the use of poisonous spray on fruit, and against the trend in automobile design which narrows the driver's field of vision by lowering the front seat.

Wartime Comment, which was not entirely by White, was not much above the level of other wartime prose, but he has since become a fervent internationalist and has written lyrically and persuasively of his convictions. The tone of the magazine, taking pictures, reporting, criticism, and fiction into account, has been increasingly liberal, pro-New Deal, and internationalist. At any rate, *The New Yorker* has grown beyond the stature of a funny magazine; there was nothing incongruous in the August 31 issue of this year, which was devoted completely to John Hersey's thirty-thousand word dispatch about the destruction of Hiroshima, later issued in book form.

Inextricably mingled with the story of *The New Yorker* is the story of Harold Ross, founder and editor. Unfortunately it is a story which nobody is able to tell. No man—no man, that is, if we make an exception of the entire field of theology—has been the subject of so much analysis, interpretation, and explanation, with so little concrete result. For more than twenty-one years he has belched and wrangled and improvised and compromised and given his subscribers a magazine every seven days. He still works hard; except for a few sports columns and foreign newsletters which come in over the week end, he works on every bit of copy that goes into the magazine. He stalks through the dirty corridors of his editorial domain, gaunt, gap-toothed, his black hair tousled and his mouth agape like that of a man who has just established contact with a bad oyster, watching the next issue grow and arguing minute points of fact, taste, punctuation, or policy. He is, arbitrarily and inexplicably, an authority on the migratory habits of eels and the customs of the harem, subjects on which he likes to expatiate for hours, usually to some anxious minion who is trying desperately to make a press deadline. It is not unusual for a writer to work in *The New Yorker* office for several years without once meeting his editor. The elevator men have strict instructions not to greet him by name, lest he be accosted by some tactless writer or artist in the same car. He is a man of no perceptible learning, and he does not seem to be inordinately impressed by experience. He has relatively few friends and a number of enemies of whom he is, on the whole, rather proud. "A journalist can't afford to have friends," he is fond of saying. In a time when people are vociferous about politics, it is difficult to decide just where he stands; probably he is a lukewarm rightist despite the underlying liberal tone of the magazine itself.

A whole generation of journalists has got into the habit of thinking of Ross as a mystery man, and it suits Ross well enough to have it that way. Actually, there is no more up his sleeve today than there was thirty-odd years ago, when he left Aspen, Colorado, to seek his fortune. It is not a pose when the editor of *The New Yorker* refers to the local smart set as "dudes." They *are* dudes, as far as he's concerned; always will be. Ross's editing might be described as the apotheosis of honest ignorance. All he asks is that a piece of writing be completely comprehensible to him. (He now asks this even of poets. "God damn it!" he suddenly yelled, one day back in 1938, "after this I'm not going to buy any verse I don't *understand!*") Ross will not pretend he understands something he doesn't understand, nor will he hope that others may be quicker than he. He has no intellectual arrogance and will happily turn over his valuable magazine to the mismanagement of somebody he has brought in off the street to be managing editor. As soon as the incumbent's incompetence becomes clear, Ross fires him—a process that takes anywhere between one and two years, the editor meanwhile continuing at full salary while his responsibilities are gradually whittled down. Ross would rather hire than fire, with the result that his editorial roster today is near a hundred, or twice what it was ten years ago. His effect on *The New Yorker,* so far as taste, policy, and other intangibles are concerned, is mainly negative. He has harnessed some of the nation's most fractious wits. *The New Yorker's* quarrel with Woollcott, for instance, resulted simply from Ross's refusal to let Woollcott devote his polished style to the narration of smoking-car stories, and old ones at that.

Next to Ross, Thurber and White have most deeply impressed

their personalities on the magazine. Thurber, because of increasingly severe eye trouble, has not been very active at *The New Yorker* for the past six or seven years, but he has left a permanent impression—a little private Thurber legend, you might say, preserved within *The New Yorker* legend. Before he appeared on the literary scene, magazine writers were not regarded as terribly glamorous figures. They were the sort of men who took pepsin tablets after lunch and wore rubbers on cloudy days. Thurber brought the neuroses to English prose. A tall, thin, spectacled man with the face of a harassed rat, Thurber managed to convey to his office associates something of his own sense of impending doom.

In E. B. White's phrase, Thurber in those days trailed a thin melancholy after him. It was catching, too. Any humorist—for that matter, any subjective writer—is a potential neurotic. In the Gothic atmosphere which Thurber established at *The New Yorker,* the potential was actualized. One after the other, a string of slapdash newspaper writers hired by Ross in the hope that they could dash off a few Profiles or Reporter at Large pieces were turned, before his very eyes, into Byronic figures who could barely summon the energy once a week to grope their way down the block to the Guaranty Trust Company and cash their drawing-account checks. It even became the thing, for a time, to be voluntarily institutionalized, and new managing editors would solemnize their promotion with a nervous breakdown.

One of E. B. White's great contributions to *The New Yorker* was his insistence, against almost overwhelming opposition, that Thurber was a funny artist whose pictures should appear in the magazine. Not even Thurber thought this; but White collected his random doodlings from his wastebasket, inked over the penciled lines, submitted the pictures to the art editor, and finally had his way. Probably more people think of Thurber as an artist than as a writer, though Thurber himself has always said he puts writing first. White, in the same defiant way, is inclined to pooh-pooh his taut and wonderful prose; he likes to think he's a poet, a title for which he is disqualified by his inordinate fondness for the word "doth."

White's Comment paragraphs can hardly be called inimitable, since they have been successfully forged by lesser staff members. Nevertheless he was the inventor, and is still the surest practitioner, of this style, which is modest, sly, elliptical, allusive, prim, slightly countrified, wistful, and (God help us) whimsical. And if White's style can be forged, the New York of which he writes remains his own property. It is a microcosm with fewer orange peels and blood-stains than its original; White regards it fondly, like a spinster looking at her tank of guppies. Slight and nervous, modestly dressed and undistinguished in feature, White is a triumph of big-city protective coloration. He is never seen at cocktail parties, though he goes to one now and then.

There is an editor in the White household, too. She was Katharine Angell when, in the twenties, she went to work editing fiction and poetry. When she and White were married, they established the first *New Yorker* dynasty: young Roger Angell, Mrs. White's son by an earlier marriage, has already sold his first piece to the magazine. Though the week-to-week drudgery of buying and printing poetry and short stories has been delegated to others, Mrs. White descends on the office every now and then for a brisk bout of editorial house-cleaning.

Wolcott Gibbs, who will thank you to pronounce his first name "Woollcott," must be mentioned among the founders of *The New Yorker* legend. Alice Duer Miller, his aunt, was a close friend of Ross's, and her efforts on his behalf landed Gibbs at *The New Yorker*. His first printed contribution was a sparkling verse parody titled "I Have a Rendezvous with Debt" and, in the fine old phrase, he has never looked back. He soon proved that any ambitious young man could become an acceptable amalgam of Thurber and White. In fact, during White's unadvertised absences from the Comment job, the principal contributor has been Gibbs; and most of his essays—*The New Yorker* staff calls them "casuals"—have been in the Thurber vein of the superior and high-strung man frightened by a piece of machinery or a woman. Under the tutelage of Mrs. White he became an excellent editor, his talent for parody enabling him to handle copy without violating the author's style. Gibbs gave up editing when he became the play reviewer.

Ross seldom talks about the early days of *The New Yorker*, and positively refuses to look at the early issues, the ones that came out in 1925-6. None of his present staff was with him then. Contributors were recruited from the Algonquin "round table" set, the lunch-time wits—Marc Connelly, Dorothy Parker, Robert Benchley, George Kaufman, and their lesser friends. They worked for all but nothing, presumably spurred on by the new magazine's slogan. "Not for the old lady from Dubuque." This touch of Greenwich Village defiance was quietly buried after a few years, and Ross would undoubtedly be happy to have it forgotten. It was this period that saw the birth of *The New Yorker* legend; the organized effort that was to produce the present-day *New Yorker* began later.

A fact about *The New Yorker* which is not part of *The New Yorker* legend is that the job of editor or staff writer is physically debilitating, mentally exhausting, and a form of social suicide.

There are no titles at *The New Yorker* except in the business department. The most definite statement possible about the staff is that the excellence of most *New Yorker* prose is due partly to the fact that it passes through the hands of men named Shawn, Vanderbilt, Maxwell, Lobrano, Whitaker, Packard, and Weekes, none of whom have any definite titles and few of whom are known to the public.

There are several factors that make an editorial job at *The New Yorker* a more desperate affair than another editorial job. The worst, of course, is the glum fact of *The New Yorker's* perfection; because perfection, in the mind of Harold Ross, is not a goal or an ideal, but something that belongs to him, like his watch or his hat.

Another factor that makes editing *The New Yorker* something of a nightmare is the number and variety of items in each issue. There are Comment and Talk paragraphs, pictures, poems, short stories, essays, a Profile or Reporter at Large, half a dozen critical departments, a dozen or so newsbreaks, and the Goings-On Department, which covers movies, plays, restaurants, and night clubs. Talk is made up according to a loose but inevitable formula requiring four short anecdotes at least, and a selection of four long stories including one "dope" story, one personality story, and if possible a "visit" or personally reported story by a Talk rewrite man. Talk must be made up so that there are no conflicts with other items in the issue: that is, no mentions of subjects mentioned elsewhere in the magazine. Thus, if one of the Talk personality stories is about a dog breeder who took a prize at the Westminster Kennel Club show, there must be no dogs in other Talk stories, nor in any of the drawings, short stories, or essays as well. Newsbreaks, poems, and other fillers—even the tiny spot drawings used as type ornaments—are scrutinized until the last press deadline, for fear of possible conflicts.

The third factor which produces a good magazine once a week and keeps editorial nerves on the stretch is an insane complexity of action. The trend is always away from simplicity. Twenty years ago a man-about-town named Fillmore Hyde used to come in and write three thousand words of Talk on Thursday afternoon. Lately, Talk has been taking up the entire working week of four reporters. The breezy titles of the various factual departments—Profiles and A Reporter at Large, as well as Talk of the Town, are merely memories of days when *The New Yorker* took life and journalism much less seriously than at present. A Profile, for instance, could be reported and written in a couple of days, once upon a time; the intention then was merely to present an offhand impression of the subject, literally a profile. Nowadays it is not unusual for a writer to spend three months gathering his material, a month writing the Profile, and another month answering queries and preparing the piece for the press. Ross is no longer content with a Profile; he requests also a family history, bank reference, social security number, urinalysis, catalogue of household possessions, names of all living relatives, business connections, political affiliations, as well as a Profile. The pieces have expanded enormously; there are numerous two-part Profiles, some three-part ones, and now and then a five-part one, such as McKelway's painstaking dissection of Walter Winchell and John Bainbridge's study of *The Reader's Digest*. Back in 1926 *The New Yorker* would probably have had some pretty caustic things to say about a publication which printed a twenty-five-thousand-word biographical study and called it a profile.

Some amateur statistician at the magazine recently estimated that if every staff writer contributed only one piece every six months, there would be a sufficient supply of Talk, Profiles, Reporters, and other fact pieces. *The New Yorker* is prodigal with drawing accounts. The indebtedness of departing writers is usually carried in the books, the fiction being that he will return someday, write seven or eight Profiles, and clear his account. Nobody, staff writer or free lance, is ever commissioned to do a piece—that is, given an assignment with a guarantee of payment.

Fiction and poetry being all but impossible to regiment, *The New Yorker* handles such contributions pretty normally. By and large, it is no harder to write a *New Yorker* short story now than it was fifteen or twenty years ago. Sally Benson once sent in a story about some adventure or other that happened to a man who lived in a cabin on a mountainside. Her author's proof included a fretful Ross query: "How he come to be living on mountainside? Better explain." Miss Benson penciled an answer: "I don't know how he came to be living on a mountainside. This is just a story I made up, and I didn't make up that part."

"Art meeting" is one of the great *New Yorker* institutions: the process, hardly changed by the passage of the years, by which the drawings are bought. It has always been attended by Ross and Rea Irvin, the first art editor. The current art editor attends; so does one of the fiction editors; Mrs. White does if she is in town. These people sit four abreast at a conference table, while the pictures, one after another, are laid on an easel in front of them. At each place is a pad, pencil, ashtray, and knitting needle. The knitting needle is for pointing at faulty details in pictures. Ross rejects pictures firmly and rapidly, perhaps one every ten seconds. "Nah . . . nah . . . nah." A really bad picture wrings from him the exclamation "Buckwheat!"—a practical compromise between the violence of his feelings and the restraint he feels in the presence of Mrs. White or a lady secretary. "Who's talking?" he will ask occasionally; this means that the drawing will get sent back to the artist, to have the speaker's mouth opened wide. Now and then Ross gets lost in the intricacies of perspective. "Where am *I* supposed to be?" he will unhappily inquire, gazing into the picture. If nobody can say exactly where Ross is supposed to be, out the picture goes.

It might be noted that the business department of *The New Yorker* is just like the business department of any successful enterprise. There is an unwritten and inviolable nonfraternization rule, encouraged by Ross and meekly accepted by Raoul Fleischmann, the owner: no business-office men in the editorial room unless by strict invitation. The advertising salesmen are happy fellows, hampered only by Ross's objection to such advertisements as those mentioning deodorants, contraceptives, or even kiss-proof lipstick. The circulation is pushing three hundred thousand, and could probably go much higher if it were not for the standard *New Yorker* advertising contract, which guarantees the advertiser that half the circulation is within metropolitan New York. Fleischmann, who put up the bulk of the original investment, has been out of the red for eighteen years. There are reports that Henry Luce, with whose magazine *The New Yorker* had been feuding for more than twenty years, is now a fairly large stockholder in the New Yorker Magazine, Inc. The why, when, and how much of the transaction have not been disclosed; but blocks of *New Yorker* stock have been available from time to time at something over fifty, there being several dozen stockholders in all. In any event, accidentally or otherwise, there have been few recent evidences of editorial swiping—at least in print—between *The New Yorker* and Time, Inc.

A guided tour of *The New Yorker* offices would reveal little of the spiritual turmoil that goes on there. It is an unusually dirty and inconvenient office, to be sure; but impersonal. There are no rugs at *The New Yorker,* no curtains, no decorations, and little feeling for order or cleanliness. Carrying on the Thurber tradition of drawing on the walls, the office boys have left quite a few dirty and meaningless hen tracks. The water coolers are filled at the mop-closet sink, though the containers bear the name of a famous bottled water. Hidden in a corner is a photostat machine; once, long ago, Ross thought that a multiplicity of photostat copies would expedite the handling of last-minute copy, forgetting that it took time for the prints to dry. The automatic pencil sharpener is gathering dust in a corner, too. The very soft pencils demanded by Ross tended to break in the user's hand after being put through the automatic sharpener. An edict went out that all Ross pencils had to be hand-sharpened and personally tested by his personal secretary. While Ross was basking in this luxury, the secretary fleeced him of thousands of dollars by presenting him with blank checks to sign and making them out to himself, lost the money on the horses, and evaded justice by way of the gas oven.

The New Yorker is, in the end, merely a state of mind, a relationship between Ross and his minions, between staff and readers. The readers are important; they contribute all the Talk anecdotes and all the newsbreaks, suggest Talk stories, profiles, and other factual pieces, and (in Ross's guilty imagination) have miscarriages at the sight of saucy pictures or stories. Ross is a puritan, and he flew into a rage, back in 1927, when *The New Yorker's* one suggestive drawing was explained to him. It was the one showing a man and a girl, carrying between them the back seat of an automobile, saying to a rural policeman, "We want to report a stolen car." It was this picture, or something equally uninhibited in the text, that caused a lady reader to have a miscarriage; or so she wrote to Ross. He has never forgotten it.

The most significant single fact about *The New Yorker* is not the financial statement, impressive as this frequently has been; it is the fact that, at present, none of *The New Yorker* people except Ross has an ulcer. It's when the boss begins delegating his ulcers to somebody else that a magazine begins to slip.

E. B. W.

by James Thurber

*Mr. Thurber, and the rest of us, for that matter, owe E. B. W. a
debt of gratitude, not only for his own unique work but also for the
fact that it was he who picked up from the floor some of Thurber's
scribblings and doodlings, and battled, over the indifference of almost everyone else, to have them published for the first time.
E. B. W. is E. B. White, or Elwyn Brooks White, if you wish to
know the worst of it. Here is an affectionate piece about him by
his friend.*

OCTOBER 15, 1938

THREE—NO, SIX YEARS AGO (how the time flies!) a gentleman came to
the offices of *The New Yorker* and asked for E. B. White. He was
shown into the reception room and Mr. White was told that someone was waiting for him there. White's customary practice in those
days, if he couldn't place a caller's name, was to slip moodily out of
the building by way of the fire escape and hide in the coolness of
Schrafft's until the visitor went away. He is not afraid of process
servers, blackmailers, borrowers, or cranks; he is afraid of the smiling stranger who tramples the inviolable flowers of your privacy
bearing a letter of introduction from an old Phi Gam brother now
in the real-estate game in Duluth. White knows that the Man in
the Reception Room may not be so easy to get rid of as a process
server—or even a blackmailer: he may grab great handfuls of your
fairest hours, he may even appropriate a sizable chunk of your life,
for no better reason than that he was anchor man on your brother's
high-school relay team, or married the sister of your old girl, or met
an aunt of yours on a West Indies cruise. Most of us, out of a politeness made up of faint curiosity and profound resignation, go out
to meet the smiling stranger with a gesture of surrender and a fixed
grin, but White has always taken to the fire escape. He has avoided
the Man in the Reception Room as he has avoided the interviewer,

302

the photographer, the microphone, the rostrum, the literary tea, and the Stork Club. His life is his own. He is the only writer of prominence I know of who could walk through the Algonquin lobby or between the tables at Jack and Charlie's and be recognized only by his friends.

But to get back to the particular caller of six years ago whom we left wating in the reception room. On that occasion, out of some obscure compulsion, White decided to go out and confront the man and see what he wanted. "I'm White," he told the stranger he found sitting alone in the room. The man rose, stared for a long moment at the audacious fellow in front of him, and then said, with grim certainty, "You are not E. B. White." White admits that his hair leaped up, but it is my fond contention that his heart did, too. I like to think that he was a little disappointed when he realized, as he was bound to, that the man was wrong. I like to insist that he resumed his burden of identity with a small sigh. (Where the remarkable interview got to from the tense point to which I have brought it here I shall leave it to my memoirs to tell.)

In the early days of *The New Yorker* the object of this searching examination signed his first few stories and poems with his full name: Elwyn (as God is my judge) Brooks White. I cannot imagine what spark of abandon, what youthful spirit of devil-may-care prompted a poet who loves to live half hidden from the eye to come out thus boldly into the open. He didn't keep it up long; he couldn't stand the fierce glare of polysyllabic self-acknowledgment. For the past twelve years he has signed his casuals and his verses merely with his initials, E. B. W. To his friends he is Andy. It was a lucky break that saved him from Elly or Wynnie or whatever else one might make out of Elwyn in the diminutive. He went to Cornell and it seems that every White who goes there is nicknamed Andy for the simple if rather faraway reason that the first president of the university was named Andrew White.

It used to be (indeed I believe it still is) a wonder and a worry to White's boss, Mr. Harold Ross, the mystic and wonderful editor of *The New Yorker*, that his favorite and most invaluable assistant avoided people, lived along the untrodden ways, hid by mossy stones, and behaved generally in what Ross was pleased to call an antisocial manner. For a restlessly gregarious man who consorts with ten thousand people from Groucho Marx to Lord Dalhousie it is difficult to comprehend the spirit of Walden Pond. As long ago as the late nineteen twenties there were hundreds of people who implored Ross to introduce them to the man who wrote, on the already famous first page of *The New Yorker,* those silver and crystal sentences which have a ring like the ring of nobody else's sentences in the world. White declined to be taken to literary parties, or to any other kind of parties, but one day Ross lured him to the house of a certain literary lady who, White was persuaded to believe, would be found alone. When the door of her house was opened to them, Ross pushed White into a hallway loud with the chatter of voices proceeding from a crowded living room, the unmistakably assertive voices of writers and artists. Ross made the serious mistake of entering the living room first. When he looked around for White, that shy young man had quietly disappeared. He had proceeded deviously through the house, to the disciplined dismay of the servants, out the back door, and over trees and fences, or whatever else may have been in his way, to the freedom he so greatly cherishes, leaving the curtsy, the compliment, and the booksy chat to writers who go in for that sort of thing.

"Isn't there," Ross demanded of him one time, "*any*body you would like to meet?" White gave this difficult question his grave consideration and said, at what Alexander Woollcott would call long last, "Yes. Willie Stevens and Helen Hayes." It is a proof of the reckless zeal and the devoted energy of Harold Ross that he instantly set about trying to get hold of Willie Stevens for the purpose of inviting him to a dinner in New York at which White and Miss Hayes were to be the only other guests. I am desolated to report that this little coming together could not be accomplished: Willie apparently knew too many people the way it was and declined the invitation with that gentle old-world courtesy of which he was so consummate a master. Ross did manage finally to bring White face to face with Helen Hayes. Our hero, I am informed, was discontented and tongue-tied during their brief, jumpy conversation and was glad when it was all over. I suppose Miss Hayes was, too.

E. B. W. was born in Mount Vernon, N. Y., and will be forty next year. He had an ordinary, normal childhood, monkeying with an old Oliver typewriter, shooting with an air gun at the weather vane on his father's barn. At Cornell he charmed and astonished his English professors with a prose style so far above Cayuga's ordinary run of literary talent as to be considered something of a miracle. The *Cornell Sun* under White's editorship must have been the best-written college newspaper in the country. After Cornell he drove a model T Ford across the country with a friend named Howard

Cushman. When they ran out of money, they played for their supper —and their gasoline—on a fascinating musical instrument that White had made out of some pieces of wire and an old shoe or something. In Seattle the young explorer got a job as reporter on the *Times,* the kind of newspaper that did not allow you to use the verb "to mangle." Accurately reporting, one day, the anguished cry of a poor husband who had found the body of his wife in the municipal morgue, White wrote, "My God, it's her!" and when the city editor changed this to "My God, it is she!" our wanderer moved sadly on to where they had a better understanding of people and a proper feeling for the finer usages of the English tongue. He became mess boy on a ship bound for Alaska, commanded by an old whaling captain, and manned by a crew who knew that a man says it's her when he finds her dead.

Shortly after *The New Yorker* was founded, its editors began to get occasionally manuscripts from an unknown young man named E. B. White who was a production assistant in an advertising agency. Harold Ross and Katharine Angell, his literary editor, were not slow to perceive that here were the perfect eye and ear, the authentic voice and accent for their struggling magazine. It took months, however, to trap the elusive writer into a conference and weeks to persuade him to come to work in the office; he finally agreed to give them his Thursdays. It is not too much to say that Andy White was the most valuable person on the magazine. His delicate tinkering with the works of *The New Yorker* caused it to move with a new ease and grace. His tag lines for those little newsbreaks which the magazine uses at the bottom of columns were soon being read joyfully aloud around town. His contributions to the Talk of the Town, particularly his Notes and Comment on the first page, struck the shining note that Ross had dreamed of striking. He has written a great many of the most memorable picture captions, including the famous one that has passed (usually misquoted) into song and legend, editorial and, I daresay, sermon: "I say it's spinach and I say the hell with it." He had a hand in everything: he even painted a cover and wrote a few advertisements. One day nine years ago he decided that some pencil drawings I had absently made and thrown on the floor should be published in *The New Yorker,* so he picked them up, inked in the lines, and, to the surprise of us all, including Ross, got them published in *The New Yorker.*

Andy White understands begonias and children, canaries and goldfish, dachshunds and Scottish terriers, men and motives. His

ear not only notes the louder cosmic rhythms but catches the
faintest ticking sounds. He plays a fair ping-pong, a good piano,
and a terrible poker (once, holding four natural jacks, he dropped
out of the betting under the delusion that there were eight jacks
in the deck and all he had was half of them). He has steadfastly
refused to learn to play bridge or to take out life insurance. Once
he offered an airplane pilot a thousand dollars to take him through
a stormy dawn from Roosevelt Field to Chicago because a mysterious
phone call had made him believe a friend was in great distress. The
pilot had to make a forced landing in Pittsburgh, so that all White
had to pay to see for himself that all was quiet along Lake Michigan
was eight hundred dollars and his railroad fare from Pittsburgh.
When a band of desperadoes stole his Buick sedan out of a quiet
Turtle Bay garage and used it in the robbery of an upstate bank,
White was suspected by the New York police of being the "brain
guy" who devised the operations of a large and dangerous mob. For
days detectives shrewdly infested his office, peering under tables,
asking questions, staring in suspicious bewilderment at the preposterous array of scrawls, dentist's dates, symbols, phone numbers,
photographs, and maps that littered his walls. Eventually they went
shrewdly away, but every time I hear the sirens scream, I think they
are coming for White. The former suspect is a good man with ax,
rifle, and canoe (for several years he was part owner of a boys' camp
in darkest Canada), and he sails a thirty-foot boat expertly. Two
of his favorite books are *Van Zanten's Happy Days* and Alain-
Fournier's *The Wanderer*. In the country he is afflicted with hay
fever and in the city with a dizziness that resembles ordinary dizziness only as the mist resembles the rain. He expects every day of his
life that something will kill him: a bit of mold, a small bug, a piece
of huckleberry pie.

Some years ago White bought a farm in Maine and he now lives
there the year around with his wife, who was Katharine Angell;
and their son. He spends most of his time delousing turkeys, gathering bantam eggs, building mice-proof closets, and ripping out old
fireplaces and putting in new ones. There is in him not a little of
the spirit of Thoreau, who believed "that the world crowds round
the individual, leaving him no vista, and shuts out the beauty of
the earth; and that the wholesome wants of man are few." Now
and then, between sunup and milking time, Andy White manages to
write a casual or a poem for *The New Yorker,* and he does a monthly

department for *Harper's* magazine. Many of the things he writes seem to me as lovely as a tree—say a maple after the first frost, or the cherry hung with snow. What he will go on to do in his forties and fifties I have no idea. If he simply continues to do what he has always done, it will be all right with me.

HEYWOOD BROUN

by Bennett Cerf

*There are enough anecdotes about Heywood Broun to fill an en-
tire book. Here are a few of them.*

DECEMBER 19, 1942

HEYWOOD BROUN has been dead now for three full years. The multitude of friends who loved and admired him from the bottom of
their hearts find it hard to believe that it's as long as that since they
saw him shambling into his favorite haunts, sloppily attired, tardy
for appointments, but welcomed with shouts of joy wherever he
appeared. His name bobs up in conversations as frequently as
though he were still alive, turning in his daily columns. And what
columns the doings of these past three years would have inspired in
him! By a stroke of cruel irony, the space they once occupied is now
devoted to the outpourings of Westbrook Pegler, who represents
everything Broun detested most. "The trouble with Peg," he explained once, "is that he was bitten early in life by an income tax."

Broun's classmates at Harvard included John Reed, Walter Lippmann, and Hamilton Fish—an omen, possibly, of the later conflicts
between his political convictions and his sybaritic personal habits.
Foreign languages were his nemesis. An irate German professor
shied an inkwell at him, but missed. His habit of fulfilling assignments at the last possible moment, if at all, failed to enchant the
Harvard authorities, and he did not graduate. His classmates
watched in awe while he threw all of his belongings helter-skelter
into a trunk, and then climbed in himself and trampled them down
after the fashion of a Burgundy grape presser.

Broun got a job with the *Tribune* and turned in some of the
greatest baseball and football stories that ever have been written.
Then he was transferred to the drama department. The day of the
transfer, he acted as official scorer at a Giant-Cub ball game in the
afternoon and covered Ethel Barrymore's opening in an Edna Ferber
play called *Our Mrs. McChesney* in the evening. At the ball game,

he scored a close play as an error for the visiting shortstop, thereby depriving the Giant batter of a base hit in the records. That evening, he roasted Miss Barrymore's performance to a fare-thee-well. The next day the *Tribune's* managing editor received two indignant communications. One, from the Giant batman, read, "What's the big idea of sending a lousy dramatic critic up here to be official scorer?" The other, signed by Miss Barrymore, concluded, "How dare you assign a cheap baseball reporter to cover the opening of a Barrymore play?"

Broun loved the theater, and the majority of his reviews were gentle and encouraging. One evening, however, an actor named Geoffrey Steyne gave a performance that displeased him. Broun allowed that Mr. Steyne was the worst actor on the American stage. Mr. Steyne sued. The whole principle of dramatic criticism was at stake in this suit; if the actor won it, obviously, a dangerous precedent would have been established. The case was dismissed, and it remained only to see what Heywood would say about Mr. Steyne on the occasion of his next New York appearance. The big night finally arrived, and the next morning initiates turned eagerly to Broun's review. He did not so much as mention Geoffrey Steyne until the last sentence of his last paragraph. This read simply, "Mr. Steyne's performance was not up to his usual standard."

Heywood was a war correspondent in France in 1918. General Pershing saw him in uniform and asked him if he had fallen into a ditch. A fellow worker once dubbed him "Six Characters in Search of a Laundry." Heywood usually forgot to put laces in his shoes. When he took them off for bowling—which he loved—he disclosed socks with such enormous holes that they looked like ankle supporters. His first wife, Ruth Hale, was just as careless as Heywood. The first time I visited their home, a step in the back staircase was broken; three years later it had not been repaired. Everybody just hopped over it, while Ruth would remark placidly, "Somebody's going to break his neck on that step someday!" I had come to collect an introduction for a Modern Library book that Heywood had promised to deliver some two months previous. He wrote it while I waited. Then we lunched together in his kitchen. We vaulted the broken step and found that the icebox contained a single can of peaches. Heywood punctured the lid with a beer opener and emptied the peaches into two saucers that he salvaged from a pile of dirty dishes in the sink. We ate standing up.

When Dorothy Parker and Beatrice Kaufman visited the Broun

Home Front, Mrs. K. is reported to have discovered a couple of deep brown, bedraggled old toothbrushes hanging in the bathroom. "Good heavens," she cried, "what are those things?" "Don't you recognize them?" said the ever helpful Miss Parker. "Those are the broomsticks witches ride on every Hallowe'en!" The last tenant of the Brouns was Ed McNamara, who plays every Irish cop role in Hollywood. "Mac," Heywood told him, "it's a shame that with a rich, resonant voice like yours, you don't ever know what the Hell you're talking about!" One night Mac came home to discover his trunk on the doorstep, and a note from Heywood written on the tag. "Dear Mac," it read, "I forgot to tell you that I sold the house!"

In 1921, Heywood joined the staff of the morning *World,* where he became scared to death of the editor, Herbert Bayard Swope. Years later, although they now were close friends and met night after night at various peoples' houses, he still held Swope—not to mention Swope's wife, Margaret—in something like awe. When Winston Churchill's son, Randolph, wangled a job on the *World* at the tender age of eighteen and called Swope "Herbert" the day he joined the staff, Heywood practically dropped in his tracks. A story he loved to tell about the Swopes concerned the day when the editor collected thirty-five men—including Broun—at the Belmont Race Track and invited them all to drop in for a drink at his Long Island home on their way back to New York. In the midst of the festivities, Broun was dumfounded when Swope turned to his guests and asked, "Why don't you all stay for dinner?" Without waiting for a reply, he turned to his wife and said, "They're staying for dinner, my dear." Mrs. Swope rang for the maid, remarked calmly, "Mary, there will be thirty-five extra for dinner this evening," and sailed majestically out of the room. "It was terrific," whooped Heywood. Later he was dispatched in the Swope station wagon to fetch six dozen lamb chops from the Manhasset butcher shop.

Some of Heywood's quips at this time are still quoted and collected in anthologies. The depression had not yet come along to toughen our fiber and sharpen our consciousness of social inequalities; everybody drifted along in a happy haze of bathtub gin and Wall Street profits. Heywood lost more money at poker games and the race track in a single day than he had had to his name a few years previous. He labeled Woollcott "the smartest of Alecs." At a Bankhead opening, he whispered into the star's ear, "Don't look now, Tallulah, but your show's slipping!" Invited to a poker game by Ring Lardner, he reported over the telephone, "I can't come,

Ring. It's my son Woodie's night out, and I've got to stay home with the nurse!" He made a disparaging statement about a fight manager in Syracuse. "You wouldn't dare come up here and repeat that," taunted the Upstater. Broun answered, "I'll be up there and say it next Friday at half past five!" "And did you?" asked the man to whom Broun was telling the story. "Of course not!" he replied. At the Baer-Carnera fight, Grantland Rice remarked, "Golly, that big fellow sure can take it." "Yeah," answered Broun, "but he doesn't seem to know what to do with it!" On the day that Babe Ruth smacked out two home runs in a world series game, and contributed a couple of sparkling catches as well, Broun's account began, "The Ruth is mighty and shall prevail!"

Heywood's dawning preoccupation with the class struggle manifested itself clearly in the Sacco-Vanzetti case in 1927. He regarded the execution of these two men as a flagrant miscarriage of justice and he wrote two burning and devastating columns about the case that belong with the great pieces of invective of all time. Ralph Pulitzer of the *World* asked him to write no more on this controversial subject, and Broun staged a one-man strike. Swope patched up the quarrel, but two years later, the wound still rankled, and Heywood accepted a fabulous offer from Roy Howard of the *Telegram*. This was when Broun first began to tell us, "You can't sit on the fence much longer. It's time to choose your side for keeps." Events of recent years have been his vindication. Referring to one fence-straddling commentator, Heywood remarked, "His mind is so open that the wind whistles through it. Nothing sticks. He's afraid to stay on any side if self-aggrandizement beckons to the other!" Heywood knew an appeaser when he saw one—years before any of us had occasion to use the word.

The last years of Heywood's life were devoted principally to the organization and promotion of the American Newspaper Guild. His customary carelessness disappeared like magic when he embraced this cause; newspapermen will never forget what he did to improve their pay and working conditions. Heywood respected all labor unions. It was against his principles to cross a picket line. One noon, however, the waiters at his favorite hangout were out on strike, and Heywood, lost in thought, passed the pickets. "Mr. Broun," said one of the waiters reproachfully, "we're on strike." "Tell me who your favorite customer is," said Broun contritely, "and I'll write him a letter and tell him to stay away." The waiter replied, "Why, you are, Mr. Broun." Heywood stormed into the restaurant, sent out luncheon to the pickets, and effected a settlement of the strike on the spot. He didn't know until much later that the proprietors had been dying to settle for days and awaited only some face-saving device to get them out of an embarrassing situation. At the height of the celebration, Broun cried, "My God, I'm due at a meeting of the Book-of-the-Month Club judges!" and rushed out, leaving behind, as usual, the galleys that were to be the subject of discussion that day. The other judges can't remember one occasion when Heywood arrived at a meeting in time. When he died, however, the directors couldn't bring themselves to appoint another judge in his place. The post is vacant to this day.

Over Thanksgiving weekend in 1938, the Averell Harrimans were hosts to a gathering of sixty at their estate in Arden. The house is located at the top of a steep hill. Heywood looked down from the summit and recalled that the year the house was built, he had eluded the guards at the outer gate, and crawled up the hill, intent on getting an exclusive interview with the ailing Edward H. Harriman, of the Union Pacific. He was caught the moment he emerged from the shrubbery, however, and hustled down to the bottom again. "Today," said Heywood, ruefully considering his build, "it's all I can do to get up the hill in an automobile." That evening, Heywood was very late to dinner. "I was down in the kitchen," he explained cheerfully to Averell Harriman, "trying to persuade the butler to strike for higher wages!"

This was the weekend that Broun and Swope decided to cross-examine Duff Cooper, another of the distinguished guests. We all gathered round expectantly, and Swope asked the first question, which Broun promptly answered—at considerable length. Then Broun essayed a query, which Swope answered. It gradually dawned on us that the interview was destined to be an exclusive dialogue between Swope and Broun. Their rhetoric flowed on, while Duff Cooper sat blinking in complete silence, like a tortoise with lumbago. Later he confided to a friend that we were the rudest people he had ever met. Of course, this was three years before he galloped off to Singapore to do nothing so magnificently while a great bastion of empire was crumbling over his head.

Two years later, we all spent another Thanksgiving with the Harrimans in Arden—all, that is, but Heywood, who was dead, and Quent Reynolds, who was reporting the Blitz from London. Swope proposed a toast that night to the two who were absent. "One," he said, "is in heaven, and the other is in hell."

Heywood had a genius for discovering strange methods to throw his money away. Once he ran for Congress on the Socialist ticket. Another time he edited a local newspaper called the *Connecticut Nutmeg.* His greatest extravagance was a play called *Shoot the Works,* which he wrote, financed, and appeared in personally. Indirectly, this play provided him with the greatest happiness in his life. One of the girls in the chorus was named Connie Madison, and Heywood adored her at sight. They were married in 1935. She called him "The Commodore," and spruced him up almost beyond recognition. Heywood's friends accepted Connie without qualification the first time they met her. George Kaufman gave her a part in *Merrily We Roll Along.* She crossed the stage once and had a single line, which read, "I wouldn't dare bob my hair. My father would throw me out!" Broun, in his review, remarked, "Miss Madison was adequate." We hope that Connie will read this piece, and accept it as evidence that besides herself, there are a thousand and more old friends of Heywood Broun's who wish he were with us in this good fight, and who will never forget him as long as they live.

THE IDLER AND
HIS WORKS

by George Santayana

For a year after Santayana's death, on September 26, 1952, his per-
sonal effects, library, and manuscripts were held in custody by the
Spanish Consulate in Rome pending the probation of his will in
Boston. Late in 1953, however, all this material was turned over to
Santayana's literary executor, Daniel Cory, secretary, disciple, and
friend of the late philosopher's for a quarter century. One of the
first things Mr. Cory found was an old valise crammed with manu-
scripts in Santayana's hand, and among them was a square brown
envelope with two words written large upon it: Unpublished *and*
Important. *It contained an essay entitled "The Idler and His*
Works," a self-appraisal of Santayana's lifework which Mr. Cory
considers ". . . a masterpiece of its kind in which he is quietly
summing up his life's literary labors and attempting to evaluate
them from the standpoint of posterity." It is probably the latter
consideration that prompted Santayana to leave this essay for
posthumous publication. The manuscript was written between
1942 and 1944 in Rome.

MAY 15, 1954

MANY OTHER PERSONS and places, not mentioned in my autobiography, have played important parts in my life and left their ghosts,
at night, in my dreams: but they had better remain there. I have
recorded only such fragments of biography as still interested my
waking mind, or perhaps might serve some antiquary curious about
the times or the types that I have painted with care. Many of them,
although potent influences over me in my private capacity, may seem
insignificant and tiresome to a reader who thinks of me as an
author: and how else should a reader think of me? Yet it is not at
all as an author or as a professional philosopher that I think of
myself. I have written a great many books and a great many reviews

314

and articles. Astonishing bibliographies of them have been compiled, astonishing, I mean, to me; I wonder how I found time for wasting so much ink and paper.

I have seldom been conscious of working hard. Most of my writing has been an instinctive pleasure, a playful impulse, as in running down a grassy slope or exploring a woodland path. The things wrote themselves; and when I dropped the pen, and rose from my writing table, I seemed to awake from a trance and to be myself again. Yet that other dreaming, industrious self, weaving words eagerly together, and excogitating arguments and opinions as if he were an animated book, is doubtless the self that I am supposed to be and that, in an autobiography, I should have been expected to write about.

No doubt that industrious, playful, automatic self was an original part of me, and a pesistent part. I am happy in mental idleness, with manual work. I envy the housemaids, so common in Southern Europe, who sing as they scrub. I feel that there is something sane and comfortable in the old women who sit knitting or turning over the roasting chestnuts at the street corners. I like to spend drowsy hours drawing, cleaning or making something, or even mending my clothes. Pleasant is solitude among manageable things. And among manageable things, the most manageable for me are words.

All my life, since I regained my freedom, I have passed the morning writing. The theme had been chosen in a moment of inspiration. The chapter, perhaps the paragraph, was already begun. Nothing was required but to turn on the current, if only the current would come, and continue the flow of language. The material act of writing entertained me; also the semi-material act of arranging and rearranging the words. Often the thought was rekindled in the process, transformed, sharpened, corrected; and out came an epigram or a terse formula for something that had perhaps been floating in my mind for years.

Various peculiarities and faults of my writings are due to this mechanical and dreamful way of composing them. All is improvised, as in poetry: hence, unless there is a drastic revision, so much repetition, so much that is desultory, rambling, inconclusive. No strict program, no order, was predetermined, no precise limits or scope. Such a method or lack of method would have been fatal had there not been sharp definition in my thought, clear principles in my judgments. As it is, though the surface be sometimes confused, as in a tapestry, the figures at a little distance stand out clearly enough; and I think that, at least in my later works, a sympathetic reader will not be seriously troubled by my meanderings. The mountains and the sea are never out of sight. I don't stop to reconsider what comes to me as I write, and I consult no authorities; but I have read much and reflected long before I begin writing.

As regards the subject matter, my work might be divided into two strands, the poetic and the academic. There may be poetic touches and irresponsible flights sometimes in the academic books, and academic themes even in the poetry: yet the two were originally quite distinct. My verses and my private philosophizing belonged to me, expressed me, and were addressed essentially to nobody else; the academic subjects were suggested or imposed by circumstances, and I appear there in the costume and under the mask of an assumed character. The acting is sincere enough, but the part is conventional. My life does not appear in my works until we turn to the *Poems, Soliloquies in England, Dialogues in Limbo,* and *The Last Puritan.* In these my inmost feelings, and the places and persons concerned in my real life, supply the subject and control the expression. It is not a question of complete portraits either of myself or of others. All has been recast in a crucible, and there appear only possibilities, dream images of my surroundings and passions, such as the mind retains more willingly than the accidental and imperfect realities.

In the academic books, besides the rhetorical veneer that I have spoken of, there is a tendency to infuse more and more of myself into the apprehension of the world and of its opinions, until in *Realms of Being* the picture of them becomes itself a confession and an image of the mind that composed it. Not that I have intentionally indulged the imagination here, as in the poems and the novel: on the contrary, I have studied to be austere and skeptical and to discount the human mind and its bias as far as possible. But this love of the bare truth, this intellectual asceticism, is itself a human passion and the secret of a regenerate life: so that the more I strip myself of myself, the better I bring to light that something in me that is more myself than I am—the spirit. I believe there is substantial though relative truth in my philosophy, since it is merely the confession of sincere and fundamental assumptions, which a living being can hardly avoid; and I hope that some more powerful and better-knit mind may arise, and restate those views as I ought to have stated them. But that could be done in a single volume, without any of the accidental trappings that encumber my compositions. All my technical writings could then be forgotten to advantage, even as my own mind prefers to forget them.

When by chance I open one of my books, especially one of the earlier ones, it seems to me the work of some other man; and I am surprised if I come to something that sounds like what I should say myself. In general the tone and tenor remain quite foreign to me. Not that I have changed my opinions. I should still say the same things, did the same questions present themselves to me in the same terms. But those terms belonged to a fundamentally foreign morality. I said in them, as well as I could, what I honestly felt; yet they constituted a literary and diplomatic veil to my latent intelligence. I seemed cold (as Bertrand Russell has observed) when my heart was burning away beneath the embers; and it has taken the greater part of a long life for me to extricate my meaning from my words, find the center of my survey, and form fresh categories and a fresh vocabulary.

Ancient philosophy was a great aid to me in this: the more I retreated in time, and the farther east I looked, the more I discovered my own profound and primitive convictions. The conventional moralizing and the prim aesthetic judgments of my earlier books need not be contradicted; the literary psychology in them may even be confirmed; but all this needs to be grounded in physical facts and at the same time shown to be purely relative to special phases of human life and to special predicaments. The surface of human experience must not be taken for its ground or for its own motive power. It is all an effect of subhuman or superhuman forces.

The liberal, empirical, psychological philosophy into which I was plunged was miserably artificial, like a modern town laid out in squares. There was nothing subterranean acknowledged in it, no ultimate catastrophe, no jungle, no desert, and no laughter of the gods. Mankind lived lost in the fog of self-consciousness, persuaded that it was creating itself and the whole universe. They had forgotten their religion; and their philosophy, when they had one, was a glorification of their vanity and of their furious impulse to make money, to make machines, and to make war. What would come of it, except perhaps to make them all alike? In my solitude I watched their mechanical arts not without admiration: they were clever children making their own toys, and as busy at it as birds building their nests or worms burrowing their holes. Verily they have their reward, if they enjoy the process. But may they not be rather multiplying their troubles, and missing the natural pleasures and dignity of man? These pleasures and dignity lie in seeing and thinking, in living with an understanding of the place and destiny of life.

Now reflection convinces me that what is called experience, the obvious and inescapable pressure of sensation, is intrinsically a dream, something arbitrary, fugitive, unsubstantial, coming out of nothing and ending in nothing. Yet since this dream is endured, and to some extent may be surveyed and remembered, there is something else on the hither side of it which I call the spirit; a witness, but not an agent, since spirit can neither bring the dream about nor avoid it nor understand why it should come. This coming, however, is a terrible assault to the spirit, for it awakes in terror and tears; so that on the further side of the dream and antecedent to it, there is something dynamic, obscure to the spirit, but overwhelmingly powerful and real, which I call matter, but which, if you prefer, you may call God. Spirit here and matter or God there, are not phenomena; they are not distinguishable and recognizable features in the dream but an outlying power in the one case and an observant intellect on the other, which is not observed but is analytically implied in the fact of observation and in the act of comparing one part of the dream with another and noting its inconstancy and confusion.

The terms employed in this apprehension of experience remain mere images or words, but for intelligence they become signs for something beneath or beyond them, matter, God, or spirit, of which they manifest the presence, power, and method of action. Such manifestation, however, is not exhaustive, as if the words or images were alone real, and signified nothing further. They do not define their object but only indicate it. Nothing existent can be defined. Definition defines only the idea, the word, or the image: the object is transcendent. Matter, God, or spirit have to be posited beyond. Only such substances, powers, or faculties can have any depth or persistence or can render our visions and definitions valid or true of anything beyond themselves.

Such was the summary system of categories by which in the end I cleared my mind, at least in principle and in intention, of all foreign confusion. In fact, however, the books in which I worked out that system—*Skepticism and Animal Faith* and *Realms of Being*—are terribly overloaded with accidental matters, the mud and the weeds that clung to me as I struggled out of the bog. Nevertheless, I hope that a benevolent reader will shed these impedimenta as he advances, and will retain at the end a clear sense of my *radical position*. It is not at all new or artificial. I did not reach it by invention or hypothesis but by retreat from all inventions and hypotheses to the inevitable assumptions and the obvious terms of all apprehension.

Then I found myself reverting to a system like those of the first Greek philosophers, who looked at the world boldly, without religious preconceptions, yet found it to be much the same world that the Indians described in their religious meditations. But the Indian like the Christian philosophers were encumbered with fantastic notions, suggested by moral predicaments to an unrestrained imagination; and it is necessary to remove these problems to the moral and poetical sphere where they belong. They are human problems and a man may well find them more interesting and important than cosmology, but this poetic or moral enthusiasm in him will not change the real conditions of his life, or the source and development of that enthusiasm itself; so that even in the interests of his private spiritual progress, he will do well in the first place not to deceive himself about his natural status. Nothing could be farther from me than a desire to quench the imagination; on the contrary, I would preserve it in all its freedom and originality. But it should not profess to be perception or science, if it would not become madness.

My philosophical system, being thus discovered within me, was latent in all the earlier phases of my opinions; and I think there is very little in my first writings that cannot be inserted into my mature system. Yet I was not clearly aware, when I wrote those innocent phrases, in what sense exactly they ought to be understood; so that some uncertainty and confusion seems to hang about my words. The words came from the heart, I was always sincere; but the heart was reacting upon alien impressions, and not speaking freely out of its clear depths. It would be necessary in each case to understand the circumstances and the connections in which such thoughts came into my mind; and then the spontaneous side of my reaction, which alone would express my innate philosophy, could be disengaged.

In my first prose book, *The Sense of Beauty,* the argument is uninspired and academic; I was writing the book for a practical purpose. Yet it was I that was writing it; so that in the incidental touches and in the style there is more of me than in the doctrine. I speak as if the sense of beauty were compounded of ingredients, so much sugar, so much lemon, and so much water making the proper lemonade. But sensations are moments of spirit, they cannot endure, they cannot be compounded; and the whole "chemistry of mind" goes on in the psyche, in the life of the body, from which the richest and subtlest intuition issues pure and whole, like the sound of a bell, or the voice singing. I had not yet read Arisobe sufficiently or understood that the psyche is the life of the body as a whole, in its unity and direction, partially and incidentally expressed in consciousness. When I spoke of "objectified pleasure," apart from the false subsistence apparently attributed to feelings, as if they could be tossed about like dice in a dicebox, there was nevertheless a true sense of the nerve of perception, which is transcendent intent or indication: the psyche receives an impression, and the intellect and will respond with a belief. So in the presence of things harmonious with its life, the psyche luxuriates, and is suffused with a vital pleasure; a part of this pleasure may be proper to the act of seeing or hearing, which at the same time evokes a visual or musical image: and since this image is a recognizable object our joy in it comes as the sense of its beauty, not as a sense of our pleasure. The beauty is probably the first thing felt by the lover, before the form in which it dwells becomes distinct and articulate in his vision. So the sun attracts and dazzles us, before we can focus the eyes on its color or its shape.

In turning to criticism, as I did in *Interpretations of Poetry and Religion,* I began to rescue the part that was my own from the borrowed part of my philosophy. The themes were public, and principally drawn from English literature and philosophy; but now the judgments passed, and the criteria that inspired them, were frankly not English. What were they? We cannot say that they were Spanish or Catholic, yet they lay in that direction; in that direction and beyond, in the humanism not of the Renaissance but of antiquity. The Renaissance was not a rebirth but a reproduction of relics; the seeds of antiquity had not been replanted in the soil of Christendom, so that they might bloom afresh into a new and complete life. There had been merely a revival, a restoration—patches of antiquity inserted in the torn garment of the Christian mind. Now in my criticism I was falling back upon pre-Christian, merely human standards; yet these in one sense even more Christian than the English standard of appreciation. They condemned "the poetry of barbarism," the worship of impulse, enterprise, effort, and blind adventure. They were anti-romantic, anti-idealistic, and demanded a "life of reason."

The long book in which I expounded what I conceived a life of reason to be suffered from the very faults that my criticism condemned: it was too impulsive, too pretentious, too casual, and based on too little learning. Admiration of ancient Greece and modern England insinuated a didactic tone into the political part, and made me seem a prophet of I don't know what Utopia. This tone pleased people in America, especially the young Jews, and perhaps caused the book to become well known in that circle when otherwise it might have been altogether neglected. It also caused the book to be misinterpreted, as if it had been inspired by romantic idealism, and not grounded, as it was meant to be, on a materialistic view of nature and life.

Such a view does not exclude the possibility of all sorts of beautiful and surprising developments in the universe. The natural world is indefinitely fertile; but its fertility is not directed by the human will; it is not governed, except in man, by human interests. The sentiment that it would justly inspire about human life and human hopes would be extremely sober. Beings that arise are likely to find means of subsistence and a chance to propagate their kind, because otherwise they would never have arisen; but in no particular case, and at no particular time, can a race or an individual be sure of continued good fortune; and no specific hope about distant issues is ever likely to be realized. The ground shifts, the will of mankind deviates, and what the father dreamed of, the children neither fulfill nor desire.

My political fancy had undergone two love affairs, two seasons in which I almost believed that I had discovered the ideal in the real. Greece and England had seemed to me, in different directions, to have come near it. I called it the life of reason. By this I meant that, on the one hand, the world had been conceived sanely in effect, though in poetical or rhetorical terms; on the other hand, the art of life had been developed in two different directions, each of them satisfying. But satisfying to whom? In Greece to the Greeks and in England to the English? Or in both, ideally, to me? On this point I had not come to clearness. If I meant that the ideals suggested to me by Greece and England, somehow fused together, seemed to me to satisfy all the just demands of human nature, then my long book on *The Life of Reason* should have painted a concrete picture of a perfect society. I should have constructed another Utopia. But I possessed neither the varied knowledge nor the firm principles requisite for such a performance. My book was only a semi-historical semi-judicial review of the most familiar forms of society, religion, art, and science in the Western world; and while a rational criterion of moral judgment did underlie the whole discussion, this criterion was not clearly set forth or strictly applied.

My mind was allowed to float lazily among plausible opinions. I intended, however, to be a consistent naturalist, and I ought to have smiled a little at my casual enthusiasms, seeing that all ideals are but projections of vital tendencies in animal organisms. Therefore, since animal organisms are of many variable sorts, the direction and goal of progress always remain optional and subject to revision. This would have reduced my lovely Greece and my lovely England to local episodes in the history of manners and morals. Their rightness would have been avowedly only relative, even if it had been complete. But it had been sadly incomplete. Soon experience in the case of England and a little more reading in the case of Greece brought my two political love affairs to an end.

This book, though loosely composed and imperfectly digested, still marks an advance from convention to radical sincerity. I perceived that morality is something normal, and that religion, like perception, clothes in spontaneous sensuous or imaginative signs the real presence of pressing dangers and favorable opportunities. The material world and our animal nature, far from being obstacles in our way, are indispensable conditions for the pursuit and safe possession of any good; indispensable indeed for the discrimination of good from evil, or their existence at all. There must be something not chosen that chooses, something not desired that desires. This dynamic surge, this primeval automatism, within us and without, sustains the whole ideal structure of our language, our thoughts, and our interests, keeps them consecutive, and brings forth the fruits that we promise ourselves and the catastrophes that we wish to avoid.

Of historical illustrations for this thesis the best I had to offer were drawn from religion. There I had more information and more experience than in other spheres. I was at home in the workings of *la fonction fabulatrice*. Moreover, I knew the difference between well-grounded inspired myths, innocently mistaken for revelations, and the vapid fancies of stray poets. In both cases we suffer illusion, because passion, and often action, reacts upon an image as if it were a physical object. But the illusion proper to waking perception and to wise myths, when once discovered, drives us all the more confidently and successfully upon the real object; whereas the illusion proper to idle musings and dreams leaves us cheated and disaffected toward reality. A great religion need not fear philosophic criticism, which will liberate its moral and speculative substance from the poetic images in which it first appeared. Ultimate truths are more easily and adequately conveyed by poetry than by analysis. This is no reason for forbidding analysis, but it is a reason for not banishing poetry.

My later books teach the same lesson, but by a different approach. They may seem to move in the opposite direction; yet only because they start from an opposite quarter in making for the same goal. This goal is a good life, according to our nature and circumstances; and it may be missed either by ignoring it or misconceiving our true circumstances or else by ignoring or misconceiving our true nature and proper good. Now for a mind coming to philosophy from religion and poetry, as I did, and as did the first Greek philosophers, the pressing reform seems to be to criticize anthropomorphism in religion and fable in science; to insist that life, reason, and spirit are something natural, and that it is only by facing our true environment, and making the best of it, that we can develop them well. Therefore, those early Greek philosophers, who were great poets and prophets of nature, figured as sour enemies of mythology: and so I too, whose turn of mind was always poetical and religious, seemed to discard all inspiration and idealism.

Yet when naturalism in regard to circumstances had been firmly rooted in my mind, the other half of the total problem spontaneously came to the fore. What, in this natural world, is the nature and possible virtue of man? On what, without folly and ultimate disaster, can he set his heart? And I was constrained to reply: Only on the life of reason, only on union with the truth, only on ideal sympathy with that irrepressible spirit which comes to light in all living beings, flowering differently in each, and moving in each toward a special perfection. And allowing for the different background introduced by my naturalism, this was very like the reply given by the most radical religious teachers, idealists, and mystics: so that I might seem to be moving away from my earlier doctrine and reverting to the traditions I had rejected. Yet I was not in the least reverting to the illusions about circumstances that accompanied those traditions; I was merely placing the spirit, the motives, and the discipline found in those traditions back where they belonged: for they were all voices of nature, elicited by human predicaments.

How rich and how full of significance in regard to the natural

world and to human life in it this spiritual music may be, I have
attempted to show once more in my book on *The Idea of Christ
in the Gospels, or God in Man.* There is less presumption than we
might at first suspect in taking Christ for a model after having
identified him with God. Reason differs from perception and sentiment precisely in transcending our human egotism and aspiring to
understand things as they are in themselves and to love in them the
good that they love. This aspiration of reason extends inevitably to
sharing the vision and judgments of God; in other words, to trans-
porting ourselves into the presence of the truth and to living, as
Aristotle says, as much as possible in the eternal. Omniscience can
neither lose nor expect anything, and lives exclusively in the vision
of all things under the form of eternity. A corollary of this teaches
us that it is only ideally that things can enter the mind. When passing events enter the mind they stick there: they become ideas of
those events. Now it is in memory and imagination that we know
the world: while we move in it, if memory and inspiration do not
retain any images of it, we are simply a part of the moving world
and know nothing of it. Physical life perforce keeps time with the
rest of the physical world and is in flux like it. But reason bridges
those gaps and makes a panorama of those variations. Though it
is impossible for us to live our lives all at once, we may cultivate
a sense of its totality, and of the totality and truth of things. In that
measure we shall have lived, as it were, in the presence of God, and
in as full harmony with his vision and will as our human nature
allows.

Let me repeat, however, that I do not propose this sublimation
of the life of reason as something obligatory: no man can achieve
it completely, and most men can hardly practice it at all. I see
nothing wrong or sad in that. It is right that most of what we are
and of what we think should be lost forever. Eternal damnation
overtakes it justly. Society will judge some minds to be too flighty
and others to be too rigid or too mystical; but those judgments have
only a relative authority. It may be true that such habits are inconvenient for certain purposes: but no man's and no society's convenience can remake or limit the world. It is always lawful for a
butterfly to be a butterfly, and it is lawful for a man like La Fontaine to be proud of being a butterfly, as when he says:

> *Je suis chose légère et vole à tout sujet:*
> *Je vais de fleur en fleur et d'objet en objet.*

Yet the butterflies had better not form a league to exterminate the sages. The sages will smile upon them, and survive.

In spite of being so much in sympathy with the sages, I am well aware of not having been one of them. As a person I was too self-indulgent and not heroic enough; as a writer I was too miscellaneous; as a thinker I was born at the wrong time and bred in the wrong way. I like to hope that someone may later revive parts of my philosophy in more favorable circumstances. Yet for my own happiness I was philosophical enough. In a commonplace psyche I kept alive a spark of pure spirit which cast an impartial light, as far as it could reach, over the *universitas rerum*. This light cannot be blamed for the quality of the objects it found to shine upon; nor can it be taxed with inconstancy for shining only spasmodically, since that is the fault of the psyche and of the world in which it was formed. Pure spirit is no complete being: only a capacity to feel and to think upon occasion. Its light must be subdued to the quality of the things it touches. Yet in touching anything, no matter how foul, the light itself is not contaminated.

In my various books I have discussed things at very unequal removes from the fountain of spirit within me. But that center was truly philosophical. I can identify myself heartily with nothing in me except with the flame of spirit itself. Therefore the truest picture of my inmost being would show none of the features of my person, and nothing of the background of my life. It would show only the light of understanding that burned within me and, as far as it could, consumed and purified all the rest.

A MONOGRAPH ON
MR. TOMLINSON

by Herman J. Mankiewicz

*The writer of this significant treatise was a member of the re-
nowned Algonquin Round Table and later achieved recognition
as a screen writer (Citizen Kane). This is the only commemoration
of Mr. Tomlinson to be found, and some readers may feel that
it is one too many.*

AUGUST 11, 1945

IN THE FIRST PLACE, I have always known I wanted to write a monograph before I died. (This is connected, I think, with my reading
of the Sherlock Holmes stories at an impressionable age, eight to
nineteen. And while I'm still within the parentheses, I herewith
present, for free, a notion to what must be millions of writers, at
this very moment gazing out across fire escapes, clothes lines, and
garbage pails, frantic for subjects for their quills. How's for a piece
that tells the truth about the Sherlock Holmes stories, how contrived, how infantile, how maybe half of one-dimensional they are?)
In the second place, Mrs. Tomlinson kept repeating it would probably be the last friendly act I would ever be able to do for Gordon
and she was sure she didn't have to tell me, if the situation were
reversed—.

Gordon Tomlinson has now been with his fathers slightly more
than three years and my monograph—the title page reads, "Gordon
Tomlinson, An Appreciation, With an Attempt at Critical Appraisal, A Memoir," Privately Printed, MDCCCXLI—appeared after
what Mrs. Tomlinson called a decent interval. It is at her suggestion
that I have prepared this slightly rewritten version, with an eye to
getting a wider circulation than was possible with three hundred
copies, of which forty-two are still at the printer's.

By unspoken agreement with Mrs. Tomlinson, I did not in my
monograph go into Gordon's enormously successful financial life. At

the age of twenty-two, as is fairly well known, he reluctantly but uncomplainingly turned his back upon a life of letters to take full charge of the family isinglass interests, in consequence of the death of his father, and his residual estate was so fabulous that three states—New York, Florida, and Wisconsin—are still snarling in the courts over their share of the inheritance taxes. His isinglass triumphs, however, had been authoritatively recorded by *Fortune* and lengthy obituary notices in all parts of the country, and so it was his literary remains—the few fugitive efforts he had found time and opportunity to put to paper, she called them—with which Mrs. Tomlinson asked me, who knew him well in and since his college days, to concern myself.

I spent an extremely pleasant two weeks as Mrs. Tomlinson's guest at their great place, Mon Repos, not far from Schenectady, New York. His secretaries had gone through his files carefully, leaving me only with his writings, and the notes and correspondences pertaining thereto. With one unimportant exception—three lengthy letters to the President of the United States, all beginning, "I don't care if you and that Gestapo you call the F. B. I. send me to Siberia for life, if it's the last thing I do," which he had never mailed and which he had promised his lawyers he would destroy, but of which, nevertheless, he had kept copies—I was able to include the entire product of his ventures into belles-lettres in my monograph.

The accumulated material seemed to Mrs. Tomlinson to fall rather naturally into three major subdivisions. I wasn't sure, nor am I now, that she didn't subdivide a bit too arbitrarily, but the point is relatively inconsequential, and I didn't argue it.

The subdivision are "Juvenilia," which would be from his seventh to his twentieth years; "The Lean Years," from his taking over of isinglass to the gigantic testimonial banquet tendered him by his isinglass associates on his fiftieth birthday; and "The Sage of Mon Repos," covering the few years still left him.

Juvenilia

The very first thing he wrote was a letter to his grandfather, at the time Attorney-General of the United States, which later found its way back into Gordon's keeping. At the bottom of the page is a notation from the Attorney-General to the President under whom he was serving: "How's this for a precocious little bastard? Please return." The letter was returned, so there must have been an answer, but it seems to have been lost.

Gordon's letter—Opus No. 1, I called it in my monograph—reads: "Dere Gramp How Ar Yu Lov Gordon Tomlinson."

It is a matter of six years—perhaps they were productive, perhaps not, it is unlikely now that one will ever know—before the appearance of his next bit of writing, this time in print. It is from the columns of *Res Academicae,* published weekly, from October through May, by the students of Washington's Crossing Academy, Washington's Crossing, New Jersey.

There are, first, four lines, credited to "Exchange":

> *"Before"*
> *There are meters of accent*
> *And meter of tone,*
> *But the best of all meters*
> *Is to meter alone.*

Immediately below this, separated by a three-em dash, under the heading of "After," there are four more lines of verse, signed Gordon Schermerhorn Tomlinson:

> *There are letters of accent*
> *And letters of tone,*
> *But the best of all letters*
> *Is to letter alone.*

It's the only time he ever included the "Schermerhorn" in his name. This is significant, in the light of his later "Tomlinson Law of Nomenclature."

There follow two clippings, each signed "G. T.," from F. P. A.'s "Conning Tower" in the New York *Tribune*. The first: "Someone, myself, to be exact, wants to know what is the present relationship of William Sulzer to the State of New York. That's not hard. He's a Governor, once removed." The second: "Do you suppose that's where Ziegfeld got his title, from Thomas Moore? You know, 'My only books were women's looks, and folly's all they taught me.'?"

A blurred, torn item from the Harvard *Lampoon*, month undecipherable, 1916, constitutes the fifth item:

> Well old pal things have been so quiet around here you
> could hear a pin drop as they say but the Bros. if they taught
> me anything they taught me doing something no matter
> what it is that's all ways better than waste prescious minutes
> that might never return so here am I in this dump if I never

see it again that's too soon writing you this letter. But you know me Al a man can be down but he's never out until the empire says three strikes and then he's still got a chance if the catcher dont hold onto the ball and some of the catchers Gleason asked come to spring training all I wish is I could get the glue consescion only there's not a chance they'll stick around but will wind up in the 3-Eye league or somewhere as happen to know hes counting on me to work every game.

There was, unquestionably, more to this, but the fragment I am causing to be reprinted is all that has been preserved.

Gordon served overseas, as a fly speck in the AEF, during what for twenty-five years arrogantly called itself The War, a title it has recently had kicked out of its teeth. In a letter to his father, written from Coblenz, in the late spring of 1918, he enclosed a copy of some lines of his, meant as a tribute to Sergeant Joyce Kilmer, that had appeared in *The Stars and Stripes,* a week after Kilmer's old regiment, the New York Sixty-ninth, had had its triumphant parade up Fifth Avenue:

> *Today the Sixty-ninth parades—*
> *I cannot see them through the trees.*
>
> *The trees who lift their arms in thanks*
> *That those they love have wandered back,*
> *And call a benediction down*
> *Upon the ones who stayed behind*
> *To guard the trees of France.*
>
> *The trees who through the winter days*
> *Unbendingly present their arms.*
> *The trees who stand so firmly there,*
> *A thin line of eternity.*
> *Nor snow nor rain can wash from them*
> *Their certain immortality.*
>
> *The Sixty-ninth parades today—*
> *I cannot see them through the trees.*

The Lean Years

Gordon became a vice-president in charge of production, executive director, and general manager of isinglass, two weeks after his twenty-second birthday, and there is no evidence of literary activity, per se, for the following eight years. To be sure, Gordon's secretaries have assured me that his business correspondence was never stereotyped and that few letters left his office without a sentence or two, pungent, incisive, penetrating, that could only have come from Gordon himself. I know this to be a fact, because my firm was engaged to straighten out an unfortunate situation wherein a Mr. Salvatore, who had ordered several carloads of isinglass from Gordon's company, relied so wholly and so erroneously on his own insufficient knowledge of English, upon receiving Gordon's gracefully grateful acceptance of the order, as to come to the conclusion he would have to look elsewhere for his isinglass, which he immediately did, with the result that he refused to pay for Gordon's isinglass when it arrived. The matter was straightened out, of course, but Gordon, for a long time, confined himself, as he bitterly told me one night at dinner, to dictating, with his eyes shut, letters of the "yours of the tenth ultimo received and contents noted and in reply to same would state" school.

The first "Lean Years" contribution is almost certainly Gordon's. I say certainly because I found it in his files, but I have been forced also to say almost, because it purports to be the work of a Hubert J. Northrupp. It was less than a page in length and I reproduce it verbatim:

Mr. Tiffle Meets A Lady

By *Hubert J. Northrupp*

It must be admitted, in all fairness, that there was no way in the world for Mr. Phineas Tiffle to know that today was going to be any different from any other day. Exactly as he had done, excepting Sundays and the two weeks in 1919 when he had the flu, for the nearly twenty-seven years of their married life, Mr. Tiffle, careful not to disturb Mrs. Tiffle, had gotten out of bed, showered and returned to their bedroom, to find Mrs. Tiffle's bed unoccupied. Exactly as on every other day, too, Mr. Tiffle had smiled gently, because the unmistakable odor of fresh coffee being brewed was in the air, which meant that Mrs. Tiffle had been on to his little game and was fixing his breakfast.

Before long, the warning whistle of the 8:14, approaching Froggin's Creek, had warned him, exactly as on every other day, that it was time to be leaving and, still exactly as on every other day, he had gulped the rest of his coffee, kissed Mrs. Tiffle a hasty and affectionate goodbye and—

So much there is and no more, save that at the foot of the page is a handwritten note: "Too many 'as on every other days'? Better rewrite?"

I am positive this is Gordon's own work. For one thing, about this same time, he had offered—they both, I'm afraid, had had a little too much to drink—to bet George Winthrop, a former Williams All-American halfback, who was then a junior partner in something or other on Wall Street, that anybody could, by locking himself up in a room for five hours, write a short story that *The Saturday Evening Post* would instantly buy. I explain the "Hubert J. Northrupp" to myself a little less satisfactorily, but still satisfactorily. At Harvard for a semester, Gordon's next-door neighbor had been a Herbert L. Southerdon, who had made Phi Beta Kappa in his junior year and had proceeded to China to be a missionary, immediately after graduation. Gordon had never liked him.

It was Mrs. Tomlinson, with her awareness that a great talent had been sacrificed on the altar of isinglass, who suggested this portion of Gordon's product be called "The Lean Years." I made a slight protest at the time, and then yielded, but I feel warranted in letting it be known here I do not agree that they were "lean" years, certainly not relatively. I truly think the one remaining item in this period, which I am reprinting almost in its entirety, is by far his most outstanding written achievement, if writing is to be regarded as the field of the mind, the spirit, and the seeing eye, put down in words.

Attached to the item in question is a note that it was rejected by *The Nation, The New Yorker, The Saturday Review, The Morning Telegraph,* and the *Detroit Athletic Club News.* I confess I do not understand what the responsible editors in charge—temporarily, beyond all doubt—of these publications could have been thinking of. (There is, further attached, a copy of a letter Gordon wrote to the editor of the *Isinglass Citizen-Herald,* stating he had thought it over and had decided he would, after all, have to reject the editor's kind offer to print his contribution, which must have been sent to the *Isinglass Citizen-Herald* as a lark by some of his friends, because he truly didn't remember having sent it. At all events, he knew the editor of the *Isinglass Citizen-Herald* would understand and he was looking forward eagerly to his luncheon engagement with E. P. Collins, the *Isinglass Citizen-Herald's* Eastern Advertising Public Relations Consultant, at 21 West 52nd Street, one o'clock, on the 24th inst.)

The item:

THE TOMLINSON LAW OF
NOMENCLATURE

It is not my discovery, it is an accepted fact, that there is such a thing as normal behavior, among people of a given class, and such a thing as abnormal behavior. The abnormal may have its roots in calculated decision or in the subconscious, but wherever these roots may be, it is obviously important that normal people be tipped off, so to speak, as to how they can recognize the abnormal. They can then pity or avoid, as they choose. At least, they will have the facts at their disposal.

The normal—by which I mean the standard, the accepted, the traditional, all of them together the decent—in regard to how a man identifies himself by name, his signature, to wit, which is the subject of this inquiry, is for him to use his first and last names, or his first name, his middle initial and his last name, or the initial of his first name, the initial of his second name and then his last name.

Well, then, and I except only the victims of court orders and unbreakable last wills and testaments:

Anyone habitually signing only his last name is a dangerous maniac who will either set the world in flames or try to. On the occasion of his first offense of any kind, he is to be treated as a fourth offender.

Anyone habitually signing his first, middle, and last names in full is to be regarded, though without prejudice, as being under a cloud. That is, at least in Anglo-Saxon countries, he can definitely not be regarded as guilty, until proven guilty, but it is a fair and warranted procedure of self defense for society to ask that, within a reasonable time, he prove himself innocent.

Anyone habitually signing three first names and his family name is to be kept under the constant surveillance of the FBI. Anyone, of this breed, who signs his first name in full, then the initials of the second and third, and then the surname, is to be required to report to the police once a month, is not to be allowed to buy or carry firearms, and is to be forbidden the use of intoxicating liquors.

Anyone using the initial of his first name, following it with a full second or third name, plus a surname, is to be required to undergo a sanity examination every sixty days. He is, in addition, to be prevented by law from residing within less than fifty miles of old folks' homes or match factories. Any-one of this category, whose first name begins with an "I" and who remains flagrant in his perversion of liberty into license, is at once to be tried, before fixed juries.

The death penalty is not mandatory and can be changed to life imprisonment in the case of anyone who refers to himself, using his surname, in the third person singular. The death penalty is to be mandatory if he, even once, puts the definite article in front of his name and continues on, in the third person singular. The death penalty, *after* torture, is to be mandatory if he speaks of himself in the third person singular, using his surname, in the diminutive.

Society has been slipshod and indifferent about its menaces long enough! Society has only itself to blame from now on, if it neglects the obvious precautionary and punitive measures the Tomlinson Law of Nomenclature clearly calls for.

This is the only one of Gordon's literary relics I have taken the presumption to edit. The fact is that he gave several examples, nam-ing names, of each of the types he was discussing.

The Sage of Mon Repos

The entire material put at my disposal for this period, from his fiftieth birthday until the very end, is one sheet of paper, in his own handwriting:

POSSIBLE TITLES FOR AUTOBIOGRAPHY

SIGNIFYING NOTHING

NEVER AGAIN

MAN AND BOY

BOY AND MAN

LIFE BEGINS AT FIFTY-SIX

IT'S NOT BEEN SO TERRIBLE

ABRACADABRA

MAX IS EIGHTY

by Alan Dent

When Sir Max Beerbohm, the English critic, essayist, and carica-
turist, turned eighty years of age, he provided this pleasant inter-
lude described by Alan Dent, drama critic of the London News
Chronicle.

AUGUST 30, 1952

ON THE DAY WHEN Sir Max Beerbohm was seventy, I arranged—
although it was the height of wartime in London—a convocation of
seventy distinguished admirers calling themselves the Maxmilian
Society. The chair was taken by Desmond MacCarthy, and the assembly was addressed by the Master himself.

On the day when he was seventy-five, I made a solitary pilgrimage
into Gloucestershire to lunch with him and Lady Beerbohm in a
charming little country house where they were staying just before
leaving again for their beloved Italy, after a war-enforced exile in
England. We washed down baby roast lamb with claret and chatted
cozily of this and that, and especially of Lord Byron. Max remarked
that he would draw no more, and would write only a little more.
And the autumn sun glowed in the mellow valley beneath our windows.

On the day when he was seventy-seven, the Maxmilians sent to
him the same number of bottles of vintage claret, burgundy, and
cognac. From all accounts, visitors from England drank a good deal
of this birthday offering.

On a hot day in June of the present year—when Max became
eighty—I paid my first visit to the famous villa at Rapallo. (I am
human enough for the notion to have crossed my mind that I might
taste the lees of one of those bottles. But a steady flow of friends
and interviewers in the interim had left not even lees.)

Sir Max became a widower in 1951, but an old friend of the
family, Elisabeth Jungmann, tends him carefully and kindly. I
found him distinctly older and frailer since our last meeting four

334

years ago; but in less than two minutes it enchanted me to find his mental vigor, his gaiety, his lambent wit, absolutely unimpaired.

It was eleven in the morning when I arrived, and the great man had yet to appear for the day. I awaited him in his study, a perfectly square little room, three yards either way, perched on the roof of his villa and commanding a classic view of the Mediterranean. Those walls were lined with books to middle height; the space above was painted a deep, deep blue to the ceiling, which was dazzling white. There were a very few ninety-ish drawings, and there was a twelve-inch-tall marble bust of Queen Marie Antoinette —laughing, elegant, proud. But it was, of course, the books that fascinated me most. The majority were inscribed gifts from their authors. One I opened before my host arrived was *A Shropshire Lad* of Housman, and in Max's own hand in the flyleaf was written this characteristic parody:

> *And now, lad, all is over*
> *Twixt you, your love, and the clover;*
> *So keep a stiff upper-lip.*
> *And shrink not, lad, nor shiver,*
> *But walk you down to the river*
> *And take your final dip.*

In the thrill of meeting Max again, I quite forgot to tell him I had taken the liberty of copying this apocryphal stanza. But I somehow opine that he will not greatly mind.

Both before and after luncheon we browsed together over his books, and he seemed to take pleasure in rediscovering things written in them by himself or the authors that he had half forgotten about. Walter Pater's *Miscellaneous Studies* was inscribed, "For Max Beerbohm *ingenioso et audaci*—Walter Pater—Oxford 1891." This was the earliest he showed me. But authors right down to the present day, whether overweening or weening, would seem to have sent to Max proud copies of their books with reverent inscriptions, and he would seem to have kept the best of them. For some of these volumes he has redesigned a title page, or added a caricature of the author, or even inserted illustrations of his own—imaginative and usually mordant. To the Pater book, at the end, he had added Some Opinions of the Press, and he read this out to me, each one with a chuckle. With any accuracy I can recall only that "The Wigan Remembrances" declared the book to have been "at once a scourge and a purge," and that the *Manchester Guardian* was supposed to liken it to "Thor's hammer on Vulcan's anvil."

We had a delicious open-air luncheon under a trellis of vines—hot hors d'oeuvres, roast veal with zucchini blossoms, strawberries and cream, and copious draughts of the local excellent *vino rosso*. I had meant to ask him many things but forgot them all in listening to his gay, unwearied observations on any topic that swam into our mutual ken. It might be Marie Corelli: "She was kind but rather common, don't you know!" (He says "Don't you know!" a good deal—a near-obsolete practice which, as Max intones it, may be taken to mean: "I think you will appreciate my meaning best if I phrase it exactly thus!") Do I have to explain, incidentally, that Marie Corelli was a sentimental novelist who crowned herself Queen of Stratford-on-Avon? Of her again Max remarked: "Her definition of a pessimist was—anyone who did not like her unduly!" He talked delightfully, too, of the old music hall in London, very particularly of Marie Lloyd and Harry Lauder, but as I made no immediate note of his phrases then I decline to recast them in recollection.

Of Bernard Shaw he observed: "He was at home only on a platform." Shaw, he said, used to have a curious habit when talking to one of twirling his fingers up and down behind his ears—the fingers of both hands at once. "They used to remind me," he said, "of white mice on wires." Mrs. Shaw he described as "so much easier to be at ease with." He recollected an occasion more than forty years ago when he lunched with the Shaws, the other guest being Mark Twain: "It was a most pleasant gathering except that GBS excused himself at the end of luncheon to keep an appointment with—of all people—a dentist!" Mark Twain charmed Max not only with his conversation but also with his Southern charm, his beautiful hands, and "his benign blue eyes." A much later acquaintance of GBS was Gene Tunney, the boxer. Max declared himself scared to meet Tunney, so much had he heard of his muscularity. All the more startled, therefore, was he to find that Tunney was a man of brain as well as brawn: "One had positively to restrain oneself when talking to him. He was an object lesson in reticence and quietness—when GBS and I were about!"

Max praised the old-fashioned Pinero when I tried to turn to the new-fashioned playwrights. He was such a craftsman, as well as such a provider of opportunities for expressive acting. "He not only gave you the good wine, but a good goblet to drink it from," said Max in so many words. Of Mrs. Patrick Campbell he observed that there were two distinct sides to that great actress when one encountered her offstage. One side he found a shade pompous and social. Mimicking her famous booming voice, he said: "That side of her lived for her Art and for the Aristocracy, don't you know!" That was the English side of Mrs. Campbell. "But," he said, "there was a delicious Italian side to her as well, in which she was far more natural and amusing."

He talked pointedly, too, of a few of our contemporaries. He said of another venerable and much-visited celebrity: "He makes the mistake of being acidly witty about people who have been kind enough to visit him. This is not wise, since you come away with the impression that he will be acidly witty about you in turn." Other things he said about other contemporaries, but they shall not be reproduced here. One's sense of decorum is sharpened when one lunches with Max. One becomes aware that one should hardly have been asked if one were totally lacking in such a sense.

He showed a little—but only a little—curiosity about the current London stage. Do they still turn the best blank verse into the best prose? he asked. And what do they teach at Gower Street (the Royal Academy of Dramatic Art)? And what do they learn there? Of the modern way of living in general he deplored the almost complete passing of the institution of Family Life. "Evenings at home in my young days," he said, "could be perfectly agreeable. Members of the same family could practice conversation—with or without music." And then, very quietly indeed, he added, "They might even come to know one another." He showed, as always, a kind uncle's interest in my own career, present and future. He asked about the rest of my holiday. Florence—ah, Florence! And Venice, too. Florence I should find to be the most *poetical* of all cities. And Venice I should perceive to be not an earthly city at all but the fulfillment of a dream.

I left, agreeing to return the following day. But I excused myself next morning by telephone since I had not the courage to say adieu. In my actual parting I noticed a certain seriousness in that face which almost consistently wears an ironic smile. It is fairly obvious that Max thinks one's adoration of him intelligent, or at least amusing. Just for an off-guard moment he seemed to be thinking it was rather touching as well.

MOTHER NATURE'S BROTHER

by J. Bryan, III

Thornton W. Burgess had written thousands of stories about Peter Rabbit and his companions of the Green Meadows when J. Bryan, III, visited him (Mr. Burgess) and wrote this article.

DECEMBER 14, 1940

THE AUTHOR'S NAME was unknown—Thornton Waldo Burgess. His title—*Old Mother West Wind*—didn't have much "pull." So the idea, a children's book of short stories presenting accurate information about animals, was doubly risky. Still, the books sold well enough for the publishers to ask him for a second one.

"Sorry," said Burgess. "I haven't got another animal story in me."

That was in 1910. But a few weeks ago a score of newspapers printed Burgess's 9,000th animal story. His fifty-seventh book, *Aunt Sally's Woodhouse Night Club*, will appear shortly. The ones already published, mostly collections of the syndicated stories, have sold more than 5,000,000 copies. They have made Peter Rabbit, Unc' Billy Possum, Buster Bear, Grandfather Frog, and some 120 other Burgess characters as familiar as household pets. They have been a powerful factor in the conservation of America's wild life, and they have taught children more nature lore than all the schools, museums, and zoos combined. In presenting him with the medal of the Permanent Wild Life Protection Fund, Dr. William T. Hornaday, Director of the New York Zoological Society, said, "Any man who can find his way into the hearts of a million children is a genius. If he carries a message of truth, he is a benefactor. Thornton W. Burgess is both."

From his tousled hair and weatherbeaten face to his moccasins and dust-draggled trousers, Burgess looks the part of a naturalist. He is sixty-six, but is far too active to fit the pattern of his years. He fits much better the pattern that his young adorers have cut for him.

Someone has said, "If the children of America could elect the President, it would be Burgess." They have already elected him their uncle-at-large. "Dear Mister Biges," wrote Betty Morrow, age five, "I lice yoo storys very much." "Of course Shakespear, Pilgrims Progress are better," wrote Elmer Peck, "but I think you have the finest animal books ever there were." They write to him intimately and affectionately, asking advice about their pets, reporting their experiences in the woods and fields, bringing him their troubles.

Letters come to him addressed simply "Farmer Brown's Boy, Green Meadows" (this is one of his few human characters); or "Thornton W. Burgess, Peter Rabbit's Godfather, U. S. A."

Almost every mail brings him stories like this one from a grateful mother: Her young son had refused to sleep with his window open. One night she read him about Jerry Muskrat, who always left airholes in the roof of his house. Thereafter the child refused to have his window closed. Or this: A little girl was afraid of the dark until she read how Timmy the Flying Squirrel and Whitefoot the Woodmouse, two of the shyest animals, came out at night because there was less to be afraid of then.

Burgess's explanation is: "Every child feels that he is superior to the smaller members of the animal world, so he will not admit that one of these little creatures knows more than he does."

It takes a man of Burgess's kindliness and genuine love of children and animals not to collapse under the burdens imposed by his reputation. When his telephone rings, he knows that half the time the caller will be an utter stranger, asking what to feed a young porcupine or how big to make a wren's house. There's hardly a week when some foundling bird or animal is not left on his doorstep.

He has sat up a whole night with a neighbor's boy, trying to thaw a frozen robin. A tremulous minister called him long distance one midnight for advice on how to release a skunk caught in a cellar rat trap.

Burgess told him, "Jimmy Skunk's a gentleman. Speak to him softly, move slowly, pick him up by the tail, and pry the trap open. Jimmy'll know you're trying to help him. He won't bother you." Jimmy didn't.

Burgess always refers to animals by the names he has given them—Jimmy Skunk, Bobby Coon, Danny Meadow Mouse, Sammy Jay, and so on. He ranks skunks highest of all—perhaps "rates" would be a more tactful word—for preparedness, independence, and usefulness. His favorite photograph of Mrs. Burgess shows her with a skunk on her lap. He is fond of saying, "Jimmy Skunk is exactly what this nation ought to be—always ready, but armed for defense, not offense."

A recent story about Jimmy Skunk was pure propaganda for national preparedness, as many readers pointed out to the newspapers that printed it. For the most part, however, Burgess propagandizes for such personal virtues as kindness, generosity, and courage. "In the old-time story," he says, "the moral was pointed at the reader. In these animal stories, the moral is pointed at the characters. That's why children don't resent them."

Burgess knows what he's talking about, too. He is an expert on zoology. He knows the color of a heron's eyes, and that certain deer will eat trout. Each of his stories is based on some fact in the habits, character, or appearance of an animal. For his early stories, he drew entirely upon his own observation, but latterly much of his material has come from research and correspondence. Everything is translated into language that children can understand and remember.

"When I say I have a friend," Burgess explains, "the homeliest fellow that I know, and his tongue is put in backwards, and when he wants a drink he absorbs it through his skin, and he sings with his mouth closed, and he is covered with warts—I catch the children's attention right away. They know I'm talking about a toad, and after that they watch toads with new interest instead of killing them."

Instead of writing "A rabbit has a white tail," he puts it more vividly: "Peter Rabbit has a white patch on the seat of his britches." This trick of personalizing animals endears them to children. Farm boys have given up trapping after reading his stories about Jerry Muskrat and Billy Mink. Once a man approached Burgess after one of his lectures and said he had a bone to pick. He loved to hunt. A few weeks before, he had come home from a day in the field and was taking a rabbit from his coat pocket when his five-year-old daughter burst into tears.

"Why, Daddy!" she sobbed. "You've killed Peter Rabbit!"

"That ended my hunting," the father told Burgess. "I don't want her ever to look at me that way again."

Burgess himself would as soon shoot a baby as shoot a rabbit, but he is by no means a zealot. His conservation campaigns are not directed against legitimate hunting, but against hoggishness and waste. During the last war he urged the young members of his Green Meadows Club to do their bit by getting land-owners to pledge acreage as bird sanctuaries—"The birds destroy the insects that eat the food we need. Help the birds!" Before the war was over, children in the United States and Canada had helped establish 10,-000 sanctuaries—or, rather, farms on which all hunting was forbidden—totaling 6,000,000 acres.

Burgess' tremendous influence on children was proved once and for all when the *Kansas City Star,* a subscriber to his syndicate, organized the Bedtime Story Club. In return for a certificate and button, children promised to "be kind to birds and animals and protect them from their enemies." It goes without saying that incidentally they were encouraged to buy the *Star.* The Club's life span was a short three weeks, not even that of the purple-eyed fruit fly (*Drosophila melanogaster*). So many thousands of children applied for membership that the cost of enrolling them soared clean out of the *Star's* budget. It dropped the Club in a panic and never mentioned it again.

There was little in his childhood to justify a prediction that a marker would one day identify the house where he was born, in 1874, at Sandwich, on Cape Cod. He was a baby when his father died, and his mother was a semi-invalid. As soon as he was able to work, he did. Money was scarce. Amusements were few. Whatever time the boy could borrow from his chores he spent in the fields or on the beach. The book of nature was hard to read at first, but at least it was free. Soon he learned to love it, although the love was mixed with envy. Years later, remembering the buoyant gulls and the carefree rabbits he said, "I often wished in those days that I was one of them."

He could not afford to go to college, so he got a job as cashier in a Boston shoe store. This "nightmare," as he describes it, lasted two years. The happiest moment of his youth was when his employer told him that business did not warrant keeping him on. Burgess doesn't think he could have stuck it as long as he did, if it hadn't been for his hobby and—when the job dissolved—his discovery that he could make it pay.

Fortunately he had a hobby—writing light verse. And one day he learned, to his astonishment, that men actually received money for composing advertisements. So nineteen-year-old Burgess inserted this in an advertising journal called *Brains:*

> What's this you're telling—
> Goods not selling?
> Try a verse of mine!

Always catching,
Always fetching.
Trade in any line!
Clever ads written in verse for ANY
and ALL lines of trade. Correspond-
ence solicited. T. W. Burgess. P.O.
Box 2069.

To his further astonishment a Boston agency hired him to parody
Longfellow's "The Courtship of Miles Standish," working in plugs
for Miles Standish Spring Water. Moreover, the printer who set up
the copy tipped him off to another customer—Austin's Dog Biscuit.
"The Origin of Shredded Wheat" brought him a few dollars more.

Burgess did two short tricks as a calendar salesman and as a bookkeeper, but his heart wasn't in them. He had drunk the headiest
brew in the world—printer's ink. After a term as newspaper office
boy, he became a reporter on the weekly *Springfield Homestead*,
writing sports, special articles, a poem, and two columns of fraternal
news. The fraternal news explains why Burgess has never joined an
organization of any sort.

Versatile and productive, Burgess branched out. *Collier's* and
other magazines began to print his overflow of copy. For nearly a
year, he had seven full pages in each issue of *Country Life* under
four different names. He began supplying verses for topical songs to
the vaudeville singers who played the Gilmore Theater in Springfield. He teamed up with a composer, and presently a song called
"Eva" was heard on every barrel-organ in the country. He could
furnish on demand any literary product from a limerick to a full-
dress obit. He even, soon after his marriage in 1905, turned out "The
Bride's Primer," a collection of little housekeeping problems.

All this time, he spent every spare hour—it is hard to understand
how there were any—rambling in the woods. His vacations were
camping trips. And he bought all the books on natural history that
he could afford. However, he might never have found his true calling but for two misfortunes. In 1906 his wife died, leaving him an
infant son. And *Good Housekeeping*, of which he was then managing editor, was sold over his head, leaving him without a job.

Each night at bedtime, he used to tell the boy a story about his
friends in the woods and fields. The child enjoyed them so much
that when he was sent to Chicago for a month's visit, he made his

father promise to send him a new story or a poem every day. Burgess kept his promise. He also kept carbons. Several of the stories seemed good enough to serve as space-fillers in the magazine, so he ran them. An editor of Little, Brown saw them and asked for others. The result was *Old Mother West Wind,* first of the series that has made Burgess's name beloved by children the world over.

The daily stories in the newspapers grew out of the sale of *Good Housekeeping.* When the magazine changed hands a few months later, he fumbled around in the advertising business until he noticed that a number of newspapers were running stories for children, simply as entertainment. Why shouldn't entertainment be combined with instruction? He made a sheaf of stories, sent them to a syndicate, and got a six-months' contract. The first story appeared in 1912, under the title *Little Stories for Bedtime.* One has appeared every week-day since, without a single break. These 9,000 stories total nearly 10,000,000 words.

Burgess starts work at 8 A.M. As soon as he finishes a story, he forgets it. Once his manuscript blew away before its ink was dry, and he had to write an entirely new one; the other was out of sight, out of mind. If a story bogs down in the works—say a story about Johnny Chuck—that night, lying in bed, he thinks of everything he knows about woodchucks, and next morning the story usually writes itself.

And Burgess has found out about woodchucks things most people don't know. A few years ago, he was keeping six young woodchucks in his kitchen. Woodchucks can't climb and they can't jump, yet he came home one afternoon and found one of them sitting on the window sill, four feet from the floor. How did he get there? Burgess was bewildered. Next day, he found two of them on top of the washing machine. This was near the window, but it offered no foothold at all. A few days later, one was discovered asleep in a basket on the top of the kitchen cabinet, which was eight feet high. The mystery was finally solved by the cook. She said they would stand on their hind legs with their backs against the wall, brace themselves against the cabinet or the washing machine, and shrug their way up to the top.

Sometimes nothing comes to Burgess for two or three days. Sometimes he does three or four stories a day. He hung up his record in 1931, when Harrison Cady, his illustrator, told him that he would go to Europe if he could get three months ahead on his drawings. Burgess holed up and rattled off eighty-four stories in fourteen days.

Surprisingly, the most difficult part of his work is the two lines of verse that head each story. This sort of thing:

> The truly great are those so smart
> They make of life a living art.

This little moral frequently takes Burgess as long as the story itself. Each story ends with an announcement of tomorrow's title. Burgess writes it with no idea of what the subject will be, and there are days when he has to struggle to make a story live up to its billing.

Burgess hopes to establish the *Burgess Story Magazine,* published desultorily at present, as a regular monthly if the public shows enough interest. "I look on it as my crowning achievement," he says. "I want to make it a power through educational entertainment in saving what remains to us of the rich inheritance of wild life which we have so recklessly wasted."

Meanwhile he and his wife live quietly at Springfield, in a house full of nature books, with a lawn full of birdhouses. Now that the 9,000th milestone is past, Burgess has set his eyes on the 10,000th. He may rest then and he may not. He hasn't decided yet. Or he may continue for only ten stories more, which would give him the distinction of beating Scheherazade's endurance record exactly ten times over.

The record for instructing and inspiring children he already holds.

ANDRÉ GIDE

by Justin O'Brien

The winner of the Nobel Prize for Literature in 1947, André Gide led a long, complex, and perhaps controversial life. His personal affairs and problems were no secret to his admirers or to his detractors. Justin O'Brien, author, editor, and translator of Gide, wrote this analysis a year after the French writer's death.

MARCH 22, 1952

A LITTLE MORE THAN a year ago, on February 19, 1951, André Gide died in Paris. Those of us fortunate enough to have seen him during the last weeks of his life marveled at the physical and intellectual vigor of the eighty-one-year-old writer. I remember a January afternoon when he was being filmed in his Rue Vaneau apartment for four hours under the blinding Klieg lights with but a single half hour break, during which he entertained us with anecdotes of his youth. And even then he would not let me leave for dinner until we had shared a half bottle of Cinzano. A week later, in a projection room on the Champs Elysées, I saw the unedited film sequences run off to the accompaniment of joking comments from a cloaked and beaver-hatted Gide beside me. But most vividly of all, because it was our last meeting, I recall that bright February morning when, a few hours before plane time, I called to say a farewell that I knew might be definitive. The tall Gilbert, his faithful domestic servant and chauffeur, was shaving him as he sat at a small table littered with papers. During the operation he continued to smoke a nervous cigarette. Through lathered lips he enthusiastically described the villa near Naples where he planned to finish the winter, now that his doctor had forbidden a projected trip to Marrakech.

He talked of the unfinished manuscript on the table between us, likening it to Montaigne's *Essays* and boasting that he had at last managed to write something quite spontaneously without even rereading his prose. We discussed writers (I had just had interviews with Montherlant and Marcel Aymé) and certain literary reviews (he admired *La Table Ronde* while finding it too much dominated by the spirit of François Mauriac). He talked of his attractive daughter's intellectual growth and promised to have his nephew send me some photographs and a privately printed book. As I suggested leaving, since he doubtless had other things to do, he detained me though admitting, "I *always* have other things to do."

A fortnight later Berthold Mahn was sketching his death mask in the same room, and Gide's posthumous life had begun. The past year has naturally produced in France a flood of recollections of the man and the writer. Whereas such memoirs had long been expected to pour forth at his death, no one counted on them to contain revelations. For, in his lifelong cult of sincerity, André Gide had long ago told the essential facts about himself, dominated, as Roger Martin du Gard noted in 1920, by "the need he feels of legitimizing his conduct by analyzing and explaining it, by seeking its underlying causes. Not for the satisfaction of proving that he was right to act as he did, but because he claims the right to be as he is and because, being as he is, he could not act otherwise."

Together with the *Journals,* the Socratic dialogues of *Corydon* and the memoirs entitled *If It Die* left nothing but the details to be filled in by others. Gide once planned and left unfinished a preface for the memoirs to explain why he published them in his lifetime. It said: "I have no confidence in posthumous publications. The devotion of parents and friends is skillful in camouflaging the dead, and I hold that very few of them, if they were to return to earth, would not have occasion to protest against the zeal that retouches and hides, or adds to, their features. I believe that it is better to be hated for what one is than loved for what one is not."

Et nunc manet in te, by André Gide, which appeared in Switzerland a few months ago, is not precisely posthumous, since thirteen copies of it were privately printed and distributed to friends in 1947. Arnold Naville even listed it in his scholarly bibliography, to the exasperation of those who could not find it anywhere. "And now she remains in thee" is the way Gide understood the title, borrowed from the Vergilian *Culex,* implying that his wife lived on solely in his memory. It is a beautiful essay of less than a hundred pages, at once self-accusing and self-excusing, which recounts the tragedy of his conjugal life. Most of the details of that intimate drama could already be read between the lines, where Gide deliberately wrote them, of his other personal writings. We already knew of the puritanical youth's marriage in 1895, shortly after his first homosexual experience and the death of his mother, to the first cousin he had loved since early childhood. As a middle-aged man he had referred to it as a marriage of heaven and hell. We had noted the pseudonym of Emmanuèle that he had given to Madeleine out of regard for her natural modesty and discretion. We had guessed at her gradual and painful recognition of his anomaly, their unconsummated union, her withdrawal from his life and rejection of his work, and even her conversion from strict Calvinism to Catholicism. And yet no one but the most jaundiced reader could have questioned Gide's many statements of his deep and exclusive love for her.

But now this essay, written in late 1938 and early 1939, only a few months after Mme. Gide's death, to which are appended unpublished extracts from Gide's *Journals* extending from 1916 to 1939, confirms our deductions and fully dissipates what some readers called the "mystery" of Emmanuèle. As we had guessed, she stood at the center of the writer's life and work. With a penetration not common in matters so close to the author's heart, Gide analyzes the progress of their painful relationship in which no explanation was ever possible. For instance, in a journal entry of January 1921 he describes one stage thus:

> With despair he recognizes that it was only through love for him that she interested herself in those things (art, music, poetry) which for him remain the supreme occupation of his life. She ceased to take pleasure in them and to believe in them at the same time that she ceased to love him.

Then in 1939 he adds this corrective footnote:

> I was right to write the above lines in the third person, as if to disown that thought or at least to detach it from me. It would have been truer to say that, eager to free herself from her love for me, she forbade herself any domain in which I had originally accompanied her and where she feared still to encounter me. There was also in her a constant need to impoverish herself.

Lest this subtle afterthought lead any reader to identify Madeleine with Alissa of *Strait Is the Gate*, it should be added that twice in this little book Gide dissociates his wife from that one or any other of his heroines. This will be a blow to Gide's prepossessed readers, especially since the reality of the Gide *ménage* at Cuverville came more and more to copy the fiction of *Strait Is the Gate* and *The*

Immoralist until Madeleine seemed actually aiming to prove the truth of Wilde's paradox that nature copies art.

There is a supreme irony in the fact that Mme. Gide, who scrupulously avoided sharing in her husband's fame and wanted no part of his writings—even to the point of burning his accumulated letters in a mad yet understandable gesture of revolt, will live on in his work. This tragic story of an existence half consciously sacrificed to the needs of genius comes to us, after all, only in his account. As Martin du Gard says in his recent *Notes sur André Gide, 1913-1951:* "She left nothing in writing, no intimate note, no message for him. No one will ever know precisely what a cross she bore, what she grasped, what she suspected, what she refused to know, what she knew despite herself, what she forgave or did not forgive. She carried her secrets with her."

No one was better qualified to write both intimately and impartially of Gide than his closest friend over the last thirty years, the author of *The World of the Thibaults,* who won the Nobel Prize ten years before Gide. His brief volume of notes drawn from his own unpublished journal abounds in sidelights on the composition of Gide's works, in revelations of aspects of his complex personality, and in perceptive descriptions of the tone of his voice, the quality of his laugh, and the now ambling, now galloping gait of his conversation. Yet Martin du Gard's affection for his old friend does not blind him to such defects as Gide's often unhealthy curiosity, his occasional selfishness, and his excessive concern with the image he was to leave behind. Three pages on a certain pompous gravity he affected briefly on his return from Communism, in order to mask his incompetence or lack of interest in certain matters, are unforgettably humorous. All these remarks were shown at propitious moments to the victim, who enjoyed them keenly, as he relished any impartial criticism of himself. And well he might have in this case, since the image this book projects is one of an ever alert and vigorous mind in an equally healthy, restless body.

A no less closely observed and almost as vivid Gide emerges from *Conversations avec André Gide,* by Claude Mauriac, a young critic and son of the Catholic novelist. Much longer than Martin du Gard's book, despite the fact that it covers a much shorter period of time, this volume is valuable chiefly for the fidelity with which it records prolonged conversations. A comparison of the meeting between young Mauriac and Gide in a café in 1937 with Martin du Gard's first encounter in 1913 brings out the difference between the two books, both drawn from private diaries: the novelist has the advantage of making us actually see and hear the personality he is evoking.

After frequent encounters in Paris from the end of 1937 until the spring of 1939, Claude Mauriac enjoyed the exceptional experience of daily association with Gide during a fortnight in July 1939 spent at the Mauriac estate of Malagar, in the vineyards near Bordeaux. There he wrote frantically to consign to his notebook the stimulating exchange between his father and the writer who had contributed so much to forming his father's taste and talent. But the reader feels that Gide enjoyed even more talking with the young man—perhaps with the diabolic pleasure, so well known to the Ménalque of Gide's *Fruits of the Earth,* of weaning him away from the conservative middle-class and Catholic atmosphere of his home. That August Gide worked in the same direction during the ten days of intellectual congress at the Burgundian Abbey of Pontigny. Obviously the young man was fascinated and occasionally even repelled by the too studied charms and too subtle cunning of his mentor.

In the background of Claude Mauriac's book, as underneath the surface of the notes by Roger Martin du Gard, one senses the disturber of youth in Gide that often made him class himself in the company of Socrates. Both of those friends record the lamentable but perhaps inevitable fact that such an influence was not always exerted in a purely intellectual or ethical sphere. *L'Envers du Journal de Gide,* by François Derais, more outspoken on the subject, deliberately presents the famous, elderly writer in a most unattractive light. Derais is the pseudonym of that little "Victor" (also a pseudonym) who plagued Gide's life in Tunis in 1942-43 and consequently occupies too many pages in the last volume of the *Journals.* If the story he now tells is true, as it probably is in the main, he is justified in reproaching Gide at least as seriously as Gide reproached him.

To the admirers of Gide who already know his own confessions of homosexuality, these books can contain no revelations, but only unwelcome, corroborative details. And even after reading all the reminiscences we should still be able, without incurring the accusation of blindness, to forget one aspect of his personal life and judge his permanent influence as dispassionately as the Royal Academy of Sweden did officially in its volume in honor of the Nobel Prizes of 1947. There we read:

Gide has often been accused of corrupting and disorienting youth; his great influence, which cannot be denied, is regarded by many as baneful. This is the old accusation that is directed against all emancipators of the mind. There is no occasion to protest it; it is enough to consider the value of his real disciples. . . . It is probably thereby, as much as or even more than by his literary work, that he decidedly deserved the signal honor Sweden has just granted him.

In a sense, the most stirring and most satisfying testimony to Gide's early posthumous reputation is the special issue of *Hommage à André Gide* brought out in November 1951 by the *Nouvelle Revue Française,* that best of European literary reviews, which was permanently suppressed in 1944. Gide had founded it in 1909 and dominated its policy until 1940, making it a model for such periodicals as *The Criterion, The Dial, Neue Deutsche Rundschau,* and *Horizon.* Occupying several shelves in all self-respecting libraries, its fifty-four volumes form one of Gide's major works. It was altogether fitting, then, that one of the founders, Jean Schlumberger, and the former editor, Jean Paulhan, should revive the periodical for one issue to do homage to its moving spirit. The plump volume of 421 pages is divided into a section of testimonies from foreign writers extending from Thomas Mann through MacLeish, Steinbeck, and Raymond Mortimer to G. Ungaretti; a section on Gide's place in letters with the best articles contributed by Saint-John Perse and François Mauriac; a collection of reminiscences by those who knew him best; and finally a group of unpublished texts of Gide. Many names are missing which with more time and better organization would have been included. With more care and a little correspondence better statements might have been secured from America instead of picking off the air the broadcasts we wrote in haste for "The Voice of America." But it is ungrateful to criticize this exciting *Homage* with its living proof of Gide's significance to the world today. Revealing as they do that that protean spirit was not quite the same to any two people, these pious pages should contribute signally to our image of André Gide. And their very variety is a guarantee for the future.

WILLA CATHER, THE SUNLIT PEAK

by Marion King

When Willa Cather lived in New York, she often visited the New York Society Library, over two hundred years old, and the oldest library in the city. Marion King, a staff member of the institution for more than forty years, supplies a vignette of the novelist.

MAY 8, 1954

FOR SOME time I had been seeing a new person in the neighborhood, a rather short, stocky lady in an apple-green coat and matching green pork-pie felt hat, which she alternated with a similar habit in red. One day, passing at close range, I recognized a famous face and began to hope that she would discover the library.

Of course she soon did, with opening words as characteristic as they were unforgettable. "I'd like to subscribe here if I may," she said. "My name is Cather. I'm by way of being a writer."

She had a husky, rather boyish voice that came in little gusts. Her hair was brown, but her fresh pink and white skin and large blue eyes gave an effect of blondness. She was sturdy and wholesome looking.

She had given up her apartment in Bank Street and was living at the Hotel Grosvenor, missing her own books she told us. We had heard a good deal about her seclusion and reserve, and we treated her with an incurious matter-of-factness that won her confidence. She began to come in often, to look over rows of books and sometimes sigh, "It's easy enough to see what you *don't* want to read."

After a while I would venture a suggestion. She liked *Miss Mole* and came back for E. H. Young's other books but found them disappointing. Once I gave her *Miss Hinch,* an excellent short tale by Henry Sydnor Harrison, and when I asked her if she liked it, she said with a smile, "I did indeed. I bought that story for *McClure's.*" I offered her only the straightforward, the veracious, and the sound.

351

I never tried her with my oblique fancies, *The Innocent Voyage, The Flying Yorkshireman, His Monkey Wife.*

Soon, when we met as she took her morning exercise, she would turn back and walk to the library door with me. My memory of Miss Cather is filled with a succession of those five-minute chats— about this and that, books of course, green vegetables once, which she wanted only in their season, and expertly cooked, not "covered with cold water and slowly introduced to heat," incompetent Congressmen, about whom she was quite vehement, the Christmas boxes she loved to make up for her Nebraska farm friends. She asked me to guess what one gift they liked above everything else. It was large white linen handkerchiefs.

Some time later, when she wanted an apartment again and found one on upper Park Avenue, she told of sitting alone in it for hours —I almost feel she said all day and night—to test its quiet, before signing the lease. Legend has it that in Bank Street she rented the apartment above hers, just to keep it empty—oh, enviable luxury!

When she was writing *Shadows on the Rock,* she came often to consult old herbals, old maps, and histories of Paris, before finally going there. She told me that book had seemed a disappointment to her friends, who sent her many scolding letters. They had wanted something else, not that. But she would always be grateful to it for carrying her over a hard stretch of life. Her mother was in her last illness, and Miss Cather traveled with the manuscript many times across the country to see her.

I think the book, lovely as it was, was the first signal of diminishment. The power if not the beauty began slowly to run out with the sands of her vitality. To me "Old Mrs. Harris" in *Obscure Destinies* was the last splendid thrust of her pen. When I met her the morning after it was published and told her how wonderful I thought it was, "I rather liked that myself," she said.

Miss Roseboro, who had been her devoted friend from the old *McClure's* days, described her once as having a heart like a great anthracite furnace. When V.R. was very ill at the last, Miss Cather asked me to find out quietly and let her know if there was any need of money, but there wasn't. I heard from someone else—not her! —that she had paid off many of the mortgages on those Nebraska farms.

She was a sunlit peak of that decade, and she stayed with us until the end of her life, two decades later.

EN ROUTE TO A LEGEND:
TWO INTERPRETATIONS
OF THOMAS WOLFE

What kind of fellow was Wolfe? How much did he owe to his family, to his home town, to his following, to his editors? Here are two different approaches to the author and his work, giving just a few of the answers. The first is by the late Edward C. Aswell, who was Wolfe's literary executor and one of his editors. The other is by the late John Skally Terry, friend, editor of Wolfe's Letters to His Mother, and Wolfe's official biographer.

NOVEMBER 27, 1948

1. by Edward C. Aswell

IN THE FALL OF 1929, two extraordinary events occurred almost simultaneously. One was the crash of the stock market on October 24 which ushered in the Great Depression. The other was the publication, six days earlier, of a book by an unknown American writer named Thomas Wolfe. It was called *Look Homeward, Angel.*

The two events were not related, yet in a strange way each shed light on the other. The depression represented the disillusionment of a nation, and *Look Homeward, Angel,* some said, represented a corresponding disillusionment in its author. This comparison was false and was based on a complete misunderstanding of what Thomas Wolfe had meant to do in writing the book. Nevertheless, many people saw it in that light; and in Asheville, North Carolina, Wolfe's home town, misconceptions were heightened by personal factors and a spate of gossip. Some of his former acquaintances read *Look Homeward, Angel* and were outraged. They felt he had betrayed his family, his friends, his town, the South; and they vented their feelings by denouncing him in bitter letters. One wrote that he was "a monster against life." Others threatened to ride him out of town on a rail if he ever came home again.

Looking back on that fantastic time of 1929, we can see clearly how things were then and why the first reactions to *Look Homeward, Angel* were less sympathetic than its author had expected. The boom years of the 1920s had been a period of crazy illusion on a nationwide scale. To untold millions the pot of gold at the end of the rainbow seemed almost within grasp. Then, suddenly, the dazzling mirage vanished, and people felt lost and afraid. It took several years for most of them to get their bearings and come down to earth again, and the return to sanity was accompanied by painful disillusionment in *Look Homeward, Angel*. The book laid bare certain spiritual realities in American life and did it, as Wolfe later wrote, "in a manner of naked directness . . . that was rather rare in books." That was what caused the trouble. The people who said Wolfe was disillusioned really meant that *they* were disillusioned. He had opened their eyes to things they had not seen before—things they had deliberately avoided looking at.

Disillusionment, the hindsight of the self-deluded and the half blind, was not one of Thomas Wolfe's qualities. No one ever accused him of being blind in any degree. His fault, if fault it was, was that he saw too much. Till the day he died he retained that luminous gift which all bright children seem to possess up to a certain age: the ability to look at life and see it as it really is, with its many and ever-changing faces, its mystery and wonder, its exhilaration and stark terror, its endless contrasts of beauty and ugliness, its haunting interplay of good and evil, its flashing colors and subtly shifting shadows. Somewhere along the way, as we grow up, most of us lose that gift. There comes a time, some nameless day and hour which we are not aware of, when what passes as education does us in, and, in our hearts, all unknowing, we accept things as we are told they are and learn to conform. From that moment our vision, our precious gift of true seeing, begins to drop away. From then on, for most of us, we are rather like those mules one sees plodding along country roads in the deep South, beasts of burden, shackled, harnessed, and wearing blinders designed to shut out the green grass beside the road by keeping the eyes fixed on the narrow path straight ahead.

Somehow—and just how it happened remains the mystery of genius—Thomas Wolfe acquired an education without acquiring blinders. He went to school in Asheville. He went to college at

Chapel Hill. He took a master's degree at Harvard. And then, with his schooling behind him and no blinders to limit his view, he began to write. He wrote about life as he had lived it and observed it. Above all, he wrote about people.

People always fascinated him. Every new person he met was a challenge to him. Why is this fellow so shifty-eyed—what is he afraid of? Why do the corners of that one's mouth turn down—what has gone sour in him? Why is A. drinking himself to death—what is he running away from? Why does B. clap you on the back and deafen your ears with hearty nothings every time he meets you—what is the emptiness in him that he must try so desperately to fill it with mere noise and bustle?

Once he had formulated the question that seemed to him the clue to each new personality, Wolfe never rested till he had tracked down the answer, and in so doing he usually managed to piece together a full life history. To Wolfe, nothing was irrelevant. He took all things human for his province. The color of a man's eyes, the way he walked, the intonation of his voice, his opinions and prejudices, his gestures, facial expressions, habits, tastes, often even his name—everything was grist to Wolfe's mill. All of it went in, to help him get at the hidden kernels of character. More often than not all of it came out, too; and sooner or later the friend or acquaintance who had responded to Wolfe's probings, who had expanded in the warmth of his presence and his very obvious interest, sympathy, and understanding, would wake up some morning to find himself a character in a book.

Anyone reading what I have just written might jump to the conclusion that Wolfe spent his life searching for material to put into books, that he approached everyone he met with a coldly calculating eye, appraising him, coaxing him into revealing intimate secrets, and at last pinning him down like a butterfly in a museum cabinet, all to suit his ulterior purposes as a collector of human specimens. That was not true. Life came first with Wolfe; the thought of books came much later. He had an insatiable hunger to find out everything he could about life, and all his years were spent in learning. His interest in people was genuine because he loved and pitied mankind and had a profound sense of the glory as well as the inescapable tragedy of human existence. Even strangers recognized that quality in him and that is why they opened up to him as flowers open to the sun.

But Wolfe the man was one thing, and Wolfe the writer was

another. Whatever he saw and heard and felt and touched became
fixed with photographic exactitude in his phenomenal memory. He
thought about it long and earnestly, turning it over and over in his
mind, examining it from all sides, infusing the bare facts with poetic
imagination, penetrating to the core of them with uncanny insight;
and then when he knew what he knew and was ready to write,
Wolfe the man did what every great writer must do: as author he
played God. He not only numbered "the very hairs of your head,"
but he also meted out a strict and impartial justice to all who had
come before the seat of his judgment. He searched out the chinks in
each man's armor, and revealed them. He scorned lies, hypocrisy,
and sham, and exposed them. He hated evil, and lashed out at it.

It was not strange, therefore, that Wolfe the man, the friend and
brother of all mankind, often brought upon himself violent reactions, including threats against his life, for what Wolfe the
writer had written. This puzzled him; he never really understood it.

The immense difference was that Wolfe's puzzlement was as innocent and naïve as that of a child who has been scolded for speaking of the family skeleton before company.

Something of all this went into the making of *Look Homeward,
Angel.* Since it was Wolfe's first book, he had gone back to the
beginnings of his life and inevitably he had written about Asheville,
though he called it Altamont; about his own strange and wonderful
family (aren't all families strange and wonderful?), though he
called them the Gants; about himself, though he renamed himself
Eugene. And just as inevitably as all the rest, some people did not
like it. For he wrote with singleness of purpose, trying to catch in
words and fix upon the printed page something deep and dark
and tortured and twisted in human nature and in the America he
loved, the bad of it along with the good of it, the sum of it being—
simply the truth of it.

But it was late in 1929 when the book came out. That was a time
when people were desperately hoping the false prophets were right
who kept saying that prosperity was just around the corner—word
magic which, if it meant anything, meant simply that folly was a
kind of superior wisdom for which there could be no retribution.
The last thing anybody wanted to hear was the truth. So, contrary
to an impression which has become quite general, *Look Homeward, Angel* was not an immediate success. In its original edition its
sale was disappointing—far less than that of any of the other Wolfe
"novels" that followed it.

Time, however, has a way of correcting human errors. The mood of 1929 passed. Little by little, the nation began to face up to reality. And little by little, *Look Homeward, Angel* became more popular. It was reissued in new editions. It was reprinted again and again. Its author began to be famous, and even the home folks who had denounced him now changed their minds. The irony of this did not escape Wolfe. Shortly before his death he said to me, "The only people in Asheville who are sore at me now are those who aren't in the book."

And today, after nineteen years, while most books of the period are dead and forgotten, *Look Homeward, Angel* is still being reprinted and its total sales have far exceeded those of most best sellers. Each new generation as it comes along rediscovers it and claims this book for its own. For Wolfe wrote about youth, and he spoke to youth more convincingly than any American writer has ever done. Thousands, reading him for the first time, have found something of themselves suddenly become articulate and universal, and with the joy of recognition have murmured: "Ah, yes, that's the way it is." Can any writer hope for a greater tribute from his readers?

2. by John Skally Terry

When fate, in the person of Madeleine Boyd, the literary agent, brought Thomas Wolfe's manuscript of *Look Homeward, Angel* to Maxwell E. Perkins, editor of Charles Scribner's Sons, there began an association which will perhaps become as famous as that of Dr. Samuel Johnson and James Boswell. Perkins was immediately enchanted by the book. He and his office staff read it avidly; all agreed as to its importance.

Perkins wrote to Wolfe in Europe, Wolfe hurried to New York, and the shaping of the manuscript for the press began. In a memorandum on Wolfe submitted by Perkins to the Harvard College Library, to accompany the William B. Wisdom collection of Wolfe's letters, bills, documents, notebooks, and manuscripts, Perkins explained, without ado, that he and Wolfe began "to work upon the book." He then told how, at the very beginning, in order to give the book unity, they agreed to cut out the opening scene first used—that which showed W. O. Gant and his brother, both then little boys in Pennsylvania, as they watched passing soldiers who were soon to take part in the Battle of Gettysburg. This cutting was done so that the book might begin with the memories of the character about whom the book was to revolve, Eugene Gant, rather than with the memories of the father. Perkins explained how this wonderful first scene was later woven most effectively in *Of Time and the River* into the memories of W. O. Gant as he lay dying in the hospital in Baltimore.

This work of shaping Wolfe's writing for publication at conferences between Wolfe and Perkins has led to false beliefs, some of them ridiculous. Therefore, some clarification is necessary.

According to Perkins the work they shared brought him some of the happiest hours he ever spent. The co-operation between author and editor continued from 1928 until 1935, when *Of Time and the River* was published. Wolfe then, in gratitude to Perkins, acknowledged his debt in one of the strangest and most moving tributes in literary history, *The Story of a Novel,* issued in 1936. This book brought further confusion as to the part played by Perkins in preparing Wolfe's material, and led to the outcropping of innuendo and falsehood which had something to do with Wolfe's leaving Scribner's in 1938 and before his last Western journey, turning over his eight-foot-high pile of manuscript of unpublished material to Edward C. Aswell, then editor of Harper & Brothers.

The extent to which the Wolfe-Perkins efforts were, and still are, misunderstood, was illustrated in *The Saturday Review* for February 7. This issue carried an autobiographical bit written by Wolfe for Georges Schreiber. An accompanying illustration showed parts of two pages of the manuscript with interlinear corrections and deletions. A legend explained that the two pages were "a working example of the Maxwell Perkins—Thomas Wolfe editor-author relationship," and there were further explanations that this was the first published demonstration of how the two worked. One of the pages photographed was signed and dated by Wolfe in his own handwriting.

Perkins had let me use, in my work as the official biographer of Wolfe, a post to which he and the Wolfe family appointed me, the whole mass of personal material left by Wolfe and now in the Harvard College Library. Since I went over all of this material most carefully and recorded what I would need, I came to know Wolfe's handwriting and methods intimately. I had, of course, before

Wolfe's death, read much of his handwriting. Therefore, when I read the legend below the manuscript illustration in *The Saturday Review*, I knew that a mistake had been made. All the editorial changes and deletions in the two pages had been made by Wolfe himself. Perkins certainly had made no editorial changes in these particular pages of manuscript.

I also knew that Maxwell Perkins, according to his own declaration to me, never made any changes in words or style; and that he never changed a sentence of Wolfe's. I had been aroused by a somewhat similar error made in the New York *Herald Tribune Book Review* of January 13, 1946. In a review by Horace Gregory of *A Stone, a Leaf, a Door*, which was a rearrangement of some of Wolfe's prose into poetic form, Gregory stated that Perkins wisely had often edited out some of Wolfe's rhetorical flights. I immediately asked Perkins if he had ever done any such thing. He assured me that he had not; that he never rewrote a single sentence of Wolfe's; that he never changed a word. What he did, he said, was give advice about material which was out of perspective, or which gave too much importance to side issues. Then he recalled to me how, once, when he asked Wolfe to work over some material on the sickness and death of the father, W. O. Gant, Wolfe brought in a magnificent piece on the doctor who treated the father; none of the material, however, really belonged in the piece, for it did not fill the gaps that required filling.

I knew as almost any careful reader of Wolfe must know, that no one could hope to change Wolfe's sentences without having the changes stand out like proverbial sore thumbs. Wolfe's lines were as personal and individual as those of a poet.

The two men, Wolfe and Perkins, working together for years, and both being very human, did not always agree; sometimes they argued violently. But stick together they did until the first two great novels published in Wolfe's lifetime were issued. Their method of working was routine. Perkins would take home the sections of manuscript which Wolfe gave him, and read them carefully. Then, after office hours—that is, after four or five P.M.—Perkins and Wolfe would meet in Perkins's little office, or they would go to the lounge of the Chatham Hotel, known as Chatham Walk, and Perkins would give his advice. The nearest he ever came to writing on a Wolfe manuscript was in drawing a line in a margin by some passage; sometimes he would merely bend down the corner of a page. Then Wolfe and Perkins would discuss the ideas held by the editor, and Wolfe, if

he found the suggestions good, would take the manuscript home
for rewriting or revision.

Perkins kept after the work and also after Wolfe until the final
unity achieved was pleasing to both. However, Wolfe was never
ready for his books to go to press, and Perkins had to use heroic
measures to convince the author that he must finally consign his
words to the printer.

Wolfe, as before stated, was not always happy about the changes
suggested. He explained in *The Story of a Novel* the way in which
Of Time and the River took form. He first brought Perkins two
enormous manuscipts, one of over 1,000,000 words; they faced the
task of bringing order out of chaos, for Wolfe had the job of revising, weaving together, and shaping and cutting. He told how during 1934 he and Perkins took the first of the two manuscripts, how
he wrote a thoroughly detailed synopsis and slowly, by adding
needed material and cutting out superfluous matter, they got the
book ready for the press by 1935. Cutting, he admitted, was always
most difficult to him, and his tendency was always to write rather
than to cut.

Wolfe's very soul revolted at some of the cutting he knew was
necessary. I remember that, one spring morning in 1934, my phone
rang at two A.M. I recognized Wolfe's agonized voice.

> John [he said], I've written all that one could write, or
> need ever write, about a train; and it's one of the best things
> I've ever written. But, by God, they tell me I've got to cut
> it. I just don't see how I can do it. This ought to stand as a
> final piece of writing about a train.

He talked to me for over two hours about the passage and how he
felt. As I listened, I visualized him sitting alone, in his fourth floor
walk-up apartment at 5 Montague Terrace, Brooklyn, five blocks
from where I lived. He just had to pour out his misery to someone.

In Wolfe's *The Story of a Novel* he explained that the section
about the train was 100,000 words long, and that, while it was important in itself, its function was subordinate and it had to be
fitted for its place in the manuscript being planned for publication.
In further explaining his task of revising the whole manuscript, he
said that he wrote over half a million words, of which only a small
part was used.

A short while after Wolfe called me about having to cut the
passage dealing with the train, I asked Perkins why he did not take

the section and publish it as a unit in itself. He replied that to do so would not be practical and that in the long run Wolfe would use the material somewhere.

At times irony and satire would develop between the two in the heat of arguments about changes. Once, for example, when they were in Perkins's office, Wolfe noticed a snakeskin hanging on the rack below Perkins's coat.

"Ah," exclaimed Wolfe, "a portrait of an editor!"

The work on which these two collaborated was at an end when *Of Time and the River* was issued in March 1935. They never got together on another project, and some resentment arose in Wolfe toward Perkins and Scribner's. Wolfe had begun to write about both in a new section of a novel; in a letter to Perkins he accused Perkins of criticizing him for planning to use such material. Perkins denied having made any such criticism; Wolfe wrote that someone had told him that Perkins threatened to disappear if Wolfe used him in his fiction.

Wolfe's frankness in his *The Story of a Novel* has led people with little understanding to accuse Wolfe of being entirely dependent on Perkins and incapable of writing alone. Perkins regretted such accusations deeply. Wolfe became convinced that he must show his independence. This conviction and other unfortunate circumstances led to rationalizations in Wolfe's mind which gave him courage to break with his first publisher and editor. The move was most painful to both author and editor; however, it was to bring Wolfe the friendship of another great editor, Edward C. Aswell, who was, as already stated, at that time with Harper's; Aswell, after Wolfe's death, performed a herculean task as editor and devoted friend, in bringing order to thousands of pages of manuscript, which were published as three posthumous books, *The Web and the Rock, You Can't Go Home Again* and *The Hills Beyond.*

Aswell dismisses as absurd the charge that Perkins ever made any detailed changes in any Wolfe manuscript. Moreover, Irma Wyckoff, who was Maxwell Perkins's secretary during the time of the Wolfe-Perkins association, declares unequivocally that Perkins never edited in detail or rewrote a particle of Wolfe's copy.

SOMERSET MAUGHAM

by Frank Swinnerton

On the occasion of Somerset Maugham's eightieth birthday, the changing fortunes of his literary reputation were chronicled in this article by Frank Swinnerton, ten years Maugham's junior and active in English literary life—both as a novelist and critic—for more than four decades.

JANUARY 23, 1954

HIS LONGEVITY, at which we all rejoice, has been a great help to Mr. Maugham's reputation. If he had been taken from us untimely we might even now be lamenting the critical blindness of several generations; whereas the truth is that Mr. Maugham is passing into old age amid the cheers of youth and the happy envy of his contemporaries. Since his mind is full of irony I am sure that his pleasure in apotheosis is much sweetened by amusement.

He can hardly have expected the event; for a great deal of his life has been spent in the shadow of popular success and more eminent seniors. When he wrote his first novel, *Liza of Lambeth,* he caught a momentary fashion for tales of mean streets. When he observed the passing of the fashion he had already seen that it held nothing more for him; and his eye had turned from the novel of what is now called squalor to the much brighter scene of the theater. Giants, however, stood in his path. He has told us that in those days they were Pinero, Henry Arthur Jones, and R. C. Carton. "For the rest the managers were content to depend on adaptations from the French or German." They did not want his first play, *A Man of Honor.*

In the end that play was produced by the Stage Society, with results which might have been expected. "The critics judged it according to their preconceptions. The more conventional abused it heartily; the earnest students of the drama praised it." It is possible that if Mr. Maugham had continued in the vein of *A Man of Honor* he could have enjoyed the esteem of the few, as St. John Hankin did for plays of rather thin wit; but "I wanted money and I wanted fame." Mr. Maugham was to learn that hell hath no fury like a high-brow scorned. Not only were the comedies he next wrote great successes, but the earnest students of the drama resented his desertion of their cause—the eternal cause of appealing only to the select few. It was this desertion, although he did not know it, which led to his critical ostracism. The earnest knew his ambition. They said, in effect, "All for a handful of silver he left us."

Mr. Maugham continued to write novels which were favorably reviewed; but both in the novel and in the theater he had eminent rivals, older than himself, who had been waiting for the change in taste which had set in after the Boer War and which became apparent to all after the overwhelming victory of the Liberal party at the 1906 election. Plays of adultery still had their strong scenes in the West End; but Shaw, Galsworthy, and Granville Barker had not long runs but critical attention; Wells, Bennett, and Galsworthy had risen to importance in the novel; Henry James and Joseph Conrad were the idols of readers for whom form and subtlety were the only excellences. "I look upon it as very natural then," confessed Mr. Maugham, "that the world of letters should have attached no great importance to my work. In the drama I have found myself at home in the traditional molds. As a writer of fiction I go back, the teller of tales round the fire in the cavern that sheltered neolithic man."

He was not an innovator, moral or technical. Where Shaw, Galsworthy, and Wells concerned themselves with society, and directed attention to faults in its structure, Mr. Maugham's exceptionally keen eye was upon the follies of individuals. Since these others were "serious" he could only be regarded as flippant. He was regarded as flippant, trivial, cynical, and nonconstructive. His name was known; the earnest greatly enjoyed his plays in the theater, because of course they were extremely amusing plays; but the British were in the mood for politics and sociology, and he was not. "I have most of my life been miserably conscious that I am not the average Englishman."

It was not that Mr. Maugham was swimming against the tide; it was that he had not caught up with it. Pinero and Henry Arthur Jones realized that it had left them in mid-channel with other derelicts; Mr. Maugham, being younger than his rivals, and certainly gratified by immense popularity, felt much more cosmopolitan than they were, and perhaps assured himself that this fashion, too, would change. He was not a failure; he was a success.

Only in the matter of prestige, in the matter of critical esteem, did he notice—tartly but philosophically—a little coolness.

That was inevitable. We had not then begun to use the word *highbrow,* which I think came from the United States after the first World War; but the passing of the Victorian age, the humiliation of the Boer War, and, even then, some decrease in the size of the world had made the English more generally conscious of European civilization than they had ever been. Ibsen's plays were being performed in the West End; Hauptmann figured at the Court Theatre under Granville Barker's supervision, Strindberg had been heard of; and it had been discovered that Russia, as well as France, had a few novelists of note. George Moore, who preferred the French manner, had said that Dostoevski was Gaboriau with psychological sauce; and Edward Garnett, in conversation with myself, described the same writer as a sort of Russian Dickens; but Turgenev was to be read in Mrs. Garnett's translations, Tolstoy was recognized as a monument, and a burning passion for Stendhal, Flaubert, and Maupassant was *de rigueur* among the intelligent young. What chance had Mr. Maugham against these enthusiasms?

Then came his juniors, the young men and women who had been born in the early or mid-eighties. Most of these were innocent of art; but they had read *The Way of All Flesh* and were familiar with Shaw's milder ridicule of parents. They perceived that disguised or fantasticated autobiography, in which early experience could be used to color chronological narrative, had well served their seniors—Wells with Dickensian fun and sociology, Galsworthy with class and analysis, Bennett with humor-filled realism—and they joined in the task of what Henry James called "squeezing the orange," which meant, according to his more private definition, producing "fluid puddings" lacking all "form" and therefore all "art."

Such young men and women leaped at once into the public eye. When invited to discuss the current novel in weekly periodicals, those who did not write novels themselves spoke of two generations only. They did not think of Mr. Maugham. Even when Mr. Maugham produced *Of Human Bondage,* which is a very fine novel indeed, he could not immediately count upon its recognition. He was not a member of the younger set; and the younger set was concentrating upon one man, a genius, who for its members represented everything that was urgent in life, sex, the novel, and poetry. This man was D. H. Lawrence.

Lawrence, as well as Freud, revealed or seemed to reveal the darker abysses of the unconscious mind. He also impressed those who came into personal contact with him as having the characteristics of a prophet. He was, I think, the first modern writer to inspire the idolatry which has become a feature of outstanding admirations in the world of art; so that criticism of him aroused passionate annoyance. It was quite impossible that Mr. Maugham, an observer of life, should be carried away by Lawrence, or should attract those who had been carried away.

He was possibly unlucky in the fact that *Of Human Bondage* was published comparatively early in the war of 1914-1918, when other matters were blinding all eyes. That was a book which demanded undivided attention. Had it been published in 1910 it could not have failed to establish Mr. Maugham as a leader in a then influential school of fiction. By 1915, when the intellectual and aesthetic part of English society was torn between military or alternative service, it was, in the history of the novel, old-fashioned. Mr. Maugham had missed the bus by five or six years.

Unknown to the world, however, and unperceived by himself, he was soon to be overtaken by another bus. The change in himself had begun earlier, when he decided that there were other continents besides Europe from which material for his craft might be drawn. Former days in Paris had made him familiar with the ways of artists, and he had been much attracted not by the paintings but by the personality and action of Gauguin. Gauguin had abandoned respectability and "gone native" in the South Seas; Mr. Maugham went to see for himself what Gauguin had seen. The abandonment of conventionality, or the desire to become what, quoting Hazlitt, he called "the gentleman in the parlor," an anonymous loser of "importunate, tormenting, everlasting personal identity," seemed to offer fascinating new experience. The result of that interest in Gauguin's escape, and the wish to "become the creature of the moment, clear of all ties," was a new birth for Mr. Maugham. Its first literary product was *The Moon and Sixpence.*

The Moon and Sixpence, published in 1919, was a great success with the public which reads for curiosity; it was the real beginning of belief in Mr. Maugham as an original writer. Though still branded as "popular," he was seen to have a personal approach to life; and as the Post-Impressionists had hitherto been regarded as peculiarly the property of advanced culture, this novel about Gauguin did much to suggest that if only Mr. Maugham had understood the art of the novel he might have done something excellent in that form. At the time, according to my interpretation of *The Summing Up*, Mr. Maugham communicated to a celebrated critic what he thought were possible claims to esteem. The critic stated those claims in an article for which Mr. Maugham expressed little gratitude in *The Summing Up*.

Glory was not yet to arrive. In 1921 Abel Chevalley's *Le Roman Anglais de Notre Temps* merely named *Liza of Lambeth* while giving extended attention to several writers younger than Mr. Maugham (including myself); in 1925 Virginia Woolf, attacking such seniors as Bennett, Wells, and Galsworthy, whose work she described as "already a little chill," listed as the only significant novelists of the time, James Joyce, E. M. Forster, Lytton Strachey, D. H. Lawrence, and T. S. Eliot. She did not mention Mr. Maugham. Even in its revised edition of 1930 the *History of English Literature*, by Legouis and Cazamian, brushed him off with dozens of lesser men, while Mr. A. C. Ward's *Twentieth-Century Literature* (third edition, 1930) confined itself to unenthusiastic references to Mr. Maugham's plays. The same author's *The Nineteen Twenties* (also published in 1930) made no reference to him at all.

Nevertheless, *The Moon and Sixpence* had been observed. So, in the theater, had *The Circle*, which was produced in 1921. Neither could wholly please those who confused professional authorship with prostitution, or those who thought success incompatible with quality; but outside the narrow world of what Arnold Bennett used ironically to call "the elite" a stir of interest and admiration could be discovered. It was to deepen and spread.

It deepened especially because, having written a few short stories in young manhood, and having noticed that people were making some fuss over a Russian writer named Chekhov whom he thought inferior to Guy de Maupassant, Mr. Maugham caught a sudden glimpse of the field in which his greatest triumphs have been gained.

Previous volumes of stories had enjoyed success; *Ashenden* proved unique. The stories in this book introduced Mr. Maugham himself; they were consummately told; critics, having unbent to them, were forced to read on with admiration. They talked among themselves. Having learned the word "escapism" from Freud or others, and having a useful cliché about "mere stories," they could not deny that Mr. Maugham had seen something of the world which was communicated in *Ashenden*. The book was thus neither pure es-

capism nor in any respect what Daisy Ashford had called "mere."
It remained correct to patronize Mr. Maugham as one who had in
youth taken the wrong turning; but patronage was colored by
admiration.

When *Ashenden* was followed by *Cakes and Ale,* an astringent
novel in which the two chief characters were recognized as having
been drawn with exquisite malice, in one case particularly from a
living model familiar to all critics, Mr. Maugham for the first time
became an important writer in their eyes. Within a year or so of
its publication both John Galsworthy and Arnold Bennett were
dead; Shaw had retired to the country; Wells had lost his force.
By 1935, when I wrote a book called *The Georgian Literary Scene,*
it was natural to include Mr. Maugham, however partially and in-
adequately, as a serious writer.

The literary fashion was already changing. It changed still more
rapidly when war came again, and when the problem of living in a
world half destroyed and soon likely to be made a waste appalled
those who survived. When Shaw and Wells proclaimed the sins of
Victorian England they spoke for the Edwardian conscience; theirs
were the plays and novels of ideas. Galsworthy, with his accounts
of breeding and ill-breeding, class, race, and justice, carried this
work toward practical humanitarianism. Bennett showed, as none
of the others did, the working of time on society and human nature.
Since Mr. Maugham's interest was rather in the follies and pre-
tenses of individuals, and he carried the almost Gilbertian flip-
pancy of Wilde into situations made familiar by Jones and Pinero,
he could not hope, and did not hope, to be taken seriously as a social
critic. He was amused; he had nothing to offer men and women to
whom Shaw was a prophet.

Nor, since his early plays and novels followed conventional de-
signs, could he win admiration from Henry James or Edward Garnett, for whom Turgenev was the great master of fiction and form,
and what James called "the refinements and ecstasies of method"
were the sole justifications of the novel. "In my twenties," Mr.
Maugham has written, "the critics said I was brutal, in my thirties
they said I was flippant, in my forties they said I was cynical, and
now in my sixties they say I am superficial." They said all these
things. Were they wrong to say them?

It was Mr. Maugham himself who said, also in *The Summing Up,*
"I am not my brother's keeper." He said, "I do not seek to persuade anybody"; and these two remarks show why he could not

enjoy the suffrages of the ethical and political schools. I have already quoted an explanation of his method of tale-telling round the cavern fire. In explanation of a later failure he said, further:

> The intelligent critics, the more serious novel readers, have since then given most of their attention to the writers who seemed to offer something new in technique, and this is very comprehensible, for the novelties they presented gave a sort of freshness to well-worn material and were a fruitful matter of discussion.

Now in Mr. Maugham's case the technique was in novels undistinguished by novelty. He several times used the comfortable method of Kipling and the early Henry James of explaining from the wings; and in *Cakes and Ale,* which followed *Ashenden,* it was Mr. Maugham who appeared in the stories as knowing whatever was to be known. He showed the characters in action; he did not intensively study their mental processes. But Virginia Woolf, James Joyce, T. S. Eliot, were all delving within—Mrs. Woolf with the poetic vagueness of one to whom sensitive impressions and memories were a delightful jumble making up consciousness, Joyce with sharp, destructive, egocentric humor and a passion for the manipulation of language as music, Mr. Eliot as a despairing conscience seeking to lose individual man in metaphysics. Mr. Maugham found all such manifestations distasteful:

> Of the other experiments that have been made the most important is the use of the stream of thought. Writers have always been attracted by the philosophers who had an emotional value and who were not too hard to understand. They were taken in turn by Schopenhauer, Nietszche, and Bergson. It was inevitable that psychoanalysis should captivate their fancy.

He did not want to psychoanalyze those whom he met in his travels and brought to book. They were simple.

> On taking thought it seemed to me that I must aim at lucidity, simplicity, and euphony. I have put these three qualities in the order of the importance I assigned to them.

Lucidity, then, was his lifelong aim. It is not a quality much comprehended by youth. Nor is the quality of detachment. Until quite recently, therefore, young men and women, especially those who were proud of their intelligence and intellectual learning, read Mr. Maugham without feeling any need to extol him.

To the metaphysical school of Mr. Eliot, however, has succeeded a generation which learned fatalism in the last very destructive war. This war affected not only soldiers; it came into every home as a daily, nightly threat of obliteration. It was everywhere, and incessant. It left whole populations shaken, and perhaps impatient of the abstract. Mr. Maugham to the newer generation represents something outside the daily; but he does not represent escape from the real. He represents something lucid, something to be understood and enjoyed. "I have a clear and logical brain, but not a very subtle nor a very powerful one." That is exactly what intelligent people now need in an author. At the age of eighty Mr. Maugham for the first time enjoys a popular admiration so great that critical admiration cannot resist it.

How long this state of affairs will last I do not know. Nor does Mr. Maugham. That his estimate is lucid and ironic cannot be questioned.

HENRY L. MENCKEN

by Gerald W. Johnson

He was hated by many who knew him not, and revered by those who knew him. A Baltimore Sun *colleague, Gerald W. Johnson, declares that the acidulous, bibulous Mencken was really two personalities. The following story describes the difference between H. L. and Henry.*

FEBRUARY 11, 1956

H. L. MENCKEN's *Prejudices,* especially the first three volumes, his *American Mercury* 1924-1934, his *American Language* with its supplements, and his *Days,* in form an autobiography but in fact a social history of extraordinary color and texture, constitute a body of work commanding the respectful attention of the literary world. As critic, as editor, as philologist, and as historian the man made original and arresting contributions to the national letters; and a writer who has scored in four separate fields is sufficiently unusual to deserve careful scrutiny and analysis. His passing may be relied on to draw all pundits to their typewriters or dictaphones.

But there was also a character known as Henry Mencken to a relatively small circle in Baltimore and to an even smaller group outside the city; and he was, at least in the opinion of this writer, more remarkable than the H. L. Mencken known to everybody. His passing on January 29 also deserves notice, not in the style of literary analysis, but in the plain speech of the unschooled, in which he was as expert as he was in the language of the Academy.

This man was conspicuously kindly and polite. The information may come as a stunning surprise to those who are familiar only with the roaring invective of which H. L. Mencken was master and the acid wit in which he barbecued heroes and demigods of all sects and fashions; but I refer, not to H. L. Mencken, the public figure, but to Henry Mencken, citizen of Baltimore. He was fully aware of this distinction and drew it sharply himself; as far as he could, he screened Henry Mencken from the observation of press and public, while thrusting H. L. Mencken to the fore.

He once told a friend that when he went into the Stork Club in New York and the diners stared and then turned to whisper to each other, he thought it was swell; but when the same thing happened in Miller's Baltimore restaurant he found himself perspiring and acutely uncomfortable. For that reason he commonly avoided the big places, especially when dining alone. What café society calls "a celebrity" appeared to his realistic eye merely as a curiosity, and he hated the idea of being a curiosity in his home town.

But he was, of course. No such vivid personality could live anywhere without being something of a curiosity, no matter how sedulously he might avoid outward eccentricity. Mencken avoided it. He was of medium height, five feet eight or nine, but stocky enough to look shorter. Clean-shaved and conservatively dressed, with no oddities of posture or gait, he should have merged imperceptibly into a street crowd. But he didn't. He stuck out, for reasons almost impossible to capture and fix in words. The best one can say is that he stood and walked and talked like other men, only more so. He was conspicuously normal.

Into that medium-sized body was packed the vitality of twenty ordinary men. He was surcharged, and the fact was evident in whatever he did, even in the way he put his foot down in walking, or the flip of a hand when he returned a greeting. It was revealed in an immense capacity for work, and in a correspondingly immense capacity for enjoyment. This enraged ascetics, of course, and they called him a sensualist, which, in the way they meant it, was nonsense.

But in another way, a quite extraordinary way, perhaps the charge had something in it. Henry Mencken's perceptions were keen, as are those of any man who is intensely alive; to observers it seemed that he could extract more, and more profound, pleasure out of one seidel of beer than most men could from a gallon; certainly he could extract energy and encouragement from apparent defeat; and certainly he could detect and savor lusty humors in situations which to most men meant only tragedy and despair. In seventy-five years he not only outlived the rest of us, he lived far longer; one is tempted to assert that he lived like Noah and Seth and Enoch, those Old Testament ancients.

This gave him a towering advantage over the majority of those with whom he came in contact, and as a rule the man who enjoys a towering advantage is a hateful fellow. The marvel of Henry Mencken is that he was nothing of the sort. H. L. Mencken was hated. Every opprobrious term in the vocabulary of billingsgate was hurled at him, and even honorable terms were applied to him with the force of epithets; he was called a Jew, a Catholic, and a Communist, but never by a Jew, a Catholic, or a Communist, always by their enemies. It would be difficult, indeed, to identify a man who didn't hate H. L. Mencken at one time or another and for one reason or another.

But I have yet to encounter man, woman, child, or beast of burden who knew Henry Mencken and hated him. He was too expansive, too free of envy, too obviously void of any disposition to grasp at personal advantage. Even those most captious of critics, writers who knew that he could out-write them, once they came within the magnetic field of his personality lost the capacity to hate. They could be exasperated by him, they could denounce him with fire and fury; but they had trouble doing it with a straight face.

The explanation is that Henry Mencken was an intellectual philanthropist. Occasionally he would follow some deliverance with the warning, "Now don't you write that. I mean to use it myself"; but as a rule he scattered ideas with the grand abandon, so astonishing to Darwin, of the fir tree in scattering pollen.

Incidentally, the writers who knew Henry Mencken were few. Every semi-literate scribbler in the country knew H. L. Mencken, of course, and those who had met him in the flesh must have numbered thousands; but in Baltimore his intimates, outside the group closely associated with him on the Baltimore *Sun,* included relatively few writers. True, he married the novelist, Sara Haardt, but there was a touch of the Pygmalion complex in that. Mencken had done a great deal toward pruning and strengthening her literary style when she was an aspiring youngster and he was probably a bit in love with his own creation. But this factor was only a touch; the charming lady from Alabama had plenty to account for the romance without seeking explanations in the subconscious. One of her charms was her extraordinary wisdom in being not merely tolerant but gracious to any odd fish that Henry chose to bring to the house.

And odd they certainly were! All the human flotsam and jetsam of the seven seas of literature eventually washed up on the big brownstone steps of the Cathedral Street house—this was during Mencken's married life, tragically brief, as Sara died within a few years—and it included, as H.L.M. once said of the lady drys, "some specimens so dreadful that one wonders how a self-respecting God could have made them." But these were at most friends of

H. L. Mencken's, more often mere acquaintances, and all too often complete strangers brazen enough to walk in uninvited.

The friends of Henry Mencken's were odd, but in a different sense—odd in that they didn't match, could not be listed in any one category. Status of any sort, social, economic, intellectual, or other, was irrelevant. They were so different that one can think of but a single characteristic that they possessed in common—they were all vibrantly alive. Whether it was Max Broedel, the anatomical artist, who rarely had a cent, or Harry C. Black, principal owner of the *Sun,* who had dollars and some millions of them; whether it was Raymond Pearl, the biologist and one of the great brains of Johns Hopkins, or William Woollcott, the mucilage manufacturer, who loudly proclaimed that he had no brain at all (although he was a finer wit than his famous brother, Alexander); whether it was a barber or a governor, any man to whom Henry Mencken took a liking was one who savored life, sometimes with a wry face, but definitely.

In the office of the *Sun* H. L. Mencken could work with anybody, although there were some who tried him to the limit. But Henry Mencken's close associates again were various: Paul Patterson, the publisher, diplomatic but as refractory as basalt; Henry Hyde, veteran star reporter, as stately as Mencken was ebullient; the two Eds, Murphy, managing editor, and Duffy, cartoonist, explosive Irishmen; and the Owens pair, John and Hamilton, chief editors, distant cousins and distantly Welshmen. They were all experts, but there were other experts around the place who maintained polite relations with H. L. Mencken, yet never caught a glimpse of Henry. Those who did had something more than *expertise;* they had zest and a fine appreciation of the flavor of life even when—perhaps especially when—it displeased them.

To us smaller fry in the organization he was consistently genial and consistently helpful, although he could be sardonic. To me one day he observed, blandly, "He is a great cartoonist, but in politics, of course, Duffy is an idiot." Since Duffy's politics and mine were identical I got it, all right.

The newspaperman, however, was not Baltimore's Henry Mencken. That character was never to be found in public places, but only in private houses, or semiprivate apartments such as the upper room over Schellhäse's restaurant, where he led the Saturday Night Club in wild forays in the realm of music, sometimes murderous enterprises such as playing the nine symphonies of Beethoven in succession—they finished at dawn—sometimes elaborate buffooneries such as orchestrating for ninety instruments Willie Woollcott's ribald ditty about the 100 per cent American; or alone at home devising preposterous communications and mementos. I had on my desk for years a three-pound chunk of rock sent through the mails at terrific expense with a preternaturally solemn document certifying it as an authentic madstone.

But the unforgettable Henry Mencken, the man who really altered the lives of the relatively few who knew him, was Mencken sitting at ease after the day's work was over, with a cigar in his mouth, a seidel in his hand, and around him a small group who were equal to the rapier play of his wit—Woollcott, Pearl, Gilbert Chinard, a very few others. In such surroundings Henry Mencken talked better than H. L. Mencken ever wrote—lightly, ironically, extravagantly, but with a flashing perception that illuminated whatever it touched, and it touched everything. A display of intellectual pyrotechnics it was, certainly, but like any fine fireworks display it created in an ordinary place on an ordinary night a glittering illusion; momentarily, at least, life sparkled and blazed, and the knowledge that it can ever sparkle and blaze is worth having. In fact, it is one of the best things a man can have.

It was not optimism. Henry Mencken, like H. L. Mencken, was a pessimist; but his pessimism was more invigorating than the gurgling of any male Pollyanna. "The trouble about fighting for human freedom," he remarked once, "is that you have to spend much of your life defending sons-of-bitches; for oppressive laws are always aimed at them originally, and oppression must be stopped in the beginning if it is to be stopped at all." It is hard to imagine anything more dismal, but I do not believe it will sap the courage of any fighting character.

Mencken would have disliked being compared to pietistic Samuel Johnson, but he played a very similar role in his own city. The difference was that Johnson always and Mencken never took himself too seriously; nevertheless, each was not only witty, "but the cause that wit is in other men." Nor did it stop with wit. They caused a zest for life to be renewed in other men; they touched the dull fabric of our days and gave it a silken sheen. Boswell, greatest of biographers, recognized but never could translate into words the quality that made contact with his hero a milestone in every man's life; and if Boswell could not do it for Johnson, what hope is there that any lesser person can do it for Mencken? One may only record the fact and pass on.

Nevertheless, it is true that when Mencken died there were those in Baltimore who were not much interested in what the world had lost—the incomparable reporter, the critic, the philologist, the social historian, H. L. Mencken. They were too much occupied in lamenting their own loss—Henry Mencken, the unique, who, deriding them exalted them, in threatening them encouraged them, in prophesying death and doom gave them a new, strong grip on life. The man who really knew him will do far more living in the same number of days than he would have done without that contact. If there is a finer gift that a man can bestow upon his friends, I cannot name it. They mourn with cause.

AMERICA'S PHILOSOPHER

by Max Eastman

At the turn of the century a young college professor named John Dewey startled educators with ideas for schooling children which were looked upon as nothing short of radical. His notions were radical, of course, and they have left their indelible and controversial mark on education in this country. Max Eastman, who worked closely with Dewey as a young college graduate, wrote this brief evaluation of the man.

JANUARY 17, 1953

"THE MOST PROFOUND and complete expression of American genius" was the phrase used by the University of Paris in conferring a degree upon John Dewey in 1930. The opinion was shared by a majority of learned men the world over, but it is not easy to explain.

Dewey was, to begin with, the man who saved our children from dying of boredom in school. His influence changed the school, as the Encyclopaedia Britannica says, "from a place where children prepare for life to a place where children live." He was also a philosopher who created the first and only system of philosophy entirely native to America.

Those two achievements are enough to fill a life. But to understand Dewey as a "complete expression of American genius" you have to know the character of the man.

I had a rare opportunity to attain such knowledge, for I began my career as his "assistant," and his pupil, in philosophy. It happened because an instructor under him had died suddenly in the middle of the year. Although I was just out of college and knew almost nothing about philosophy, Dewey satisfied himself that I was capable of knowing something about it; and as he said, "There is one kind of coeducation that everybody believes in—the coeducation of teachers and pupils." On that theory he lifted me out of a hall bedroom in Greenwich Village and set me down in an office adjoining his at Columbia University. For four years he was my closest intellectual friend.

In those days Dewey looked like the portraits of Robert Louis Stevenson; with the same flat hair and black mustache, and the same luminous eyes. Dewey's eyes were wells of dark, tenderly intelligent light such as would shine more appropriately out of a Saint Francis than a professor of logic.

I remember how he used frequently to come into class with his necktie out of contact with his collar, or a pants leg caught up on his garter. Once he came for a whole week with a rent in his coat which caused a flap of cloth to stick out near the shoulder like a cherub's wing. His hair always looked combed with a towel, but no one cared.

He would come in through a side door, very promptly and with a brisk step. The briskness would last until he reached his chair, and then he would sag. With an elbow on the desk he would rub his hand over his face, push back his hair, and begin to purse his mouth and look vaguely off over the heads of the class, as though he might find an idea up there along the crack between the wall and the ceiling. He always would find one. And then he would begin to talk, slowly and with little emphasis and long pauses, and frequent glances up there to see if he was getting it right.

The process was impersonal and rather unrelated to his pupils —until one of them asked a question. Then those glowing eyes would come down from the ceiling and shine into that pupil, and draw out of him and his innocent question intellectual wonders such as he never imagined had their seeds in his brain.

Drawing out was never better done than in Dewey's classrooms. His instinctive deference, and unqualified giving-of-attention to whatever anybody, no matter how humble, might have to say, was one of the rarest gifts of genius. He would conduct long correspondences with obscure people—carpenters, plumbers, cigar-store keepers —from all over the world, discussing the problems of life with them as though they were the heads of universities. Pecking away with two fingers on a worn old portable typewriter, he seemed to me to embody the very essence of democracy.

Dewey was not only American, but you might almost say average American. Nobody would ever call him brilliant. He published thirty-eight books and 815 articles and pamphlets—a pile twelve feet, seven inches high—but if he ever wrote one quotable sentence it has got lost in the pile.

He was born in Vermont. His father ran the general store, and had a sign up: "Hams and Cigars—Smoked and Unsmoked." His mother was a Universalist, which means one of fifty to sixty thousand Christians kindhearted enough to believe we shall all be saved. The family was no more poor than rich, but if John wanted any spending money he had to earn it—which he did by delivering papers after school.

He swam and skated on Lake Champlain, but not any too well. He liked to play, but was no good at "set games"—not competitive enough, I think. He was a great reader, but did not care for "set lessons," either. He didn't get high marks. People were more impressed with his sweet temper and selflessness than his brains.

He used to say that he wouldn't have gone to college if there hadn't been one right there in Burlington to slide into. He slid through his first three college years, too, without throwing off any sparks. He joined the White Street Congregational Church with sincere religious feeling but no profound experience of conversion. He was a good boy and wanted to be better, and thought God would help him—that was all. He was an impeccable Sunday-school teacher.

Toward the end of his junior year in Vermont University this placid life-process was crashed into by an event that unsettled the whole scheme. The crisis was a short course in physiology with a textbook written by Thomas Henry Huxley, Darwin's great disciple and defender. In reading Huxley's account of how man's actions are determined by his nerves and brain, Dewey felt himself to be in a different world from that in which as a Sunday-school teacher he was telling boys how they should be determined by the soul. He was swept off his feet by the rapture of scientific knowledge. And yet he could not stop thinking of life in the old terms of moral aspiration. There seemed to be some chasm between these two worlds, a chasm over which this lanky, shy, black-eyed boy yearned in the intense way that most shy boys do over their best girl.

As a result, his senior year at college was an ardent adventure. He plunged heart and soul into his studies. He led his class and got the highest marks on record in philosophy. By the end of that year there was little hope left in the Dewey family that John would turn out to be anything more useful than a philosopher.

After graduation, John went down to Oil City, Pennsylvania, to teach in a high school. One evening while he sat reading he had what he called a "mystic experience." It was not very dramatic. There was no vision—just a supremely blissful feeling that his worries were over. When he tried to convey this emotional experience to me in words, it came out like this: "What are you worrying about, anyway? Everything that's here is here, and you can just lie back on it."

"I've never had any doubts since then," he added, "nor any beliefs. To me faith means not worrying."

At the end of the year Dewey went back to Burlington with a new tranquility in his heart, but still the old tension in his head about that chasm between the material and moral sciences. To close that chasm was the main preoccupation of his intellectual life. That is what his philosophy was created for. He taught that all thinking, even about the stars and the universe, is "instrumental," and its truth is nothing more than its success in bringing human beings to their ends. Thus he sought to give moral judgments the same force and validity possessed by judgments of fact. Like other average Americans who take life seriously, Dewey was intensely concerned about being good. He wanted goodness to be harder and less molly-coddle than it was in the White Street Sunday School, more like playing your part as a citizen-soldier of democracy. He wanted it to have a firmer hold on the thinking mind.

That fall he borrowed $500 from an aunt and went down to study philosophy at the brand-new university founded by Johns Hopkins in Baltimore. When he received his Ph.D. degree in 1884, President Gilman offered him some advice: "Don't be so bookish; don't live such a secluded life; get out and see people."

At the University of Michigan, where he went as an instructor, Dewey did begin to "see people." Among the first he saw was a coed named Alice Chipman, who lived at his boarding house. She was a strong-minded girl, an ardent woman suffragist, deeply religious but of no church, and brilliantly intolerant of "bunk." It was good luck —or was it good sense?—that John Dewey loved and married such a woman. She had an adoring admiration of his genius, but she had also a female impatience of the cumbersome load of ideological considerations that he had to carry along when arriving at a decision. Her own decisions were swift, direct, harshly realistic. She put "guts and stuffing"—the phrase is Dewey's—into what had been with him mere intellectual conclusions. She kept pulling him down into the real world where, as his own philosophy insisted, a man ought to be.

There were five children romping around the house during the most creative years of Dewey's life. They did not disturb his meditations in the least. Indeed, Dewey was at his best as a logician with one child climbing up his pants leg and another fishing in his inkwell. He had a way of doing two things at once without getting nervous that was almost like a parlor trick.

He encouraged his children to cope with difficulties created by their own activities. In his house at Ann Arbor, Dewey's study was directly under the bathroom, and he was sitting there one day, absorbed in a new theory of arithmetic, when suddenly he felt a stream of water trickling down his back. He rushed upstairs to find the bathtub occupied by a fleet of sailboats, the water brimming over, and his small boy Fred busy with both hands shutting it off. The child turned as he opened the door, and said severely, "Don't argue, John—get the mop!"

In 1894, Dewey went to the University of Chicago, which had offered him the chair of philosophy, psychology, and education—a combination then unknown to the academic world. In Chicago, Mrs. Dewey organized and became the principal of an elementary school in which Dewey's theories could be tried out. Here was not only the "learning by doing" but also the *thinking* that Dewey sought to promote. He wanted children so placed that problems would arise out of their own natural interests. They should themselves select the information relevant to the solution of a problem and themselves apply it experimentally.

Education has moved in that direction now for half a century, and throughout the world John Dewey is recognized as the author.

In these days it is hard to imagine the clamor raised in 1896 by the idea of a laboratory school. "A school where they experiment with the children—imagine!" He could hardly have shocked the parents of the nineties more if he had proposed vivisection in a kindergarten. Even when closely examined, his idea seemed to be to let children do just what they wanted to, which was generally regarded as equivalent to letting them go to hell.

Dewey was, perhaps, slightly utopian in his rebellion against the old puritanical pumping-in system of education, summed up by his contemporary, Mr. Dooley, in the remark that "it don't make much difference what you study, so long as you don't like it." But he did not believe in consecrating children's whims, much less in forcing them to have more whims than is natural to them. He had more horse sense than some of those who now conduct "progressive education" in his name.

The school was a flourishing success, but a falling-out with the president of the university put an end to it after two years. Dewey resigned in 1904 and accepted a professorship at Columbia University, where he remained the rest of his academic life. The migration eastward was a good thing for John Dewey. Ideas were sprouting up through the bricks at Columbia in those days, and Dewey's mind was happy there. Also, he found it easier, living in New York, to be a factor in the nation's political life, as is appropriate to a philosopher who believes that the truth of an idea lies in its practical effect. And by taking a fourth-floor apartment at the corner of Broadway and Fifty-sixth Street he managed to surround himself with enough noise so that he could get some thinking done.

Later, he moved out to Long Island and preserved his contact with reality by raising eggs and vegetables and selling them to the neighbors. He enjoyed telling how one day a hurry call came from a wealthy neighbor for a dozen eggs, and the children being in school, he himself took the eggs over in a basket. Going by force of habit to the front door, he was told brusquely that deliveries were made at the rear. He trotted obediently around back, amused and happy. Later he was giving a talk to the women's club of the neighborhood, and his wealthy customer, when he got up to speak, exclaimed in a loud whisper, "Why, he looks exactly like our egg man!"

Dewey's long life was a spectacle of unwavering devotion to his principles. This was dramatically illustrated when, as he was approaching his eightieth year, he stood against the Communists in an act of moral courage not easy to match in the history of philosophy.

Stalin, in the notorious Moscow trials of 1936-38, had extorted confessions from the leading old Bolsheviks that they had plotted with Trotsky to overthrow the Soviet government. Under cover of these "show trials," Stalin shot thousands of his old comrades in arms and made fast his dictatorship. Dewey headed a Commission of Inquiry which went to Mexico, where Trotsky lived, and held prolonged hearings on the question of the plots and Trotsky's guilt. The inquiry was in effect a trial—a trial of Stalin and a determination of the real meaning of his regime. Its decision that the Moscow trials were a fake, that Stalin was a treacherous tyrant, would, had it been heeded, have saved the free world from a decade of almost fatal blunders.

Communists, of course, described Dewey as "senile." The *New Masses* regretted that a great philosopher had made a fool of himself in the sunset of his life—a remark on which Dewey's comment was "Twilight is the usual expression."

The charge of senility looked a little foolish when he published, almost simultaneously with the 800-page report of the Dewey Commission, what may appear in history as his major work, *Logic, The Theory of Inquiry,* a book of 546 pages.

Dewey was never senile. There was never a quaver in his voice or a quiver in his handwriting. He married a second time at eighty-six. A footnote to the last letter I received from him reads: "We have two children, a boy of five and one half and a girl of eight, brother and sister, war refugees. As we've only been married a little over a year we think we've done pretty well." At a banquet tendered him on his ninetieth birthday he made the most vital and vigorous speech of all those present. He was still clearheaded, still thinking and writing —with children still romping around him—when he was stricken with pneumonia and died on June 1, 1952, in his ninety-third year.

ALL ABOUT
GEOFFREY T. HELLMAN

When Geoffrey T. Hellman's book, How to Disappear for an Hour, *came out, it was warmly praised in* The Saturday Review. *The editors felt that an accompanying biography of the author would be fitting; the following interesting facts were submitted by one close to Hellman and were printed in conjunction with the review. They explain, furthermore, the importance of Hellman on the literary scene, and why he could not possibly have been excluded from this anthology.*

SEPTEMBER 27, 1947

GEOFFREY T. HELLMAN was born in New York City, in a home of culture and refinement, on February 13, 1907, and is thus an Aquarius type astrologically—like Lincoln, Franklin Roosevelt, and several million people who have never amounted to a hill of beans.

Young Hellman began to write at the Westminster School, in Simsbury, Connecticut, when he was thirteen. His first published work, which appeared in *The Westminster Review,* was a poem called "The Storm." Its concluding line ran: "And nary a sheep did die." The thought behind this is typical of Hellman's kindly philosophy, which embraces all of God's creatures. "A sheep is a real person," he says.

He continued to write relentlessly at Yale, where he became columnist of *The Yale News,* and an editor of *The Yale Record* and *The Yale Literary Magazine.* He disappeared from Yale in 1928, having been voted the Second Wittiest Man in his class. He rarely left his room except to stroll to the Elizabethan Club, and received three sardonic votes for Best Athlete. Thornton Wilder, who had read his college effusions with sympathy, gave him a note of introduction to Irita Van Doren, editor of the New York *Herald Tribune* Sunday book supplement, which read in part: "Catch him young." Mrs. Van Doren caught him at twenty-one, and for several months he wrote book reviews for the *Tribune.* Armed with these, he solicited employment at *The New Yorker* office in the winter of

1929 and was hired as a reporter in the Talk of the Town department. He began to write Profiles the following year (the first was on Graham McNamee), and has, to date (September 1947), had fifty of these, in seventy-two parts, published in *The New Yorker*. In 1936, he drew the attention of the Talk of the Town to the fact that a dog was listed in the New York *Social Register*. The ensuing paragraph caused world-wide repercussions and was *The New Yorker's* outstanding scoop until it printed John Hersey's article on Hiroshima, a decade later.

Hellman's initial salary as a Talk of the Town reporter was thirty dollars a week. His boss, Ralph Ingersoll, who in 1929 was *The New Yorker's* managing editor, advised him that at the end of six weeks he would either fire him or give him a substantial raise. Six weeks passed, and nothing happened—or at any rate nothing happened to Hellman. However, Ingersoll subsequently offered to put him on a free-lance basis, and in this way Hellman's returns from reporting rose to an average of twice this sum. One day Ingersoll called him in and asked him if he played squash. No, said Hellman. "Ever see anyone play squash?" said Ingersoll. Hellman shook his head. "How would you like to be our court games editor?" Ingersoll asked. Hellman nodded, and for several years in this capacity covered squash racquets and squash tennis, as well as those esoteric games hard racquets and court tennis.

Hellman concentrated on colorful and implausible anecdotes about leading players and generally relied on Allison Danzig, the court-games specialist of *The New York Times*, to tell him what the score was, or who had won. Court tennis is played in New York only at the Racquet Club, where, arriving to inspect his first match, Hellman, not being a member, was besought to use the back door. Hellman is a Yale man and he declined to do this. In the interest of complete coverage, however, he sublet the legwork on these jobs to a friend who belonged to the Racquet Club, Christopher T. Emmet, Jr. Emmet wrote out 2000-word accounts of court-tennis matches which his employer had to condense into three or four inches of space. At the end of a year, Emmet complained to him that his fees from Hellman had amounted to less than his Racquet Club dues ($240); he had remained a member of the club, he said, only in order to report on court tennis. Hellman advised him to resign, which he did. Emmet has since become a well-known social thinker and radio commentator.

After a couple of years at *The New Yorker*, Hellman disappeared from the office for nearly a year. His disappearance arose from the circumstance that he was one of the first *New Yorker* writers to think about money, or at any rate to mention this subject to the management. In 1931 he asked Harold Ross for an increase in pay. Ross, wishing to play a joke on him and on Raoul Fleischmann, the magazine's publisher, urged him to see Fleischmann about this. Hellman had never met Fleischmann; he was too innocent to realize that Fleischmann had never seen a reporter on such a matter. He asked for an interview, and Fleischmann greeted him cordially. "How's your mother?" Fleischmann asked. Fine, said Hellman, tugging his forelock. "Lovely girl," said Fleischmann. "Haven't seen her for twenty or thirty years. Used to know your grandfather; fine old gentleman." The conversation, which was brief, continued on such a sociable plane that Hellman felt it would be tasteless to bring up the matter of pay. Instead, he left *The New Yorker* to join the staff of *Fortune,* where, after a few months of relatively plain sailing through assignments on the trout-fishing, horse-show, emerald, and whaling businesses, he ran into a request for 10,000 words on the Federal Reserve System. Hellman's attitude toward this system was, and remained, one of extreme reserve. Following a shaky interview with Eugene Meyer, who soon fell into a puzzled silence, he bogged down on the fifty-third word ("rediscount"), relinquished the assignment (by request of the management) to Archie MacLeish, and returned to *The New Yorker,* hat in hand, rates somewhat raised.

There, with two hiatuses, he has been ever since. The first hiatus occurred in 1936-38, when he spent two years as an associate editor of *Life.* He contributed a number of Close-ups to this magazine, including ones on Franklin and Eleanor Roosevelt, Alfred Hitchcock, and Heywood Broun. The second hiatus consisted of three years in Washington between 1942 and 1945. These were spent writing for the Office of the Co-ordinator of Inter-American Affairs, the War Department (he helped write the *Official Guide to the A.A.F.*), and the Office of Strategic Services. Hellman served on the Planning Staff and the History Project of OSS, and in this last connection helped collect, write, and edit a million-word top-secret history of the organization. OSS was a very mysterious outfit, and Hellman has no idea what happened to this history.

I asked Mr. Hellman how long it took to write a Profile. "The quickest one I ever did took two days," he said, leaning back in his chair and puffing a costly cigar. "It was on Joe Crane, the world's champion parachute jumper. One of the most time-consuming was a three-parter on the Metropolitan Museum of Art, which took several months. The one on Dr. Gilbert Grosvenor, which I have included in *How to Disappear for an Hour,* took the longest, because it was as much the story of the *National Geographic*—thus involving the buttonholing of a large cast of characters and the reading of forty years of *National Geographics*—as the story of an individual. The research on a profile takes much longer than the actual writing as a rule; most of it has to be discarded. Sometimes you talk to a hundred people before you begin.

"The various themes in this book," he continued, "were chosen for the hell of it—*i.e.,* because they appealed to me and made me happy while I was writing about them. I am generally in a state of euphoria while working, which is very unfashionable in this day of apprehensive speleologists, but I cannot see that it does any particular harm."

Hellman works seven or eight hours a day and typewrites everything with one finger—the index one of the right hand. In cold weather, while writing, he wears a sweater which he bought at Niagara Falls, and which looks as though it had been worn by someone who had just gone over the Falls in a barrel. He smokes pipes constantly while working, and only then, and believes that this has become a useful associational device—like the bell-ringing which causes the saliva of a properly conditioned dog to begin to flow. He is convinced that it is as important to select what you take into your mind as what you take into your stomach, and for this reason tries not to entertain too many thoughts on too many subjects. He has been notably successful in this.

Hellman has been an amateur lepidopterist for thirty-five years and has formed a large collection of butterflies and moths, chosen purely for their looks. He fills a hatbox with cocoons every winter and can hardly wait for spring, when the imagos emerge.

GEOFFREY T. HELLMAN

ROSS LOCKRIDGE, JR.—
ESCAPE FROM
MAIN STREET

by Nanette Kutner

When Raintree County *was published more than ten years ago it was a tremendous success, bringing fame and money to a young teacher and his family. But Ross Lockridge, Jr., was unable to cope with this experience. His suicide shocked every knowing writer in this country. Nanette Kutner, who had interviewed the Lockridges a few weeks before Ross took his life, kept asking herself the question everybody was asking, "Why did he do it?" Two months later she returned to Bloomington, Indiana. Here is her version of the "why."*

JUNE 12, 1948

LATE LAST JANUARY, when I set out to interview Ross Lockridge, Jr., none of the press agents assigned to publicizing his *Raintree County* knew his whereabouts. The people at the Book-of-the-Month Club said he had settled in California; they had just issued a release that had Lockridge announcing, "California is a wonderful state in which to rear children." Metro-Goldwyn-Mayer, owner of the film rights to his book, wired me that he had already left California. Houghton Mifflin Co., his publishers, suggested that I telephone his father in Bloomington, Indiana. His father told me that Ross, Jr., was now living in Bloomington, where he had bought a house.

So I said to the editors of *Today's Woman* magazine, "You can't miss. For six years a young English instructor, married to his childhood sweetheart, supports her and four kids on twenty-five hundred a year. All the while he's writing a book. When it's published he wins a quarter of a million dollars! The important point," I insisted, "is that he doesn't go berserk. He and his wife settle down and buy all the things your readers want to buy—the house, the car, the furniture, the electric icebox. What more could a woman's magazine want?"

The editors agreed to send me to Bloomington to interview Mr. and Mrs. Ross Lockridge, Jr.

I had no trouble arranging an appointment. Ross wrote me, typing the note himself, and I went to Indiana at my convenience. I mention this because one press agent had assured me, "Lockridge is so vague you can't pin him down," and another had said, "He thinks he's the great American genius." If Ross Lockridge, Jr., exhibited such traits, then he was a schizophrenic personality. He cooperated with me completely, even offering to make hotel reservations for me. To me he seemed wistful, surprisingly boyish, delighted to talk to "somebody from the outside."

As my taxi drove up a small hill and stopped before his gray shingled house, starkly new, my thoughts reverted again to the perfect slick-magazine story that I was going to write. Then I met the Lockridges, Ross and his very pretty, blond wife, Vernice.

We sat in the living room that had the neat, barren look of a freshly decorated hotel parlor. Although they had been living in the house a month, no personal pictures hung on the walls. With the exception of two copies of *Raintree County* and a copy of *Red Plush* standing in the otherwise empty, glassed-in shelves of the secretary, there was not a book in sight, nor a bookcase.

I spoke of *Raintree County*. "It's like a symphony."

Ross nodded appreciatively.

"Ross says that about *The Magic Mountain!*" exclaimed Vernice. Then she blushed as if she had talked too much. "I never read a thing," she added hastily. "I haven't time."

Ross spoke of the reviews his book had received, especially the two which appeared in *Newsweek* and *The New Yorker*. They thoroughly angered him. "I don't think those fellows read the book through," he said.

Vernice told me how they had geared their lives to the writing of *Raintree County*. "We tried to go out once a week. We had to rely on the kindness of a neighbor because we couldn't afford a baby-sitter. We were so broke Ross wrote on the back of his discarded papers. He would come home and write between classes, with the children running toy trains under his legs. It was grind, grind."

He smiled. "I wouldn't advise anybody to try it. I wouldn't do it again."

When I suggested that his work had been influenced by Thomas Wolfe, he agreeably admitted that it was true. "I feel that I have a better historical background than Wolfe had," he added.

He spoke about the months he had spent revising the manuscript. Vernice explained, "M.G.M. thought it would sell more copies if it were shorter."

"I could revise it eight more times," he said. "If you read it aloud . . . it scans. Now that it's finished I feel . . ." His voice died away expressively.

"Like having been eight years pregnant," he said.

"Although we were living in such close quarters—three rooms— Ross never talked to me about the book," Vernice volunteered. "Oh, I had a vague idea what it was about. But I didn't really know until I typed it."

Ross spoke of Dorothy Canfield Fisher, one of the Book-of-the-Month Club judges, and how much he would like to meet her.

Later, when I wrote Mrs. Fisher about Ross, she told me that "his reaction to suggestions from the Committee of Selection of the Book-of-the-Month Club was mature, not self-willed, not stubborn, very reasonable and intelligent, rather unusual with a young and untried author."

I asked him how he was getting along with his new book. He said that it was "terrible going." He pointed to an adjoining pine-paneled room and his paper-littered desk.

I asked if he had done anything in the recent war.

"Had too many responsibilities. Physical disabilities . . ." he mumbled.

Vernice's fresh voice took up the cue. "I can tell you *I* was glad when he was rejected. I was in the hospital having my second baby."

He was still mumbling, something about not having wanted to stand on the sidelines while the rest of the world . . .

I sensed a feeling of guilt. Perhaps this was the reason he had scrapped his first two years' work on *Raintree County*, starting all over again so that he could shift the time from the twentieth to the nineteenth century. Maybe it was easier for him to forget his guilt writing about the past.

He told me *Raintree County* was going to appear in a condensed version in *Omnibook*.

"But why?"

"Money."

Yet he certainly was not a commercially-minded writer. He did not even have an agent.

"A writer can do better for himself," said Vernice.

He did not belong to the Authors' League.

"Is that a kind of union?" Vernice asked when it was mentioned.

He spoke of his cousin Mary Jane Ward. "Oh, she made plenty of money out of *The Snake Pit,* but she could have done better with her movie deal."

Ross told me he gave some of his prize money to relatives, and that Vernice's mother had bought a washing machine.

"Ross gave me a lot, too," Vernice said. "This minute I have more money in the bank than he has."

What did Ross Lockridge, Jr., buy for himself with his money?

"With the M.G.M. award, some neckties and my first suit in five years," he told me. "With the Book-of-the-Month money, a second suit."

Did he buy freedom in which to breathe, to relax, to refill the creative vessel? Or did the money turn him into an advertising agent's idea of the perfect husband, a man with cash ready to purchase linoleum, gas heat, and three tiled bathrooms?

Upon winning the Book-of-the-Month selection, the Lockridges deposited their children with relatives and went to California. For like his dreamy hero, Indiana-born John Wickcliff Shawnessey, Ross Franklin Lockridge had watched others go West and was curious as to what was out there.

What did he and Vernice do in California? They hired a Ford, lived in a motel, and visited the M.G.M. studios, where they saw a Margaret O'Brien picture being filmed.

Vernice said she was disappointed that they hadn't seen Margaret. "But we saw Edward Arnold rehearse a scene. And I sat in Robert Preston's chair!" She was shocked at the prices of the California houses. "Fifty thousand for a place no better than this one! Why, they call two lots a ranch!" She giggled. "I wrote home and asked my sister if there were any houses for sale in Bloomington."

I looked closely at Ross Lockridge, Jr.'s patient echo. Her young, soft beauty, her sweet dignity, masked the quiet granitelike stubbornness I encountered when I asked a question she did not want to answer. I noted her self-consciousness and defiance as she told me, "My father was a bookkeeper," then, thinking better of it, changed the word to "statistician." She was proper and precise when she altered a mention of "brassière and drawers" to "undergarments." She appeared thoroughly happy as she caressed a mammoth rib roast with garlic and told me that now she could afford to "hire a woman to help with the work."

Ross Lockridge, Jr., loved her from the time they were in high school and she was afraid to speak to him "because he was the smartest boy in my class."

"She's Nell Gaither," Ross told me. "She definitely influenced Nell."

But Johnny Shawnessey never married Nell; his heroine was an unattainable dream.

I met Ross's mother, there to help mind the children while I conducted my interview. She displayed her Phi Beta Kappa key prominently, a mother proud of her son who had always won things —races, typing championships, scholarships to the Sorbonne, to Yale, to Harvard.

I met his sturdy historian father, who other Indiana professors tell me is "an extreme extrovert." To his father Ross must have owed much of his knowledge, yet he ignored him in the book dedications. There again Ross followed the tradition of the good son, the good husband.

During the course of the afternoon I kept meeting the children: Ernest, asking for his allowance; Larry, wanting to know if I had hot meals on the train; Jeanne, running in and out of the room, piping, "Is it time to pass the cookies, Mom?" and the baby, who was dressed and diapered by his writer father.

All the Lockridges were normal, nice, pleasant, kind; as American as the "Elsie" books, as banana splits and apple pie, as Thanksgiving dinners, and fireworks on the Fourth. And as smothering as your Aunt Tillie's feather bed.

It was late afternoon when he drove me back to my hotel, drove badly, with sudden stops and starts. On the wheel his hands were nervous and unsure.

He looked thin and pinched. "I can't sleep," he said. "I take sleeping pills."

"Maybe you ought to get drunk," I suggested.

"Maybe you've got something there."

But he wouldn't join me in a drink, insisting, "*You* grab yourself a couple of quick ones before dinner."

Back in my hotel room I could see the courthouse built of native limestone, curiously reminiscent of the one in *Raintree County*.

We dined together, Ross, Vernice, and I, in a tearoomy kind of restaurant. Ross explained, "There are no interesting places to eat around here."

After dinner he drove me to the outskirts of Bloomington and pointed out the tall, tree-embroidered white frame house of his parents. It might have been a cousin to the two pictured on the inside cover of his book.

In front of my hotel we said goodbye. "Now I'll lie awake the whole night," he declared. "Vernice, here, she sleeps like a log. I haven't slept since I won those prizes."

Those were the last words he spoke to me. Later I received several letters from him.

In the first, he thanked me for visiting him and his wife "and for bringing a lot of illumination." He added, "Things go on much as before here, with everything down around our ears more and more. I hope to get out of the woods sometime, though it seems right when I need rest most I get least of it. Such is the way of the world, if I may be permitted a fragment of philosophy, having exhausted practically all my philosophy in *RC*." In another letter he refers to himself as being "ravaged by illness, additional family responsibilities, etc." (The *etc.* is his.)

In February, just before my article in *Today's Woman* went to press, he sent me a note in response to a query of mine about the make of his automobile. "The car is a Kaiser," he wrote. "Take care. I'm trying to." A few days later Ross Lockridge, Jr., aged thirty-three, took his life in that Kaiser.

Two months later I returned to Bloomington.

A near neighbor said, "We knew something queer was going on. Why, I've never set foot in their living room. They kept saying Ross was tired and wanted to be left alone. He used to drive his car from the garage to the street and back again as many as fifteen times in succession."

Vernice, peaked, trembling, had dinner with me. "Now it's my turn not to sleep," she said. "You never saw the real Ross," she said. "He lost all his vitality. He was sick since October. Sleeping pills strong enough to knock me out for twenty-four hours gave him only two hours. He couldn't eat either. They worked him so hard, rewriting the book for M.G.M. He couldn't do anything after October. He wanted to go to a sanatorium, but we had put ourselves in the hands of a family doctor who said it would be a disgrace to send Ross to any such place and that he would be all right if he just kept to a normal routine."

I went to see his mother, seated on the wide porch under the wonderful old trees. "I don't cry," she said. "I am Eva Alice of the book. And I'm the mother too. Did you notice, he didn't dedicate it TO me, it was FOR me. He said, 'Mother, I want you to be the first to read it.' He came here that last day. I said, 'What's bothering you, Ross, can't you tell your mother?' I made him laugh too. I don't think he killed himself," she added, her mouth a tight line. "He might have met with foul play; why, he had as much as one hundred and thirty dollars in the house."

His father, quick to tears, the ruggedness dwindled, lunched with me. "The boy put his heart's blood into the book; he had nothing left. I knew this would happen. A doctor warned me of suicide. So I prayed for him, prayed every day on that porch. He was a good boy, my boy, never drank, swore, or smoked."

The very factors that had made his story a good woman's magazine feature were, it seems to me, the factors that undermined him. I remember thinking of Oscar Wilde and his "Each man kills . . . ," and Tom Wolfe, as a student, shouting, "Don't let them get you!" They "got" Ross Lockridge, Jr., because he was a sweet person, lacking ruthlessness, the prerogative of genius. If he had cut more ruthlessly into *Raintree County,* the book would have been better. He was no one-book author; he never would have been content to live as a Margaret Mitchell lives. But he could not find a remedy for the letdown that invariably comes after completing a big job, the letdown Trollope understood so well he never submitted a novel until he was deep into the next.

Obviously, Ross Lockridge, Jr., should have escaped, if only for a while, from the environment that constricted him. He should have boarded a ship for South America, for China, anywhere but Hollywood. No matter where he went, he should never have lugged Bloomington along. But even if he had left it physically, he probably would never have been able to escape it mentally. Like his own Johnny Shawnessey, he knew "his victory was not in consummations but in quests." So the inner conflict stretched and tore him to bits. He "could no more uproot himself from this memory-haunted earth than he could pluck body from soul."

THE LITERARY LIFE
AT SEVENTY-FIVE

by William McFee

One of our finest sailor-authors, William McFee, was born in London in 1881, apprenticed an engineer at seventeen, ran away to sea at twenty, and sailed until 1922, when he quit the sea and settled down in Connecticut. His first book, Letters from an Ocean Tramp, *was published in 1908, and he produced a steady stream of writings from then on. Incidentally, McFee contributed a book review to SR's first issue, August 2, 1924. No more content to be swallowed up by old age than by the ocean waters, on the occasion of his seventy-fifth birthday he delivered up the virile, rebellious remarks found in this article. When it was published in* The Saturday Review, *it was subtitled "A Whine from the Chimney Corner."*

JULY 14, 1956

THOSE WHO HAVE REACHED or will reach my age will understand that when you reach it, no matter how youthful you may feel, you are for the vast majority of people just another old man tottering on the edge of the grave, and many of them wonder why you hang around. This is particularly true of writers in America, where vogues and fashions change so rapidly.

Writers are not highly regarded in America. I know this sounds odd, but it is true. Everyone uses a pen, and everyone believes he or she could write a book if there were only time. Recently I heard the expression, "I could write a book about that place." Another person, after reading a book about his own profession, said he could write a better book. The point is, each assumed as a matter of course he could write a book, but he would never claim to be able to carve a statue or compose music or paint a picture or design a building. Even if they do not offer to write a book they have a plot for a novel, which they present to a writer, free.

I am sure many writers, still living, who were once great commercial successes sometimes wonder what has hit them. Why did their vogue suddenly end? I recall a certain enormously successful English playwright, Henry Arthur Jones, who cried to a fellow dramatist, "They don't want me any more!" Arnold Bennett, another spectacularly successful playwright, notes calmly in his journal that he thinks his vogue as a writer of plays is ending. Bennett was an uncanny realist about himself. But this sudden, shattering obsolescence is more prevalent in America than in Britain, where loyalties last longer.

This illusion that one's vogue and financial prosperity are permanent is particularly common among writers for the great national weekly and monthly magazines. They become condescending, and even arrogant, toward those lesser breeds who gain a pitiful popularity in highbrow organs like *The Atlantic Monthly*. I remember one of them commiserating me for having to sell a story to the *Atlantic*. Anyone who did not, as the saying went, "make the *Post*" was practically nonexistent as a writer. I used to know some of these men and correspond with them. One was good enough to tell me that the trouble with Conrad was, quite simply, he did not know how to write. What Conrad needed, he believed, was a *Saturday Evening Post* writer to go over his copy and make it salable. That particular writer is no longer writing. He is in Florida real estate. You would not recognize his name if I mentioned it, although in those days, twenty years ago, he received $3,000 for a short story. And I can remember an editor of a popular magazine who said in a symposium that Max Beerbohm's story "Enoch Soames," about a writer who sold his soul to the devil for posthumous fame, would need revision and rewriting before he, the editor, would accept it. It was a good idea, he admitted, but Beerbohm didn't know how to work it out.

It must always be borne in mind that the average editor, when he starts on a manuscript, is a man of ideals. He has an ideal writer in his mind, and how you measure up to that writer depends on his reaction. At one time the ideal writer for a popular magazine editor was James Oliver Curwood. I have known an editor kiss his hand in ecstasy about Curwood, and tell me I should study that guy. At another time it was Edna Ferber who was an editorial star. No nonsense about Edna. They might yak-yak about Conrad, but give him Edna. Now I fancy it is Paul Gallico. Editors don't expect to get that kind of perfection every time, but if only the other writers would try. . . .

Oh, the editors! If the mortality among writers is tragic that among editors is cataclysmic. They come and they go as if through a revolving door. When I first retired from the sea and bought a house in Westport, then a quiet village on the Sound, every other man I met at a cocktail party had been editor of *Collier's.* The place was full of them! And a writer of seventy-five, if he has a manuscript to offer, finds he is submitting it to an editor who was wetting his diapers when he himself was doing his best work. That is very testing, especially when the editor returns it for an obviously disingenuous reason. The real reason is, the generations cannot communicate one with another. But a modern editor, who can feel his successor breathing down his neck, is in no mood for philosophic analysis. His cultural equipment keeps him nervously aware only of today's headlines. I think one of the most sinister evidences of this is an item that appeared in a California paper when Colette died. It ran simply, DISCOVERER OF AUDREY HEPBURN DIES.

I realized years ago that a new day was dawning. Somerset Maugham recently remarked of a once fabulously popular novelist that he could not sell a story today. He is still around, that novelist, but it is true. His style would not be acceptable now. The thing to do when you find yourself no longer in fashion is to take up insurance or Fuller brushes or real estate, something people really want. Authorship is not like most businesses. It has no good will. A writer has to produce his work himself, except in special cases, like the elder Dumas or the husband of Colette. A manufacturer of Scrabble might lose his trade, but not with the lightning speed of the changes in the book market. Some of you may remember a book called *The Specialist.* Six hundred thousand copies. Its sale resembled a Midwestern twister, and harder to explain. I doubt if you could give it away now, let alone sell it. The public is not only extremely unpredictable. It is exasperatingly fickle. It will buy hundreds of thousands of copies of a book, and while the author may write twenty more as good, or even better, they will stay away in droves. The author will be known by that one book for the rest of his life.

There is the classic case of Conan Doyle, desperately trying to extricate himself from the coils of a creation he loathed, Sherlock Holmes. When he doubled and tripled his price for writing Holmes potboilers the editors went him one better, and the public would not be denied. In despair he killed the fellow, but was compelled

to invent a resurrection. The character was, although Doyle did not
know it, immortal. And his hard-plotted, well-written historical
novels went unregarded. I personally knew such a case, Hugh Loft-
ing, the creator of Dr. Doolittle. They were so popular with the
younger set he had to keep on grinding them out while he wanted
to write serious novels.

The public will stay away in droves even from a book which by
every standard of excellence and acceptance should be a success.
Often I have heard my wife say of a book I was reviewing and rav-
ing over, "It has everything. It *must* sell." It not only did not sell, it
died aborning. I used to keep a shelf of such books. It was a sort of
cemetery of literary miscarriages.

A man who has reached my age reacts against anniversaries out of
modesty. He has seen so many reputations rise like balloons and
sink out of sight. So many of them turn out to be will-o'-the-wisps,
beginning with a bang and ending with a whisper. He becomes increasingly aware of the meretriciousness of all literary fame. He certainly becomes skeptical of his own pretensions. In my own case I
think I achieved philosophical resignation by my relations with
H. L. Mencken, when he was running *The American Mercury*. He
was a fine editor. He had an unerring eagle eye for what he called
"the hole" in a story. He was a sound counselor for filling up the
hole. But he was an unpredictable reviewer. Of one of my novels he
said it was an absolutely first-class piece of fiction. Naturally I threw
out my chest. I was young and inexperienced then. My next novel,
he said, should be burned by the common hangman. I deflated my
chest. On looking back I am not sure it was that bad. Besides, the
common hangman might have liked it.

Now in England it is, or was, different. Fame takes longer to mature and stays with you longer. If you keep writing books for fifty
years you do achieve fame of a sort. If you still hang around and
grow a long gray beard you become a Grand Old Man of Letters,
and when you become senile your books will be reprinted.

I can recall an amusing case in my youth, George Meredith. The
subject of trial marriage or, as they called it then, companionate
marriage—what the Scotch call hand-fasting—was being ventilated in
press and magazines. Some of you may remember Judge Lindsey.
Well, some bright journalist recalled that the old gaffer down at
Box Hill, if he was still alive, once wrote a novel called *The Amazing Marriage*. Maybe he meant a trial marriage. The bright journalist went down and got an interview while the old boy sunned

himself in his garden. He brought back the astonishing news that
George Meredith approved of trial marriage. Novel readers were
excited. They had no idea Meredith was *that* kind of writer. They
jammed Mudies's rental library. Hadn't they *anything* of Meredith's? It created a temporary revival. That was around 1908, when
I published my first book.

Even more astonishing is the quirk of fate which shoots one
author to a pinnacle of celebrity, or notoriety, and leaves another
deep in oblivion. Take the Gissing brothers. George Gissing, a very
serious novelist, became famous by a novel about what he called
The New Grub Street. I think his personal career, like Scott Fitzgerald's, was a help. At the end of his life he wrote a short non-
fiction book, an excellent book, which caught public fancy. But his
long historical novel *Veranilda,* on which he lavished a wealth of
classical erudition and hard work, never got off the ground. He was
a friend of H. G. Wells's, who put him in a novel. He was a friend
of Frank Swinnerton's, who wrote a fine biography of him.

But what about his brother, Algernon Gissing? Thirty years ago
I mentioned him to Henry Seidel Canby, who said briskly he had
never heard of him. I said he had written thirty novels and I had
read two of them. He repeated he had never heard of him. Algernon
lived in a village called Broadway in Worcestershire, and he was
an authority on the region. He never did anything spectacular. He
just wrote one novel after another, and nobody but me has ever
heard of him. Not one of those novels is in the Yale Library. On
the other hand, while the Yale Library has a full collection of
George's works and other material about him, I doubt if he is any
better known that Algernon. Time is a great leveler.

And, speaking of time, I am not one of those cheerful optimists
who believe in the inevitable continuous evolution of literature as
we have known it since the nineteenth century. That is a short view.
I am sure the scribes who created that immense library of cuneiform
clay cylinders collected by a Mesopotamian monarch 4,000 years
ago believed that their profession would last forever. It did last a
long time. So did the profession of their successors, the Egyptian
public-relations men who concocted lying histories of nonexistent
victories for the Pharaohs who hired them. In our case it is only
500 years since the invention of movable type. Why should we assume that the era of printed books is going to last forever? I am
glad I shall not live to see it, but I sometimes have a nightmare of
a time far beyond "Nineteen Eighty-Four" when electronic brains

will drone out newer and more awful stories than Mickey Spillane's, throwing them direct on millions of television screens. Men will always want stories, and it is quite possible technology will eventually eliminate not only the printed word but the creative intelligence.

There are other reasons for shying away from anniversaries, but I have said enough about that. I would rather discuss briefly what could be called some of the curiosities of literature, such as, for instance, the extraordinary chanciness of some fame. It rivals betting on horses. What makes a book famous? Or what makes it sell? Some publishers feel that if they can make you believe it was written by a teen-ager or a convict in a penitentiary or the inmate of what the Elizabethans called a house of fair reception you will rush to pay $3.50 for it. There was a time when Mr. Gladstone, the great British Liberal statesman, could make a book's fortune by writing a post card praising it. There was a time when the then Bishop of London could sell an edition by preaching a sermon against it. When Arnold Bennett was book reviewer for Lord Beaverbrook's *Evening Standard* he could sell a book, too. The first printing would be sold out next day. Mind you, the first printing might be only a few hundred copies, and novels were not $3.95 in those days. But he had started the book. Now I doubt if a reviewer can sell as many as a dozen copies by a good review.

These cases are not too farfetched. But what about a book like *Lorna Doone?* When R. D. Blackmore wrote it he was just another novelist. That was 1869. He wrote a number of other good novels. I have read some of them. But the publication of *Lorna Doone* was almost contemporary with the engagement of a popular princess, Louise, daughter of Queen Victoria, to a popular young man, the Marquis of Lorne, son and heir of the Duke of Argyll. It was, moreover, a love match, and in those days the public had a fantastic interest in the Royal Family. In some miraculous fashion that public got the idea that *Lorna Doone* had something to do with the engagement of the Marquis of Lorne. The book was doing well, but then it became a runaway. The royal engagement and the love story of John Ridd and Lorna became identified in the public mind and heart. Now you can buy cookies called Lorna Doones, which is fame of a sort.

Another curiosity of modern literature is this. In the old days it was the dogged, talented writer who finally got his foot in the door of the temple of fame and by luck or cunning kept it there and established his position. Rags to riches; from an attic in a slum to a Georgian house in the country. That was the way writers like Dickens, Zola, Kipling, Bennett, Hardy, and so on climbed to fame and—sometimes—Westminster Abbey.

But since the book clubs have come into the game the whole business works occasionally in reverse. I don't mean that you get into Westminster Abbey first and end up in the poorhouse. What I mean is, you can easily get the nod from a book club with a first book and achieve a circulation that would make Dickens, Dumas, and Marie Corelli turn over in their graves. You reach the pinnacle in one jump and then find yourself down in the dusty arena struggling for a living. It becomes a real problem to adjust yourself to the new conditions—from riches to rags. A very testing situation, and peculiar to our modern literary life.

I mentioned the curious fate of *Lorna Doone* ending up as a cookie. I know other cases of such immortality. In Danbury, where I shop, my favorite tavern is called The Mad Hatter, Danbury being a hat town. It is embellished with pictures of Alice in Wonderland. Such celebrity, like the Prince Albert coat, the Gladstone bag, the Brougham carriage, and the John Ruskin cigar, sometimes takes off and travels completely dissociated from the original in the public mind. I doubt if anyone having a drink at The Mad Hatter, glancing at the pictures of Alice at her extraordinary party, has any memory of the book or its author, any more than smokers of John Ruskin cigars recall *The Stones of Venice*.

I must make another digression. A gentle comment on the tendency of modern publishers to assume that they operate a philanthropic institution for indigent writers, that they pay much higher rates than their predecessors. This is simply not so. What is so is that the occasional large earnings of certain writers receive extravagant publicity. I remember an artist friend telling me, bug-eyed, of the fabulous earnings of a writer he had read of in *Life*. He looked blank when I said that, compared with the earnings of writers like Zane Grey, Harold Bell Wright, Ethel M. Dell, and Edgar Rice Burroughs, Mr. Thomas Ernest Hemingwolfe had earned little and not long. Those other writers earned large sums year after year after year. And hardly any income tax. My friend had never heard of them. Growing excited, I went on to astound him by recounting the earnings of George Eliot 100 years ago. For seven novels, several of them only leased, so she still owned them, she received just under £56,000. The pound sterling was then five dollars, and the purchasing power was five times what it is today. So George Eliot received the equivalent, in our money, of $1,400,000. No income tax, no literary agent getting his 10 per cent.

Enough of that. I can close on what some might call a high note, but not a shrill one, by mentioning the most important member of the partnership. It is neither the author nor the publisher. It is the public. It is recognized by most people now that you cannot advertise a book into success. Nobody knows *what* makes a book sell. There was once a great scheme, and it seemed watertight, to eliminate the frightful hazards of the publisher, abolish what one publisher called "moribund remainders." A corporation was formed to limit the list to best sellers. There were to be no lemons, no geese, only swans, in this new venture. A dozen phenomenally successful novelists were rounded up, given fat contracts, and the directors sat back to rake in the money. I often wonder what happened to that corporation. I could tell you the name of it if I wanted, but it doesn't matter now. The famous best sellers were not happy away from their own publishers. They all went back after a while. This is by the way. What I wanted to point out is that public taste changes so subtly, and the publisher has to be alert to see it. You would have trouble selling *The Rosary* now, although when it first came out here it took an entire large printing plant to cope with the demand. Now the public clamors for stronger and gamier meat. It is a short view to blame the publishers. They have to have a sixth sense which anticipates the next jump in public taste. At present, owing to Freud and Kinsey and the tensions of the age, conventional citizens are lapping up more sex than usual; or, rather, they want it spelled out more explicitly than ever before except in books which used to be sold from under the counter. Now they are piled high *on* the counter, and high-school girls discuss things that when I was at school were kept in medical clinics. Remembering what was called daring sixty years ago, this attitude of suburban, conventionally living people and their children, living unexciting lives from cradle to grave, which causes them to read avidly about vicarious lust, infidelity, lesbianism and homosexuality, and what Hollywoods calls "sleeping around," makes me wonder what comes next. I doubt if this will last very long. But when I told a literary agent that a book I was writing contained no fornication he immediately lost interest in me.

Perhaps I have let too many cats out of the bags already. All I intended was to make a few random reflections on the literary life as it appears to me at seventy-five. I did not, as so many young Americans do, plunge into writing even before I left college. I have to confess that I never went to college. I was a sea-going engineer from twenty-five to thirty-eight. I had published four books before I left the sea and, as we say, swallowed the anchor. I became a professional writer reluctantly and by accident. It was a fluke. Now, in old age, I sometimes wonder whether I would not have had a happier and more useful life if I had stayed at sea. Only sometimes. Now and again I take up one of my own books and read a bit, and I feel that it is not so dusty. If you can say that, at seventy-five, you are a writer. Or you have been a writer. You have achieved as much success as you deserve. And, at that, it no longer seems so very important. As Somerset Maugham said when he was seventy-five, you don't care. You are on the wing.

AMY LOVEMAN

by Norman Cousins

To many people, Miss Loveman and The Saturday Review *were the same. From the very first issue she made a place for herself in the pages of the magazine as well as in the hearts of her friends and associates. She died in her seventy-fifth year, typically maintaining a full working schedule until only a few days before her passing.* SR's *editor wrote this tribute to her memory shortly afterward.*

DECEMBER 24, 1955

I SIT HERE AND stare at the sheet in my typewriter. It is Sunday. The city is quiet and the office is empty. Some thirty feet away is Miss Loveman's office. Her desk is as she left it last Tuesday, except for some accumulated mail. Perhaps half the envelopes will contain poetry; ever since Bill Benét's death Miss Loveman has handled poetry for *SR*. In the mail, too, will be letters from publishers about their new books. But, most typically, letters from friends. The letters will probably thank her for some act of extraordinary kindness. Nothing was more remarkable about Amy Loveman than her gift for friendship or the ease with which she did things for other people. People would say she was the only person they knew who could be thoughtful without having to think about it.

In the lower left-hand drawer of her desk is a large folder we have gone through together many times. Memory lane. Letters from men and women like John Masefield, Theodore Dreiser, Lord Dunsany, Ellen Glasgow, Sinclair Lewis, Willa Cather, Bernard Shaw, H. G. Wells, Bertrand Russell, Osbert Sitwell, Edwin Arlington Robinson, Vachel Lindsay, Carl Sandburg, Robinson Jeffers, Upton Sinclair, Thomas Wolfe. In the top drawer some photographs, generally between boards, of the people she worked with and loved, people like Henry Seidel Canby, William Rose Benét, Christopher Morley, William Allen White, John Mason Brown, George Stevens, Harry Scherman, and members of the present *SR* staff and their families.

In the second drawer on the left, her reports for the Book-of-the-Month Club. For years Miss Loveman had carried efficiently and gracefully the burdens of two full-time jobs. How many books she had to handle and read all during that time for *SR* and BOMC she herself never dared to guess. The bad books, and there were many of them, failed to exhaust or depress her. Now and then she would come across something of quality and her reward could not have been more complete if she had discovered an unpublished novel by Jane Austen.

Still looking at her empty office: on the bookshelf behind her desk conveniently within reach are her favorite reference books, the most conspicuous of them being the Dictionary of American Biography. She could relive the moments in history when the big men had to make their big decisions and she could retain a sense of freshness and excitement in her appreciation. For her, Winston Churchill was like a summing-up of everything that's right with the human race. She liked the epic forward thrust and the mammoth optimism of the man; she was enchanted with the Churchillian contempt for the difficult and his sense of outrage toward the impossible.

"Whatever may be said about me," she said about herself last week, "no one can say I'm not an optimist. I have always been an optimist. And I've never been disappointed."

From the start she had been optimistic about *The Saturday Review*. In the file in her office is a specially bound copy of the first number of the magazine, and not far from it the artwork for the symbol of the phoenix rising from the ashes. The symbol was to become something of a trade-mark for the magazine. It had been William Rose Benét's idea and he used it as an integral part of the heading for the department he conducted in *SRL* until his death in 1950. It was a decorative but jaunty bird, looking more as if it were indignant because its tail had been accidentally singed than if it were the fabled creature taking shape from the dying embers.

It is easy to imagine Amy Loveman admiring the spunky quality of the artist's conception of the bird. For in those days one had to be an optimist. She was part of a group trying to do something that had never been done successfully before: publish an independent weekly national literary review. Henry Seidel Canby, William Rose Benét, Christopher Morley, and Amy Loveman had been the editors of the Literary Supplement of the old New York *Evening Post* and had won fame throughout the English-speaking world for the high standards and literary excellence of its essays and reviews.

Miss Loveman liked to tell about the time that Cyrus H. K. Curtis, publisher of the New York *Evening Post,* who spent most of his time in Philadelphia, walked down Wall Street and was astounded to observe the brokers as they bought their newsstand copies of the *Evening Post.* The brokers ejected the Literary Supplement with a practiced flip of the wrist and deftly folded the paper with the same hand. Mr. Curtis then decided that the supplement was not contributing as substantially as he had hoped to the cultural development of the captains and the kings of the financial district. He informed Dr. Canby that the supplement would be discontinued.

The first part of that story may be apocryphal, but one thing that is certain is that at least one of the customers read the Literary Supplement and wanted to keep it alive. Thomas W. Lamont was enthusiastic about the propects for the continuation of the supplement as a separate magazine and was willing to write the checks that would make it possible. Three other young men of energy and confidence were connected with the new venture then starting up: Henry R. Luce, Briton Hadden, and Roy Larsen.

The first issue of *The Saturday Review of Literature* was dated August 2, 1924. The masthead listed Dr. Canby as Editor, Miss Loveman and William Rose Benét as Associate Editors, and Christopher Morley as Contributing Editor. The small type announced the fact that *SRL* was being published weekly by Time, Inc., of which Henry R. Luce was President and Henry Seidel Canby Vice-President. Prospective advertisers were invited to write to Noble A. Cathcart; prospective subscribers to the Circulation Manager, Roy E. Larsen.

The format of the new magazine was newspaper-supplement size, printed in three wide columns of distinctive type. The leading editorial said that modern criticism must "be like a modern university where one seeks Principles, but also works in laboratories of immediate experience amidst the vivid confusion of experiment. In one guise a graybeard philosopher searching for the Best, but also in the mood of youth, watching the three-ringed show under the great tent of Today—yet discriminating in both—that is the double function of criticism and this Review."

In that first issue Miss Loveman wrote a review of a novel, *Woodsmoke,* by Francis Brett Young. All the qualities which were to win her distinction as a critic were observed in that review: the attempt to see a book not only in the reviewer's terms but in terms of what the author was trying to do; the sense of balance and fairness that prevented her from seizing upon a single startling aspect of a book and raising it to a monopoly status; the existence at all times of basic critical values carefully developed out of a remarkable working knowledge of the best in literature; and a final neat loop of appraisal that could be grasped readily by the inquiring reader.

There was something else in that first review that was beautifully characteristic of the reviewer. Miss Loveman praised Mr. Young for a story that drew its strength from the author's "sympathetic vision of a world in which human nature, cast back upon elemental conditions, retains even at its most pitiful a certain essential dignity."

In that one sentence is to be found the essence of her own optimism. She could contemplate all the violence and meanness and mobilized evil of the age, yet never forget the ultimate strength that was to be found in human decency. She was not appalled by the dualism in man; all that mattered to her was that moral catharsis and the chance to do better came with the gift of life.

At the time *SRL* began Amy Loveman argued strongly but without stridency for idealism without self-deception, for awareness of living issues without meaningless immersion, and for recognition of the power of hope. She had no patience with the cynicism that went in and out of fashion; she thought nothing was more wasteful than defeatism—whether in literature or life. This large view never left her.

The early connection between *SR* and Time, Inc., didn't last very long. Apparently the theory that two new struggling weeklies were easier to publish than one didn't hold, and it was decided that each would fend for itself as best it could. The story of Time, Inc., has been told elsewhere. *SRL* in those early days found some 20,000 readers who became devoted to it and quickly formed a cheering section. And it performed the kind of service for the world of books in America that had never before existed on a national scale. The editorial franchise was the market place of good taste. But it was a limited market place, despite the intensity of the response, and only Mr. Lamont's generosity enabled the magazine to continue.

During the first fifteen years Amy Loveman assigned most of the books for review, wrote reviews of her own, handled a regular department in the magazine called The Clearing House, in which she answered requests from readers for out-of-the-way information, edited copy, pinned up the dummy, read page proofs, and put the magazine to bed at the printer's. She answered most of the office mail, made sure that Henry Canby, Bill Benét, and Christopher

Morley ate their lunches on time, kept the publishers and authors happy by going to their parties, and supplied that most valuable of all functions in a magazine office—finding the lost manuscripts of anguished authors who somehow forgot to make a carbon copy.

Once, early one evening, Christopher Morley cried out in horror that a valuable photograph had suddenly disappeared from his desk. He had borrrowed it from an English publisher and had promised to return it within two weeks. The problem was promptly turned over to Miss Loveman, who made the usual search, then expressed her hunch that the photograph had slid off the desk into the waste-paper basket, which had been emptied an hour earlier by the cleaning women.

Miss Loveman rushed downstairs and discovered that the dump truck had been gone thirty minutes. She obtained the address of the dump, hurriedly proceeding there by taxicab. For the next two hours she picked her way through a mountain of crumpled paper, cigarette butts, apple cores, remains of box lunches. But in the end she emerged triumphant from the city dump with the missing photograph. When she telephoned the good news to Chris Morley he almost cried for joy.

Years later Miss Loveman and I were on a somewhat similar pilgrimage—this time searching for a book manuscript in a ware-house where *The Saturday Review* keeps its old files. For almost three years we had been bombarded by an author with requests to return to him a manuscript which he claimed was worth at least $50,000. Now he was instituting suit. With only a month before the case would go to court we spent a week end looking through the office, then decided we would have to go through the countless thousands of old papers in storage at the warehouse.

It was winter and the warehouse was unheated. I begged Amy not to come. She would have none of it, reminding me that in twenty-five years at *The Saturday Review* she had never been ill a single day. Like my predecessors, I had learned to respect her power of decision. We made a pretty sight that afternoon, climbing over mounds of files and papers at the warehouse. We didn't find the manuscript but we had a wonderful time.

Three weeks later—ten days before the trial—*The Saturday Review* moved to larger quarters and the missing manuscript fell out from behind a desk. The lawsuit for $50,000 against *The Saturday Review* was dropped. We were pleased, but the author didn't seem as elated as you might expect after an only copy he valued so highly had suddenly reappeared.

At the time I joined *The Saturday Review* late in 1939 Mr. Lamont's backing had long since ceased. We needed enlarged public support. Related to this was the fact that a war had just begun in Europe and there was no point in talking about literary values unless we had a world in which the life of the free mind was possible. This meant new connections with the big issues of the times.

The founding editors couldn't have been more magnificent in their concurrence and support. Mr. Canby, who had left the editorship several years earlier, agreed to come back as chairman of the new editorial board. Harrison Smith, President, who was responsible for my coming to *SRL,* provided unequivocal backing. Bill Benét asked only to be put to work.

But nothing was more inspiring than the kind of help and support and devotion a green young editor got from Miss Loveman. No magazine is really edited during office hours. The work actually begins after the telephone stops. Night after night Amy Loveman would work with me on the magazine, reading proofs, dummying the pages, encouraging me in the new concepts that were being developed in *SRL*. Indeed, she was far ahead of me, almost prodding me at times to strike out in new directions. She agreed completely with the need to make books a part of the world of ideas and issues. Whenever a publisher would complain that we were abandoning the classical position of critical detachment she would ask for the privilege of reply.

"America's age of innocence is gone," she wrote in an editorial. "The mood of the nation has changed from assurance to anxiety, at times even to fear. . . . But at least knowledge has come that only by the abandonment of its vaunted isolation, only by accepting responsibility in the councils of the nations, can America realize its ineradicable faith in a world in which freedom and peace are the portion of all. In that faith it links today to yesterday."

Amy Loveman lived to see the journal in which she had invested so much of her life become solidly self-supporting. In the hospital, two days before she died, she inquired about the size of the print order. I told her it was 192,000. Her voice was weak but she repeated the number slowly, then said that this was really only the beginning, and asked about plans for future growth.

It was this forward-looking quality that attracted to her so many young people. They were around her constantly, confiding in her, seeking infusions of courage for their hopes and new enterprises. Children couldn't get enough of her. She had never forgotten the brightly colored contours of a child's world; and she loved to journey through it whenever she could.

Equally remarkable was her ability to effect rapport with people regardless of age or their rung on the social or cultural ladder. Several years ago she got into conversation with a taxicab driver who, after inquiring about her occupation, revealed that his main interest in life was poetry, and that he wrote verse whenever he wasn't actually driving. There was a spirited conversation about techniques in poetical expression. When Miss Loveman arrived at her home the driver said goodbye, adding it was nice to be able to meet someone in the same line of business. The incident delighted Miss Loveman and she told it often.

Almost everywhere she went she met people who wrote poetry. Invariably they would follow up the meeting by submitting verse for publication in *The Saturday Review*. Miss Loveman had the incredibly difficult job of returning 98 per cent of these submissions, and it is a tribute to her genius in human relationships that her rejection letters never lost her a friend.

She never got tired of reading poetry; indeed, I doubt that there is more than a handful of critics who have had to read more of it— good, bad, and in-between—during the past thirty-five years. With it all, she never wrote a poem in her life. "I wouldn't dare to," she said, "knowing how well supplied the world already is with bad verse."

I am still looking through the doorway into her office.

In the top center drawer is a folder containing some correspondence that was turned over to her in June 1942. The correspondence had to do with a surprise party in her honor. Originally the party was not to be larger than fifteen or sixteen persons. We planned to give Miss Loveman a gold medallion for her contribution to literature in particular and cultural values in general. But dozens of letters came in from people asking to share in the tribute. Each letter established the writer's admiration and affection for Miss Loveman. Finally it became necessary to hire a small ballroom at a large hotel.

Miss Loveman knew nothing about the surprise party until she was escorted into the hall.

Tributes at the dinner came from Thomas Lamont, Elmer Davis, John Mason Brown, Harrison Smith, Henry Seidel Canby, Christopher Morley, William Rose Benét, Oswald Garrison Villard, Dorothy Canfield Fisher, Simeon Strunsky, Bennett Cerf, and *SRL's* editor. It was a chance to confess our love in public and we made the most of it. Several days after the dinner we gave her a neat bundle of the letters requesting that we enlarge the dinner—letters reflecting the overflow of genuine affection. She treasured the packet and kept it in her top drawer.

There were other honors. Columbia University gave her the University Medal for Excellence in 1945. Wheaton and Wilson colleges gave her honorary degrees in literature. In 1946 she received the Constance Lindsay Skinner Achievement Award.

It is doubtful, however, whether anything gave her greater satisfaction than to be able to work with new writers, helping to remove the roadblocks in the way of publication. Her advice was precise, crisp, practical, built on a solid foundation of reasonable explanation. And underlying everything else was an almost epic kindness. This combination of incisiveness and kindness characterized her entire life.

Amy Loveman was less cluttered emotionally than any person I have ever known.

Her horizons were unblurred by petty assertions of a sovereign ego. Her concerns pointed outward, and it carried over to others. I can't recall ever hearing a petty argument in her presence. I can think of many animated conversations in her home or office, but I can't recall a single instance when people did not respond to her presence by liberating themselves from trivia.

Her nobility was a universe; and to know it was to soar inside it. No wonder that so many people came to her; there were peace and purpose in her life and incredible strength, and it gave nourishment to others. The human mind feeds on great expectations, but there must also be great reassurances. These reassurances have to do with the natural goodness of man. Such assurances are forever sought but are not easily come by. The evidence for them cannot be spun out of abstract evidence or persuasion. They exist in living tissue or not at all. Amy Loveman carried this proof; it was visible; it was recognized; it could be shared.

On the right-hand side of her desk are some souvenirs of a trip to Europe last summer. She went with her brother Michael. It was her first visit since the summer of 1914. She was especially eager to see England again, and nothing was more of a lure in England than Jane Austen Country. No writer in any language had a greater hold on Miss Loveman's affections than Jane Austen. She was fascinated by Jane Austen's ability to reconstruct a life with such meticulous regard for the anatomy of human emotion. The fact that Jane Austen could engage the attention of the reader without a circus of aberrations or bloodletting or rampant irrationality—this to Miss Loveman was the mark of a real novelist. This ability to make a casual life compelling seemed to Miss Loveman to represent a major challenge in fiction.

A year earlier, in the summer of 1954, it had become necessary for Miss Loveman to undergo surgery in an attempt to arrest the illness that was to cost her life. She had taken with her to the hospital a single book: Jane Austen's *Emma*. It was to be her sixth rereading of the classic.

The operation prolonged her life by perhaps a year and a half. Within a few weeks after coming out of the hospital she was back at her desk again—both at *SR* and Book-of-the-Month Club. She was thinner—much thinner than we had ever known her—and her skin had faded. But she proclaimed that she had never felt better and spoke excitedly about her plans to go to Europe with her brother. She saw just as many people and gave no evidence of disability.

The trip to Europe added to her portion in life. There was a sense of fulfillment in her manner when she returned in the fall. But time was running out. She continued to lose weight and took longer to get from one place to another. She amazed her good friend and physician, Dr. William M. Hitzig, by insisting on her ability to continue in her work. And even when taking a few steps required almost superhuman power she insisted that Dr. Hitzig not trouble to visit her at her home; she would go to his office.

"I feel so guilty about taking up Dr. Hitzig's time," she said. "When I look in his waiting room and see people who really need his help I almost feel like apologizing to them. Dr. Hitzig is a miracle man and I'm afraid I'm keeping him from working miracles where they are really needed."

She lived alone but she refused to allow a nurse to stay with her. In this way the weeks passed until one day she telephoned the office to say she felt somewhat tired and would not be coming to work.

Dr. Hitzig, who deeply respected her determination to keep going, did not order her to the hospital until very near the end. She refused ambulance service, insisting on walking to the car. I held her by the arm and felt nothing but frail bone. She seemed to exist on sheer will power.

Then, on the way to the hospital, she asked, "How is Pat? I was so sorry to hear about his illness." Patrick Mahoney is the night elevator man in our office building. "Pat is such a nice man," she said.

She took with her to the hospital her Book-of-the-Month Club reports. "I'm not sure I'm going to be able to get out in time for the meeting of the judges Friday," she said, "but my work is here and it's up to date."

On Friday morning she spoke to Mr. Scherman and gave him all the last-minute information about her Club reports. On Saturday morning the nurses reported she was becoming increasingly weak. But in the afternoon she rallied. She chatted with her three brothers, Herbert, Ernest, and Michael. Ernest and Herbert had brought their wives; Michael is unmarried. After they left, she started to read the galley proofs of a book for the Club. Early in the evening she told Dr. Hitzig she was happy with her nurse and her room and the general hospital care.

Shortly before midnight she fell into a coma. The end came at two A.M. Sunday, December 11, 1955. The memory and wonder of her will endure and it will sustain us.

SIR WINSTON CHURCHILL:
NOBEL PRIZE WINNER

by Samuel Eliot Morison

*One historian appraises another. Samuel Eliot Morison has been
for many years Jonathan Trumbull Professor of History at Harvard, and is official historian of the United States Navy in World
War II.*

OCTOBER 31, 1953

THE ENTIRE HISTORICAL PROFESSION is honored in the honor to Sir
Winston; for it is the first time in half a century that an historian
has won the Nobel Prize for Literature; in 1902 it was bestowed on
Theodor Mommsen. Restricted as this prize is to "literature of an
idealist tendency," few historians would even qualify, since few are
able to apply "idealist" tendencies to the past. Even if we define
"idealist" as synonymous with "creative," what historians might
have won the prize—assuming, of course, that the prize had always
existed? Herodotus certainly, and Thucydides. Gibbon would have
rated, and Macaulay and Lord Clarendon, the Winston Churchill
of Charles the Second's day. Our own Parkman and Prescott,
certainly. For Italy, Ferrero; for France, Henry Martin; possibly
Sorel. And of living historians, George Macaulay Trevelyan. But I
cannot for the life of me think of another I would have voted for
if I had been a judge.

There is no question but that Churchill is a great historian. He
has verve, style, honesty, imagination, and, above all, superb craftsmanship.

How did he learn the craft? The young men and women today
who are training to be historians wish to know. Well, my answer is,
background, innate capacity, experience, and a vigorous course of
self-teaching; that each was essential, but no one would have worked
without the others. Sir Winston is a descendant of the great Marlborough; and the son of Lord Randolph Churchill, an important

figure in Victorian politics; and, on the distaff side, he is a member of our oldest hereditary society, the Cincinnati. Thus he absorbed history *through the skin*. History was in the air during his youth. People discussed it at his parents' table. He knew from childhood that he was heir to a great tradition. And right here is an important lesson for us. We have plenty of intelligent youths in the United States and Canada with a background similar to Churchill's, but we do not recruit them for Clio. We choose graduate students from the top-grade college graduates and wonder why they do not do better when it comes to writing history. The trouble with these lads is that, no matter how bright they may be, they never can catch up with the sort of thing that Winston had from birth. Call this snobbery if you will; it is the truth.

So we are back at the question, how did Winston become a great historian, the only one to win the Nobel Prize for Literature? First and foremost, this infiltration of history "through the skin." Second, a prodigious memory, which enables him to repeat verbatim a lecture that has interested him, or a whole Shakespeare play. Third, Harrow-on-the-Hill. He has told us about that school in *My Early Life* (1944). He hated the classical education forced on him, but he had to go through with it. He hated to translate Caesar, Ovid, Vergil, Horace, and Martial, even with a trot. And he doubled his work in what we call English Composition, because he swapped tasks with a good classicist who did his translations, while he wrote the other fellow's English themes. Most of all, the encouragement of a wise headmaster and the English system of education, which requires every teacher, no matter what his subject, to teach English. In the United States only the teachers in the English Department teach English; the others let their students get by with any old gobbledygook; an aspiring historian has two strikes against him at the start. Winston hated Latin, but I will wager that when he read Caesar's *Commentaries* the boy said to himself, "I'll have something like that to write one day, and I'll do it even better." Which he did.

Winston's school record was so poor that his father refused to let him go on to Oxford or Cambridge; sent him to Sandhurst for an Army career. That and the Royal Navy were the only respectable alternatives in those days for English boys of his class who did not make good in public school. Winston went through Sandhurst and obtained his commission. Then began his real literary education. It was in the winter of 1896-97, in his twenty-second year when, as an officer of the Fourth Hussars, he was stationed at Bangalore in

India. He had already "picked up a wide vocabulary . . . and a liking for words, and for the feel of words fitting and falling into their places like pennies in the slot"—a gift that he never lost. Now he wished to find out about things, and concepts. *Ethics*. What did that mean? He had to read Aristotle to find out. *History*. What was that? He had to read no history at school except a wretched abstract of Hume. So he sent for sets of Gibbon and Macaulay and devoured them. His cousin and my friend Sir Shane Leslie, to whom he gave one of his volumes of Gibbon, tells me that the margins are covered with Winston's questions, remarks, criticisms. All that was vital for his literary future. He had read critically the two great stylists among modern English historians. He was too sensible to try to imitate their style. But the beauty, the muscular strength, the majestic cadence of their style did something to his mind, and there are distant echoes of Gibbon and Macaulay in his latest volume. Here is another lesson that our American historical students have never learned. Gibbon to them is "old stuff," Macaulay is "old hat," Parkman is "drum and trumpet history," and so on. They never read through an historian who is pre-eminent for his style. Without one inspiring example how can they become first rate themselves?

Churchill's first serious history, *The River War: an Historic Account of the Reconquest of the Soudan,* which came out fifty-four years ago, was not a great book. It was just the average sort of contemporary history, with a rather unusual flair for vivid description. For instance: "Since they [the Seaforth Highlanders] would not run, their loss was heavy, and it was a strange sight—the last vivid impression of the day—to watch them struggling through the deep sand, with the dust knocked up into clouds by the bullets which struck all around them. Very few escaped, and the bodies of the killed lay thickly dotting the river bed with heaps of dirty-white. Then at 8:25 the 'Cease Fire' sounded and the battle of the Atkara ended."

This is good writing; but any first class-newspaper correspondent could have done as well; and no critic reading *The River War* predicted, "Here is a great historian." Churchill had to work constantly to improve his style. It would be a fascinating study to follow him, book by book; but we have no time for it here. His competence developed with his political experience. Polybius, twenty-one centuries ago, wrote that historians should be men of action; for without a personal knowledge of how things happen a writer will inevitably distort the true relations and importance of events. Basil

Williams quotes a French writer, *"Ecrire l'histoire, c'est agir; et c'est pourquoi il courient que l'historien soit homme d'action."* But most of our men of action today have neither the time nor the capacity to write; Churchill found the time and had the capacity. He wrote when he was out of power about the Duke of Marlborough, and he wrote when he was in power about the events that he observed; and he went right on improving.

Neither of his greater histories, his memories of World War I or his "Second World War" is impartial, and he never pretended that they were; but they are honest. They describe events as he saw them, and in the most arresting and intriguing prose. Turn, if you will, to *Their Finest Hour* ("Second World War," Vol. II) pages 383 and following, and read the story of how Professor Lindemann (now Lord Cherwell), Winston's *éminence grise*, brought in one of his former pupils to explain what he knew of one of the Germans' secret weapons, the "Knickebein," and how the British dealt with it. Could anything be more fascinating? Turn to *The Hinge of Fate* (Vol. IV), on the battles of the Coral Sea and Midway. He boiled it all down from one of my own volumes—and handsomely acknowledged his debt in the preface—but I could never have done it so well myself. And the ringing conclusion to these two great naval battles is all Churchill:

> The annals of war at sea present no more intense, heart-shaking shock than these two battles, in which the qualities of the United States Navy and Air Force and the American race shone forth in splendour. The novel and hitherto utterly unmeasured conditions which air warfare had created made the speed of action and the twists of fortune more intense than has ever been witnessed before. But the bravery and self-devotion of the American airmen and sailors and the nerve and skill of their leaders was the foundation of all. As the Japanese Fleet withdrew to their far-off home ports their commanders knew not only that their aircraft-carrier struggle was irretrievably broken, but that they were confronted with a will-power and passion in the foe they had challenged worthy of the highest traditons of their Samurai ancestors and backed by a development of power, numbers, and science to which no limit could be set.

Note his use of vibrant words and phrases—splendour—twists of fortune—will-power, and passion; note the reference to history, of which he was always conscious even if, in this case, it was Japanese history; and he even gets in a tribute to American production and science. Not only sentence and paragraph structure but choice of words—*le mot juste*—are vital elements in Churchill's craft. Tens of thousands of people, not only English-speaking but from all parts of the world, read Churchill when they will read no other history of World War II. Churchill was not at Coral Sea or Midway; he had little time to know what went on in the Pacific; but he recognizes brave deeds and the effect of great decisions when he hears of them, and he places our achievements in the Pacific on the same plane as those of the sailors and soldiers of his King in Africa, Asia, and Europe.

According to the news release about the Nobel Prize, it was conferred on Churchill not only for his books but for his oratory. And his oratory is indeed superb. We all know his aphorisms such as "blood, sweat and tears." One of the finest set speeches I have ever listened to was his when given an honorary degree at Harvard in September 1943. Note the boldness and truth of this one paragraph:

> Twice in my lifetime the long arm of destiny has reached across the ocean and involved the entire life and manhood of the United States in a deadly struggle. There was no use saying: "We don't want it, we won't have it; our forebears left Europe to avoid those quarrels; we have founded a new world which has no contact with the old"—there was no use in that. The long arm reaches out remorselessly and everyone's existence, environment, and outlook undergo a swift and irresistible change.

After the official ceremonies were over Churchill was asked informally to address the young soldiers and sailors then training at the university. He was unprepared; he had not even been told that this was expected of him; but this is what he said, in part (and, remember, this was before Salerno, before Tarawa, before Normandy):

> I have no reason to suppose that the climax of the war has been reached. I have no reason to suppose that the heaviest sacrifices in blood and life do not lie before the armed forces of Britain and America. I know of no reason for supposing that the climax of the war has been reached even in Europe, and certainly not in Asia. . . . I bid you all good fortune and success, and I earnestly trust that when you find yourselves alongside our soldiers and sailors you will feel that we

are your worthy brothers in arms. And you shall know that
we will never tire nor weaken. We shall march with you into
every quarter of the globe to establish a reign of justice and
law among men.

In that time and setting this was the most eloquent extempore
address I have ever heard.

Nobody, and certainly not Churchill, will claim that his "Second
World War," of which the sixth and final volume will shortly appear, is "objective." He was too close to events, too much a part
of them. He had neither the time nor the staff to sift everything to
the bottom; consequently some assumptions of the time are accepted
as facts, when the facts turn out to be different. But the general
impression is correct. It is splendid history; magnanimous to our
enemies, understanding and generous to England's allies, even to
those who have sadly defected since 1945; vibrant with the passion
and fervor of the time; written in muscular, virile prose.

So, here's a "Hurrah!" for the Nobel Prize Committee, and a
three-times-three for "Winnie." And if any historian, British or
American, won't join in the cheer, let him be condemned to sit
forever in a college library, reading Ph.D. dissertations!

FAULKNER: SORCERER
OR SLAVE?

by Edith Hamilton

The renowned celebrator of the timeless world of the classics presents her critical views of the Nobel Prize-winning novelist and his novels about "ugly people in an ugly land."

JULY 12, 1952

"I DETEST NATURE," Picasso has said. He is the spokesman for the art of the age, our age, for the music we are listening to, the pictures we are looking at, the books we are reading. Today the usual and the normal, which is to say the natural, is being discarded. What is called abstract art has taken a foremost place. One of the most recent prizes was given to a sculptor for her figure of an animal shape, not like any animal that ever lived, but a representation of an indeterminate animal vaguely applicable to many kinds of living creatures. The sculptor had turned away from nature to depict an image she had conceived, a form existing only in her mind. When Picasso detests nature he is doing the same thing. He shuts out the detestable world his eyes show him and takes refuge in the inner world of himself where he perceives shapes only dimly connected with things that have actual existence.

Our artists are escaping from reality. This is no new thing, to be sure. In almost all ages there have been artists who escaped. What is new in our age is the direction they are taking. In the past a detestation of nature, a determination not to be dominated by fact, led persistently to the land of heart's desire where everyone and everything was good and true and beautiful. Now it leads to just the opposite, where nothing is good or true or beautiful. Of course one is just as much an escape as the other. It is just as far from reality to shut out all that is agreeable as to shut out all that is disagreeable. Both extremes are equally unreal, and both are equally romantic.

Romance is the refusal to accept things as they are, "the world being inferior to the soul," as Bacon says. All art bears either the romantic stamp or the classic. To the classic artist his chosen field is things as they are. He is repelled by anything unfamiliar and extraordinary, and he detests extremes. Greek art, of course, is the preeminent example of classic art. The Greeks had no desire whatever to turn away from nature. They did not see the usual and the normal as commonplace. The way they looked at them is perfectly exemplified in the statue of the girl bending over a basin to wash her hands. She is classic art in herself; beauty is embodied in a completely ordinary act. The Greeks saw beauty and significance in nature. If they took a romantic subject like the Iliad, they brought it down to earth and worked it out in ordinary surroundings which to them were not drab and dreary but interesting. Both trends, the classical and the romantic, have their dangers, which perpetually threaten to destroy them and often have destroyed them. The specter that haunts the classic artist is putting form ahead of spirit, style ahead of matter, polished convention ahead of free realism. The danger to the romantic, equally present whether he turns his back on ugliness or on loveliness, is sentimentality. It is easily recognized in the first case, but not in the second. There is a general impression that to describe things as dull and drab and unpleasant is realism and farthest removed from the roses and raptures of sentimentality. That is not true. The extremely unpleasant can be extremely sentimental. Sentimentality is always false sentiment. It is such a danger to the romantic artist because he has escaped from the domination of fact, and sentimentality is falsehood to fact. When an artist detests nature, he has thrown away his best defense against that danger. Nature is not sentimental.

When Edgar Lee Masters describes a baby:

> *She was some kind of a crying thing*
> *One takes in one's arms and all at once*
> *It slimes your face with its running nose,*
> *And voids its essence all over you,*
> *And there you stand smelling to heaven—*

he has fallen into one extreme of sentimental unreality as truly as Swinburne has into the other when he writes:

> *A baby's eyes—*
> *Their glance might cast out pain and sin,*

> *Their speech make dumb the wise,*
> *By mute glad god-head felt within*
> *A baby's eyes.*

Neither Masters nor Swinburne, of course, were in the least concerned with what a baby is really like. They had escaped from that limitation. Perhaps each in his way was seeking for some other truth than the truth of nature, but all we know is that the result was falsehood for both of them, pure sentimentality, as much in the case of the nasty baby as in the case of the baby with the momentous eyes.

Before the publication of the *Spoon River Anthology* Swinburne's was the prevailing mood. Thereafter the other extreme came into fashion. At present there is a brilliant group devoted to it, and the most brilliant of all is the Nobel Prize-winner William Faulkner. He is our leading romanticist today; he too detests nature.

Mr. Faulkner's novels are about ugly people in an ugly land. There is no beauty anywhere. Whether he deliberately excludes it or does not perceive it, no one can say; but at least he says himself that a blossoming pear tree in the moonlight looks like hair streaming up from the head of a drowned woman, each hair distinct in the water from the others. He describes the scent of a blooming shrub, still wet with dew, as sickening. To walk through the woodlands in summer in "a gloom dimmer than the gray desolation of November" is to feel "malicious little eyes" watching (birds? squirrels?) while under foot the oozing earth crawls with snakes.

But the land is worse, far worse, than all of these unpleasant features put together. It ruins the people it nourishes. A dark curse lies on it. It was "already tainted before any white man owned it . . . from that old world's corrupt and worthless twilight as though in the sailfulls of the old world's tainted wind which drove the ships." Columbus', presumably. The initial curse, connected with the dispossession of the Indians, appears to be—Mr. Faulkner is not quite clear about it—inherited by the North as well as the South, but its full effect is shown concentrated in the South. "Don't you see?" young Ike McCaslin cries in "The Bear." "Don't you see? This whole land, the whole South, is cursed, and all of us who derive from it, whom it ever suckled, lie under the curse."

The people, thus doomed, are like the land that dooms them. It is part of the fate that molds them. "Our rivers, our land: opaque, slow, violent, shaping and creating the life of man in its implacable and brooking image." At this point Poe comes irresistibly to mind, "The dank tarn of Auber—the misty mid region of Weir—the ghoul-haunted woodlands of Weir." It is the point in the realm of romance where extremes meet, Poe's lovely and lost Ulalume and Mr. Faulkner's curse-ridden men.

And his women? No one adjective or two can describe them. I confess his attitude to them puzzles me. I know nothing like it in literature outside of *The Golden Bough*. Frazer's account of the way some primitive tribes feel toward young women, the mixture of violent attraction and equally violent repulsion, is just what Mr. Faulkner feels. Young women are not really human to him. He calls them "the Symbol of the ancient and eternal Snake." They are an embodied Menace to Man. Old they are more tolerable, but even in childhood, earliest childhood, they are already initiates of darkly secret rites. "They are born," Mr. Faulkner concludes, "already bored with what a boy approaches only at fourteen or fifteen with blundering and aghast trembling."

There is something familiar back of all this. As I see Mr. Faulkner, he was brought up in a community where religion took the form of condemning most things: Thou shalt not . . . I see him listening as a little boy to accounts of a jealous God, an implacable judge, who punished sin by inflicting suffering, before whose "awful and irrevocable judgment seat"—so he calls it—trembling human beings would have to stand even though they were "predestined," foredoomed to be saved or lost. Most of them to be lost, for humanity was born sinful. The only way to escape inexorable punishment here and hereafter was through the grace of God, mysteriously bestowed upon some, those chosen out for eternal bliss, and as mysteriously withheld from others, those not chosen. A man could not earn this saving grace; he could never deserve it; and yet without it he could not resist the evil which infected him on the day of his birth. Nevertheless if it was not given him the fault was his.

These are ideas which have in many periods darkened the world. Children brought up in their shadow will not be apt to see the things that are lovely or many things that are good. In such an atmosphere beauty and enjoyment are suspect, and sex of course is still worse. The relation between the sexes, indeed, always becomes a crucial difficulty. It had to be tolerated. There had to be children, fleshly though their origin was. At this point the Church could be counted on to give a helping hand: marriage was blest of God. Somehow they always made out, but only superficially. All that had to do with the flesh was tainted and all that had to do with sex was the most fleshly and the most tainted of all.

This was a heavy burden to be placed on the shoulders of a little boy who thought about the things he was told. How could a blooming pear tree give him pleasure? Pleasant things were not only futile; they could be a fair cloak hiding what was ugly, and of course the cloak soon ceased to be fair. The eye can be trained not to see. Beauty and all things desirable can vanish out of sight.

Inevitably, gifted as he was, Mr. Faulkner worked his way through this maze of confused instincts and feelings and thoughts. He did it by a logic of his own. People were predestined; that part was true. They did not act of themselves; they were driven. "A volitionless servant of fatality," he calls one of his characters. His own peculiar twist was that they were always predestined to hell. Heaven was nonexistent.

So too he had his own way of dealing with the conventional but precarious balancing act, aided and abetted by the church, between a point where women were spiritually sexless, chastely elevated above the flesh and only yielding to the gross male, and a point where they were shameless Sex embodied, tempting man to his fall. That tenuous connection between contradictions he cleared away by the reasonable method of dismissing the first kind of woman, but temperamentally he cannot take to the middle of the road, and so he swept all females together, little girls too. Eves, every one of them, forever holding out the apple to bewildered Adams.

Of course he repudiated the doctrines back of these notions. Mr. Faulkner will not be found in any little church today listening to the imprecatory psalms. But the ideas of God and man they express molded him and made him what he is. He is to the very depths of him a Puritan, a violently twisted Puritan, a perverted Puritan, and that means something very strange indeed.

In *The Sound and the Fury*, Quentin finds out that his sister has been having relations with men. "Have there been very many?" he asks and she answers, "I don't know. Too many," and begs him to look after their father. With that a plan to help them all leaps into his mind. "I'll tell Father," he says to her, "then it'll have to be because you love Father then we'll have to go away amid the pointing and the horror the clean flame I'll make you say we did you thought it was them but it was me." But, extraordinarily, the idea of incest between his son and daughter is not comforting to father. In fact he rejects it. He tells Quentin, "i [sic] think you are too serious to give

me any cause for alarm you wouldn't have felt driven to the ex-
pedient of telling me you have committed incest otherwise did you
try to make her do it." Quentin answers No: "i was afraid she might
and then it wouldn't have done any good but if i could tell you we
did it would have been so and then the others wouldn't be so." The
father accepts this as making the matter perfectly clear and tells his
son approvingly that he is not lying now. After a little disquisition
on the unimportance of everything, he bids Quentin, "go on up to
cambridge right away" and "you will remember that for you to go
to harvard has been your mother's dream since you were born and
no compson [the family name is Compson] has ever disappointed
a lady."

Comment seems unnecessary, except perhaps to point out that the
passage is notably characteristic of Mr. Faulkner. All that chiefly
distinguishes him is there, his stylistic vagaries along with his peculiar brand of Puritanism, his twisted notions of good and bad, and
his kinship with the more romantic writers among the earlier Victo-
rians, whose heroes also would never disappoint a lady.

Back of the extremely bleak view he takes of all things here below
stands the conviction, older than Puritanism, as old as antiquity,
present in all ages, among all nations and races, that there is an
inseparable trinity: the world and all that is therein, the flesh and
all that are born therefrom, and the devil.

His special gift as a writer—and it is a great gift—is that he can
make anything live, no matter how ordinary and trivial, if he chooses
to do so. When he takes in hand what he deals with best, a flood,
a fire, a storm, he can carry his reader away with him past all damn-
ing points of criticism. Indeed he can do that without any aid from
convulsions of nature. In his most popular novel, *Sanctuary,* he is
able to sweep one through most improbable events and people and
keep up the interest which, in the preposterous circumstances the
book spotlights, is an achievement.

Sanctuary, however, was a new experiment for Mr. Faulkner. In
his earlier novels, usually considered his best, which were, with one
exception, written before that highly colored piece of fiction, he
paints a drab, monotonous world. Necessarily so, for there are no
contrasts in the picture. There is violence, indeed, and cruelty and
all manner of sexual doings, but they merge into the general scene,
dimmed like everything else. They are an ugly, insignificant part of
what is ugly and without significance. All these books merge with
one another. There is the same heavy gray atmosphere, the same

undiversified country, the same inconsequent little human beings making the same futile gestures; the writer's art used not to heighten and magnify, but to dull and diminish. Plot, character, the story-teller's tools from Homer on to the latest *Saturday Evening Post* serial, do not interest Mr. Faulkner. How many readers could give a clear account of what happens in any of these novels? Certainly not a single individual in them stands out and is alive. Power of choice, the great individualizer, Mr. Faulkner will not allow them. They are all volitionless servants of fatality, and thereby unimportant, even to their creator.

Wherein his special gift is most brilliantly shown, what he can make come alive most vividly, is an experience,—just that, an experience which the reader feels as if it were his own, independent of the person in the book it is attached to, who is there only to give it a locality. There is no feeling necessarily of sympathy with the character or even of understanding him, but only of being one-self put through that suspense, that terror, that remorse.

It is a gift few writers have had. It is especially Mr. Faulkner's for two reasons. First, his characters with few exceptions are not sympathetic or understandable, so that it is easy to detach the emotion from the embodiment of it as it would not be to detach horror from Raskolnikov or passion from Anna Karenina. In their case it is what they are feeling that takes possession of us; we have forgotten ourselves. None of Mr. Faulkner's characters have that independent life. The second reason is that he avoids the profounder emotions. Love and the suffering bound up with it is not a subject he cares to treat. It is absent even when its presence is urgently required, as in *Requiem for a Nun* where a baby who has been murdered drops out of the picture which has for its center the baby's mother. Her suffering is concentrated on herself; the baby is forgotten.

With the power he has to tell a story, his ability to create tension where he chooses, the storyteller's best gift, he seems deliberately to set up obstacles in the way of his story. His obscurities, his sentences that make no sense, are herein a minor matter. He will never put into incomprehensible words anything that is essential to under-standing what he wants to get over. But he will keep on interrupting it, breaking it in two. He loves to release a torrent of words that have nothing to do with what has gone before. Suddenly, for no apparent reason, they rush out, tumbling over each other, eddying around the reader like a flood, carrying him this way and that, all sense of direction lost. The feeling of hurry is increased by an absence of capital letters and periods. The impression given is that the writer cannot stop to end a sentence or write a capital. The reader finds himself breathlessly trying to keep up with him while holding on to the story left pages behind. The sense of immediacy, which Mr. Faulkner when he wants can give to anything, has without warning been transferred to some unlikely and irrelevant account of an ancient train of cars, perhaps, or the building of a jail, or the contents of an old ledger, all of them there as if the surge of words, words, words had taken possession of the writer too and was driving him on along with his reader.

These interruptions to the story are much less distressing, of course, when there is nothing of importance to be interrupted. If one is reading a tale told by an idiot, for instance, one does not especially mind being shifted away from the subject, such as it is, to a description of fishing. But in Mr. Faulkner's latest novel, *Intruder in the Dust,* there is, surprisingly, a good plot, even an exciting plot, how a boy saves a Negro from being lynched for a murder he did not commit, and there are scenes in it as tense as anything Mr. Faulkner has written. It is infuriating, when one is waiting to see if the boy digging up the murdered man will be quick enough to stop the lynching, to be plunged into long pages describing over and over again what Mr. Faulkner calls accurately "the land fixed in monotonous repetition." One is reduced to wishing that the story could be printed in some special kind of type and the meanderings of Mr. Faulkner's thought in some other kind. Or better still, that he had employed earlier the same technique as in his latest book, *Requiem for a Nun.* This is a play, and it appears that when Mr. Faulkner comes to the drama, even he cannot stop at a breathless moment to give the history of an old jail, then return to the moment and go on to another crisis and in the middle of it pick up the jail again. He has put all the material about the jail together and simply interlarded the acts of the play with it. The play is almost as easy to read as if the other material were not there.

This play is the only book he has published since he received the Nobel Prize. At the award ceremonies the speech he made was notably brief, less than a page in any of his books, and yet it may well outlive them all. "That singular swing to elevation" which Schopenhauer noted in great literature, is as marked in it as it is absent from his writings. As he spoke he came back to what he called "the old universal truths, love and honor and pity and pride and compassion and sacrifice," from which he has wandered so far in his books. Without these, he said, a writer "writes not of love, but of lust." In what book ever did he himself write of love, and in how many books has he not written of lust? He went on to say that such a writer, one who has not learned "the old verities and truths of the heart," will deal with "defeats in which nobody loses anything of value, of victories without hope and worst of all without pity and compassion."

Many figures in his books throng to mind with these words: Rosa Coldfield in *Absalom, Absalom!* the final defeat of her death after a life of so little value that for forty-three years it had been only "a stubborn and amazed outrage"; Henry Sutpen's victory over Bon in the same book which brought him back to live "as if he were already a corpse; waking or sleeping it would be the same forever as long as he lived." These two can stand for all the victories and defeats Mr. Faulkner has recounted. No values are ever at stake; no victory ever brings hope or pity or compassion. Everything there is ends in futility. Darl says toward the end of *As I Lay Dying*: "How do our lives ravel out into the no-wind, no-sound, the weary gestures wearily recapitulant, echoes of old compulsions with no-hand on no-strings; in sunset we fall into furious attitudes, dead gestures of dolls." The passage deserves quoting not for itself but because it expresses Mr. Faulkner's creed. It could be matched over and over again in his books.

On the other side there is only courage. His characters are helpless. Their "every breath is a fresh cast with dice loaded against them," by "the dark diceman" who cares nothing for human anguish. Even so, they accept their inevitable doom with heads carried high. That is all.

In his speech Mr. Faulkner said that the writer's duty and privilege is to help men endure by lifting their hearts, not only by reminding them of what is good and great and enduring, but also by being a pillar of strength to them in their struggles toward it. In his books he reminds us only of the futility of all things human, and the cerain defeat of all men's struggles. When he accepted the prize in those words of singular nobility and profound truth he was pronouncing the condemnation of the work which had won him the prize.

The speech met with wide acclaim. It seemed to reveal depths he had never sounded before, and what he would do next was eagerly awaited. *Requiem for a Nun* was published in the following year. Its great importance comes from the fact that it was written after the speech.

Two women are the protagonists in the play, a Negro prostitute and murderer, and the girl who was a chief figure in *Sanctuary*, Temple Drake, grown up now and married. The thesis Mr. Faulkner sets forth is twofold. One, the less prominent, is that old but terrible companion to so many religions, expiation. Sin can be expiated; the debt incurred thereby to God can be wiped out if the sinner suffers enough. Temple, induced to confess all the evil ever in her, says she has confessed for no purpose except to suffer: "Just suffering. Not for anything; just suffering. Just because it's good for you." Suffering as such is good, cleansing, powerful in itself to make white what was black. Temple must confess although her confession will do nothing for anybody: "We don't come here to save Nancy. What we came here for is just to give Temple Drake a good fair honest chance to suffer—just anguish for the sake of anguish."

This is the idea deepest in the Puritan ascetic, in all asceticism. Men of themselves can wipe out evil and achieve goodness if they are willing to torture themselves. They do not need forgiveness. "I have blotted out thy transgressions as a thick cloud and as a cloud thy sins: therefore return unto me." Mr. Faulkner's guilt-ridden men, curse-driven men, could never accept anything so full of pity and compassion, so natural in a Father to His children, as unearned forgiveness.

Expiation, however, plays a minor part in the play. The main thesis is that the end justifies the means, that ancient falsehood which has been the cause of the most hateful deeds men have done to each other. It is stated directly and clearly. Mr. Faulkner has dropped all his mannerisms. He tells the story as simply as possible, and his special gift of making an experience come alive has never been more strikingly shown. He needs no actors to carry over to his audience what he is telling them. They are not watching suffering people; they are suffering themselves, without any help from theatrical devices, almost it would seem—the dialogue is pitched so low, the language is so ordinary—without any help from the author.

In the last scene, which is in a prison the night before the Negro's execution, she and Temple talk to each other in brief sentences, the thought hardly expressed, the words completely commonplace, but intensity is there, rising, ever rising, through all they say.

And yet the text of this sermon Mr. Faulkner is preaching is not that a crime is pardonable, but that it is admirable, if it is seen by the criminal as the only way to stop another crime conceived of as greater. Nancy, the Negro, strangles Temple's six-months old baby because she believes that the child's death will stop Temple from eloping with a blackmailer and a thief. Nancy is the Nun who is lifted by her deed up to a level high above the others.

She has murdered a baby, with what Mr. Faulkner calls "that simple indeviable aim," and thereby she has become one with the saints and martyrs. Temple's friend and lawyer tells her that Nancy is dying "to prove that little children shall be intact, unanguished, untorn, unterrified." At the very end the odds are that she has saved Temple's soul too.

What has become of the great ideas in the Nobel Prize speech, "the old verities and truths of the heart, the old universal truths"? The lawyer's speech is the very acme of sentimentality. The play not only culminates in it, but is founded upon it. The danger which threatens all those who detest nature and escape from reality has dogged Mr. Faulkner always. In his latest book it has overtaken him and overwhelmed him.

MY FATHER

by Monica Mann

*A word portrait of Thomas Mann, with some special insights into
his character, by his daughter.*

JUNE 4, 1955

MY FATHER WILL BE eighty years old on June 6. I got to know him
when he was forty. If I was naughty he would shame me with an
admonishing lift of his brow, a gentle tap of his ring and manicured
fingernails, and his clearsighted, penetrating look. You can be sure
that I was ashamed. The mere idea of it was enough for me.

The mere thought of it had its own power. When I went to the
cellar where Lina would be shining his shoes—rather ordinary shoes,
to be sure—they seemed something very much alive to me. I imagined
how these shoes—meticulously tied—walked in sharp rhythm over
the paths, carefully sidestepping all puddles and stones. How
thoughtfully they were scraped on the mat and lined parallel in
front of the door. My father's belongings had an inescapable fate.
They radiated life. His energy, clarity, subtle irony, and inner
warmth always remained true to the objects belonging to him. The
desk laden with ornaments and utensils reflected that elongated,
gold-bespectacled, dreaming face of Father as characteristically as his
yellow Empire chair—cigar smoke and throat clearing, the dog's
leash—a shrill musical whistle, the cup of tea—a comfortably
measured sipping, the silken housecoat—a disciplined *Gemütlichkeit,*
the Bluethner grand piano—gentle *Tristan* melodies.

Everything has its time and importance. Umbrella and walking
stick seemed to look expectantly only to him, as did the cigar trim-
mer, the Waterman pen, the gingercakes, the Goethe volumes. The
black-and-gold pendulum clock seemed to wait only for the moment
when his dependable, caressing hands would wind it. If Papa was
sick the clock looked hurt and depressed in its corner. Equally hurt
was the patient, because the routine had abandoned and betrayed
him: he could not work. It hung over his slim, unshaven, somewhat

trembling face like a cloud. My father always wants to work. Work is his saintly friend from whom he will never part. Since I have known my father there has hardly been a day that he did not work.

He was always delicate and susceptible, but, yet, basically healthy, I guess. I believe that there are delicate men who have, as it were, a secret inner vitality and who are sensitive and possessed of a deep-seated, immeasurable calmness. My father is one of these men. Whether there are ups and downs at home or abroad, whether he is tired or sad, it does not matter—after breakfast he will sit down with his saintly friend to work.

In every will there is pleasure. Without pleasure one cannot will. There is, for instance, a will to live which is also the love to live. Therefore, the will to work is also the love to work. This strong drive bespoke my father's nature and became his nature. At heart he is a gay man. He loves to be everywhere and everything. When he writes, life belongs to him. He hunts it like an eagle and dips his pen into its blood. But he does it out of love. That beautiful eagle's blood continues to live in his books though the eagle must die. He is a sportsman of the spirit, tenacious and courageous. He is also a child who plays with blocks, puts one on top of the other until a cathedral stands in front of him.

My father's work consists of linking life which he experiences—and he does have some experiences—with that which he does not experience so that it becomes art. He hardly knows how to distinguish one from the other. At times he thinks he has invented something but has really experienced it, or believes he has pictured something he lived when he really invented it. This matter of invention is not very clear at all because it may represent a probing or prophesying of something that exists or will exist, or because one might have experienced it before birth. Creative writing is extremely mysterious.

When I sit together with my father he radiates a deep inner curiosity that suggests a sense of knowing. It is almost uncanny. His silence—he is frequently silent—demands expression but actually seems superfluous. It seems at best like an affirmation of what he knows; his curiosity is pretended and polite. He plays the child which sees and hears everything for the first time. Somehow he may be one, but a child as deep as a well.

Once, in *Hamlet,* we saw the duel scene when Hamlet's arm bleeds. Later Dad said to the actor, "That was blood on your arm, wasn't it?" The actor answered debunkingly, "It was toothpaste."

I think that at that moment my father experienced a real disillusion. Even though he was fully aware of all the technical stunts and tricks of the art, he faced it with *pure faith* and thus felt deceived and betrayed. Yet in such gall as this deception displayed and as it was admitted by the actor, he felt some deep satisfaction. What a devil of a fellow he is! How he leads people around by the nose! With toothpaste he makes them see royal Danish blood. Dad may have also thought, I create my world for you, and you believe in it. That is basically the same sort of pretense.

In his intense and almost pious dedication to creating the world in words there is something of a childish, even diabolical glee in imitating, in nose-pulling, in bluffing. I could well imagine that if my father should see a piece of jewelry of unique beauty and unique value and then should see another identical to a hair, but false, he would lovingly look at the imitation, exclaiming, That is really wonderful! For its cunningness I prefer it to the genuine. Moreover, I keep it with a better conscience since the irreplaceable value of the genuine would almost be a sinful burden on me.

That's how it is with the genuine and the imitated life. The genuine is relieved of its burden by the imitated, depreciated in its worth, but also raised. You might read a book of Conrad's and think you were at sea. That is enough. And yet the reality of the sea itself was thereby made keener. Since the day of the phonograph record it is easier to appreciate live music. Since my father lived in the imitated world, he found the real world twice as exciting. When he would leave the room of alchemy he would breathe real fresh air with twice the warmth and pleasure, but in the long run it would tire and irritate him, even overpower him. He had then to exchange it again for the fictitious world, again and again, but thus one was set afire by the other.

Nor was he in any way just a doctor of alchemy, but a real man of life. Few loved as much as he to take walks in the lovely countryside, to look at beautiful store windows—particularly at nice leather and pastry goods—or to see a child laugh, hear an old woman curse, a boy sing, the wind roar, or to watch the glow of the autumn foliage, flowers in bloom, birds in flight, two dogs at play. But he was also fascinated by the appealing, the strange, and the sad—he breathed in everything and found it unexpectedly again in his study.

I was never present when my father did his writing. I suspect that he used a magically prepared paper that would whimper softly when he wrote something wrong. For he seemed to have a great respect for the paper—his manuscript looked so clean; practically nothing was revised. He wrote everything correctly on the first try in his adroit, profound gothic hand which in its abstractness was difficult to read. But the drawn symbols seemed to be in rhythm with the thought.

He never wrote with a typewriter. Nor did he ever drive a car. Yet Dad is no old-fashioned man. He would dare to accept an invitation from the president of Mars and risk the voyage with armor and monster mask. Even without that he has enjoyed flying. He has said that it felt like being in a luxurious sanatorium attended and cared for tenderly by lovely stewardesses. Many times he has flown over the Atlantic and across the United States.

He has never been in a war, never really under fire, but in spirit he has been. Certainly he must have fought with himself and battled courageously for harmony in art. Once somebody marveled at the patience with which he carries his work to completion, and I heard him reply, "Patience is courage." I know roughly what he meant, and yet I am inclined to think that he mistook this courage a little for the calm and resoluteness with which I have credited him. Out of such calm came the rhythm, continuity, validity, and timelessness of his work.

Time has never touched him at all. With his eyes fastened upon the eternal sky he has let this nervous, fleeting something pass by the window. Time cannot age him. My father is not a hunchbacked old man with a long white beard and shaky hands—on the contrary. Hardly gray, erect, his hands steady, his mind and voice clear as ever. Perhaps with time his inward radiant glance has become more confident. I think that nowadays my father often looks satisfied.

Perhaps it is only today that the marriage of his work and his life has been consummated. They have become harmonious. Maybe in the past there was, in spite of everything, some jealousy, disunity, and strangeness between work and life. Only after a long, steady, side-by-side existence, while both proved themselves to each other, have they finally been reconciled and wedded. Now they know that one existed for the other, life for work, work for life. And recognizing the latter may have imparted kindliness and assurance to his eyes.

MISTER HEGGEN

by Victor Cohn

Thomas O. Heggen, the young author of Mister Roberts, *was found dead in the bathtub of his New York apartment on the morning of May 19, 1949. On the washstand of the bathroom stood an almost empty bottle of sleeping pills. The twenty-nine-year-old writer had experienced remarkable success since resuming civilian life after the war. His novel had already sold some 850,000 copies, and the play (on which he collaborated with Joshua Logan) was still attracting large audiences after more than 500 performances on Broadway. The explanation of such a tragedy as Heggen's may be simple, or it may be complicated—and it may never be made. Here is one small clue to the puzzle, contributed by a classmate and friend of Heggen's. Victor Cohn is the well-known science writer for the Minneapolis* Tribune, *winner of many awards and of much praise for his work in the field of scientific and medical journalism.*

JUNE 11, 1949

WHEN I FIRST SAW Tom Heggen he was slouched and wearing an old green corduroy jacket. That was in the fall of 1939, and he was a junior at the University of Minnesota. During the next two years he was seldom without the jacket or the slouch. He was hollow-cheeked and hollow-chested and more sensitive to the truth about the people around him than anyone I have ever known.

We sat together every afternoon on the rim of the copy desk of the *Minnesota Daily,* our college paper, in the basement of worn, old Pillsbury hall. It was a place full of memories and traditions, but Heggen did not care about clothes or tradition or journalism classes or anything else that most of us took somewhat seriously.

Studies and grades meant nothing to him, but he would skim a text and listen in on a bull session, and pass an examination the next morning. Drawing partly on a few library books but mostly on his imagination, he would produce a long term paper in a single four- or five-hour session at a *Daily* typewriter.

Heggen took journalism because he considered writing and news-paper or magazine work the easiest way he knew to exist and do what he pleased. He gave the subject as little attention as any-thing else—except the informal study of people, serious fiction, and serious carousing—yet he was easily expert at headline writing, editing, make-up, and typography. He thought most of his teachers and most of his classmates were fools, but he had tremendous respect, even reverence, for anyone or anything he considered in-telligent and honest. The best works of Ernest Hemingway were in this class. Arthur Koestler was in it. So were Thomas Wolfe, F. Scott Fitzgerald, the Marx brothers, a bottle, or a brief romance (never a very long one) with an attractive woman.

He spent much of his time in silence, either watching and listen-ing or simply immersed in what was partly deep thought and partly almost a trance. He had great black moods. He was greatly concerned with people and their pitiful little attempts to lead simple, reason-ably happy lives in a confusing world. Heggen never said or wrote a word on this subject except after long pondering.

And he could write. You hear it said of many writers that their "words flow," but I have personally never known it true of anyone but Heggen.

I never knew him to write about anything but tragedy. The story I remember most clearly was about a boy on the bum. The boy's close friend was killed by a freight train, or in some similar way, and the story was about this boy's terrible, wordless sorrow. If Heg-gen had a feeling for any human emotion, it was pain. He could brood over other people's little troubles, seldom his own, for days.

His great work, *Mister Roberts*, is a tragedy. It has funny passages —and the play made from it emphasizes these—but if it had included funny things alone, it would have been just another profitable war book. The real story in *Mister Roberts* is the story of a young man whose life and dreams were shattered by the war, who had a large and precious chunk of time snatched irretrievably out of his life— and who therefore suffered infinitely from the long boredom of war because he kept this painful knowledge pent up, never letting it become a surface thought for an instant, and even developing the remarkable facility of standing silent for hours on end (during watch on a Navy ship) without thinking a single thought of any kind.

The humor in *Mister Roberts*—and there is not much more hilari-ous reading anyplace—is all cruel humor, funny because it is tragic.

The men on the ship are all heartsick and unhappy, and their escapades are like hysterical laughter at a funeral. It is the eternal humor of the drunken porter in *Macbeth* or the sad clown of Charlie Chaplin.

Mister Roberts was itself the result of months at sea. During four years in the Navy Tom Heggen was on one ship or another most of the time. I think he must have thought the book out over a long, long period, one thought at a time, then one day sat down and started writing, in as much comfort as one can achieve in a lieutenant's little cabin.

He gave me the manuscript of much of *Mister Roberts* just before it was published and said, "Here's a half-assed novel I've written." The book was printed just as he set it to paper on first writing, with only a small penciled change here and there.

During the entire war Tom was concerned with the problem of expressing the war's whole spirit in one novel—a sort of *A Farewell to Arms* of World War II. He said often that he did not think it could be done. There were too many men in this war with too many different experiences. I don't think he ever changed this opinion. Yet I felt the first time I read the book that he had succeeded. The one feeling common to every man in the service—expressed either in Heggen's deep introspection or in the average sailor's and GI's lonely letters home—was the feeling of losing out on the good life you had coming, of being caught hopelessly in powerful events. The feeling was common to those who stormed the atolls and those who never heard a shot.

Heggen does not say this specifically, but his whole book cries it. I think it is the only book of either war that does, and I think that by Tom's own standard it is painfully intelligent and honest.

THE MAGIC OF
UNCLE REMUS

by Eileen and Robert Mason Pollock

*More than three quarters of a century ago Joel Chandler Harris,
a young Atlanta newspaperman, created Uncle Remus. Even today
the stories are translated and read around the world, for the characters in them easily survived the decline that usually afflicts dialect tales. They have innate humor and earthy wisdom that are as
pure as they ever were. In this story the Pollocks describe a visit
to the Harris homestead.*

FEBRUARY 18, 1956

ON A RECENT TRIP to Atlanta, Georgia, we reacquainted ourselves
with one of the most memorable characters ever to walk through a
storybook—Uncle Remus. We had run across his trail in various
parts of the world, for his appeal has leaped the barrier of both
ocean and language. In Egypt, India, Spain, Finland, Brazil, and
England he holds an enthusiastic audience, and in Norway there is
a children's radio series based on his stories.

We had first met Uncle Remus as children: a lean old Negro
philosopher—his weatherbeaten face wreathed with a fringe of
white beard—who sat outside the slave quarters and wove enchanting stories for the plantation owner's seven-year-old son. Suddenly
it all seemed very near again and very real. And the stories themselves, as Uncle Remus had told them in a colorful dialect sprinkled
with words like *reckembembunce* or *slanchendicklar*, seemed nearest of all.

His were tales that turned nature into a fantastic fairyland with
animals who acted and spoke like human beings. The "creeturs"
of Uncle Remus's world had formal names: Brer Rabbit, Brer Fox,
Sis Wolf, Sis Cow, or just plain "Mister"—Mister Lion, Mister
Rooster—and with elaborate formality they addressed each other by
their full titles at every encounter. It never occurred to us to doubt

437

that Brer Tarrypin carried an umbrella or Sis Goose wore spectacles and an apron, for Uncle Remus made it all sound plausible.

Brer Rabbit, Uncle Remus's most popular character, was no ordinary bunny. Sly, mischievous, clever, and under all circumstances appealing, Brer Rabbit "smokin' his seegyar" or "chawin' his terbacker" moved lightheartedly from one adventure to another, somehow managing to wriggle out of each dangerous situation by using his head, for, as Uncle Remus explained, under Brer Rabbit's hat was "a mighty quick-thinkin' appleratus."

Brer Rabbit was much on our mind as we drove out to Wren's Nest, home of Joel Chandler Harris, who created Uncle Remus over three quarters of a century ago. There on the lawn stood a large, colorful signboard, showing Uncle Remus perched on a stool with a little boy opposite him.

He could well have been spinning the story in which Brer Rabbit found himself solidly stuck to the Tar Baby—a figure made of soft tar mixed "wid some turkentime"—which Brer Fox, his old enemy, had rigged to trap him. "I'm gwine ter bobbycue you dis day, sho," the fox gleefully boasted.

But the impish, sassy little rabbit slyly planted an idea in the mind of his captor: " 'I don't keer w'at you do wid me, Brer Fox,' sezee, 'Roas' me, Brer Fox, but don't fling me in dat brierpatch.'

" 'Hit's so much trouble fer ter kindle a fier, Brer Fox,' sezee, 'dat I speck I'll hatter hang you.'

" 'Hang me des ez high as you please, Brer Fox,' sezee, 'but do fer de Lord's sake don't fling me in dat brierpatch,' sezee."

More frantic pleases convinced Brer Fox that this was the ideal punishment for Brer Rabbit before making a meal of him. The rest is history. Flung into the brierpatch, where he knew Brer Fox dared not venture, Brer Rabbit "holler out: 'Bred en bawn in a brierpatch, Brer Fox—bred en bawn in a brierpatch!' en wid dat he skip out des ez lively ez a cricket in de embers."

We were still gazing at the signboard when a busload of school children drew up before it. They had traveled more than 200 miles to visit this memorial where thousands flock each year from every state in the Union and countries as far away as Australia and Japan.

Like us, they journey to find the spirit of Uncle Remus and to see mementoes of Joel Chandler Harris, the young newspaperman who once lived here and who, seventy-six years ago, gave literary life to Uncle Remus in the columns of the Atlanta *Constitution*. Almost overnight Harris became an internationally famous author. The only man who refused to acknowledge that fame was Harris himself. From the time he was a boy he had been shy and modest. Success changed nothing. When one of his small sons came to him in tears because he had heard his father called a "genius" and thought it meant something bad, Harris consoled him with a chuckle. The lad could dry his eyes, he pointed out—there was not a word of truth in the accusation!

Some of the tales of Uncle Remus have been translated into Swedish, French, Bengali, Dutch, Spanish, Japanese, and a number of African dialects; the total number of books is estimated to be well over a million. To satisfy the growing demand for these stories, Houghton Mifflin recently brought out an 875-page book, the first to contain the complete tales of Uncle Remus. These tales have not only entertained myriads of readers but have made an important contribution to the science of folklore, for the fables told by Southern slaves in America have been discovered in similar versions in Siam, Egypt, the Arab countries, and South America. Some of them appear in the mythology of American Indians, and even feature a mischievous rabbit who might be Brer Rabbit's twin. The mystery of where the fables originated has remained unsolved, but one thing is certain: Uncle Remus struck a chord in his unique renditions of them and is doubly loved because of it.

Uncle Remus was the inspiration for Walt Disney's full-length motion picture, *Song of the South,* and of his internationally syndicated cartoon strip peopled with Brer Rabbit, Brer Fox, Brer B'ar, and the rest of the colorful "creeturs."

On the library wall of Wren's Nest today hangs a faded picture of "Uncle" George Terrell, a slave on a plantation called Turnwold near the village of Eatonton, Georgia, where Harris was born on December 9, 1848. When work was done and night enveloped the plantation young Joel would make his way down to the slave quarters to sit in the flickering firelight and listen wide-eyed to Uncle George and the other slaves spin tales that had come down to them from their fathers and grandfathers.

Joel drank in fascinating animal yarns that ran the gamut from an explanation of why Mister Possum has no hair on his tail (it was left behind in Brer B'ar's teeth when Mister Possum beat a fast retreat) to Brer Rabbit's defeat of Mister Lion by luring him to a pool and prodding him into attacking his own snarling reflection in the water. But there was more to the stories than near-violence: there was laughter, and an earthy, chuckle-provoking wisdom that was to color the character of Uncle Remus two decades later. Once when the little boy seemed overly impressed with the strength of the elephant and the ferocity of the tiger, Uncle Remus sagely pointed out that Brer Rabbit could outdo them both, for, " 'Tain't de biggest en de strongest dat does de mostest in dis world. De cuckleburr got needer life ner lim', yit when it git in de sheep wool it kin travel fast ez de sheep."

In the dimly lighted hall of Wren's Nest we saw the cavernous rolltop desk that once sat in the office of the Atlanta *Constitution* where Uncle Remus was born. Harris had been asked to carry on a humor feature abandoned by another writer, but he was unhappy with someone else's brainchild. His mind went back to Turnwold and the songs and stories of the slaves, whose rich accents still echoed clearly in his ears. Out of those memories he brought to life Uncle Remus.

As newspapers around the nation began to reprint the stories, Americans who had known the Southern Negro only as a broad caricature in a minstrel show discovered the poetry, imagination, and sensitivity which were blended into the humor of the genuine article. Yet when a representative of the Appleton Publishing Company journeyed from New York with an offer to put the Uncle Remus stories in a book, Harris was doubtful that they would be popular. But his colleagues on the newspaper were so enthusiastic that some months before the book appeared they circulated a prospectus among the paper's employes urging them to buy a copy of *Uncle Remus, His Songs and Sayings.*

By the time the third volume of Uncle Remus was ready for publication Harris had other things he wanted to write. He came to a decision: Uncle Remus had spun his last tale; his voice would be heard no more. But he failed to reckon with the public. He was deluged with pleas to let the beloved old man go on recounting his delightful stories.

It was an appeal Harris could not ignore, and the world expressed its appreciation. A steady stream of notables made their way up the long walk of Wren's Nest to pay tribute to Joel Chandler Harris: James Whitcomb Riley, Joaquin Miller, Walter Hines Page, even the President of the United States, Theodore Roosevelt. Andrew Carnegie, visiting in 1906, wanted to meet the man who "has given a helping hand to all the world. He's won the hearts of all children, and that's glory enough for any man."

Carnegie was right. Today, almost fifty years after Harris's death, children are still enthralled with the magic of Uncle Remus. Like the laughing youngsters around us in Wren's Nest gazing at a replica of the "brierpatch" and Brer Rabbit's descendants "lippity-clippitin'" inside its fenced enclosure, children around the world look at bobtailed bunnies and remember Uncle Remus's explanation of how Brer Rabbit lost his fine bushy tail. They recall how he met Brer Fox "amblin' along wid a big string er fish," and being "monstus fon' er minners" himself, took his old enemy's advice on how to catch some: "Go ter de creek atter sundown, en drap his tail in de water en set dar twel day-light, en den draw up a whole armful er fishes."

Brer Fox neglected to mention the creek would freeze overnight. Brer Rabbit discovered this for himself in the morning when he tried to pull his tail from the water and left it behind in the ice—according to Uncle Remus, "dat w'at make all deze yer bobtail rabbits w'at you see hoppin' en skaddlin' thoo de woods."

Logical? It seemed so years ago when as children we read the tale on a rainy afternoon. And as we glanced out the window of Wren's Nest at the bobtailed rabbits it still made a kind of magic, enchanted sense. Suddenly we realized the charm of Uncle Remus is like that—you never outgrow him. We had journeyed back into memories of our childhood to find him—only to discover that we had never lost him at all.

POOR PILGRIM,
POOR STRANGER

by Robert Tallant

*One of the strangest cases of a double life was revealed when the
author known as William March died a few years ago in New
Orleans. He was one of the most widely anthologized short-story
writers of our time, known especially for the first one he ever
wrote, "The Little Wife." His novel about World War I Marines,
Company K, was highly praised when it came out in 1933. The
other William March was—well, read this almost incredible tale by
the Southern author, Robert Tallant.*

JULY 17, 1954

THERE WAS A SHEET OF PAPER in his typewriter. At the top of it he
had typed the heading "Poor Pilgrim, Poor Stranger," and beneath
it he had written this paragraph:

> The time comes in the life of each of us when we realize
> that death awaits us as it awaits others, that we will receive
> at the end neither preference nor exemption. It is then, in
> that disturbed moment, that we know life is an adventure
> with an ending, not a succession of bright days that go on
> forever. Sometimes the knowledge comes with repudiation
> and quick revolt that such injustice awaits us, sometimes
> with fear that dries the mouth and closes the eyes for an
> instant, sometimes with servile weariness, an acquiescence
> more dreadful than fear. The knowledge that my own end
> was near came with pain, and afterward astonishment, with
> the conventional heart attack, from which, I've been told,
> I've made an excellent recovery.

So did William March describe, probably as well as any man can,
his reactions to his own death. For he did not make that excellent
recovery. Early in the morning of May 15, 1954, presumably within

the same day's cycle during which, a writer to the end, he put down the words above, another heart attack occurred.

Hours before Robert Clark, an artist friend, who occupied an apartment in the same house, found the paper in the typewriter, he found Bill March. Sleeping in a room directly above March's bedroom, Clark awoke at five-thirty and heard Bill turn over in his bed. At eight o'clock he came downstairs and went into Bill's room. Bill lay with his face buried in his pillow. Afterward it was decided that he had been dead about an hour. Within a short time after that there was excitement in Dumaine Street in the New Orleans Vieux Carré. First doctors came, then police sirens whined through the narrow street, and at last came the coroner's men. The curious neighbors crowded in front of the cottage as Bill March was carried out, a naked white foot protruding from beneath the white sheet with which the rest of his body was covered.

To many people it seemed a good way to die, quietly in bed, in all probability in his sleep. To many people who knew Bill March it seemed a good *time* to die. His last book *The Bad Seed,* was a success as novels go, perhaps more successful than any book he had written. It had received glowing reviews; it was on the *Herald Tribune* best-seller list; it was listed in the "And Bear in Mind" department of *The New York Times* Sunday book section. A few critics had even called *The Bad Seed* an American classic of its kind. Alistair Cooke had said that William March ". . . is the unrecognized genius of our time." Moreover, Bill had known all this and it had made him happy. It did not matter that in private conversation he had been heard to say that he thought *The Bad Seed* was the worst book he had ever written. What seemed most important to him was that within the last few years he had accomplished what might be called a writing comeback after a decade of writing almost nothing.

Also it seemed to many persons that Bill March's life had been both full and successful. At sixty years of age he was wealthy. He had not made his money as an author, to be sure, but his writing had brought him fame in critical circles, with readers of the sort whose approval mattered most to him, and among other writers. There is even a possibility that it may be an enduring fame. His admirers have remained persistent. They recall short stories he wrote twenty-five years ago. He knew that this was so. For instance, when Martha Foley included none of his work in her *Best of the Best* there were protests to this omission. Within the past year he was still receiving letters from persons who had read his novels and short stories of years ago. It was the kind of applause every really creative writer wants. So he had money and literary recognition of a high caliber. What more could a man want? In addition to these advantages, he looked ten years younger than his age; when he chose to be he was an engaging and amusing raconteur; he appeared to possess unusual energy and stamina; he was sought after by people constantly, not that he wanted to be, for often he wanted to be alone and unnoticed. Yet to those who did not know him well this, too, appeared an advantage to be envied. So they said he had already had everything, and that he died on the rise of his new book's success, and that it was a good time to die.

But the last time I saw Bill March he was enraged at the idea that his end might be near. It was about two weeks after his first heart attack, and I went to see him at the hospital. He talked of a new book he was planning. First he had decided to call it *Poor Pilgrim, Poor Stranger,* then he had changed his mind; he was going to call it *The Gift.* He kept saying that he could not die now. All he wanted, he said, was ten more years. He had five books in his head, and it would take him that long to complete them. The idea of his heart's going bad was ridiculous. He had always worried about his blood pressure and his eyes, he told me, as he had told me many times before, and once he had suspected he had cancer, which had been proven fear and nothing more, for he knew he was a hypochondriac. He believed all his ailments, including this heart attack, were psychosomatic. I agreed with him and went away, and I did not see him again within the five more weeks he lived.

In a sense two men died that morning in Dumaine Street, for few men have lived so completely two lives as did the one I usually called "Bill March." He was born in Mobile, and his full and real name was William Edward March Campbell; he was "William March" in some circles and to some friends, "William E. Campbell" to other circles and other friends, yet both among still others. This dual identity was always confusing when it was necessary to introduce him to people.

William E. Campbell was a founder, former vice-president, and major stockholder of the Waterman Steamship Line. After a year or more in the Marine Corps during World War I, and the acquisition of a distinguished record which won him the Navy Cross, the Distinguished Service Cross, and the Croix de Guerre, he went to work for Waterman. Within a short time he became traffic manager, then vice-president. He acquired stock and it increased in value. From 1932 to 1937 he represented Waterman in Germany and in England. Then he returned to New York, where he lived for the next decade.

William March was born in about 1928, when William E. Campbell decided to use that name as a writer. Yet he had done some writing even before that. During his war service overseas he had written the book and lyrics for a musical comedy, which he called *Getting Too-Loose*. It was staged at the University of Toulouse and was, he always declared, a magnificent success. But his serious writing began with the 1928 publication of a short story, "The Little Wife," and the completion of a novel, *Flight to Confusion*. He destroyed the latter without submitting it to any publisher. "The Little Wife," however, has never been forgotten; it was broadcast as a television play this year.

Company K, a novel about his own company of Marines during World War I, was called by some reviewers the best novel written about that war, and it sold well when it appeared in 1933. This was followed in 1934 by *Come in at the Door*, in 1936 by *The Tallons*, and in 1943 by *The Looking Glass*. But during these years he was becoming better known for his short stories than for his novels. His stories were appearing steadily in all the better magazines, and few writers of our time have been more widely anthologized in the O'Brien and O. Henry annuals, in many others, finally in his own collections of his own short stories, which included *The Little Wife and Other Stories, Some Like Them Short*, and *Trial Balance*. *Trial Balance*, he often said, contained all that was "worth preserving" of his enormous short-story output. There are fifty-five stories in the book. One of his ambitions was to write and publish forty-five more, thus rounding out a hundred worth preserving. He had, also, he said, a hundred fables he wanted to see in book form. I never saw them.

After fifteen years of being his fan I first met William March four years ago. He had taken a furnished apartment in the French Quarter in New Orleans. When a friend offered to take me to see him I was excited at the prospect of meeting him. I suppose most writers have certain literary gods. For years he had been one of mine. I had read and reread everything of his I could get my hands on. I had collected him. I did not even know he was also William E. Campbell. I knew nothing about his personal life at all. When I asked David Mynders Smythe, the writer friend who was taking me

to call on him, and who had known him in New York, what he
looked like, David replied that he looked like a preacher with
wicked eyes.

It was a rather neat description. I met a man of medium height,
of slim physique and erect carriage, with a thick crop of wavy, gray-
ing hair. He looked much younger than what I knew his age to
be, and his whole appearance was mild; his voice was soft; his manner gentle. Only his eyes were different. They gleamed from behind
his glasses, probing, studying everyone in the room, and, as I came
to know later, analyzing everyone. Then, as I became conscious of
what the quiet voice was saying, I discovered it was a highly barbed
monologue that was pouring out at us, witty, mischievous, brilliant,

For Bill March loved to talk, and he talked a great deal about
himself, curiously perhaps as if he were another person. He dug
deeply into others, too, but mostly, and I think preferably, into
himself. As I came to know him better I heard bit by bit the entire
story of his life, and nothing was omitted. I believe he had total
recall. He would talk of something that had happened when he
was three years of age as if it had taken place yesterday. He talked
of his childhood, of his parents, of his brothers and sisters (he was
one of eleven children, of whom seven survived him), of his service
in World War I, of his years with Waterman, of his writing, even
of the time when his emotional life got the best of him for a while
and suspended his writing, suspended his life. He would tell all
this to nearly anyone. During an evening he would also tell the
entire story of a novel he was planning to write, and because he
was a gifted raconteur this was never a dull experience.

During the first few years after I came to know him he did not
live in New Orleans all the time. He rented furnished apartments,
but he called Mobile home, and he came and went, sometimes
vanishing for weeks at a time, but always reappearing in New
Orleans. At last he decided the French Quarter suited him, and
about a year ago he bought the house in Dumaine Street and moved
all his possessions from Mobile, although he still retained a legal
residence in that city.

Among his other things Bill brought his pictures to the small
creole cottage, as its type is called in New Orleans, and which was
the first home he had ever owned in his life. This collection of
pictures was considered by many authorities to be one of the finest
of its sort in the United States. Mostly French moderns, it contained
Rouaults, Soutines, Modiglianis, Picassos, a fine Utrillo, and others.

He had begun the collection during the decade when his life was in a period of greatest turmoil, and when he was not writing. He had taught himself about paintings simply by reading about them and by visiting galleries and dealers. By the time he reached New Orleans he was willing to match his knowledge of the schools in which he was interested against anyone, and he valued his collection at a half-million dollars. He was positive in his judgment of his paintings' worth. Soutine was his favorite, and he thought Soutine would one day be recognized to be as great as anyone who ever painted, as Titian, as Rembrandt.

In comparison to his pictures he had little else of great value. His furniture was pleasant but of the commonplace, store-bought variety. Unlike most writers, he did not even have many books. He did not even own copies of his own books. Those he had once had he had given away. Once when we were having a drink in the patio of the house he had just acquired he said, "Do you know I don't have a single old manuscript? I have no files, or anything of that sort. I had stopped writing. I was through with it."

Somehow New Orleans seemed to start him writing again. Here he wrote *October Island,* which was published in 1953. It was an expansion of a short story that was published in *Good Housekeeping* years ago. Immediately he began the writing of *The Bad Seed.*

It seems to me he had begun to live again. Suddenly he was talking of the other five novels he was carrying about in his mind, of the forty-five more good short stories he wanted to write, of the hundred fables he wanted to see published. Formerly he had made frequent trips to New York; now he ceased going. It was a waste of time, he said. He had never cared much for social life; he loathed cocktail parties. Now he eliminated his social activities almost completely. He saw comparatively few people, usually only some who lived in the neighborhood of whom he was fond.

Every night promptly at ten o'clock he walked a few blocks to his favorite bar, a place called Café Lafitte in Exile, and had two drinks. During the past year he claimed this was his only recreation. He might sit for several hours talking to people he knew who happened to be there or to Tom Caplinger, the proprietor, but he kept to his ration of two drinks. Friends learned that this was the place they could find him, and if they wanted to see him enough they could go there any night at ten o'clock.

On the night of his death, when his body was already gone to Tuscaloosa, Alabama, for burial, I went to Café Lafitte in Exile. It is one of those bars that is virtually a club, where everyone knows everyone else, and if by chance a stranger appears he soon knows everyone there, too. That night everyone was talking about Bill March. They both discussed him and argued about him. Someone would say it was a good way to die and a good time to die, and someone else would say it was not. They talked of his writing and things he had said, and why certain ways of his had been as they were, and why others were not so. Accounts of his passing were clipped from the newspapers and tacked on the walls. At least two people wept. In a way this was his wake. I think it all would have pleased Bill, poor pilgrim, poor stranger.

WALTER DE LA MARE

by Laura Benét

This short biographical memoir was written about the English poet shortly after his death, by a friend of De la Mare's and a member of a poetical family herself.

SEPTEMBER 22, 1956

WITH THE SUDDEN GOING of Walter de la Mare a poet unrivaled in his own field passes from the scene. He was not only a gentle, wise, and hospitable being possessed of immense charm and fun, but no poet in his native England, or indeed in the world, had his gift of fantasy, his intense hunger for the land just across the border of reality, that land of light and shadow made memorable in both his poetry and his stories. Despite the vogue of modern verse so different in quality and content, Mr. de la Mare in his later years attained the honors and recognition he richly deserved. He was one of the favored twenty-four persons who hold the Order of Merit. Four universities had made him a Doctor of Letters, he was an honorary Fellow of Keble College, Oxford, also an honorary Fellow of the American Academy of Arts and Letters. For half a century up to the last months of his eighty-three years he continued to bring forth books illumined by the spiritual awareness of one who loved this life well. Yet he walked also a farther land, darkly unknown to us but of which he had astonishing intimations.

De la Mare was born in Charlton, Kent, a connection of the Robert Brownings on his mother's side. For years he was a statistician in the Anglo-American Oil Company in London and wrote one book, *Henry Brocken,* on scraps of that firm's paper. In 1902 he published his first effort, *Songs of Childhood,* under the name of Walter Ramal. For some time he was considered solely as a writer of unusually perceptive and delicate verse for children, but in 1908 the Asquith Government recognized his talent and granted him a small pension. Later on, in 1922, his longest novel, *Memoirs of a Midget,* received

449

the James Black Tait Memorial Prize and he was enabled to devote himself to the loved occupation of writing.

As poet, anthologist, and tale-teller, his was a prolific genius, and volume followed volume as the years marched forward: *The Return;* the inimitable rhymes in *Peacock Pie;* collected poems; fantasies such as *The Three Royal Monkeys, Desert Islands,* and *Lord Fish; Early in the Morning* (that rare book on the childhood of unusual people); the remarkable anthologies *Love, Behold This Dreamer,* and *Come Hither* and finally, in 1949, his collected tales and the final achievement of his poetry in *The Burning Glass* and the *Winged Chariot.*

The tales, like the poems, illustrate the two sides of his imagination. He is a *revenant,* looking deeply into the intricacies of the human soul, able to apprehend it in a peculiar way—yet he is a realist. How comprehendingly he deals with hardhearted childhood and the lonely pathos of the mad in that unforgettable picture "Miss Duveen," sustains the malicious horror in "Seaton's Aunt" and suspense in "Missing," a murder story. How piteous is the dedicated artist in that marvelous saga "The Tree," how actual the young wife and mother in "Physic." He is able in the same breath to tickle our sensibilities with the humorous portrait of Jones in "The Corner," and to strike terror by the grim journey in the poem "Solitude."

> *And islands*
> *Peaks of such beauty that*
> *Bright danger seems to lie in wait,*
> *Dread, disaster, boding fate; . . .*
> *And every thorn*
> *And weed and flower*
> *And every time-worn stone*
> *A challenge cries on the trespasser,*
> *Beware,*
> *Thou art alone!*

No one since Coleridge could create this atmosphere.

Yet no mortal ever reveled more than did this poet in the coming of the light, in every tiniest revelation of earthly loveliness in sky, wind, water, flower, tree, and human beings—especially those who by reason of certain strange characteristics became members of his world.

There is not space to quote from a longer poem, but for simplicity "Why Then Comes In" is perfect of its kind:

> *Long-idling Spring may come*
> *With such sweet suddenness*
> *It's past the wit of man*
> *His joy to express. . . .*
>
> *To share, to live, to be*
> *Merely a reflex of*
> *Earth's old divine delight*
> *And peace and love!*

My meeting with De la Mare was a happy privilege. I was traveling with my mother in England in 1932, and my brother, William Rose, had given us a letter of introduction to the poet. He replied to it with a most cordial invitation to come for a day to Taplow Priory, not far from Windsor. From the instant we met I was struck by the expression of his extraordinary eyes, which seemed somehow to convey everything man had ever thought or felt. Twenty years later, when his wife was gone, I met him twice in his home at Twickenham and both visits were joyful and friendly occasions.

In parting (how little I thought it was our last meeting on *terra*) I said, "One thing I must know, for at times in your poems I sense an uncertainty: Do you believe in another life?"

He looked at me reproachfully, yet with amusement, "Let us leave out that word *believe*," he said. "One doesn't *believe* in butterflies. They simply *are*. Why, of course. And more and more I do every day and night. I see it in dreams."

To me Walter de la Mare's poem "The Gnomon" might well be his epitaph:

> *I cast a shadow. Through the gradual day*
> *Never at rest it secretly steals on;*
> *As must the soul pursue its earthly way*
> *And then to night be gone.*
>
> *But Oh, demoniac listeners in the grove,*
> *Think not mere Time I now am telling of;*
> *No. But of light, life, joy and awe and love:*
> *I obey the heavenly Sun.*

THE ODYSSEY OF
NIKOS KAZANTZAKIS

by Kimon Friar

*A longtime friend and co-worker of the great Greek author's,
Kimon Friar translated* The Odyssey: A Modern Sequel, *published
in English in 1958 and immediately hailed as a modern classic.*

NOVEMBER 30, 1957

IN THE SUMMER of 1952, in an obscure student's hostel in Florence, I
met Nikos Kazantzakis and his wife, Helen, for the first time. We
plunged immediately into excited talk on many philosophical and
trivial subjects, as only fellow Greeks can, until after a half hour
he exclaimed, "But you must have read *all* my work! You seem
familiar with all my thought!" I had read and translated into prose,
however, only those forty small sections of his epic, *The Odyssey,*
which the best artist of modern Greece, Ghika, had chosen for illustration, and yet I also felt that I had never before met a man so
completely the father of my own thought. His epical poem of twenty-
four books and 33,000 lines takes up the story exactly where Homer
left it. Odysseus cleanses the suitors' blood from his body, leaves
Ithaca once more, runs off with Helen, and destroys the decadent
civilization of Knossos in Crete. After many adventures in Egypt
he follows the Nile to its source, builds the Ideal City, which is
immediately after destroyed by volcanic eruption, then turns ascetic
and in his travels to the southern tip of Africa meets various symboli-
cal representatives of the Primitive man, the Hedonist, the Ascetic,
Don Quixote, Buddha, and finally Christ. He then builds a small skiff
and sails to his death amid the icebergs of the Antarctic regions.

Kazantzakis had been invited to visit China by the Chinese
Government, and in June of this year, amid his packed valises, he
wrote me from his home in Antibes on the French Riviera: "Again
I am taking the road of insanity [that is, of Dionysian ecstasy, of

spiritual adventure], which has always remained for me the road towards the highest wisdom." Though he had been suffering precariously from lymphoid leukemia for the past few years and was now seventy-two years old, he was eager to see the changes in the new worlds of China and Japan, both of which he had visited in 1934. From Peking he sent me a card of a bird perched on a blossomed cherry bough, and wrote in part: "My heart is like this bird that sings of spring . . . I force my body to obey my soul, and thus I never tire. We shall return to Europe via the North Pole." In order to visit Hong Kong, he was given a smallpox vaccination, and as he flew on to Tokyo, and then to Anchorage, Alaska, on the North Pole route, Death entered his body through the vaccination puncture on his right arm and worsened to deadly infection as he flew past the Arctic regions. By one of those astounding coincidences which topple rational thought, Kazantzakis in old age had flown to the northernmost extremity of the earth to meet Death exactly as the autobiographical hero of his *Odyssey* had confronted Death in Antarctic regions, and thus harmony had been preserved in antipodal and frozen balance.

He was rushed to a hospital in Copenhagen, then taken after a few weeks to the University Clinic in Freiburg, Germany, where he had often gone for leukemia treatments. The infection had spread to his right side, his lower lip and tongue had swollen, and after four days of influenza with a 105-degree fever, he died at 10:20 on the evening of October 26. At dawn on the following day, his wife wrote me that he had "slept away, lovingly, beautifully, kindly, without complaint. . . ." His last days had been filled with joy by visits from the man whom he most admired in the living world, Albert Schweitzer, who for years had sponsored Kazantzakis as candidate for the Nobel Prize in Literature. Although in Europe Kazantzakis is known only for six of the novels (in America only by three, *Zorba the Greek, The Greek Passion,* and *Freedom or Death*) which he began to write in his last years primarily to amuse and please his wife in the stagnation and near starvation of the German-Italian Occupation of Greece, he has come within a vote three or four times being granted the Nobel Prize. Unfortunately, the great bulk of his best work still remains entombed in a language none of the Nobel Committee can read, that of modern Greek, and in which he has written three books of philosophy, five books of travel (on Spain, Russia, England, Egypt-Mount Sinai, China-Japan), and eighteen of drama, most of them in poetic form. In addition he has translated innumerable works into Greek from the French, Spanish, English, Russian, Italian, German, and Ancient Greek, including Homer's *Iliad* and *Odyssey*, Dante's *Divine Comedy*, and Goethe's *Faust*. All his thought, however, and his greatest effort, have been summed up in *The Odyssey*, surely one of the masterpieces of the modern world.

In June 1954 Simon and Schuster sent me to Antibes to collaborate with Kazantzakis in a translation of the *Odyssey* into prose. There I spent four months with him, reading each word of his epic together as I took voluminous notes, and there and then, though it would mean three of four years of constant dedication, I decided that only a poetic version could capture the richness of the original. A Fulbright Research Scholarship in Modern Greek Literature at the University of Athens took me to Greece in October, and there I remained for nearly three years with Kazantzakis in the Alps of Yugoslavia, until in an Odyssey of my own through most of Greece and the Greek islands I finished my first draft of the poem. When we met again in Antibes for a month last April, he told me, as he had often told me before, that he would meet death gladly if once he could hold the bound volume of the English version in his hands and know that his mature thought could now scatter the ashes and sparks of his words among mankind.

I have been privileged to meet many great literary figures of our day, but I have never before felt so immediately and persistently in the presence of greatness as before him in day after day of close collaboration and discussion when souls are tried, tested, and revealed. In aspect he was arresting, extremely tall and thin, of a bony and ascetic angularity, with shaggy tawny-gray eyebrows, and the only eyes I have ever seen which the clichés "piercing" and "eagle-eyed" adequately describe. His greatness was lambent and transparent with the simplicity which one always posits for true greatness yet rarely expects to find, a serenity that accepted all and dwelt in a higher tension beyond trivialities. He dressed simply, ate sparingly, and was by temperament a monk (he had lived for two years in contemplation on Mt. Athos) and has summed up his ascetic philosophy in a work of poetic epigrams, *Spiritual Exercises*. And yet, like Yeats, he had a passionate admiration for violent men of action, for those, like his hero Zorba, who reveled in all the deliriums of flesh and freedom. Born in Crete between the crossroads of Europe, Africa, and Asia, he saw all life with the double vision of tension between opposites, an explosive conflict that ascended eternally toward higher and higher spiritual reaches in an abyss of nothingness.

To read *The Odyssey* together was to accompany Kazantzakis in the search of the modern man for his soul, for that is the true theme of his book. If I were to sum up all his endeavor and thought, I would say that he attempted to bring matter and flesh into an ever closer refinement of spirit, to follow man's own progressive idea of Godhead refined from atavistic fears and powers, from the dualisms of beast and God, from polytheism to the concept of one creator and then back again to the Godhead of man's proud mind and God-creating spirit. For Kazantzakis God was not an exterior entity toward which man proceeds but a continuously created and recreated aspect of spirit within man himself. For him there was no immortality but simply the dissolving of his particular rhythms into those of the universe, and thus for him, more than for most authors, whatever of his was to remain would endure or die in his words on the printed page. Death was his constant companion, as Death was also the constant companion of Odysseus throughout his spiritual journey. When Odysseus meets the representative type of the Buddha who accepts death in negation, he declares that only on the abyss may man build the affirmative structure of his life, and cries out, "But I hold Death like a black banner and march on!"

INDEX